THE RUSSIAN LANGUAGE IN BRITAIN

BY THE SAME AUTHOR:

I. S. Turgenev's 'Mumu' with Introduction, Notes and Vocabulary (Editor)

Nikolai Leskov and the 'Spirit of Protestantism'

A Guide to the Soviet Curriculum

Portrait of a Soviet School under Glasnost

Bold Shall I Stand. The Education of Young Women in the Moravian Settlement at Ockbrook since 1799

Post-school Education and the Transition from State Socialism (Editor, with W. John Morgan)

TRANSLATIONS FROM THE RUSSIAN OF NIKOLAI LESKOV:

Vale of Tears

Schism in High Society. Lord Radstock and his Followers

The Priest Who was Never Baptized. Stories factual and fictional of Russian life in the nineteenth century

THE RUSSIAN LANGUAGE IN BRITAIN

A historical study of learners and teachers

by James Muckle

Bramcote Press
Ilkeston, Derbyshire
2008

©James Yeoman Muckle 2008

All rights reserved. No reproduction, copy or transmission of the whole or part of this publication may be made without written permission.

The author is grateful to the British Academy for financial assistance in carrying out the research on which this book is based.

First published 2008 by
BRAMCOTE PRESS,
81 RAYNEHAM ROAD,
ILKESTON,
DERBYSHIRE DE7 8RJ
UNITED KINGDOM

Printed by the MPG Books Group in the UK

ISBN 978-1-900405-15-7

CONTENTS

Illustrations	vi
Preface	vii
1. The Russian Language and its British Speakers to the End of the Eighteenth Century	1
2. Towards the Emergence of the Organized Study of Russian in the Nineteenth and Early Twentieth Centuries	21
3. The 'Boom' in Russian Studies and its Rise and Fall from 1914	52
4. Russian Between the Wars: Treading Water, but Still Afloat	81
5. Wartime Again. A Slow Revival	103
6. Poised for Expansion. Russian from the Late 1940s to the Early 1960s	124
7. After Annan. The Road to Atkinson. The 1960s and 1970s	161
8. Change, Decline or Consolidation? The Last Three Decades	195
9. What is the Position of Russian in Britain Now, and Where is it Going?	223
Bibliography	247
Index	268

Illustrations

It has not proved possible to trace the copyright-holders of all the illustrations, or in some cases to discover which of the photographs are in copyright. The publisher will make appropriate arrangements if approached by the relevant persons. Known sources and acknowledgements are:

Ludolf's *Grammatica Russica* (Oxford University Press); Horsey (Internet: several locations); Buck and Heard (from their publications); Schnurmann (Cheltenham College); Anna Semeonoff (Rev. Robert Semeonoff); Pares (from *My Russian Memoirs*); Storr-Best (Firth Park School); Gregory (source uncertain); Milne (Katherine Dickie); Haywood (Judith [Haywood] Roberts); Rix (Robert Pullin); Wade (May Wade); services Russian, 1950s (first three: Crail Museum, newspaper source untraced), last two: photographer unknown); Ukrainians (source untraced); after-school Russian (Muckle); MAPRYaL congress (Soviet source unknown); olympiada (RIA-Novosti); *Angliiskoe podvor'e* (Muckle); JSSL Bodmin (source unknown); exchange teachers (Muckle); Hill and audience (photo by Edward Leigh, Cambridge University Library); rehearsal of *Zoikina kvartira* (Nottingham University Slavonic Studies Department).

Captions on the illustrations are self-explanatory and the text of this book (and the Bibliographies) refer to most of the persons depicted, but readers may like the following additional information. Fred Gregory (d. 1969) was a founder-member and sometime Chairman of ATR, author of teaching materials, and member of the Annan Committee. The following five were all school teachers of Russian at some time, were all awarded the Pushkin Medal 'for services to the Russian language world-wide' and were prominent office-bearers in ATR. Alan Haywood (1915-1991): textbook author and innovative examiner, Harry Milne, MBE (1914-89): author, campaigner and publicist for Russian in Scotland and the whole UK, David Rix (1935-2004): schoolteacher, teacher-trainer, course and textbook author, Terence Wade (1930-2005): professor at Strathclyde, prolific author of teaching and reference materials, Daphne West: textbook author and school head. W. Gareth Jones is emeritus professor at Bangor, literary scholar and author. Alan Richards taught Russian in secondary and further education; was a campaigner for the subject and languages in general, and officer of ATR.

Elizabeth Hill (1900-96) and audience: no-one who has seen this can say what occasion it was. Recognizable in the front row are Dr John Fennell (1919-92, second from left), later professor at Nottingham and Oxford, Edward Sands next to him, and V. P. Saulus two places beyond Sands. Dr Malcolm Burgess is partly visible on the extreme left one row back, and Dr Peter Squire is faintly discernible at the very back on the right. (All four were on the staff at Cambridge).

PREFACE

To learn a language is to pay a compliment to those who speak it as a native tongue. The compliment may be unintended, accidental, or even unwilling, but a compliment of a sort it almost inevitably is, and it is usually taken as such by native speakers, who are delighted when foreigners make the attempt to speak their language. Non-Russians may learn the Russian language for pragmatic commercial or political reasons, out of curiosity, out of interest in languages in general, or because of fondness for the culture expressed through the language. The compliment is particularly prominent when British people take up Russian, since the language is not offered in British schools and colleges in the same way as are French and German: to study it usually requires both conscious choice and initiative. One of the things we look at in this book is the motivation for undertaking the study and the social, cultural, and political influences governing, encouraging, or discouraging it.

To learn any language, not excluding Russian, is at best an arduous task. Arduous, but not necessarily impossibly difficult. Some students take to language study more easily than others, but for the most part what distinguishes the apparently 'gifted' linguist is a high level of motivation, application to the task, determination, and persistence. When we read of linguists who have mastered eight, ten, or even twenty languages (and some are mentioned in this book), invariably they have striven single-mindedly to achieve their ends. The best Russian-speakers who began their study before the twentieth century were, in addition, often working with inadequate study materials and perhaps no qualified teacher, or even no teacher at all. Determination enabled many of them to overcome these obstacles.

Many British people who have set out to learn Russian report a fascination with the language itself: that 'великий, могучий, правдивый и свободный русский язык' (great, powerful, honest and free Russian language), of which Ivan Turgenev wrote in a poem in prose entitled 'Русский язык' (The Russian Language) from 1882, which every Russian school child can quote by heart. I have not been able to trace any comparable hymn of praise to the *English* language by an English, Scottish, American or any other poet or writer who uses it as his medium of expression, yet several British students and teachers of Russian have written warmly of the strength and beauty of the Russian language, and some of their remarks are recorded in this book.

Russian novels, poetry, drama, music, opera, dance, and culture generally have been widely admired, as have Russian achievements in science, technology, psychology and medicine. Long-term residents in Russia from other countries often profess a fondness for the Russian people; it is remarkable that Russian departments in several universities owed their establishment to the generosity of businessmen who had spent extended periods in Russia, and whose liberality was clearly not motivated entirely by the desire to make money.

It may be countered that the learning of Russian in Britain has (and not only in the years of the recent 'Cold War') been done for military or defence purposes. This is true, but we are faced with a paradox here. A century of what one historian has gone so far as to term 'Russophobia' resulted in the study of Russian for military purposes; but when it abated for a while in 1914, when Britain and Russia became allies in the First World War, this was the point at which Russian studies in Britain increased exponentially, if briefly. Even before that military men who had studied during longish periods of residence in Russia developed a fondness for the Russians and some scepticism about their superiors' suspicions of Russian ambitions. The famous National Service Russian courses of the 1950s, intended on the one hand to provide interpreters for any future conflict, and on the other to train collectors of intelligence, obeyed the law of unintended consequences. Many of the five thousand or so young men who had been through these courses went after demobilization into professions in which their Russian was important to them, and while many may have been to some extent hostile to Soviet attitudes, they certainly did not comprise an embittered anti-Russian group in any field of activity in which they eventually made their name. Nor did they, despite the paranoid effusions of some of the spycatching community, form a dissident and disruptive body in society in the way certain pro-Soviet pressure groups did during the Second World War.

This book, then, may be seen in one way as a record of the changing and developing relationship between Britain and Russia as reflected in the attention paid by Britain to the Russian language. Political and military events undoubtedly have had an influence on our story. Yet, without the fascination which Russia has ever exerted on those Britons who have become involved with her, there would be no story to tell.

A few words about the scope of this study and some definitions: the main focus is upon British people who have, for whatever reason, taken up the Russian language. 'British' is interpreted very loosely as including any inhabitants of the British Isles. The English and Scottish diaspora in Russia—those who emigrated to Russia and stayed there for good—figure in these pages to a much smaller extent, and the major emphasis is placed on those who contributed to knowledge of Russian language and life back in Britain through their writing or teaching, whether or not they themselves returned to Britain. Of course, the teaching of Russian has been immeasurably advanced by Russians who made their home in Britain: they too appear in the story. Some travellers to Russia remained hostile to the country, and there are even emigrants who long remained impervious to the language. Such people have actually obstructed British understanding of Russia. Others became Russified to the extent of taking citizenship. Some of these disappear, in the sense that contact with the native land is severed; a few others, however, become workers for good understanding between the nations. An example is James Arthur Heard, to whom deservedly some considerable attention is devoted in Chapter 2. He did what some British civil servants used to deplore: he 'went native'. In my own lifetime I have heard a diehard British official paradoxically (since he had devoted his life to the foreign service!) declare that 'any British person who settles abroad cannot be worth his salt'. I fervently hope that such dismally perverted attitudes are no longer found in the British diplomatic service in the twenty-first century.

Many readers of this book will be disappointed that some outstanding teachers of Russian are only cursorily mentioned, not mentioned at all, or at least not named, in its pages. A moment's reflection will be sufficient to reveal that to name every worker for the cause would be impossible. It is heartwarming to speak to people who say they owe an enormous amount to inspired teachers at school and university. The splendid fact to any educationist is that what they owe has to do not only with a knowledge of Russian, but with broader issues: contact with a vivid personality, or infection from that person with a love of some aspect of Russian civilization.

In the course of telling the story, I have tried to recognize Russian writers past and present who have expressed their love of their own language in prose and verse: Sumarokov, Trediakovskii, Lomonosov, and Turgenev in particular. Anna Akhmatova's poem Мужество (Courage), written in the dark days of 1942, expresses the poet's love of the language, and sees it as a liberating force and a priceless possession to be passed on to future generations. It deserves quoting in full here, and may stand as the epigraph to this whole work:

> Мы знаем, что ныне лежит на весах
> И что совершается ныне.
> Час мужества пробил на наших часах,
> И мужество нас не покинет.
>
> Не страшно под пулями мертвыми лечь,
> Не горько остаться без крови,
> И мы сохраним тебя, русская речь,
> Великое русское слово.
>
> Свободным и чистым тебя пронесем,
> И внукам дадим, и от плена спасем
> Навеки!

Acknowledgements. My own keen interest in the Russian language and in its study and teaching in Britain goes back over fifty years, so in a way this book had its real origins long before I formed the plan of writing it. I wish to acknowledge the support, stimulation and encouragement I received from colleagues, many of them outside the Russian field, throughout my teaching career. Without the environment thus created, I should never have wanted to complete this project and write this book. I am grateful to Emeritus Professor Malcolm Jones, who has taken great interest in the project and has commented on drafts of several chapters, as well as helping in other ways. Staff of the UNESCO Centre for Comparative Education Research at Nottingham University and Professor John Morgan have been unfailingly encouraging.

I should like to express my thanks to a long list of other people who have assisted in various ways. I am particularly fortunate to have certain friends and colleagues who served on official bodies concerned with Russian in schools and universities, with examinations, and with the English national curriculum: they were often able to give me—always discreetly—the 'low-down' on the deliberations of these committees. They include Malcolm Jones, Robert Pullin, and Alan West.

Librarians and archivists have been a tower of strength. There must have been times when insistent demands for help in locating items in the labyrinth which is British government activity made the life of the staff, especially Angela Shearsmith, of Documents Division in the Hallward Library at the University of Nottingham seem quite unbearable, but she and her colleagues almost invariably came up with the relevant papers. I am grateful to Richard Davies at that most valuable resource, the Leeds Russian Archive. Some of the papers I have assembled in compiling this project will be deposited there in due course. Ray Scrivens, Brian Cooper and Godfrey Waller at Cambridge University Library met and briefed me on the University's holdings and on the Elizabeth Hill papers; Dr Patrick Zutschi went to considerable trouble to get permission for an illustration to appear. Thanks go also to Michael Ball at the National Army Museum, Stuart Hadaway and others at the RAF Museum at Hendon, to staff at Birmingham Central Library, and at County and other regional Record Offices in Derby, Matlock, Nottingham University, Nottingham Central Library, and Leicestershire. I have been welcomed and assisted in the archives of the Royal Society of Arts by Claire Batley, by Ralph Gibson at the RIA-Novosti photo archive, and by John Cunningham, Jean Turner and Barbara Ellis at the Society for Cooperation in Russian and Soviet Studies.

Curricular, teaching, and advisory centres which have provided valuable information and statistics which might otherwise not have come to light include: Christopher Higgins at the AQA, Ross Laing and Sarah Conroy of the SQA, the Northern Ireland Education Office, Joanna McPake and Sheila McLachlan (Scottish CILT), Sarah Joy (CILT), and Tom Spencer (Schools Statistics, Scottish Government).

Many individuals have discussed my ideas, or have answered specific questions and provided, sometimes at considerable trouble, illustrations, memories of relations or friends who were Russian teachers, and information which has been used in the text. Many have written their Russian-teaching autobiographies. In alphabetical order they are: Professor Richard Aldrich, Nicola Allen (RSA), Robert Avery (Defence School of Languages), George Avis, Jill Barlow

(Cheltenham College), Professor Roger Bartlett, Iris Bellmann (Deutscher Russischlehrerverband), Calder Benzies (Daniel Stewart's College), George Bird (formerly of JSSL and JSLS), Liz Blackman MP, Sue Bradman (Crail Museum), Nadezhda Bragina, Christopher Brandie, Nick Brown (Specialist Schools and Academies Trust), Aldyth Cadoux, Jenny Carr (Scotland-Russia Forum), David Chamberlain, Sue Coatman, Rob Crawford, Aaron Cripps (Defence Academy), Professor Tony Cross, Mel Dadswell, Katherine Dickie, Thomas Dickins, Alan Dickson, Dr John Dunstan, Geoffrey Elliott, Nicholas Evans, Dr Nicholas Fennell, Walter Grauberg, Christopher Grzybowski, Professor William Harrison, David Haysom (RAF Linguists' Association), Camilla Hezelgrave, Peter Hoare, Brian Hollis, Dr David Holohan, John Ingram, Andrew Jameson, Professor Edgar Jenkins, Graham Johnston, Dr David Keep, Professor Michael Kirkwood, John Langran, Vera Liber, Trevor Lloyd, Tatiana McCrum, Professor Cynthia Marsh, Peter Meades, Patrick Miles, Eric Miller, Michael Morris, Mike Mulvaney, Professor Brian Murphy, Dora O'Brien (Great Britain-Russia Society), Lt-Col David O'Connor, Professor Paddy (L. M.) O'Toole, David Pearce, Harvey Pitcher, Vivien Pixner, John Porter (Leeds Russian Archive), David Potter, Michael Pursglove, Alan Richards, Clive Richards (Air Historical Branch, RAF), Dr Ian Roberts, Judith Roberts, Suzanne Rogers (Nottingham University Library), Peter Rooney, Professor Robert Russell, the Rev. and Mrs Robert and Jean Semeonoff, Dr Harold Shukman, Ken Smith, Dr Sarah Smyth, Dr Peter Squire, Dr Gerald Stone, Dr Alan Suggate, Lady Jeanne Sutherland, Elaine Thawley, Henry Thompson, Dr Peter Thwaites (RMA Sandhurst), Dr Glyn Turton, Derek Twigg MP (Ministry of Defence), May Wade, Geoff Wadhams, Dr Daphne West, Professor Marcus Wheeler, Roy Williamson, Thomas Wilson, Tanya Yurasova.

I do not care for dedications in books, but I do wish to pay tribute to those teachers who introduced me to Russian and who fostered my enthusiasm for the subject through excellent teaching from beginner level to doctorate. They are: George Shutt at Manchester Grammar School; George Bird, V. Diakovsky, J. Godlewski, J. Klavins (I do not know their first names) and Peter Meades at JSSL Bodmin and Crail; Mr Paegle at RAF Wythall, Dr Peter Squire and Dr Alexis Vlasto at Cambridge University, and Colin Johnson at Leeds University. I am grateful to all of them.

The research on which this book was based was carried out with some financial assistance from the British Academy, for which I am grateful.

Practical matters

Annotation and Bibliography.

The **Bibliographies** contain all works referred to more than once in the text and footnotes, as well as items which are of some importance to the subject matter even if they are not cited specifically. In the **footnotes** the source will be given by the author's name and if necessary a short title, provided the work appears in one of the Bibliographies. References to peripheral sources not included in the Bibliographies will carry a full citation.

Abbreviations are particularly common in the field of education, and are liberally used in this book: AQA, ATR, BASEES, CILT, MLA, SSEES, and the like. Systematic use of these shortens text, footnotes, and bibliography, which is the main reason for using them. No reader can be expected to keep them all in his head, and they are all to be found, spelt out, in the Index.

Transliteration is an insoluble problem. Slavonic scholars have for centuries debated and quarrelled over how to transliterate Russian, and more than one system has existed: confusion up to around 1960; after that the 'Czech' system was used by linguistics scholars, and by others the British Standard, which always seemed to me the most elegant and acceptable. Then about 20 years ago Slavists in higher education decided to wrong-foot everyone by changing it yet again, instantly rendering the alphabetical arrangement of reference works slightly obsolete, giving much scope for error by those of us who had got used to the old system, and providing excellent opportunities for them to bully their undergraduates. While regretting that my learned colleagues had nothing better to do, to some extent I have reluctantly felt obliged to drift with the tide. Readers who are expecting 'Yuriy', 'Yaroslav' and so on, should therefore get used to 'Iurii', 'Iaroslav' and the like. But, of course, all names quoted from material published before we went transliterationally 'metric' will have to be left as they were before. Chaos therefore reigns, as it always did, and probably always will.

A largely **chronological approach** has been adopted in telling the story, but this has occasionally been departed from when information would appear unduly fragmented if it were stuck to rigidly. The theme is Russian in *Britain*, so I have tried to deal with Scotland, Wales and England alongside each other. Ireland, which was part of the United Kingdom when the story begins, is likewise referred to for the most part in parallel. I apologize to Irish Slavists if they feel I have not given their work due attention. The information on Ireland has been assembled with their help.

AUGUST 2008   JAMES MUCKLE

Chapter 1

The Russian Language and its British Speakers to the End of the Eighteenth Century

The most copius and elegant language in the world
SIR JEROME HORSEY

The Early Years of Anglo-Russian Relations

THE first significant contact between England and Russia occurred in 1553 as if by accident. Sir Hugh Willoughby and Richard Chanceler or 'Chancellor' had set off in three ships to try to discover a North-East passage to Cathay and the Far East. They bore a letter from King Edward VI to all kings and princes 'in all places under the universal heaven', inviting these potentates to engage in trade with England.[1] The ships were separated in a great storm; two of the ships bearing Willoughby and his men disappeared and they were to die of cold and starvation on the coast of Lapland. Chancellor's ship, the Edward Bonaventure, made it to Archangel, from which port he set about establishing trade links with what he discovered was 'the Countrey called Russia, or Moscovie',[2] then under the iron rule of Ivan IV (Vasilievich), later to earn the appellation *Ivan Groznyi*, variously translated as John the Dread or Ivan the Terrible. Ivan had assumed full power after the regency of his mother relatively recently, in 1547; he reigned until 1584.

This was certainly not the first time people from the British Isles set foot in the realm of Muscovy. The royal and princely families of Europe were to a greater or lesser extent intermarried a thousand years and more ago. Iaroslav the Wise (reigned 1036-74) maintained relations with Western European nations, including possibly Anglo-Saxon England. A notable dynastic marriage took place in 1074: Gytha, a daughter of King Harold II Godwinson, after her father's death at the Battle of Hastings and Harold's sons' failure in the succeeding years to regain the Kingdom from William the Conqueror, was taken by her brothers to the court of their cousin, Swein of Denmark. It is said that Swein sent her to Smolensk to marry the future Grand Prince Vladimir Monomakh. This marriage

---

[1] Willan, *The Early History of the Muscovy Company*, p. 4.
[2] Hakluyt (ed. Hampden), p. 49. Hakluyt's *Voyages* were extremely extensive; in this chapter I quote mainly from Janet Hampden's edition, using other sources when necessary.

is not confirmed by any Russian source, but 'appears to be generally accepted'.[3] As an Anglo-Saxon princess, even the daughter of a deposed king who had been defeated and killed in battle, and as a cousin of the Danish king, Gytha was a promising match for Vladimir. She is believed to have borne him at least eleven children. Coincidentally there is a Danish connection with the first Scot identifiable by name to have been in Muscovy: he was Peter Davidson, a servant of the King of Denmark, who was sent as ambassador to confirm an alliance between Denmark and Ivan III in 1493. Other Scots and English lived and worked in Muscovy or served in the armies of its princes before the time of Chancellor's expedition.[4]

Chancellor and his men had not specifically planned to land or to stay long on the territory of Muscovy, but clearly decided to make the best of the situation and to present King Edward's letter to the Tsar. To engage in trade assumes a common language or languages, but at that time there may have been no-one in England who could communicate with the Russians in their own tongue. Yet Chancellor reports that 'the barbarous Russes asked likewise of our men whence they were, and what they came for: whereunto answere was made, that they were Englishmen sent into those coastes, from the most excellent King Edward the sixt...'[5] In what language this exchange took place we do not know. Chancellor paints a vivid picture of his party's reception later by Ivan at court in Moscow, and he seems to know what was going on at the ceremony, and what was being said, but it is impossible to make out how he knew this. We can only surmise that he was informed of the proceedings in a language he did understand, and that likewise his men communicated with the 'barbarous Russes' in some tongue known to both parties.

Chancellor's men, however, did not all remain tongue-tied. It would appear from the section of his account entitled 'Of Moscovie, which is also called Russia', that some of them tried unsuccessfully to locate the Riphean mountains, part of the Urals, a colossal distance from Archangel or Moscow, which were written of in antiquity, but long believed to be more mythical than real. Very interesting for our theme is Chancellor's aside: 'Our men which lately came from thence, neither sawe them [the mountains, presumably], nor have yet brought home any perfect relation of them, *although they remained there for the space of three moneths, and had gotten in that time some intelligence of the language of Moscovie.'*[6] (My emphasis—JM). These men would appear to be the earliest English on record to have attempted to learn the Russian language in order to

---

[3]Ian W. Walker, *Harold: the Last Anglo-Saxon King*, Stroud: Sutton, 2000, pp. 193-195. The Soviet scholar A. S. Orlov, in his *Vladimir Monomakh*, Moscow-Leningrad: Izd. Akad. Nauk SSSR, 1946 (p. 10 and footnote) confirms the marriage.

[4]Fedosov, p. 29 (re: Davidson); and *passim*.

[5]Hakluyt (ed. Hampden), p. 49-50.

[6]Hakluyt (ed. Hampden), pp. 53-54.

return home with that knowledge and consequently facilitate relations between the two nations.

Published correspondence between English and Russian monarchs shows that a variety of languages were used for official communications.[7] In a reference to the message sent by Ivan to King Edward (who, unknown to all concerned in Russia, had died by this time) we read: 'This letter was written in the Moscovian tongue, in letters much like to the Greek letters, very faire written in paper, with a broad seal... Under this letter was another paper written in the Dutch tongue, which was the interpretation of the other written in the Moscovian letters.'[8] 'Dutch' in the sixteenth century was used to refer to both Low and High German, that is 'Deutsch', and the documents presented by Tolstoi in *The First Forty Years...* include some written clearly in High German. A mission to Russia in 1555 carried letters from the new Queen Mary and her husband Philip II of Spain written in English, Greek, Polish and Italian. One senses a degree of desperation here: which of these tongues would the Tsar or his staff comprehend? Later embassies suggested writing in addition in 'Dutch' and Latin.[9] Philip and Mary did in fact later write in Latin. It was not until 1570, when Ivan was seeking to marry Queen Elizabeth or another English noble lady,[10] that he asked the Queen to write in Russian, while he promised to reply in English or Latin. (Incidentally, Chancellor states that Latin, Greek and Hebrew were all unknown to the Russian clergy,[11] the rank and file clergy, one assumes he meant.) Elizabeth wrote in 1586 to Ivan's successor, Tsar Fedor, in Latin.

In his classic work, *Britain's Discovery of Russia 1553-1815*, M. S. Anderson states that England played no part at all in the Westernization of Russia before the mid-sixteenth century, and that up to this time England knew literally nothing of 'Muscovy'.[12] The establishment of the Muscovy, or 'Russia', Company and the burgeoning of trade between the two countries changed all this. In consequence of the voyages which now took place with consistent regularity and the development of trade between the two countries, a number of diplomats, officials and merchants found it necessary to become proficient in the Russian language. It was known by a variety of names: the Moscovian tongue, Russic, Russish, Russe and Russ, the last of which was used regularly well into the nineteenth century. 'The Sclavonian tongue' is also found. This, however, raises an important and interesting issue. By the time of the events described here the Russian languages used, while all mutually intelligible, differed to an important degree. For ordinary use in the family and everyday life there was Russian, the

---

[7] Yury Tolstoi, *The First Forty Years...* is a useful collection of the correspondence of the period.

[8] Hakluyt Voyages II, quoted by W. S. Page, *The Russia Company...*, p. 24.

[9] Pennington, p. 680.

[10] See Skalkina, 'Neudavshee svatovstvo,' in *Rossiia i Britaniia*, pp. 12-13.

[11] Hakluyt (ed. Hampden), p. 68.

[12] Anderson, pp. 4-5.

language spoken by the 'barbarous Russes' encountered by Chancellor and his men. Alongside this from the ninth century there existed Church Slavonic, the language into which the Bible had been translated by Christian missionaries, the language of the Orthodox liturgy and theological writing. This language was more or less intelligible to ordinary Russians, but obviously distinct from it. Both of these languages developed over the centuries as languages naturally do. There was also very importantly a 'literary language', a 'high style' adopted by anyone writing anything literary in intention; linguists further distinguish a *prikaznyi iazyk*, or 'chancery language'—officialese, differing sharply from the literary style. All these modes of speech and writing influenced each other strongly in both vocabulary and syntax, and there were infinite gradations between them: historians of the Russian language enjoy analysing surviving texts and estimating their level. Moreover, far more examples of the higher and official styles than of the ephemeral everyday speech have survived, by the very nature of the matter. It is scarcely surprising if our novice linguists were often unsure of themselves. The 'Sclavonian tongue' as a term of reference may have meant Church Slavonic, or the literary style, or it may have been used for Russian when the speaker, quite forgivably, did not understand the finer points of all this.

Anderson surmises, and the notion is echoed by A. B. Sokolov, that many of the Muscovy merchants would not have succeeded in learning the language, or even have tried. Nevertheless, we have the names of a number of linguists, some of whom were diplomats too: Richard Johnson spoke well enough to be taken for a Russian when communicating with Lapps, John Merrick (d. 1638), Francis Cherry, John Elmes ('the Tolmach, or interpreter for the English tung', in the words of one memoirist), Logan, Stephen Borough (the master of the Edward Bonaventure, the ship on which Chancellor sailed in 1553) and most of all his nephew Christopher Borough, whom the scholar Anne Pennington considered to deserve the title of the first English Slavist.[13] In saying this she relied on a series of manuscripts in Russian and Church Slavonic held in the Bodleian Library, one of them possibly in Christopher Borough's hand, but certainly with many annotations by him, which prove he was learned in Russian, and could distinguish it from Church Slavonic, White Russian and Ukrainian. A voyage in 1571 led by Anthony Jenkinson had an interpreter called Daniel Sylvester. When the Tsar complained that he had not received an answer to his secret message to Elizabeth (presumably concerning the possible marriage), Jenkinson uses the excuse of poor interpretership: 'If the reply is not all that the Emperor desires it must be for the want of a good interpreter.'[14] This can not have referred to Sylvester, since Ivan found him as fluent in Russian as he was in English.[15]

---

[13] Pennington, p. 686. Several of these names are mentioned by Hakluyt and by Academician Alekseev, in his 'Angliiskii iazyk v Rossii i russkii iazyk v Anglii'. See also C. L. Wrenn.

[14] Page, p. 155.

[15] Anderson, p. 11.

Sylvester was unfortunately killed by a thunderbolt in the 'English house', where the merchants had their headquarters, in 1576; his papers were all destroyed in the same incident. Ivan saw this as a sign from God that relations with England were contrary to the divine will, and a temporary cooling-off took place.[16]

Sir Jerome Horsey is credited by historians with a particularly good knowledge of Russian, as a result of his twenty or so years in the country. However, in the following passage, in which he describes how he learned it, there are one or two doubtful statements:

> After I had ben and seen som part of France and the Low Countries, in thir florishing but most trowbsom tyme of warr, I arived in Muscovia, comonly called Russia. Though but a plaine gramarian, and havinge som smake in the Graek, I ateyned by the affinitie therof in shortt tyme to the readie and famillier knowledge of their vulgar speach, the Sclavonian tonge, the most copius and elegent language in the world. With som small breviacion and pronunciacion, yt coms near the Polish, Lettois, Transilvania, and all those adjacent countries; and yt will serve in Turcky, Percia, eaven to the knowen Indies, &c.[17]

A certain confusion may be perceived here: the 'Sclavonian tongue' is scarcely a correct term for the Russians' 'vulgar speech'. While Russian (however termed) was indeed useful in neighbouring Slavonic countries, it can hardly have 'served' in Turkey, Persia or the Indies. Moreover, however much 'smake in the Greek' Horsey had, it can scarcely have helped him very much with Russian, except for some of the alphabet. Nevertheless, Horsey's description of his travels is certainly a remarkably detailed and penetrating study of Muscovy. It is to him that we owe the famous account of Queen Elizabeth's fascinated reaction to the sight of the Charter of Privileges given by the Tsar to the Russia Company.[18] On receiving the formal privilege, the Queen

> Made me kneell by her; perused the lyminge and carectors of the privaledge, havinge some affinitie with the Graeke; asked if such and such letters and asseveracions had not this signification; saied she,—'I could quicklie lern it.'— Preyed my lord of Essex to lern the famoust and most copius language in the world; after which comendacion his honor did much affect and delight it, if he might ateyn therunto without paienstakinge and spendinge more time then he had to spare.[19]

Sensible fellow! Indeed the word 'copious', a favourite epithet of Horsey's for the Russian tongue, is defined by the Oxford Dictionary in relation to the 1670s as 'abounding in language or words', and it refers to the daunting task any

---

[16] Sokolov, pp. 39-40.

[17] Horsey, in E. A. Bond, p. 156.

[18] Unfortunately the document is believed to have been destroyed in the Great Fire of London, 1666.

[19] Horsey, pp. 232-233. The 'lyminge' is presumably the *limning* or illumination of the manuscript.

5

learner has in mastering the vast vocabulary. The unfortunate Horsey had another 'dangerous'—in the old sense of 'difficult to deal with'—task:

> Yt pleased her Majesty and her counsaill to comand my service yet farther in a mor difficult and daingerous imploiment then ever I have been exposed hertofore, in regard only of the languages and experience those seaventen years had taught me, which my lord treasuror and Mr. secraetarie Walsingham desired to have sett down, to heer and perceave the pronunciacion and differenc each had with the other; some exactly and familliarly ateyned unto, other som, by conversinge with the ambassodors, nobelmen and merchants, but in part, as Percian, Grecian, Pollish and the Garman...[20]

There follow some very short examples of 'Sclava' (Russian), Polish, German, Persian and Livonian: the Russian is presented in facsimile; it and the other phrases are extremely difficult to make sense of. This may be the printers' incompetence rather than any failing of Horsey's.

Horsey gained the respect of Elizabeth for his resourcefulness in conveying secret correspondence from the Tsar. He is said once to have concealed letters in transit, preserved in vodka in the false sides of water-flasks. On arrival at court, he extracted and dried the correspondence, sprinkling it with perfume to remove the smell; Elizabeth, however, detected the vodka and happily saw the joke.[21]

It is difficult to estimate the quality of interpretership in these distant days. Giles Fletcher, Elizabeth's ambassador to Tsar Fedor, was sent by the Queen to pour oil on troubled waters in 1588. He reported:

> My articles of petition delivered by woord of mouth, and afterwards by writing, with all other writings wear altered and falsified by the Emperors Interpreter, by meanes of the Chancellour Andreas Shalcalove, speciallie whear it concerned him self, manie things wear putt in, and manie things strook out, which being complained of and the points noted would not be redressed.[22]

Shchelkalov (sic) was in charge of foreign affairs for the Tsar; he was in dispute with one of the Muscovy merchants, and Fletcher doubtless felt he should do as much as he could to placate him. In this case it is clear that malice affected the quality of the translation. Several decades after the events described, we have evidence of interpretation which was not entirely competent. When two Russian envoys came to King James in 1617 to negotiate a Charter of Trade Privileges, we learn that these Ambassadors delivered long speeches in the Russian language, speaking 'very lowde and readyly'. As each speech was uttered it was interpreted by an Englishman, though one witness of the ceremony, Sir Gerard Herbert, says

---

[20] Horsey, p. 235.

[21] At least, it's a good story which may well be true: Sokolov, p. 42.

[22] 'Fletcher's Report on his Embassy' [September 1589], in Fletcher, *Of the Russe Commonwealth*, pp. 43-44.

in his account that 'the interpreterr, whether abashed or imperfaict in the language, or not so well comprehendinge, was not so readie or facound in his interpretacion, but made shift to goe through to the ende.'[23] At least, letters from Russian tsars in the seventeenth century were written in Russian, and there were British public servants available who were capable of translation. Academician Alekseev, writing in 1941, reports: 'Russian archives contain a series of documents about English youths who with the aim [of becoming interpreters] studied in the Russian State.' British records also confirm the presence in London of official interpreters.[24]

In the sixteenth and seventeenth centuries, as a result of the Muscovy merchants' enterprise, a foreign trading community, including English and Scottish persons, was well established in Moscow, and it must be presumed that some of them at least had learned Russian. The extent to which this was so is not ascertainable. The foreign community had a rather rough time under Tsar Aleksei Mikhailovich (reigned 1645-76). Xenophobia was rife, the intolerant clergy clamoured for forced conversion to Orthodoxy, and at least one *cause célèbre* concerned a British young woman, wife of a man who had converted, but who herself refused to accept Orthodoxy and was cruelly imprisoned and persecuted.[25] Despite occasional treatment of this sort, the British were inclined to stay in Russia, and the Tsar knew that their presence was beneficial to his country economically. Corralled in a *nemetskaia sloboda* or 'foreign quarter'—so as not to contaminate the Orthodox Russians—they survived quite well. It is the title 'nemetskaia sloboda' which is interesting. *Nemets* today means a German; then it was any foreigner, but the word is related to the word for 'dumb', that is, unable to speak Russian. It appears, therefore, that many in the expatriate communities then and much later did not learn Russian.

Those that did wish to learn it had no published books to help them. No Russian wrote a grammar of his own language until 1755, and the first surviving Russian grammar by a foreigner appeared in Oxford in 1696. It seems that would-be learners had to do the best they could by learning entirely orally, compiling their own grammatical or phraseological aides-mémoire, lists of useful words and the like. There must surely have been many such notes and lists, and the vast majority were probably discarded when the person who compiled them left Russia or died. However, two manuscript vocabularies at least have survived: they date from the mid-1590s and 1618-20.[26] Mark Ridley, a court physician in Moscow from 1594-99, compiled a Russian-English dictionary of about six thousand words along with an English-Russian list. The Rev. Richard James was

---

[23] Konovalov, p. 66.

[24] Alekseev, p. 79. The English record Alekseev cites is E. Green, (ed.), *Calendar of State papers Dom 1633-1634*, London 1862, p. 181, but this reference appears to be inaccurate.

[25] Fuhrmann, pp. 47-51.

[26] See Simmons, Unbegaun, Wrenn.

chaplain to Sir Dudley Digge's embassy and was in Moscow between 1618 and 1620. Scholars who have examined the vocabulary compiled by James report that the words are listed not alphabetically, but in order of collection. James seems to have had a better ear than Ridley, to have been able to interrogate his interlocutors to verify his facts, but to have had a rather shaky appreciation of Russian grammar, since words are often given in oblique cases, as if he did not distinguish one form of the word from another. Historians of Russian value these vocabularies for the information they provide of the state of the language at the time; for us it is equally interesting that men spending extended periods in Russia made the effort to document a language of which they must have found it very difficult to acquire any overall structural grasp.

It is at this time that we have the first tentative reference to the teaching of Russian in a formal context. In a book of 1615 entitled *The Third University of England*, Sir George Buck lists the subjects taught in colleges and schools in London. Chapter 37 is entitled 'Of Language'; he writes:

> There be also in this City Teachers and Professors of the Holy or Hebrew language, of the Chaldean, Syriac and Arabic languages, of the Italian, Spanish, French, Dutch and Polish tongues. And there be those which can speak the Persian and Morisco, and the Turkish and the Moscovian Language and also the Sclavonian Tongue, which passeth through seventeen nations. And in brief divers other Languages fit for Ambassadors and Orators and Agents, for Merchants and Travellers, and necessary for all Commerce and Negotiation.[27]

It will be seen that Buck does not say that the languages listed after 'And there be those...' were *taught*, merely that people could speak them. There were 'professors' of Polish—it was therefore presumably taught. However, the context—a catalogue of the languages which could be acquired in London at the time for commercial and diplomatic purposes—surely indicates that teaching could be had. The 'Sclavonian' tongue is mentioned separately; Buck's 'seventeen nations' are doubtless meant in this instance to be those countries where a Slavonic language other than Russian is spoken and where he imagines a traveller may get by, using a smattering of one of the native Slav tongues which were, to some extent at least, mutually comprehensible.

The deposition and execution of King Charles I and the establishment of the Commonwealth in the mid-seventeenth century brought to an end the favoured position of the Russia Company: trading privileges for the English were abolished in 1649 under Tsar Aleksei Mikhailovich. The Russian throne was a notoriously insecure seat, and events in London cannot but have made Aleksei uneasy. British and Soviet scholars, however, agree on two things: no nation in Western Europe was better informed about Russia in the second half of the sixteenth and the first two or three decades of the seventeenth centuries than the

---

[27] See first page of Illustrations.

English, and the English were better informed about Russia than the Russians were about England. Alekseev declares that the English were more proficient in Russian than the Russians were in English. He regrets the later steep decline. M. S. Anderson is positively scathing about the way the British allowed their pre-eminence to diminish so quickly. He castigates two British ambassadors, Dudley Digges (1618) and Christopher Cocks (1623) for incompetence and disobedience. Russia became an object of distaste to many British travellers and temporary residents: the severe climate, the obstacles placed in the way of internal travel, the xenophobia of the people, the severity of the penal system, a people who 'were moved by instinct and appetite rather than by intellect and reason.' 'With comparatively few exceptions English judgements of Russia in the seventeenth century were overwhelmingly adverse'. Anglo-Russian contacts are characterized by 'remoteness and estrangement' and an attitude of 'complacent indifference' ensued, which was not dented until Peter the Great rose to prominence.[28]

Little has been said so far about any specifically Scottish contribution in this period to the teaching and learning of the Russian language. From the year 1603 the crowns of Scotland and England were united, of course, though the parliaments remained separate for over a hundred years. The Russians have more recently obstinately dubbed all Britons *'anglichane'*—strictly speaking, 'Englishmen'. Dmitrii Fedosov, a Russian scholar who has worked in Scotland, has in an immense labour of love compiled his eccentrically typeset and proofread *Concise Biographical List* of hundreds of Scotsmen and women who went to Russia from the middle ages onwards. In the seventeenth century and in a few cases earlier the vast majority of these served in the Russian army and navy, often mercenary soldiers who were captured by the Russians and willingly enough 'turned'. Fedosov remarks that this distinguished them sharply from the English, who were overwhelmingly engaged in trade; he further demonstrates that Scotsmen were much more likely to naturalize, remain in Russia, and serve their adopted country wholeheartedly than the English, who, with exceptions, worked for Anglo-Russian trading and other relations as Britons, probably returning home eventually. One may dispute this judgement on the grounds that Fedosov's list may include many English expatriates: the surname is often no firm indication of ethnic origin; allowing for intermarriage with both English and Russians, the Scots or English blood must surely have become diluted in many cases. His statement that 'it is my conviction that in terms of national character Scots have much more in common with us Russians than the English do, and I know this view is shared by many on both sides' must be accepted as fact insofar as it records a matter of perception, but it can scarcely be defended empirically.[29] Nevertheless, Fedosov undeniably shows a different behaviour pattern on the part of Scots in Russia. Those who joined the Russian armed

---

[28] Anderson, pp. 33, 39, 44, 48.

[29] Fedosov, 'Preface', second page, unnumbered in original.

services must have learned Russian. One, Peter Hamilton, is known to have served as an interpreter for the Russian Admiralty around 1715-1725.[30] They doubtless learned it in the barrack-room, the wardroom, or the officers' mess, but we have no evidence about this. Published memoirs by Scotsmen tend to be by diplomats and travellers rather than émigrés. It can be said that neither Scots nor English made any substantial contribution to the study and teaching of the Russian language in the eighteenth century—not by publishing any scholarly or practical work, at least.

Learning Russian from the end of the Seventeenth Century to 1800. A Great Advantage Squandered by the British.

A milestone in Russian studies at the end of the seventeenth century was the publication of Ludolf's *Grammatica Russica*. The title only of an earlier work was included in a bibliography published in Frankfurt am Main in 1682, but since no copy survives we have no knowledge of its nature, its quality, or its contents.[31] Ludolf's was the first ever grammar of Russian to survive written in any language, and it deserves a place in a history of the study of Russian in Britain because, even though the author was German and the book written in Latin and it seems that most of the copies may have been sold abroad, Ludolf was a long-term resident in England and his grammar was published by the Oxford University Press.[32] Moreover, Ludolf includes about 25 pages of 'Phrases et modi loquendi communiores'—a brief phrase-book of the greatest interest. In terms of the reality, and truth to life of the conversations presented, no phrase-book since has ever bettered them.

A fair amount is known about Ludolf (1655-1712) and his activities.[33] He was born in Erfurt, studied in Jena, and first visited England in 1677-78. At different times in his life he was Secretary to the Danish envoy in London and to Prince George of Denmark, Queen Anne's consort. George granted him a generous pension after he suffered a mental breakdown; for the rest of his life he pursued ecumenical and evangelistic religious aims. It seems that both linguistic interests and the desire to foster rapprochement with Orthodoxy were strong motivating features in his Russian activities. He spent eighteen months in Russia from January 1693, when he made many Russian friends, met Tsar Peter, studied the religious situation, and acquired an amazingly comprehensive (if not absolutely perfect) knowledge of Russian. He settled permanently in London in 1700.

The Grammar (for which the Oxford University Press had to import a cyrillic font) consists of about a hundred pages following fourteen of preliminary matter.

---

[30]Fedosov, p. 53.

[31]Unbegaun, 'Introduction', p. viii.

[32]The Press published a facsimile edition in 1959: see note below.

[33]B. O. Unbegaun, 'Introduction', especially pp. xiii-xv.

Thirty-odd pages of grammatical description (all in Latin) are followed by twenty-five of the phrases; next comes the religious section 'De Cultu Divino', then a list of cardinal numerals and a short vocabulary of 'natural things'. A special edition, of which two copies survive, contained a formal dedication to Tsar Peter I and a short Russian-German vocabulary of military terms.

It is the realism of the little conversations in the phrase-book which is so striking. The flavour is conveyed by this exchange between master and servant:

> Take my shoes to the cobbler and have them repaired.
> *You've had them a long time; you need some new ones.*
> I don't need your advice; do as I say.
> *Sorry.*
> ...
> Help me to take my boots off and hang them up so they'll be dry by tomorrow.
> *You'll spoil them if you put them near the fire.*
> That's no business of yours; if I spoil them it'll be my own fault. Wake me tomorrow at four, and bring me some clean water—today you forgot.
> *You sent me out on an errand; I can't do two things at once.*
> If you hadn't been dawdling you'd have been back before I got up.
> *I came racing back like a mad dog.*
> I know you always answer like a fool.
> *It's better to be a fool than a thief.*
> Fools often steal as well, and even if you don't, you don't look after my things.
> *You can hire another man if you like.*
> Get the fire going and light a candle.
> *It's light now. When it gets dark I'll light up.*
> These candles don't burn very well, they're too thin. I need thick ones. Snuff them now.

This manservant recalls Zakhar in Goncharov's *Oblomov*—opinionated, obstinate, truculent, and intermittently servile. Any traveller to Russia, most notably in the Soviet age, has had to deal with waiters, shopworkers and the like with an uncanny likeness to this man. No modern phrasebook conveys the irritations of being a foreigner in Russia quite so vividly as does Ludolf's. His instructive Russian sentences beautifully convey the mounting irritation and frustration of the master as he tries to cope with his intractable factotum.

We have little evidence, alas, that Ludolf's grammar was widely studied in Britain, or that travellers and expatriate residents were helped by it. Only three hundred copies were printed; how many of them were sold to English native speakers cannot be known. It did attract approving comment in a number of

(54)

Глава д҃.	Cap. 4.
Междѣ хос̑аина и слѣги.	Inter Dominum & Servum.
Кормилъ ты ло- (1) шадь	Cibaſtine equum?
Пормилъ, а еще не напоилъ.	Cibavi, ſed nondum aquatum duxi.
Далчево ты не по (2) ране всталъ?	Quare non maturius ſurrexiſti?
Твое здоровїе знаетъ когда ты вчерасъ домон прѣ-халъ.	Tua dominatio ſcit, quando heri domum veneris.
Хотїа ты рано (3) спатъ лежишъ однакожде некогда прежде седмого часа тебя вижѣ.	Quanquam mature cubitum eas, tamen nunquam ante ſeptimam horam te video.
Въ передъ ленивъ не буду.	Impoſterum ignavus non ero.
Далчево ты не то- (4) пилъ печь.	Quare fornacem non calefeciſti?

Cap. 3.

Zwiſchen dem Herrn und Knecht.

(1) Haſtu das pferd gefuttert? Ja, aber ich habe es noch nicht getrancket. (2) Warumb biſtu nicht früher auffgeſtanden? Der herr weiſs wenn er geſtern zu hauſs gekommen iſt. (3) Wenn du gleich früh ſchlaffen geheſt, ſo ſehr ich dich doch niemahl vor ſieben uhr. Ins künfftige will ich nicht faul ſeyn, (4) Warum haſtu nicht eingeheitzet?

нетѣ

A page from the *Grammatica Russica* by H. W. Ludolf, Oxford, 1696. This extract is from 'Phrases et modi communiores'; Russian dialogue with Latin and German translations. The word *netu*, bottom right simply indicates the first word on the following page.

The image appears here by kind permission of Oxford University Press and is from the facsimile edition of this work published by the Press in 1959.

Western books, mainly German.[34] However, Ludolf's book was a beam of light in a dark place. Alekseev writes: 'In the next two hundred years not a single book appeared on the Russian language in England which could match the significance of Ludolf's work, (this is perhaps a *slight* exaggeration!) and knowledge of the language for many a long year stood on a much lower level.'[35]

By 1750 three more grammars had appeared, none of them written in Russian, by Belorussian (writing in Latin), Russian (writing in German) and Swedish authors respectively.[36] The first Russian-language grammar of the Russian language was by that great eighteenth-century polymath Mikhail Vasilievich Lomonosov: his *Rossiiskaia grammatika*, St Petersburg, 1755. It was, of course, intended not for learners, but as a scholarly description of the language for native speakers of it. There is, however, what appears to be an eighteenth-century French-language translation and adaptation of it with a title suggesting that it may be used for learning the Russian language.[37]

There is little to report on the study of Russian by Britons during the eighteenth century. Not only did Britain not produce a Russian grammar, but there was no English and Russian dictionary either. The British public were to some extent interested in events in Russia. As always, attitudes were equivocal: Peter's war against Sweden was unpopular, his growing naval strength was seen as a threat and, moreover, he was suspected of giving comfort to the Jacobites—though in fact he did nothing to assist their cause. The conclusion of the Great Northern War in 1721 was 'the beginning of a fundamental change in the attitude of British opinion towards Russia.'[38] We shall see that spying on Russian diplomatic representatives in Britain had taken hold by 1719.

Later in the century Catherine II was not without her admirers here, though, again, Russia's treatment of Poland was regarded with distaste. Anderson stresses that the picture of Russia the British public had was imprecise because it relied mostly on writers without any knowledge of Russian.[39] The question of literary exchange is interesting: one Thomas Consett translated some works by Theofan

---

[34] Unbegaun, p. xi.

[35] Alekseev, p. 84.

[36] Unbegaun, pp. xi-xii.

[37] I am grateful to Peter Hoare, former Nottingham University Librarian for drawing my attention to the existence of this work. The catalogue of foreign language books of the Russian National Library (RNL) gives the same author and title for all three editions, 1768, 1791, and 1795: Charpentier (c.1740-1800), *Elemens de la langue russe ou Méthode courte et facile pour apprendre cette lange conformement à l'usage*, Saint Petersbourg: de l'Imprimerie de l'Académie Impériale des sciences. Mr Hoare points out that ambiguous claims are made for its provenance: Cambridge University Library notes that its copy of the 1768 edition adds 'by M. V. Lomonosov; translated by Marignan; edited by Charpentier. Cf. dedication, preface. Translation of *Rossiiskaia grammatika*.' The RNL catalogue states that the first edition was 'printed at the author's expense.'

[38] Anderson, p. 67. For a study of Russia in relation to the Jacobites, see Rebecca Wells, *The Jacobites and Russia 1715-1750*, East Linton: Tuckwell Press, 2002.

[39] Anderson, p. 87.

Prokopovich, Peter the Great's steadfast episcopal supporter, in 1727. There were 245 known translations of English books into Russian, but only 48 of these translations can be shown to have been made directly from English: most were re-translated from French translations, and were consequently at two removes from the original. The first English translation of a work of imaginative Russian literature appeared in 1793: of Catherine II's *Ivan Czarowitz, or the Rose without Prickles That Stings Not.* The translator was Matthew Guthrie (1743-1807), a veritable polymath of Scottish birth—army doctor, literary man, scientist, historian, who was made a Russian nobleman with hereditary status.[40] Three tales by Karamzin appeared in 1800-01. A bare handful of non-fiction works was translated.[41] It would appear that the two nations were slow to develop a willingness to learn each other's language.

However, there was one field in which British government employees with a knowledge of Russian were active. Anderson states that the British government had no regular Russian translator to call upon until 1764.[42] His evidence for this statement is to be found in Home Office papers from 1772:[43]

> ANTH. TODD TO THE EARL OF ROCHFORD: Returning his warmest thanks for the obliging manner in which His Lordship expressed himself in regard to his nephew, Mr Maddison. Mr. Francis Willes has since called to say that he had been appointed Under Secretary of State, and that upon entering on his new office he would allow 200 L. of his salary of 400 L. a year as decypherer, to some persons to do the work for him, intimating as much as that his, Mr. Todd's, nephew might have a preference.
>
> His nephew's situation is this:- [... At] the latter end of 1762, [...] he was sent by the King's express commands to St. Petersburg to learn the Russian language, as he already understood the German. He arrived there in the midst of that winter, and accomplished the task so as to return hither in the spring of 1764; since which time he has constantly attended the despatch and arrival of the mails at the General Post Office, to copy the Russian letters, there being no person ever before that time for it; nor is there yet, except his brother, to whom he has taught the language. In the course of these eight years he has made out three of the Russian Minister's cyphers; two in their own language, and one in French. Though he claims no merit as a decypherer from the discovery of the last, as he was enabled by the course of the Russian correspondence to point out such papers (with which he was furnished from his Lordship's office) as made the success of that undertaking certain, yet it may fairly be said to be solely owing to him, and it was even then a work of labour. [...]

---

[40] Fedosov, p. 50. Cross identifies Guthrie as the pseudonymous 'Arcticus', who contributed around fifty items to an Edinburgh journal in the 1790s. See Cross, 'Arcticus and *The Bee*...'.

[41] I have drawn heavily on Cross, *Anglo-Russica*, in this paragraph: see pp. 7, 19, 26, 26-28, 83, 108.

[42] Anderson, p. 88.

[43] Dom Geo. III, pcl 85, no. 75, pp 552-553.

The statement that the British Government had no permanent Russian translator is not confirmed by this passage. Maddison is claiming expertise not as a translator merely, but as a cryptanalyst, a codebreaker. Other sources confirm the interest of the first three Kings George in cryptography.[44] That Maddison was sent to Russia to acquire the language is typical of government servants and military men right up to the First World War, and even later. The use of postal intercepts by the security services in Britain was first recorded in 1324.[45] In the first Elizabethan age such prying into private communications was notorious, and was even referred to by Shakespeare: 'The King hath note of all that they intend/By interception which they dream not of' (*Henry V*, IIii). Under the Stuart monarchs the system came into its own: the Post Office gradually became a monopoly, and monitoring of the mails was regarded as an essential means of maintaining the security of the realm.[46] In the 1820s the Office was even spying on the King's correspondence and that of the Royal Family. The so-called 'Secret Office' was closed down in 1844 after public and press outrage made its continuation impossible.[47]

John Maddison (1741-1808) had a distinguished career in the Post Office, eventually being made head of the Secret Department. He was 'a shy, reserved bachelor, collecting coins and curios',[48] a personality type which fitted well the duties of translator and cryptanalyst. The claim of there being 'no person ever before that time for [dealing with Russian mail]' is not true: it is well known that when Peter the Great introduced cryptology to Russia, British cryptanalysts were not slow to decode Russian cyphers. The first recorded British solution of a Russian code was in 1719, long before Maddison's time, and has been published in facsimile.[49] The battle went on: the earliest Russian codes were primitive and very easy to decrypt; but under Empress Elizabeth (reigned 1741-62) they became much more sophisticated and secure. As Maddison found, both Russian and French were used at different times up to the very end of the century; consequently linguists with knowledge of both Russian and French must have been active in the decoding. Examination of surviving records in the British Library[50] suggests that the mathematical skill of the decryptors was considerable, but their ability as translators from Russian may not have been so good. Some of the interceptions in the folders are of uncoded private correspondence; scribbled translations between the lines are confined largely to

---

[44] Much in this paragraph is based on the published findings of David Kahn, *The Codebreakers. The Story of Secret Writing*, New York: Scribner, 2. ed., 1996, esp. pp. 171-172 and 614-615.

[45] Bernard Porter, *Plots and Paranoia. A history of political espionage in Britain 1790-1988*, London: Unwin Hyman, 1989, p. 10.

[46] Marshall, 'Intelligence and the Post Office'.

[47] Ellis, *passim*.

[48] Ellis, pp. 93-94.

[49] Kahn, p. 614.

[50] Additional Manuscripts 32,288 and 32,292.

the courtesies ('your esteemed letter', 'your excellency'), and little more. There is, however, a letter of 1727, the first part of which is in open Russian and the second in code—which has been decoded into cyrillic. Other cyrillic jottings on the documents do show, however, that some of the cryptanalysts were familiar with the Russian language. There is a complete translation of a letter in Russian from Peter II to George II upon Peter's accession in 1727, partly into English and partly German, this last for the King's benefit, presumably. It is competently done—but by an Englishman or a German? No translator or decryptor is named in these papers. The Russians used French for their diplomatic correspondence increasingly, though not exclusively, from about 1758; this was really rather foolish of them, as it surely made the job of spying a little easier for the British.

What is true is that Britain's Russia-based intelligence was weak and seems to have been heavily reliant on friends and allies in the German states (Prussia, Württemberg, Saxony and others). An attempt in 1725 to establish a secret political agent in Russia was so obvious that the person concerned, Captain John Deane, was expelled within a month of his arrival.

It is fairly clear that many British expatriates in Russia did not feel the need to learn much Russian. Many, but not all: at the same time as Maddison was perfecting his language skills in Russia, another very young Englishman, John Newton, was finishing a six-year stint as teacher of English in the naval academy in St Petersburg. At the age of about 21 in 1761 he engaged in trade and other free-lance pursuits [в свободных науках] until, thanks to his outstanding linguistic skills he was enrolled by the leading statesman Nikita Panin as an interpreter in the College of Foreign Affairs, which established his career as a Russian diplomat in the service of Catherine the Great.[51] But for most Britons in Russia, French or German would suffice, and in fact by the end of the eighteenth century many noble Russian families had adopted the fetish of speaking French, or a sort of broken French, in 'good' society. An anonymous Russian visitor to England in 1796 wrote that no foreigners bothered to learn Russian: 'When they come to our country they should be obliged to learn it, but they despise it when they see that we ourselves consider it a distinction to know their languages better than our own.'[52] Just how widespread the habit of speaking French was is difficult to know. It applied most in metropolitan areas; anecdotes exist of provincial gentry whose French was near to non-existent. In one famous case a fraudulent children's tutor allegedly moved from family to family teaching his native Finnish for thirty years before any of the local gentry found out it was not French.[53] Russian ever remained the official state language, and, of course,

---

[51]Newton's very brief account of his life and career is reprinted in Skalkina, pp. 92-93. It is perhaps significant that Newton's ability in Russian led him into service of the Russian, not the British state.

[52]Quoted by Cross, *Anglo-Russica,* p. 108.

[53]The story is told by E. J. Simmons, *Pushkin,* London: Oxford UP, 1937, p. 25. Pushkin himself, in a fragment of prose fiction, 'Russkii Pelam', indulges in mockery of French tutors: A. S. Pushkin, *Polnoe sobranie sochinenii,* VI, Moscow-Leningrad: Izd. Akad, nauk SSSR, 1950, p. 596.

had to be used in speaking to the lower orders. The chasm between the classes was widened by the language barrier thus erected and by the fact that the serfs and lower orders despised the French anyway.[54]

And yet in the same century innovative writers and scholars urged their compatriots to *use* their native language. Part of the difficulty may have been the state of the Russian language itself: for centuries there had been disagreement. Linguistic science was in a primitive state, and in the early years of the eighteenth century it was widely thought that Church Slavonic, the language of the church, the liturgy, theology and the Bible was distinct from the secular Russian used in government and administration; 'literary' Russian fell in between. The immensely complex developments of the language at this time are traced by Ian Press in a recent book; he points out that mid-eighteenth-century writers ceased to see Church Slavonic and Russian as being in opposition to each other; rather was the 'civil language' [...] based on the church language.' 'The old bookish tradition is now free to influence the language, secure in its status.' Moreover, Press attributes political and ideological reasons to the establishment of a linguistic norm: the strong nation-state which was developing in the eighteenth century 'need[ed] a standard language to maintain cohesion.'[55]

A number of leading literary figures, some of whom are now remembered best for their theoretical writings on language and style, made a conscious attempt to establish a standard literary language while engaging in discussion and polemic. Trediakovskii, Sumarokov, Kantemir, and principally Lomonosov, did not agree on what style should be established for literary works, but their discussion of the whole issue was significant. The matter may also be seen as a strong reaction against the use of foreign languages in society. 'Our tongue is sweet, and pure, and splendid and prolific', wrote Sumarokov in his verse 'Epistle I (on the Russian language)':

We need a tongue such as the Greeks had, and as the Romans had too, a language like that of Italy and Rome today, and as beautiful as French became last century; Russian is capable of becoming such a tongue![56]

---

[54] Hosking, pp. 156 and 287-288.
A clue to the linguistic situation in some British expatriate families long established in Russia is given by a reminiscence of Jean Paterson. She was a daughter of Catherine II's distinguished 'Scottish admiral', Samuel Greig; when she took up philanthropic work in the early nineteenth century, she made a particular effort to brush up her *childhood* Russian for the purposes of prison work. [Wendy Rosslyn, 'Benevolent ladies and their exertions for the good of humankind', *SEER*, 84(1), 2006, 52-82', p. 75, my emphasis—JM] Presumably that 'childhood Russian', even in Russia, had been used mainly or exclusively with the servants.

[55] Press, pp. 186, 187, 195.

[56] Sumarokov, pp. 114 and 112.

Sumarokov's elegant alexandrines, which he wrote doubtless in tribute to his French models, are rendered here in mere prose. Lomonosov confirms his feeling and injects a further element of patriotism into the argument:

> The language which the Russian State uses to rule a large part of the globe displays in its very nature abundance, beauty and power second to no other European language. And there is no doubt that the Russian tongue can be brought to the same level of perfection which we admire in the other languages.[57]

The Russian literary language was, in D. S. Mirsky's words, 'in a state of standardless chaos'.[58] Lomonosov's proposal to fix the standards gained some considerable support, at least for a few decades. He argued for three styles of writing: a lofty language with Church Slavonic elements for tragedy and ode, a 'middle style' for poetry, and a more demotic manner for comedy and fable. A later generation rejected this scheme, when Karamzin advocated a single style—in effect, a development of the 'middle' style—tending to French elegance (and vocabulary) and rejecting Lomonosov's Germanic and Latin syntax. Against the opposition of several very gifted writers, Karamzin's view prevailed; Pushkin himself tended in this direction. It is interesting that over a century after the controversy was settled, a Russian writer of the stature of Mirsky openly expressed serious reservations.[59] For our purposes it is relevant principally to realize that Russian writers directed their attention keenly to the tool which they used and to the way it could be developed. A Russian Academy modelled on the Académie française was founded in 1783, which interested itself strongly in the Russian language; it produced a dictionary in 1789-94: 'everything conveyed by language [had] a place within it.'[60] A grammar followed in 1802.[61]

We cannot leave Lomonosov without recalling his most memorable utterance about the Russian language, which, he said, possessed 'the splendour of Spanish, the vivacity of French, the strength of German, the tenderness of Italian, and the richness, brevity and vivid imagery of Greek and Latin.'[62] Russians are often able to quote this dictum from memory.

French was not the only foreign language beloved of the Russian upper classes, though it was certainly the favourite. English and German were also popular, English particularly in the years of 'Anglomania' which began during

---

[57] Lomonosov, p. 43.

[58] D. S. Mirsky, *A History of Russian Literature*, L: Routledge and Kegan Paul, 1949, 43.

[59] Mirsky, p. 60.

[60] Press, p. 187.

[61] Hosking, pp. 287-288.

[62] '...великолепие испанского, живость французского, крепость немецкого, нежность итальянского, сверх того богатство и сильную в изображениях краткость греческого и латинского языка.'

the Napoleonic Wars and developed during the nineteenth century.[63] English or Scottish children's nurses and male tutors were widely employed in Russian noble families. British children's books and educational toys were also much prized in Russia.[64]

To this fondness for foreign languages in Russia, we may add the prejudice as well as the ignorance of many British expatriates and travellers (and not only them) towards the Russian language. 'Even in the character of their alphabet there is a kind of barbarism which is truly revolting,' wrote one. 'Russian is the most abominable language that ever was,' wrote another. Both these quotations come from the early years of the nineteenth century, and we shall see that such prejudice continued well into the later years of that century. British conviction of their own superiority provides a rationalisation for idleness in attempting to master the language. One British observer, however, can be found who thought the language 'concise, nervous, musical and flowing.'[65]

It would be good to finish this account of the study of—or failure to study—Russian in the eighteenth century on that pleasant note; however, we turn to bathos. As stated above, it appears that not a single book on the Russian language and no translating dictionary appeared in Britain between Ludolf's grammar and the year 1800. In this respect Britain was behind the Russians, who produced a number of textbooks and grammars of English between 1790 and 1811.[66] The grotesque work which saw the light of day in 1800 was *A Commercial Dictionary of the English and Russian Languages*, by Adam Kroll, who describes himself on the title page as 'member of the Russian (sic: he seems to mean "Russia") Company'. Publication details are: London: Printed for S. Chappel, Royal Exchange, by T. Plummer, Seething Lane. The price was the enormous sum for the day of twelve shillings. There is no date on the title page or verso, but the preface is dated 12 August 1800.

This publication is far less and far more than a dictionary. The 'dictionary' section is in fact a relatively limited vocabulary of about 650 words intended to be of use to merchants and their agents. This vocabulary does not appear in cyrillic type: the strangeness of the Russian letters is felt by the author to be a deterrent to the user. All the words are given in chaotic transliterations; thus *iron* (zhelezo) is 'shelesso', *books* (knigi) 'kneega' [sic], *bottles, empty* (butylki porozhnie) 'bootelkeé, porushnea', *bristles, hogs' all sorts* 't'schetina Sakich sortoff' (this garbled phrase may be taken as representing 'shchetina vsiakikh sortov'). It is hard to believe that this can have been much use to those seeking to sell their wares in Russia. The compiler's knowledge of Russian seems to have

---

[63] Alekseev, pp. 95ff.

[64] Alekseev, pp. 97-99. The story of the British nannies in Russia, especially but not exclusively in the late nineteenth and early twentieth centuries, has been engagingly chronicled by Harvey Pitcher, in his *When Miss Emmie was in Russia*, Newton Abbot: Readers' Union, 1977.

[65] These contrasting opinions are quoted by Anderson, pp. 87-88.

[66] Alekseev, pp. 92-93.

been limited; his name, moreover, is German-sounding, and the transliterations may owe something to a German accent.

However, the book is immensely informative in other ways; the vocabulary is only the start of its 135 pages. There are statistics of Russian exports to Britain and other countries, lists of goods prohibited from export or import, ships arriving at St Petersburg (more than half of them British at this time), the coinage, means of conveying goods to the interior, originals (these actually in cyrillic) and translations of various Government edicts on trade, duties payable to the King of Denmark on goods for Britain passing the Elsinore Straits, and advice to ships' masters and private travellers arriving at or departing from St Petersburg. Apparently they had to expect their luggage would be sealed and not released for up to twelve days, and advance notice of departure had to be advertised in Russian and German in the Petersburg papers so that any Russian having financial claims might make them. If the book did not foster linguistic knowledge and understanding, it obviously provided other types of valuable information to assist the trader.

It was in the nineteenth century that Russian studies really began to make a significant impact in Britain. This impact was felt strongly in the military area, in commerce, in diplomatic relations, and in the universities. However, before we turn to these areas, there are other tales to tell, which comprise the beginning of our next chapter.

Chapter 2

Towards the Emergence of the Organized Study of Russian in the Nineteenth and Early Twentieth Centuries

From the gigantic strides, which this mighty Empire is making in literature, science and the arts, we may reasonably anticipate the period, when its rich, harmonious and energetic language will be studied by the other nations of Europe for the sake of its original productions. As yet, we have seen only a few rays of the literary scene, which is dawning on the North, but their brightness sufficiently bespeaks the glory of its meridian splendour.

JAMES HEARD (1827)

Some pioneer teachers and grammarians

BRITISH would-be learners of Russian still lacked opportunities for assisted study when the nineteenth century began. The provision of dictionaries and books for the learner had not begun. In 1808 there appeared in Moscow an extensive thousand-page *New Dictionary English and Russian*, by Nikolai Grammatin,[1] intended primarily for Russian learners of English, but better than nothing for English students of Russian, always supposing they knew of it and could obtain a copy. From 1846 several editions appeared of *A New Pocket-Dictionary of the English and Russian and of the Russian and English Languages*. This work has no declared author or authors, and describes itself as 'Stereotype edition, Leipsic'; there is no date, but the British Library's copy bears the date stamp '18 DEC 50'. It is a substantial small-format book of about 800 pages, with some 22,000 head-words in each half. As such it must have been of considerable use to its purchasers, if their eyesight was good enough to read the very small print.

Two Russian grammars for English-speaking learners appeared in the 1820s. As these were the first, they deserve consideration here; the second more than the first. *A Manual of an English and a Russian Grammar*, St Petersburg, 1822, is a slim volume of 153 pages, and the British Library's copy appears to have belonged to a John Subron of Ekaterinoslav, whose pencilled annotations show that he made some use of it. The author conceals his identity as 'W.H.M.D.' The use of a *nom de plume* raises the suspicion that the author might have been a

---

[1] Details of these books may be found in the relevant section of the Bibliography.

lady anxious to avoid the charge, all too common at the time, of 'impropriety', 'vanity' or 'immodesty' in publishing something under her own name,[2] but this appears not to be the case, as the author refers to himself as 'he' in the Preface, and nothing in the book suggests female authorship. It is intended for English residents in Russia, 'particularly those who are engaged in merchantile pursuits.' It is riddled with misprints (at least 150), for which the author apologizes, citing his distance from Petersburg as the reason for inadequate supervision of the printing.

Only the fact that it is, as far as we know, the very first grammar by an English-speaker for English-speakers, claims our attention for this book. The writer works hard in trying to describe the Russian language, but there are many errors and clumsy attempts at explanation. The information given on pronunciation is grossly inaccurate in several ways which cannot be explained by changes in pronunciation since 1822; some strange details in the declension of nouns may be discerned; the section on verbal tenses is full of confusion and misunderstanding, and the concept of 'aspect' is absent, even under another name. As an example of useless information, two 'pluperfect' and 'compound' tenses are expounded, though 'The present Academy, in order to simplify their grammar have thought proper [not] to retain [them].' They had in fact not been used for hundreds of years. In general, it is a descriptive grammar and lacks any examples of usage except for short phrases; it gives no cultural information such as the use of the second person pronouns, the words are not accented and accent is not mentioned, it is not arranged progressively to aid the beginner, there is no index, and it would be well-nigh impossible to learn much Russian from it. But it was the *first* such grammar.

To be quite fair to W.H.M.D., we must remember that the Russian language in the 1820s was just beginning to settle down from the state of flux which Lomonosov and his fellow-writers had grappled with seventy years earlier, and with charity some of its failings may be attributed to the difficulties a foreigner must experience in bringing order into the description. A much better attempt at a self-instructional manual published in St Petersburg a few years later is of considerable interest for the history of the study of Russian, not least by reason of the career and personality of the young author. He has left an account of how he taught himself to speak Russian and to use the language in an exacting professional career. That author was the notable, but largely forgotten, figure of James Arthur Heard. In 1817 Heard, then aged only about 18, was persuaded to go to Russia to run a school on the principles of 'mutual instruction' instituted by Andrew Bell and Joseph Lancaster[3] to be set up at Gomel' on the estates of

---

[2] Wendy Rosslyn, 'Benevolent ladies and their exertions for the good of humankind', *Slavonic and East European Review*, vol. 84 no. 1, 2006, 52-82, esp. pp. 53 and 63.

[3] For information on the Lancasterian system of mutual instruction, see any good history of education or James Muckle 'Alexander I and William Allen: a Tour of Russian schools in 1819 and some missing reports', *History of Education*, vol. 15, no. 3, pp. 137-145

Count Rumiantsev. His first task was to master the Lancasterian (or 'Lancastrian') system, which he did by gaining his certificate of competence in June 1817; his second was to acquire the Russian language. The body which supported him was the British and Foreign School Society (BFSS).[4] He is quoted[5] thus:

> In 1816 four students were sent from the Pedagogic Institute of St. Petersburg to study the different elementary methods adopted in England and Switzerland [...]
> From them I received instruction in Russian in return for assistance in their study of English. I soon discovered what an arduous task I had before me, especially as there were no books whatever to help the English student while the Germans and French had both grammars and dictionaries.

'Arduous task' or no, Heard clearly made considerable, if at first rather slow, progress. His eventual total success is evidenced by his later distinguished career in Russia. The Russian students were in Britain under the auspices of the BFSS. With Heard's help they made rapid progress in English, within five months passing their examinations both in the language and in Lancasterian pedagogy.[6]

Heard left for Russia. It took him twenty-two days to reach Gomel' from St Petersburg. He was kindly received there by a Mr Clark and a retired General Derbiashin, who spoke excellent English. Later in his narrative Heard mentions using a Russian and French dictionary to extract monosyllabic words in order to teach them to his Russian schoolchildren. In the third winter of his stay, he was still hard at work on his Russian, having found 'a nice English boy to study Russian with me, the son of an Englishman named Harbottle, who had lately come out to look after a farm.'

Heard endured hardship and relative poverty (the Count seems to have been a wholly disorganized individual who had not begun to think through the necessary measures to the setting up of a school, and who paid Heard in paper roubles instead of the silver ones he had been led to expect), but he survived a winter of inactivity and frigid temperatures in a draughty hut with a serf-boy servant. When he eventually had it out with the Count, Rumiantsev said that most of the inhabitants of Gomel' were Jews, and he had wanted to start a school for his (Christian) serfs, whom it would be hard to assemble from outlying

---

[4] On the Society's work in Britain, see H. B. Binns, *A Century of Education*, London: Dent, 1908; in Russia, see: B. Hollingsworth, 'Lancasterian schools in Russia', *The Durham Research Review*, no. 17, September 1966, pp. 59-74.

[5] 'Mr Heard's Lancastrian school in Russia', *Proceedings of the Anglo-Russian Literary Society*, 1902, vol. 35, pp. 49-59. The anonymous editor of this paper introduces it by writing: 'Time and space do not permit of the reproduction of the whole of [Heard's autobiographical] narrative, but an abridged form of it may interest members of this Society.'

[6] *Report of the British and Foreign School Society*, 1817, pp. 30-31. For the record, the students' names were Obodovskii, Busse, Svenske (of whom more later) and Timaev, two of whom were Lutherans and two Orthodox—as the names might suggest.

villages. Heard pointed out that there were two hundred orphans on the Count's estates—why not start a boarding school? The Count, jolted into activity, allocated a building; while it was under construction, the boys were accommodated in an unoccupied wing of the Count's house, with Heard and a classroom for 45 boys. The eventual success of the venture made Heard's reputation in Russia, and led to his help in founding numerous Lancasterian schools in several cities.

It is to be regretted that we know so few details of Heard's life, but what we do know is of great interest. He lived until 1875. He and his whole family (he married one Elizaveta Lomnovskaia around 1830 and had at least four sons, one of whom in turn became a distinguished Russian educator, and a daughter)[7] took Russian citizenship in 1845. He was awarded the Order of St Stanislav. James's further career—as educator, translator, novelist[8] and consultant to a railway company—concerns us principally in regard to his work as a linguist. His gifts are graphically illustrated by the fact that his translation into Russian of *The Vicar of Wakefield* was regarded as the best available at the time (1846). The poet Zhukovskii is said to have enjoyed his company and conversation.

Heard must have turned his mind to writing his *Practical Grammar of the Russian Language*, St Petersburg (1827) and an accompanying *Key* in the mid-1820s. He was well under thirty years old when he undertook this task. His formal education was very limited. His elder brother was a Royal Navy man, who was killed at the battle of Philadelphia during the War of 1812 against the United States. Another brother was also a sailor who discovered Heard Island south west of Australia and had it named after him; he later died at sea. Their mother was adamant that James should not go to sea, though he wished to; teaching became his profession. The family was of relatively humble social status; James's training was of a very basic nature, and in fact school teachers of working-class origin were regarded with some apprehension by leaders of society, in case they should get ideas 'above their station'. This applied less to the largely Quaker and nonconformist BFSS than to the established church, and indeed, someone must have encouraged James in intellectual pursuits, since his grammar is the work of a man not just of high intelligence but of broad culture.

The *Practical Grammar* of Heard is the first by a known British professional educator, and a linguist of unusual skill. He acknowledges the help of Charles Svenske, one of the Russian Lancasterian teachers he coached in English a decade earlier, and a debt to the Academy Grammar, a work by Grech on

---

[7] I am indebted to Dr John Dunstan for information copied from the baptismal records of the Anglican Church in St Petersburg, held in the Guildhall Library, London.

[8] His very readable epistolary novel, *The Life and Times of Nathalia Borissovna, Princess Dolgorookov*, London: Bosworth and Harrison, 1857, was, to judge by one of the narrator's remarks, intended for children. It paints a vivid picture of Russian life in and around the courts of tsars from Aleksei Mikhailovich to the Empress Elizabeth, but reaches a bleak moral conclusion—that stories do not always end happily. It has been reprinted in the twentieth century.

Russian declensions, *Opyt russkikh spriazheniiakh*, *Grammaire russe* by Reiff,[9] and two grammars by German writers called Vater and Tappe.[10] 'The road to some sciences leads through delightful scenery, but the path that leads to the knowledge of a language is dreary and uninviting, and requires to be strewed with flowers,' he writes in his Preface. The arrangement of the grammar and the way the students are to reinforce their knowledge is unusual, to say the least. What it consists of is basically a descriptive grammar—nouns, pronouns, verbs, etc., leading to syntax in conclusion—interspersed with 'themes'. These are in fact English to Russian translation exercises, with the exception of the very first, a reading passage from Karamzin's *Letters of a Russian Traveller* in parallel columns of Russian and English. However, when the student had read all about, for example, the six cases of masculine nouns ending in a hard consonant, he must work through the translation of 'select sentences, gradually increasing in difficulty as the scholar proceeds'; all necessary vocabulary is provided at the foot of the page, so all the student needs to do is manipulate the case-endings of the phrases in italics, thus: 'God is the creator *of the world*. The soul *of man* is immortal. Reason was given *to man* to control his passions. Happy is that youth who has found *a true friend...*' (The religiose and moralistic tone here is not untypical, but it does not overwhelm.) When all the noun endings have been presented, Heard provides 'promiscuous' exercises: 'Here is the reign *of winter*. In the beginning *of October* everything is covered *with snow*. The neighbouring hill scarcely shows its sterile *summit...*(etc.)'

There is no selection or limitation of vocabulary, nor is there any logical arrangement of it. The 'themes' (exercises in morphology, in effect) dictate the words the student must manipulate—and the whole thing is an exercise in manipulation. Heard falls into the trap which WHMD did, and which many much later and more eminent scholars did, of sometimes describing the language as an English speaker might expect it to be, rather than looking at it as it is. Thus we have the present tense of the verb *to be* given in full, with the first two persons placed in brackets without the necessary explanation that they had not been used

---

[9] Nikolai I. Grech (1787-1867) was of Prussian origin, was known in Russia as publisher of conservative journals, and as the first person to attempt a history of Russian literature. Grech was a prominent linguist and critic; he wrote several handbooks of Russian grammar and syntax, no fewer than three of which appeared between 1827 and 1830, one of which was translated into French by Reiff and published in St Petersburg in 1829; later in the century his own grammars were regarded as standard: see Bibliography. It may be that the grammar Heard acknowledges was actually Reiff's translation of Grech. Carl Philipp Reiff (1792-1872) was Swiss, long resident in St Petersburg, teacher of languages, author of grammars, compiler of multilingual dictionaries. His *Grammaire russe* first appeared in 1821, but was reissued in 1851; grammars in English and German appeared in 1853; the dictionaries appeared until 1862.

[10] These authors can be identified, though exactly which of their books Heard used is not always clear. J. S. Vater's *Practische Grammatik der Russischen Sprache* appeared in Leipzig in 1808. A. W. Tappe published a German-languge grammar of Russian in St Petersburg in 1835, an earlier edition of which Heard had presumably seen.

for centuries. The author presents *all* types of noun and verb, regular and irregular, usual and unusual, without any concession to the learner who needs to absorb these gradually. There is no 'cultural' information. Only highly motivated and academically-minded students could have learned Russian from this book.

And yet... it is hard not to be attracted by the charm of some of the writing. The conclusion of Heard's Preface is quoted as the epigraph to this chapter. He writes of 'the irksome dryness of grammatical rules', and he certainly tries to 'strew the path with flowers'. Most of all is this revealed in the *Key to the Themes Contained in Heard's Russian Grammar,* which he published alongside his primer. Apart from the answers to the translation exercises, there is a vocabulary of about 1,500 words arranged by subject matter: for example 'spiritual objects' (from 'God' to 'a free-thinker'), natural objects, the animal kingdom, the human mind, virtues and vices, clothing, habitation, etc. There are sections on titles and ranks, weights and measures, and there are several very useful and practical dialogues. These lack Ludolf's humour and characterisation, but they must have helped many a traveller to negotiate the pitfalls of Russian life. The volume closes with 'Reading lessons in prose'—very well annotated stories by Muraviev, Benitskii, Izmailov and Batiushkov—and 'reading lessons in verse'—poems with translations, by Karamzin, Krylov and Khemnitser, along with Kozlov's translation of Byron's 'Good night', Zhukovskii's translation of Goldsmith's 'The Hermit', and an unattributed translation of Gray's 'Elegy in a Country Churchyard'.[11] These choices clearly demonstrate Heard's knowledge of and taste in Russian contemporary literature.

The most significant points about Heard's Grammar do not concern its structure, but the spirit in which it is written. The year, it will be remembered, was 1827. There is a beautifully engraved dedication to the Empress Alexandra Feodorovna (consort of Nicholas I) in which the book is described as an 'attempt to facilitate the acquirement of the Russian language to a nation whose friendly and mutually advantageous intercourse with the Empire has been uninterruptedly maintained since the sixteenth century.' It is therefore, unlike the grammar of WHMD, unashamedly a contribution to international understanding, not merely a handbook for the use of British residents in Russia who needed to speak to shopkeepers and carry on their daily business. The epigraph which stands at the head of this chapter betrays a love of Russia and her culture, not merely a dry knowledge of grammar. Heard, as a courageous pioneer of Lancasterian education in Russia, is here campaigning for mutual peace and understanding, which reflects his Quakerish background.[12] His humanity and his empathy with the

---

[11]The first few stanzas are from Zhukovskii's 1802 version, later numerous amendments appear; five of the seven stanzas of the Epitaph are changed, two of them substantially. It may be that Heard's adaptations were meant to assist the learner, and included more literal extant versions, of which there were several (see Zhukovskii, *Sobranie sochinenii,* I, Moscow: Izd. khud. lit., 1959, p. 416.)

[12]It cannot be confirmed for certain that he was a Quaker. The BFSS was not so exclusively. It can probably be said that Heard was close to the Quaker position.

Russian heritage shines through the demanding, academic and even—let us face it—boring pages of his grammar. James Heard should be recognized as a worthy pioneer of the teaching of Russian.

Before leaving Heard, we should remark that he is unusual in that he compiled materials for the teaching of English to Russians as well as for the teaching of Russian to English native speakers.[13] Indeed, he also published grammars for French and German learners of Russian.

Heard's Grammar sets the scene for the institution of Russian language studies in Britain in the later nineteenth century. He and writers of grammars who followed him clearly had self-instruction in mind. But formal teaching of the language too could scarcely take place without the provision of teaching material. Teachers, of course, can and do compile their own courses, but before the age of the photocopier, this was not easy. Grammars and dictionaries in particular were needed. After the appearance of Heard's grammar, no other grammar by a person with an English-sounding name appeared until the 1880s, though Reiff's 1853 work for English speakers (see note 9) was much used and appreciated. At least two others by German-language authors (Alexejew—a Russian enough name—and Bolz) appeared in German in 1872 and 1880. Henry Riola was a Russian—though his name does not suggest it. He and Pietro Motti (described on the title-page of the 1922 edition of his grammar as 'Knight of the Crown of Italy'), an Italian whose work was first published in Germany, but later by Nutt in London, produced courses which were used for some years. An English translation of a French translation of a Russian-language grammar appeared in 1882, and in the same year A. Ivanoff's *Russian Grammar [...] translated for the use of English students* saw the light of day. In 1884 there appeared by Ivan Nestor-Schnurmann, *The Russian Manual*. Schnurmann and Riola will reappear later in our story; if the methodology followed in Schnurmann's grammar is odd,[14] at least we can say he was concerned to present his material in a way conducive to learning. F. Freeth's very brief 75-page *A Condensed Russian Grammar for the Use of Staff-officers and Others* appeared in 1886, but this title is something of a mystery, as the book has nothing specifically military about it, thought it doubtless reflected the growing interest among the military in the Russian language, which will become a major theme in our story. The same year saw the appearance of Kinloch's grammar, which is, like Freeth's, purely

---

[13]His works for Russian learners of English are: *Frazeologiia angliiskogo iazyka ili sobranie upotrebitel'nykh soobshchenii*, SPb., 1840, *Etimologicheskii angliiskii bukvar'*, SPb., 1844.

[14]From his introduction: 'Before proceeding to the grammar, the student is advised to read over repeatedly the Exercises... as they give the derivation of every word, its simple meaning, how it is compounded, and what part of speech it is. Then let him in each instance refer to the grammatical part of the Manual and learn the rule relating thereto. The student will now find the exercise put into an interrogative form, to which he will be able with very little effort to reply in Russian. Thus he will find he has learned the grammar merely by referring to the different rules.'

descriptive, though much fuller (250 pages), and which contains an as yet unique feature: a section of handwritten Russian in different styles so the student may learn to cope with manuscript text.[15] The year 1889 saw the appearance of W. R. Morfill's *A Grammar of the Russian Language*, which academic slavists see as a milestone in Russian studies; Motti's grammar also appeared. Like Kinloch's, Motti's was described as a 'Conversation' grammar and had an appendix for 'tradesmen, travellers, Army officers [etc.]' The 'progressive' grammars (that is, those which were for people trying actually to learn the language, as opposed to scholarly descriptions of Russian) often claimed to be based on some fashionable 'system', such as those of 'Gaspey-Otto-Sauer' (Motti) or Ollendorf. Just what exactly there was of significance in these 'methods' is often difficult to see.

After the 1846 *New Pocket Dictionary*, there appeared Aleksandrov's *Polnyi Anglo-Russkii slovar'* in four editions from 1879, with about 16,200 headwords dealt with in helpful detail, decently and clearly printed and a great advance on Grammatin—but still primarily intended for the Russian learner of English. A commercial dictionary was published, and a polyglot seven-language medical vocabulary by Theodore Maxwell in 1890. After this we have: in 1906 a military and naval dictionary, in 1909 an engineering dictionary, in 1910 *Hill's Modern Pronouncing Dictionary of the English and Russian Languages*, compiled by two men with Russian names (Hill was the publisher); in 1911 a pocket dictionary by Linden and in 1913 *Hill's Russian-English (English-Russian) [sic] Vest-pocket Dictionary and Self-instructor* by S. I. Lyubov. This looks like a lot of dictionaries; yet sixty years and more later academics were still complaining that Britain had produced no really good translating dictionaries, and students in the 1960s were *still* mainly relying on dictionaries of Russian or Soviet provenance.

Most of the pre-1914 dictionaries and grammars have been forgotten, but the course which became very popular was *Bondar's Simplified Russian Method Conversational and Commercial*. It first appeared in 1911, and there were regular reprints and five new editions until 1954. David Bondar was a Manchester teacher who turned the teaching of Russian into a small industry, especially during the First World War. Dull though this book was, it was thorough, and its success was probably due to the 43-page long commercial section, which gave the student a firm grounding in business correspondence in Russian. The book was certainly snapped up by universities and technical colleges as interest in Russian grew after 1914.

Motivation to learn and the national need for Russian

Who, though, wanted to learn Russian in the later nineteenth and early twentieth centuries, and how did the language find a place in the curricula of educational institutions? As we have already begun to discover, and as we shall find in the

---

[15] Alexander Kinloch was later Secretary of the Anglo-Russian Literary Society.

twentieth century, British-Russian relations and the way the two nations perceived each other played and continue to play an equivocal part in the story, and the relationship between attitudes to Russia and the desire to study the language was by no means straightforward. James Heard's love of Russia expressed in his grammar was not an eccentric aberration. There were many in Britain who shared his enthusiasm, or who sought to interpret Russia to their compatriots. The Rev. Henry Lansdell's once popular travel books were seen in diplomatic circles as likely to 'do something towards softening the asperity which then existed between England and Russia.'[16] More enduringly well-known writers, Harold Williams,[17] W. T. Stead[18] and D. Mackenzie Wallace[19] wrote in more measured style about Russia. Their works were to some extent influential, but they were swimming against the current. The reports of E. R. B. Hodgetts, the greatly respected Reuters and *Times* correspondent, were frank about conditions in Russia without demonstrating anti-Russian feeling. Why did the 'asperity' to which Lansdell referred exist, and who felt it? One historian, John Howes Gleason, has charted the rise of 'Russophobia' in Britain to 1841.[20] He argues that it is based partly at least on misunderstanding of Russian policy by politicians and public and unease in Britain about the authoritarian political philosophy of Russia. He further attributes it to 'an inescapable *guerre des idées* between the liberal west and the autocratic east of Europe', but at the same time to 'trade rivalry, the absence of profitable and waxing commercial intercourse, the accident of event and personality, the pursuit of policies which appeared to conflict in execution even if their basic inspiration did not, and the genius of those men who happened to possess political authority or to play an important part in the formation of opinion that made a ponderable contribution to the process of Russophobia.[21]

The two nations had come to blows in the Crimea in the 1850s and nearly did so again in the 1870s over Turkey and the Balkans. Autocracy and oppression in Russia fluctuated in intensity in the last half of the century, but the impression conveyed by the popular British press was one of fearsome experiences in prison, deportation in chains, Siberian exile, 'a fate worse than death' for women prisoners, and restriction of free speech and of human rights. Revolutionary activities not excluding terrorism were to some extent even condoned in the British public mind and regarded as heroic resistance to a cruel régime. Government was ambivalent—and divided. On the one hand it was necessary to

---

[16]Lansdell, Henry. *Russian Central Asia.* London, 1885, p. 2.

[17]Williams was the correspondent for the *Daily Chronicle*, and was held by Sir Bernard Pares to be the greatest of all connoisseurs of Russia of his time.

[18]W. T. Stead, *Truth About Russia.* London, 1888.

[19]D. Mackenzie Wallace, *Russia*, II volumes. London/Paris/New York: Cassell, 1905.

[20]Gleason, *The Genesis of Russophobia.*

[21]Gleason, pp. 288-289.

have smooth diplomatic relations with Russia; on the other, Russia was seen as a direct threat to British imperial interests in Asia. Moreover, since Russia did not threaten Britain in Europe, Britain had no European allies against Russia: no other nation cared to support British imperial interests.

Britain was perceived as siding with Japan in the Russo-Japanese war of 1905. After this, the British Foreign Secretary, Sir Edward Grey, sought to improve relations through the Anglo-Russian Convention of 1907. The Government, however, was split between those who took Grey's view and 'those in his own party who disliked Russia on principle'—the likes of Lord Curzon, who saw Russian diplomacy as 'one long and manifold lie', and his successor as Viceroy of India, Lord Minto, who had 'a pathological distrust of Russia'.[22] In these circumstances, it is refreshing, perhaps even surprising, to read in the anonymous introduction to the Board of Education Report on Education in Russia (1909) of 'a great and friendly nation'. The author these words was presumably Sir Michael Sadler,[23] the scholar and distinguished educationist.

The 'asperity which then existed' was similarly accentuated in the popular mind by the pulp literature of the period, which has been studied by scholars in some detail. One lurid futuristic novel of 1911 portrayed an invasion of the South coast of England by the brutal soldiers of a terrifying alliance of France and Russia. Though the people who read such drivel were scarcely those to influence the teaching of Russian, it must be said that more serious novelists painted a not dissimilar and still distasteful picture: Joseph Conrad in his 1911 novel *Under Western Eyes*, which portrays both oppressive and sinister Russian officialdom and unprincipled, unrealistic and ineffective resistance to it by émigré ninnies, wrote of 'hate and fear, the inseparable companions of an uneasy despotism'.[24] Conrad, a Pole who had in childhood experienced internal exile and the death of his parents as a result of confinement in penal settlements, was scarcely the man to improve attitudes to Russia through his writing.

So for nigh on a hundred years there was a strong strain of antagonism in British society towards the Russian government, to public policy there, and to the whole official mind-set. At the same time the country experienced the emergence of interest in Russian culture, which may be seen not as a paradox, but as a manifestation of sympathy for those oppressed by autocracy. The works of major Russian writers were being translated into English,[25] and were widely appreci-

---

[22]These opinions of Grey, Curzon and Minto are quoted by Neilson, pp. 12, 16-17 and 18.

[23][Darlington, Thomas—name not credited on title page]. *Report on Education in Russia*. London: Board of Education, 1909. *Special reports on educational subjects no. 23*; Command Paper Cd 4812, 'Introduction'.

[24]Joseph Conrad, *Under Western Eyes*. Part First, Chapter I.

[25]Garth M. Terry, 'Dostoevsky studies in Great Britain: a bibliographical survey', in M. V. Jones and G. M. Terry (eds). *New Essays on Dostoevsky*. Cambridge: Cambridge University Press, 1983, pp. 215-244, esp. pp. 215-217; Garth M. Terry, 'Tolstoy studies in Great Britain: a bibliographical survey', in M. V. Jones (ed)., *New Essays on Tolstoy*, Cambridge: Cambridge University Press, 1978,

ated. The translator of very many of these works, Constance Garnett, was deeply attracted to Russia by friendship with refugees and political activists including Stepniak-Kravchinsky, a revolutionary terrorist and, it must be admitted, a murderer. Some of Turgenev's major works had been translated in his lifetime: he died in 1883, but Garnett's versions of his works were what really made both his reputation and hers in Britain.[26] Popular as Turgenev was, the authorities (and he himself) had feared anti-Russian demonstrations when he was granted an honorary degree at Oxford in 1879. Fortunately, the occasion was entirely happy.[27] Thirty-seven volumes of Lev Tolstoy were published in 1901, 1902 and 1904. The first major translation of Dostoevsky had appeared in 1881, in a translation by Marie von Thilo, and was of *Notes from the House of the Dead*—a forbidding enough title already, but the English title twisted the knife even further: it was *Buried Alive or Ten Years Penal Servitude in Siberia*. None the less, it was the appearance in 1912, thirty years after its author's death, of Garnett's translation of *The Brothers Karamazov* which was quickly recognized as a milestone in the impact of Russian literature on British readers. It was to be followed by many other Garnett translations of Dostoevsky. Her work has stood the test of time: twenty-first-century scholars firmly place her work at the head of translators' achievements, not to mention her phenomenal output: as many as half a million words translated in a year. Yet in these works the image of a country of suffering and gloom was to some extent reinforced in the British mind. However, much more important for the intellectual community was the challenge these great novels made to the mind and the notion that Russian literature was eminently deserving of scholarly study. Garnett's publisher, Heinemann, had been equivocal in supporting the venture, and Garnett, who herself doubted whether Dostoevsky would be a success with the British reading public, was obliged at first to accept rather niggardly financial terms for her work.[28] In the event, the novels in her translation were a great publishing success.

It is interesting to note in passing that Garnett's knowledge of Russian was oddly patchy. While she could translate huge numbers of words, she was often reluctant to write a letter in Russian, and was modest about her oral command of the language.

We therefore have this picture: a reasonably powerful level of public fear of and distaste for 'official' Russia, but a fascination with Russian literature and culture, and lurking behind both the realization that relations need to be improved and trade developed. The forty-five years before the outbreak of the First World War comprised a period which saw the study of the Russian language emerge in

---

pp 223-250, esp. p. 223.

[26] Richard Garnett, pp. 361-362.

[27] See *Turgenev's Letters*, translated A. V. Knowles. London: Athlone Press, 1983, p. 191.

[28] Richard Garnett, pp. 259 and 265.

Britain in more than one area. The first of these was centred upon the military: this was principally based on self-instruction or individual initiatives. Outside the army and navy, study was undertaken by other people, diplomats and businessmen for example, with special professional and practical reasons for needing the language. A few universities soon became active in the field; here intellectual and academic motivation was prominent while the vocational aspect of Russian-language study was reinforced. As for schools and colleges, there was little to report, but a very small amount of groundwork in preparation for later expansion of Russian language instruction can be seen. We shall look at each sector in turn.

Teach yourself Russian Nineteenth-century style. Military men, diplomats and civil servants

'I know you are the Muskos regiment/And I shall lose my life for want of language,' says Parolles in *All's Well That Ends Well*, believing himself to have been accosted by Russian soldiers. The fear that the 'Muskos' were waiting on the frontier for their chance to appropriate India engendered British determination not to be caught with 'want of language'. There was also considerable tension over Russia's support of her Slav brethren in the Balkans against Turkey in the 1870s, and diplomatic duelling over Afghanistan, which led to the Second Afghan War of 1878-80. Fears of a Russian attack on British India are now regarded by some historians as little more than a war of nerves, but at the time the War Office and the Admiralty were sufficiently wary to begin to encourage promising young officers to take up Russian. The scale on which this was done dwarfed what little teaching there was in the universities before 1914. There was particular interest among Indian Army officers.

Certification was eventually placed in the hands of the Civil Service Commission (CSC). The CSC's annual reports do not detail the languages in which officers qualified, but list the examiners the Commission used by subject. The first year in which an examiner in Russian is mentioned is 1885.[29] Archives for this period have been lost both at Sandhurst and the Staff College, so it is uncertain exactly when Russian was first taught there; it was certainly taught in the College in the 1880s, maybe earlier. Henry Riola claimed to be 'Professor of the Russian Language at the Staff College' on the title page of the second (1883) edition of his *How to Learn Russian*.[30] In a later Report of the CSC a 'new regulation' is referred to by the Commissioners, whereby naval officers may be granted three months for residence on the Continent to improve their knowledge

---

[29] Examiners who served at different times from before 1900 included Edward Cazalet, H. Riola, and E. R. B. Hodgetts.

[30] Riola was born in Taganrog and was resident in London from about 1870. His naturalization papers (1876) do not explain his un-Russian name (spelt 'Henri' therein) and otherwise tell us nothing about his origins and activity. (National Archives: HO45/942/59105.)

of French, German, Italian or Spanish—but not Russian.[31] The Commission's need for an examiner in Russian indicates that it must have had a role in some sphere of military and/or Civil Service entry. In the 1886 Civil Service *Report* an exchange of correspondence is reprinted to the effect that officers should be allowed to present themselves for examination in *any* European or Oriental language, and receive either a 'pass' or 'interpreters'' certificate. In 1887 it was decreed: if service duties permit, special leave of absence for the purpose of going abroad will be granted annually to a limited number of officers in order to make themselves proficient for becoming interpreters. 'This will not apply to officers who have passed in the more ordinary European languages'.[32]

That Russian was widely studied by military men is indicated by the existence of quite a few of the early grammars, which were intended for army or navy students: Riola, Freeth, Schnurmann and Kinloch were all active in such teaching, or intended their books for this purpose. The first army officers to qualify in Russian were Captains F. Beaufort, J. M. Grierson, and J. W. Murray, whose names appear in the Army List for 1887; in 1888 four more names are added, including that of Lt-Col. Robert Collinson d'Esterre Spottiswoode (1841-1936). It is fortunate indeed that Spottiswoode allowed himself to be persuaded by his family to write and publish his *Reminiscences* when he was over ninety years old, and to deposit them in the National Libraries. His chapter on 'Russia' is the best—and possibly the only—full record we have of the experience of learning Russian at that time and in these circumstances. Military man Spottiswoode certainly was, but his comments on his own learning process are thoughtful and illuminating. His account mentions socializing with several of the other officers in Moscow at the time, but his approach to learning was highly individual: it deserves some little attention here.[33]

After service in Egypt and Sudan, where he was mentioned in despatches, and shortly after his marriage at the age of over forty to a young widow, Spottiswoode sought a new stimulus rather than enter the humdrum existence of home military service as a major. Lord Wolseley at the War Office, with whom he served in Sudan, asked him to study Russian. In November 1885 he set off to Russia with his new wife, knowing not one word of the language. Some of his fellow officers had received a grounding at Staff College. Once the Spottiswoodes settled in Moscow, 'life became easy, and everything else too, except the language.' It might appear from his account of his and his wife's social life that he was not serious about Russian, but this would be far from true. He spent a few weeks being introduced to Russian by British expatriates, in particular Walter Thornton, who had been born in Russia and was a near-native speaker and

---

[31] *Report of HM Civil Service Commissioners*, London: HMSO, 1885, Command Paper C. 4405, pp. 40-42.

[32] *Report of HM Civil Service Commissioners*, 1886, Command paper C. 4753, pp. 8-12, and 1887, Command paper C. 5120. p. 39.

[33] Spottiswoode, pp. 122 ff.

member of a family business house, but then Spottiswoode decided to entrust his wife to a female friend and banish all English from his life. He took lodgings with the village priest and his wife and six children at Khimki; he was lonely and bored out of his mind, '*but I did it*' for six weeks (his own italics). Returning to the Thornton household, he took lessons from a lady 'governess', and he and his wife (who was also trying to pick up some Russian) would frequently visit the theatre for practice in listening to Russian.

When the three fellow-officers whose names we have mentioned left to present themselves for examination, Spottiswoode took stock of his own situation. He had had Latin grammar 'flogged into him' at Edinburgh Academy, and felt he had the firmest possible grasp of the structure of Russian. But after eleven months in Moscow, oral fluency and translation skills were still less good. Lord Wolseley granted him six more months; Spottiswoode sent his wife home and took lodgings with a Russian family that knew no English. At the same time he moved socially in Russian military circles, and even, he hints in his narrative, reported back to Lord Wolseley on his conversations with indiscreet interlocutors, such as General S. M. Dukhovskoi, chief of staff of the Moscow military region, of whom Spottiswoode made a friend. When time was up, he returned to London and employed a Mr Carnegie, who had been brought up in Russia, to coach him and speak Russian all the time until after the exam, his account of which runs:

> The examination was stiff, and the culminating point was the finale when the examiner, a Mr [Brayley] Hodgett[s], read in English an essay on 'Ironclads', if you please, of all things. We had to write it straight off into Russian, sign it, and hand it up. Final result, which was not very long in being communicated, was that I had qualified as an interpreter. In due course I received a cheque officially for £200!

Spottiswoode had expected to be sent to Central Asia, which was the whole point of his training as a Russian interpreter, but instead he was to his surprise posted to Cork in 1887, 'and there I am still as I write these lines today, 26th September 1934!' It was a very happy outcome, but surely represented a tremendous waste of effort and training from the Army's point of view.[34]

Other Russian interpreters include Lt-Col William Aldworth, an Anglo-Irishman, who died a heroic death at the battle of Paardeburg in South Africa in 1900. Reginald Burton provides an informative case-study. Aged 26, on leave from the Indian Army in 1891-92, he fell in with another young officer who was studying Russian with Ivan (or Johann) Nestor-Schnurmann (1852-1917), a Rus-

---

[34]Kinloch's 1890 Russian grammar is dedicated 'to my first pupil, Colonel Spottiswoode (late of the 10th Hussars) in recognition of the strenuous manner in which he grappled with the language and gained the "Interpretership" in a single examination.' Oddly, Spottiswoode does not mention Kinloch at all in his memoir, though he gives the names of the other Britons who helped him with his Russian. I wonder if 'Carnegie' is in fact Kinloch, and that—writing forty-seven years after the event—Spottiswoode simply misremembered the name.

sian Jew who had come to England in 1880 and made a career out of coaching army officers in Russian. He had just been appointed to run a Jewish house at Cheltenham College[35] and was the author of the *Russian Manual* of 1884. Bored while on leave, Burton joined his new friend in the lessons. The grant of furlough for study depended on achieving 25% in a preliminary War Office test; Burton had no problems in qualifying. He went to Moscow to live and study with a Russian family. (The usual choice of Moscow was due to the phenomenally high cost of living in St Petersburg, which drove some British diplomatic staff to seek a transfer elsewhere in the service.)[36] Burton made excellent progress; however, he found the atmosphere in Russia oppressive, foresaw that the corruption, widespread ignorance and misery would lead to a 'strike for freedom'. He left in September 1893, continued to work for his interpretership qualification, and passed with a more than creditable mark of 87%. The Army rewarded him with the sum of £242—but, as with Spottiswoode, failed ever to make use of his ability in Russian. His further military career was distinguished: he reached the rank of Brigadier General by 1920 and died at the age of 86 in 1951.[37]

These men belonged to a significant and rapidly increasing number of successful aspirants: the *Army Lists* for 1890 name 49 qualified Russian interpreters, by 1895 there are 85, in 1900 103, in 1905 about 130, and in 1909 127; the 1910 list gives the names of 142 first-class and 42 second-class officer interpreters in Russian, 27 of whom had received their certificate before 1890. I cannot explain this sudden dramatic increase, except that lists previous to 1910 had not mentioned 'second-class' interpreters. Of the surviving 27, eighteen were first-class interpreters holding the rank of Lieutenant-Colonel or above; the earliest officer among them still serving in 1910 was Major-General Grierson, whom Spottiswoode had known as a Captain in 1887-88. At least half of these officers were in the Indian Army, which confirms where the fears and interests of the British army as regards Russia lay at that time. However, a use was found for five Russian interpreters during the Russo-Japanese War; four served as observers attached to the Russian armies, and one to the Japanese.[38]

The first naval officer to study in St Petersburg was Lieutenant Ernest Goldfinch Rason who qualified in Russian in 1887. After a long period in the doldrums as far as promotion was concerned, by 1890 he had been raised to Commander and was placed in charge of HMS Cockatrice 'for service in the

---

[35]'Ivan Nestor-Schnurmann', *Jewish Encyclopaedia*, a somewhat inaccurate source in this case. For more reliable information I am indebted to Ms Jill Barlow, Archivist of Cheltenham College, to the Cambridge University Archive, and to his naturalization papers of 1889 held in the National Archives (HO 144/307/B5569). These papers give his first name as 'Johann'; though he regularly used 'Ivan'.

[36]Hughes, pp. 21-22.

[37]On Burton, see David O'Connor. I am grateful to Lt Col O'Connor, who himself trained in Russian at Cambridge University in 1958-59 as a regular officer, for sending me the text of his article, on which I have relied heavily in this paragraph.

[38]For this information I am indebted to as yet unpublished research by Nicholas Evans.

Danube', where he might conceivably have been able to make some use of his Russian; in 1892 he was still the only naval officer listed as qualified as a Russian interpreter.[39] In that same year he was appointed British Resident Commissioner in the Franco-British Joint Naval Commission of the New Hebrides (now Vanuatu), before retirement a few years later with the rank of Captain. The Navy Lists for 1907 and 1909 enumerate twelve or thirteen active naval and marines mostly senior officers, who were qualified Russian interpreters, and two more are listed as 'studying [Russian] abroad on full pay.'

The CSC *Reports* annually list examiners in Russian (occasionally as many as three in one year). This pattern of study in Russia and examination was followed by officers each year until the outbreak of war in 1914. One of them was George Bowen, of whom Bruce Lockhart paints an attractive pen-portrait in his *Memoirs of a British Agent*.[40] Colonel James Blair learned Russian and was appointed Assistant Military Attaché to the British Embassy at Petrograd till 1917. In 1918 he was made Chief of Staff to the British military mission in Siberia, supplying the ill-fated Admiral Kolchak; his final duty was to withdraw the mission in 1920.[41]

A not dissimilar course of study to that followed by Burton two decades after him was undertaken by the future General A. P. Wavell (1883-1950). Wavell came to be regarded as one of the most intellectually able generals on the British side in the Second World War. On graduation from staff college Wavell was asked by his superiors to learn Russian. He arrived in Moscow in February 1911 knowing nothing. It seems there was still no organized programme for any of these officers from Spottiswoode onwards; Wavell found lodgings and instruction in Russian on his own initiative with a Mme Ertel', widow of the writer of that name who had died in 1908. A daughter in the household was Natalia, who later became well known as Natalie Duddington, a translator into English of classic Russian novels. Wavell studied with Mme Ertel' in the mornings; he enjoyed the intellectual atmosphere and life (but not the heavy cuisine and the Russians' total reluctance to take exercise). On his return to Britain he achieved class I in the civil service interpreters' examination.

The Army and indeed the country made good use of Wavell's Russian as it had of Blair's. While studying, he had attended Russian army manoeuvres, and on his return he wrote a handbook on the Russian Army. A year or two later he returned to Russia to attend military exercises, once getting arrested for possession of a (British) War Office letter, which the authorities thought was

---

[39] Elliott and Shukman, p. 15, alerted me to the existence of Rason, whose further career may be traced in successive Navy Lists. There were 89 officers qualified to act as interpreters in 1892, many of them for Hindustani and Swahili; Persian and Arabic also figure.

[40] first published in 1932, most recently reprinted: London: Pan Macmillan, 2002, pp. 68-72.

[41] An obituary of Blair appears in the *Slavonic Review* vol IV, 1925-26, pp. 482-483.

incriminating.[42] In 1916 he was military attaché to the Russian army in the Caucasus. Churchill took him on his first visit to meet Stalin in Moscow in 1942, where he was able to make 'an excellent speech in Russian' at a Kremlin dinner.[43] However, knowledge of Russian and the ability to make a formal speech are not everything; Wavell lacked social skills. The British ambassador apparently had the greatest difficulty in persuading him to converse informally with Russians on social occasions: the British officers reportedly remained in a huddle, determinedly apart from their Soviet hosts.[44] However, this may not have been typical: a curious consequence of these extended periods of residence in Russia by officers is that it often greatly increased their feeling of warmth towards the Russians they met. This may not have been intended by the military authorities, but it is reported by many of them.[45]

The year after Wavell lodged in the Ertel' household, his place was taken by Robert Bruce Lockhart, the self-styled 'British Agent', who was not a military man, but had just been appointed to the consular service in Moscow. He commented that a certain number of Russian families specialized in teaching Russian to British officers. 'Most of them were squalid middle-class homes with nothing to recommend them in the way either of comfort or of intellectual uplift.' The Ertel' family were an exception:

> Madame Ertel' was [...] very intellectual, with a keen interest both in literature and in politics, fussy in a crisis, but a born teacher [...] Her daughter [was] a dark-eyed temperamental young girl more like an Italian than a Russian [...] Every day I had a lesson from Madame Ertel' and her daughter, and under their skilful tuition I made rapid progress.

Bruce Lockhart further comments on the political views of the family; he found he was living in 'an anti-Tsarist stronghold', where 'they would sometimes sit far into the night discussing how to make the world safe by revolution. But when the morning of action came they were fast asleep in bed. It was very harmless, very hopeless, and very Russian.'[46]

---

[42]On Wavell, see John Connell, *Wavell, Scholar and Soldier to June 1941*, London: Collins, 1964, pp. 65-81.

[43]Churchill, III, p. 468, and IV, p. 444.

[44]Kitchen, pp. 134 and 136. Kitchen also states that in the first discussions between Churchill and Stalin the quality of interpreting was inadequate on both sides, and the interpreters were replaced. Courtney (p. 45) reports that Stalin's speech at a Kremlin dinner was 'viciously tinctured with references to Churchill's own handling of the Gallipoli campaign, but whose poisonous implications were quite lost in the awful hash of [...] translation.' Churchill, to judge by his own account of the incident in *The Second World War*, IV, p. 444, appears to have taken the garbled remarks as a compliment; Glees (pp. 61-62) suggests that Stalin was obliquely implying that Churchill's failure in the Dardanelles was due to faulty intelligence—and that he would fail again for the same reason.

[45]See for example: *Proceedings of the ARLS*, no. 8, 1894, p. 49.

[46]Bruce Lockhart, pp. 64-66. (See note 40).

The political views and standing of those who taught Russian were at this time, and remained for many years, something of a problem. Lockhart was warned by his superior to be careful. Wavell seems, however, to have gained nothing but benefit from contact with the Ertel' family; it doubtless prepared him for some later brushes with tsarist authority.

We have just moved into the time of the First World War and therefore out of the period covered by this chapter, but in fact this method of study involving long periods of residence in Russian-speaking families continued even into the late twentieth century, as we shall see. In 1914 the young novelist Hugh Walpole came to St Petersburg as a journalist and at the same time officer in the medical section of the Russian army. He memorably described Russian as 'a language like idiots talking beautifully in an asylum—it *is* most beautiful'. 'I am very lucky in that the mistress of the house is a nice woman and an excellent teacher. I work at Russian for about four hours a day and have it with my meals, asking for potatoes and then being told that I have to use the genitive. It is a lovely language, rich as gold brocade and full of lovely words.'[47] Though his mastery of Russian remained shaky, Walpole was in 1915 put in charge of the Anglo-Russian Bureau, a propaganda institution which was set up to encourage the press to report favourably on British efforts to assist the Russian military.

We do not know from what primer if any these officers and others acquired their very first introduction to Russian: it may be supposed they bought whatever grammar they could find. Frequent references to Reiff imply that this was regarded as standard. Those taught by Schnurmann, Riola, or Kinloch must have used their teacher's own material. Moreover, some of these officers clearly added to the literature themselves, as occasional publications in this period of military vocabularies and the like show. There will always be learners who plough their own furrow, even when opportunities exist for organized study of the language.

One or two diplomats or consular personnel have been mentioned above—Bruce Lockhart, Walpole—as well as military men who took on a partly diplomatic role. It might be assumed that British Embassy staff studied Russian in a similar way to the servicemen, since an important part of their duties was to monitor and translate the Russian press; few at home in the Foreign Office in London knew Russian. However, of the four British ambassadors between 1900 and 1918, only one had a very good knowledge of the language (Sir Charles Hardinge); one remained almost totally ignorant of it for all the eight years of his stint in St Petersburg (Sir George Buchanan).[48] Moreover, it is astonishing to find that, at any one time in the early years of the century, only two members of the British diplomatic corps had good enough Russian to qualify for the one

---

[47]Letter from Walpole to Henry James, quoted in Rupert Hart-Davis, *Hugh Walpole, a Biography*, London: Hamish Hamilton, 1985 [first pub. 1952], pp. 125-126. Walpole used his Russian experiences in two novels, *The Dark Forest* (1916), and *The Secret City* (1919).

[48]Hughes, pp. 17-20.

hundred pounds' allowance per annum paid by the Foreign Office. This was better than the one staff member in the 1860s who understood Russian.[49] The great majority, then, relied on Russian 'minders' with fluent English, or on the diplomatic French and German they doubtless possessed. This unquestionably skewed the impression of Russian conditions they obtained and passed on to London. In addition some senior diplomats avoided any contact with elements in society which might be termed dissident, for fear of offending the Russian government. Consular officers in the provinces, whose findings might have been of greater importance, often had their reports disregarded, or at best little heeded. Buchanan relied to some extent during the First World War on Bernard Pares (of whom more later) and on the journalist Mackenzie Wallace for information about underground organizations. They had, in Hughes's words, 'the freedom of the journalist and the authority of the diplomat.'[50]

One of the most strikingly successful civilian learners of Russian was Thomas Darlington (1864-1908), a Her (later His) Majesty's Inspector of Schools, an outstanding scholar and linguist. Darlington was asked by Michael Sadler, who was then Director of Special Inquiries and Reports at the Board of Education, to visit Russia and compile a report on education at all levels there. The Report,[51] which was not published until 1909 after Darlington's death, is an outstanding piece of extended writing; it is the first detailed analysis of education in Russia by an English-speaking observer. What interests us here is the way he acquired the Russian language to enable him to carry out his investigation. William H. E. Johnson describes it:

> He engaged the services of an émigré Russian, Count Markov, who lived at his house for six months, accompanied him on all his school visits, and sat for hours at a time in his office, conversing about education. Many times these lessons consisted of Markov taking copious notes on a conference which Darlington conducted in English, and then teaching the latter to say the same things correctly in Russian [...] He astonished the Minister of Education, N. P. Bogolepov, by conducting his first interview entirely in Russian.[52]

We further learn that Darlington visited Tolstoy at Iasnaia poliana and conversed with Countess Tolstaia for half an hour without her realising that he was not Russian and that he had been learning Russian for less than a year.[53]

---

[49] A. S. Thompson, 'The British Embassy at St Petersburgh', *Proceedings of the ARLS*, no. 9, 1895, pp. 42-62; see p. 46.

[50] Hughes, pp. 31 and 32.

[51] See Darlington, *Report on Education in Russia*.

[52] Johnson, 'Thomas Darlington—his life and work as a scholar and His Majesty's Inspector', in Janusz Tomiak (ed.), *Thomas Darlington's Report on Education in Russia. Papers from the seventy-fifth anniversary conference, 1984*, London: School of Slavonic and East European Studies, 1987, pp. 1-7; this quotation is from p. 4.

[53] Johnson, pp. 4-5.

The Introduction of Russian to the universities

Russian figured in the curriculum to varying degree in three English universities at the end of the nineteenth and beginning of the twentieth centuries: Oxford, Cambridge and Liverpool. It was at Liverpool that by far the most adventurous steps were taken. The controversy surrounding its inception at Oxford is, however, of the greatest interest.

The teaching of Russian at the older universities followed hotfoot upon the institution of modern languages in general at degree level in those institutions. Much earlier attempts to establish the teaching of western European languages in the reign of George I at both Oxford and Cambridge in 1724 had come to grief. The aim had been to benefit the state: the civil, diplomatic and consular service. Since the state had no organized civil service and since there were consequently not sufficient posts to offer the young men recruited, the experiment failed. It is interesting to note that the project was unpopular because the men were selected by merit, a fact which was disapproved of by a society in which patronage was the norm.[54] In *A Tale of Two Cities* Dickens coins a telling phrase in Chapter X in relation to one of his characters who had taught French to undergraduates at Cambridge: he was seen 'as a sort of tolerated smuggler who drove a contraband trade in European languages, instead of conveying Greek and Latin through the Custom-house.'

At Oxford a legacy from Sir Robert Taylor came to the University in 1835: this was for establishing a foundation for teaching European languages. A professor, a librarian and two teachers were appointed. The first professor was Francis Trithen, appointed in 1848, and he was interested in Russian: his first course of lectures was on 'the language and literature of Russia'. Alas, Trithen very soon succumbed to serious mental illness, and in 1850 Max Müller, specialist in comparative philology, was appointed professor. French and German were allowed in the Final Pass School only. Standards were generally agreed to be low, and Müller felt that things would not improve until there was cooperation from the public schools, a view which was not shared by all at Oxford: there were those who believed that the University should be adopting a more positive stance.

Apart from the brief tenure of Francis Trithen, we are not yet speaking of Russian or any other Slavonic language. However, the Earl of Ilchester died in 1865, leaving the University one thousand pounds, 'for the encouragement of the study of the Polish and other Slavonic Languages, Literature and History, with the view of promoting the knowledge of European politics in general, and more especially of benefiting the diplomatic service of this Country.' We note again the reference to 'diplomatic' reasons for the study of language. The preference for Polish was quickly forgotten. Ilchester Lectures began in 1870, and were seen as a significant contribution to interest in modern languages at Oxford. Yet in

---

[54]Firth, *Modern Languages at Oxford 1724-1929*.

1877 Lord Selborne's Commission on the University recorded average enrolments for French at no more than 12, German at 16, Italian 5.5 and Spanish 4. Russian does not yet appear.

Of great interest for the theme of this book is the controversy about the reform of the universities of Oxford and Cambridge which began in the 1830s. Resistance to any notion that government had the right to a point of view was fierce, and both vice-chancellors refused all cooperation with a Royal Commission in the early 1850s. Despite this, acts of Parliament on Oxford (1854) and Cambridge (1856) forced the issue, and new triposes and honours schools were set up in moral sciences, law, natural sciences, and history. The stranglehold of the Anglican Church was broken when the religious tests were abolished in 1871—to the outrage of some clerical dons, who saw this as opening the door to moral turpitude. Gradually the conservatives died off, but there were enough of them around at Oxford in 1887 to frustrate an attempt to found an Honours School of Modern Languages. The vote was 92 to 92: a tie, which meant the motion was lost. It is very hard from the perspective of the early twenty-first century either to understand the reasons why the study of modern languages was opposed, or to contain one's exasperated amusement at the antics of the dons who debated the issue. One participant sardonically commented: 'The superstition still lingers among us that Classics is the unique means to an education.' This superstition was shared by no less a man than Mr Gladstone, who said in 1861 in relation to modern studies:

> Their true position is ancillary, and as ancillary it ought to be limited and restrained without scruple as much as a regard to the paramount matter of education may dictate [...] The materials of what we call classical training were prepared, and we have a right to say were advisedly and providentially prepared, in order that it might become, not a mere adjunct, but the complement of Christianity in its application to the culture of the human being, as a being formed both for this world and for the world to come.[55]

This claim—'providentially prepared'; 'the complement of Christianity...for...the world to come'—and from such an august source is staggering. However, for Classics teachers what was more important was that they feared losing their incomes and posts. Modern languages were declared too easy. Scorn was poured on modern languages as a subject of university study.[56] There were controversies as to whether or not the curriculum should include philology, philosophy, and history. But the main argument was that 'the study of Latin and Greek literature would seriously suffer.'[57] In any case, in the new competitive examinations for entry these, along with mathematics especially at Cambridge,

---

[55] Quoted by Green, *The Universities*, pp. 54-74.

[56] Referred to by Leathes, pp. 3-4.

[57] Frith, p. 74f. See also Freeman, 'Literature and Language', an acerbic commentary on the controversy.

were the only subjects recognized. 'The more higher education improved, the less chance there was for the introduction of new studies in equality with the old. For they said the old were better.'[58]

Where was Russian in all this? It scarcely figured. The controversy was over French, German, and to a lesser extent Italian and Spanish. If 'the "Letto-Slavic" group of languages (as the Oxford dons called it) was mentioned at all, it was looked at as simply something funny by those who think it the mark of a wit and a superior person to mock at whatever he does not understand.'[59] The phrase 'something funny' is interesting, in that as recently as 1961 an Oxford don (a Russian specialist) was heard to declare in a public lecture that he never had been able to share the view that there was 'something funny' about Russian as a subject of study.[60]

It may be imagined that the usefulness of modern languages, Russian among them, in professional terms would have been accepted as a good reason for their inclusion in the university curriculum. There were those, however, even among the supporters of modern languages, who deplored any connection with usefulness. Some of these same people were not in favour of any test of oral proficiency in the languages:

> I regret also a most ill-advised provision for making the examination include a 'colloquial' use of the languages taken up. I regret still more the reason which was given for such a course, namely that it would be useful for candidates who meant to enter the diplomatic service. [...] The point is that the university has nothing to do with the diplomatic service or with any service. [...] It has [...] nothing to do with any profession or calling of any kind. [...] Some stop should be put to this lowering of the University by adapting its system to suit this or that calling.[61]

While the controversy was raging in Oxford, the innovators at Cambridge had overcome opposition and initiated a Medieval and Modern Languages Tripos. It was not enormously popular in terms of the numbers of students who enrolled, and in fact the somewhat half-hearted opponents in Oxford of the second attempt in 1903 to establish a School of Modern Languages claimed it had been a failure. At that time about a dozen men and rather more women were presenting themselves for examination in modern languages in Cambridge. Nevertheless, a statute establishing an Honour School of Modern Languages was passed at Oxford in 1903; the first graduate in Russian was Neville Forbes, in 1906, who later became Professor. Russian was added to the Medieval and Modern

---

[58]Leathes, p. 3.

[59]Freeman, p. 557.

[60]I heard a tape-recording of the lecture by (I believe) Dr Ronald Hingley.

[61]Freeman, pp. 558-559.

Languages Tripos at Cambridge when a new scheme was adopted in 1907. The scheme was passed by an overwhelming majority of 154 to 11.[62]

We return to the year 1870, a crucial date for Slavonic Studies in Oxford and in the British universities as a whole. It will be recalled that Trithen devoted his first lectures to the language and literature of Russia in 1848, but Russian studies got under way, as yet only in a general sense, with the first Ilchester lectures in 1870. The first lecturer was William Richard Morfill (1834-1909), who is regarded by many Slavists, not all of them Oxonians, as a crucial figure in the establishment of Slavonic scholarship and of the dominant language, Russian, in the university system. On three occasions he was Ilchester lecturer, but he was not appointed to the University until 1889; he was promoted professor in 1900. When a boy at Tonbridge School, presumably in the late 1840s, one of his teachers gave him a Russian grammar. Gerald Stone suggests it may well have been Heard's, which was virtually the only available grammar with English text.[63] Morfill went on in his lifetime to write grammars of Russian, Czech, Polish, Bulgarian, and Serbian, and he also published on Slavonic literature and the history of Slav countries. Stone, who writes very appreciatively of Morfill, comments that some of his works are somewhat banal and that his observation of scholarly standards in his treatment of sources do not meet modern criteria, but he reminds us that Morfill was a pioneer.[64]

In 1890 Morfill delivered an inaugural lecture as 'Reader in Russian and the other Slavonic Languages'. This document, entitled 'An Essay on the importance of the study of the Slavonic languages' and published by the University Press, is of considerable interest, both for its content and also as the first public argument in Britain for the subject. Morfill's approach is that of a dedicated don: he must establish the academic importance of the Slavonic languages in the face of scepticism (as we have seen) from the classicists who ruled the roost in Oxford in 1890. He divides his advocacy of Slavonic Studies into three, the first two of which are allowed the lion's share, but the third—a very brief section on the 'practical' arguments—is powerfully and persuasively, if briefly, phrased. Morfill first establishes that scholars (exclusively non-British continental academics) have set the study of the Slavonic and Baltic languages on a firm footing and that they have provided sufficient material to enable comparative diachronic linguistic study to take place. He surveys Slav literature, from folklore (very much the current subject of interest at the end of the nineteenth century) to contemporary writing. In conclusion he advances the argument that Slav languages are important for 'political and military purposes'. He argues that lack of familiarity with Russian ideas led the nation into blunders such as the Crimean

---

[62] *Modern Language Teaching*, vol. III no. 3 (1907), p. 159.

[63] Stone, 'The History of Slavonic Studies in Great Britain...', p. 382.

[64] Stone, pp. 382-384.

War, and he mocks British failure to understand the motivation of Bulgarians and Serbs in supporting Russia in that war.

> In order to interpret properly the Eastern question, which never settled is still hovering over us, we must know the Slavonic mind, the Slavonic languages and literatures. Otherwise these races will be an enigma to us. For the statesman and soldier this knowledge is a necessity.

Commercial reasons for the study of the Slavs are absent from Morfill's argument.

It should be remembered that Morfill clearly commanded much respect in the University and that the inclusion of Russian in the new Honour School owed a good deal to that. For the theme of this book, it is his *Grammar of the Russian Language* which is of interest. His approach to the language may be deduced from the layout of the book. 'It is a scientific treatment of the Russian language which is attempted on this occasion'. (p. vi) The only previous grammar he mentions is that by Ludolf: there is no acknowledgement to any other previous linguist, British or foreign. Structure is clearly far more important to Morfill than usage: again the reader is given the obsolete present tense of 'to be' without any warning or explanation; a misleading statement about *niet* is made—it is 'the particle of negation'; the long-forgotten pluperfect tense figures, which is of interest to the historian of the language, but not to a student learner. Not until 'Syntax' is reached (p. 63) do we find any sentence-length examples of the use of the language. At one point the author gives up:

> There is considerable laxity in the sequences of tenses in Russian, past and present tenses being constantly mixed up. The following sentences will help [the reader] to understand the laws of the language in this respect.

Some good examples follow; but surely a scholar—even a pioneer—should be capable of *some* explanation of Russian usage in respect of sequence of tenses? The grammar ends with over forty pages of prose and poetry by standard authors, but, unlike Heard's grammar, there are no annotations or translations. Finally a vocabulary of about 2,800 words is included.

In all this we note significant differences between university Russian and the vocational training which our military officers received and, indeed, gave themselves. Morfill's grammar is not concerned with teaching Russian so much as teaching *about* the language from the point of view of an academic philologist. It reflects no system of teaching methodology, and pedagogically it is no further forward than Ludolf—one may even say Ludolf's 'Phrases et modi loquendi communiores' put him well ahead of Morfill in this respect. Unlike the army students who strove to learn to speak, Morfill did not support the testing of oral proficiency in Russian. The 'scientific treatment' was an adequately demanding intellectual task for students, and until it proved insufficient in this respect there was no need for an oral test. His book falls clearly into the tradition of a learned treatise, not a practical teaching instrument. It seems, however, that he was a good teacher; though he had small numbers of students, there were some distinguished scholars among them. In fact, his real achievement seems to have been to raise the scholarly status of Slavonic studies at Oxford, thus laying a foundation for future development. Morfill deplored the lack of interest in the study of the Slavs in Britain, and seems to have been better known in the Slavonic countries than here.[65]

The introduction of Russian at Cambridge is considerably less well documented than at Oxford. In 1892 A. A. Sykes commented in a barbed and witty article, that Oxford is 'a little ahead', while he mocks the 'mediaeval and insular ignorance' of Russian which prevails at Cambridge University.' There Sykes found 'about a dozen Slavonic books' in the University Library, and in the whole University there were only two dons who had taught themselves the alphabet in order to catalogue them (and then fell out over transliteration!), a BA and an undergraduate 'who had got as far as the verbs and then given it up as a bad job', an 'ex-tourist or two who had been there and left most of their Russian behind', a Newnhamite and a hairdresser, not a member of the University.[66]

To the rescue came the same Mr Schnurmann as had coached Reginald Burton and others at Cheltenham. From 1896 or 1897 he took the arduous train journey for two days a week during full term at a salary of £50 per annum; he was paid out of Foreign Office funds under the auspices of the Special Board for Indian Civil Service Studies. While his main function was to teach potential interpreters, he was also required to set aside two hours a week 'for the purpose of giving assistance to any member of the University who may desire to study Russian, Bulgarian or Bohemian.'[67] In 1899 there were no student interpreters, and the arrangement lapsed. However, there was a strong feeling that Russian should be taught in the University for both practical and cultural reasons, and Sir David Salomons offered fifty pounds a year for five years to pay a teacher. A lengthy and unpleasant controversy followed over the person to be appointed. Schnurmann was an unsuccessful candidate. Dr A. P. Goudy, a graduate of Edinburgh and St Andrews, who had been teaching at Liverpool University College, was appointed in 1900 against determined opposition from dons who thought a Cambridge man (Ellis Minns) should have been appointed. Goudy served until 1936.[68] In 1905 an unlikely source of funding was quickly found—the Worshipful Company of Fishmongers—which guaranteed further support for twenty years. In the early years of the twentieth century there was a Russian

---

[65] Typescript extracts from Russian-language obituary by Grot, enclosed with Stone, *Slavonic Studies at Oxford: a Brief History*, [mimeographed documentation for a public exhibition], Oxford, 2005.

[66] 'From a Correspondent: Learning Russian', *The Globe and Traveller*, 8.8.1892. The attribution to Sykes comes from a cuttings book from the archives of the ARLS.

[67] Archives of Cambridge University: UA CUR 28.12 item 97.

[68] Cambridge University Archives UA CUR 113/V, Russian. The selectors insisted on Dr Goudy as their choice, and despite a heap of *non-placets*, Goudy was elected by Senate by 149 votes to 105. Elizabeth Hill's inaugural lecture many years later implies, without saying so, that Minns was the more deserving scholar.

scholarship at Gonville and Caius College, open to undergraduates already at the College. The same scepticism as at Oxford towards the need for spoken proficiency in the language was typical of Cambridge also; before 1909 there was an *optional* test of pronunciation only, and in that year an optional conversational examination was introduced. Not until 1917 did 'wider views prevail':[69] the Tripos was renamed 'Modern and Medieval', and candidates could only be admitted to the examination in a language if they had previously satisfied the examiners in the oral examination.[70]

It may well be that the hostility at Cambridge and Oxford to any vocational purpose in the teaching of languages, represented antagonism to other newer universities, whose degrees Oxford and Cambridge did not even fully recognize well into the mid-twentieth century. It was one of these, the University of Liverpool, which was shortly to eclipse the older places, when Bernard Pares burst on the scene and within a few years established a department with more staff and students than all the others put together.

The story is a refreshing contrast with the pettifogging controversies that went on at the older universities. In the first place, the foundation of a Russian department in Liverpool owed a lot to provincial civic pride. There were a number of rich businessmen who endowed chairs of Russian for little other reason than to give expression to their sense of public responsibility; in the case of Liverpool the principal donor was John Rankin of Rankin, Gilmour and Co., a company with interests in timber in Canada and in shipping. Pares was too modest to reveal in his memoirs that Rankin offered to pay the salary of a professor only if Pares was appointed. The appointment was made in 1908, and the Chair bore the title of 'the Bowes Chair', after another benefactor of Liverpool University. It was not the very beginning of Russian there, as Dr Goudy had been teaching Russian to non-degree students in the University College, which became a full university in 1903. It has been suggested that the foundation of the Liverpool department at this time owed something to public interest in the Russian 'revolution' of 1905. At the same time it is argued that the British government was pro-Japanese, and that it passed intelligence to Japan, to the extent that Britain contributed to a Japanese victory in the Russo-Japanese war.[71] Here is another example of the division of opinion about Russia: was she a threat or a potentially friendly ally to be cultivated? It is interesting that Britain's rivalry with Germany emerges as an influence. Germany was seen as a supporter of Russia—Britain therefore had to be on the Japanese side. A recurrent refrain in Pares's writings is Britain's folly in allowing German views of Russia to infect our perception of a potential friend and trading partner.

---

[69] Leathes, pp. 3-4.

[70] University of Cambridge, 'Report of the Special Board ...', esp. p. 565.

[71] Chapman, 'Russia, Germany ...' in Erickson, pp. 41-55.

Two significant matters should be mentioned in connection with Pares's innovations at Liverpool. He was a proponent of what he called 'nation study': the courses at the University were in language, of course, but while literature was taught, so also were history and economics. In this respect Pares set a tradition which many a Russian department in later years emulated: even at Cambridge history and thought were included in the Tripos. The second significant matter concerns a concordat which Pares concluded with the Liverpool College of Commerce. By this agreement the salary of a teacher of Russian was assured, and the Russian language was taught in both establishments. At the University, there were a professor, two lecturers and a research fellow engaged in teaching.[72]

There two other British universities at which Russian was taught before the First World War: Manchester and King's College, London. Nicholas Orloff, of the Russian Embassy, taught a few students annually at King's from 1889 (in response to War Office pressure), and a philologist, Dr W. J. Sedgefield, taught Russian in the English Department at Manchester from 1907.

In Sedgefield's 1907 inaugural address, 'The Study of Russian', he highlights Russian folk poetry and tales, as did Morfill in his Oxford inaugural, but he introduces a new argument: in Russia 'something new [is] being made.' The Russian is 'a new kind of man'. 'Ideas are germinating which may profoundly influence the history of the coming centuries.' (pp. 412-413) Sedgefield was quite right, though whether those ideas were what he expected is another matter.

Schools, colleges and private initiatives

There may just possibly have been isolated examples of Russian being taught informally in schools before 1914, but no documentary evidence is easily discernible. At that time, what we now consider to be 'secondary' education was carried on mainly in the 'public' schools, that is the independent boarding schools, and in the long-established 'free' grammar schools in the cities, some of which had started charging fees in the nineteenth century. While many towns had a municipal 'secondary' school, the state and local authorities never fully considered, in England at least, that it was their province to provide secondary education for all until the 1944 Education Act. Most pupils who did not go to the secondary school continued in extended 'elementary' education until the age of 14. Moreover, while in the independent sector there was virtual equality in the provision of places for boys and girls, in county and municipal schools older boys of secondary age outnumbered girls by as much as four to one.[73]

Before turning specifically to Russian in institutions for younger teenagers, we must establish the context of modern language teaching in general, which at the time in the vast majority of schools meant French and to a lesser extent

---

[72] Advertisement in *The Russian Review*, [1914], vol. III no. 1., flysheet.

[73] in Derbyshire, for example: Michael Sadler, *Report on Secondary and Higher Education in Derbyshire*, Derby: Administrative County of Derby Education Committee, 1905.

German. The independent and grammar schools must be considered separately from the public elementary institutions at this period. The free grammar schools in industrial cities knew very well that the local business houses needed linguists who could facilitate overseas trade. Such considerations meant little to the legal system, however. It took an act of Parliament, the Grammar Schools Act of 1840 to legalize the teaching of French and German in such schools: a judge in the Court of Chancery had ruled in 1805 that no part of a grammar school's endowments could be used to pay teachers of modern languages, or indeed of anything other than the 'learned languages'—Greek and Latin. If offered, modern language instruction had to be paid for as an extra. The suit in Chancery had taken ten years to resolve, and it arose from an internal dispute at Leeds Grammar School. That school went through a bad patch while the minds of all there were concentrated on the legal case; but the implications of the judgement, which formed a precedent, 'carried dismay to all interested in the advancement of education'. Leeds and other grammar schools, however, found skilful ways around the problem: so long as every boy (and we are talking about *boys*) studied the classics alongside whatever else he studied, all was well. The parallels with the controversy in the older universities scarcely need pointing out. If French and German were the subject of such a prolonged dispute, one might imagine there was little hope for Russian, even a hundred years later.[74]

The Clarendon Commission of 1864 began the movement for modern languages as a 'liberal' subject for study in the senior elementary schools, while firmly asserting the superiority of the Classics; the Taunton Commission of 1866-68 defended modern languages as *equals* to the Classics. Prior to 1872 French and German were seen as subjects for the middle-class élite, particularly for girls, who learned to communicate in speech, while boys were taught to communicate in writing—excessive stress on grammar established the academic rigour of the subjects while rendering many boys unable to carry on simple conversations. In this deprecation of 'colloquial' language, we see another pale reflection of the controversy in the universities. French, however, became firmly established in elementary schools from 1872; prior to this attempts to introduce language study to schools with commercial aims had been stopped by the Board of Education and the courts as 'extravagance with ratepayers' money', and no more than four percent of elementary school pupils had studied a language. The working classes were not to be denied, however, and the Bryce Commission of 1895 commented: 'There is evidence of some demand [...] for modern language instruction among skilled industrial workers, and enrolment in language courses in evening

---

[74]See Davis, pp. 45-46; P. H. Kelsey, *Four Hundred Years 1552-1952, the Story of Leeds Grammar School*, Leeds: privately published, pp. 11-12.

continuation schools and in higher grade elementary schools bears this out.'[75] When, shortly, the 'boom' in Russian came along, it was precisely in evening continuation schools and in other centres of vocational training that it became strong, if briefly so.

One voice calling for the teaching of Russian in schools and colleges in the 1890s was the Anglo-Russian Literary Society (ARLS), which had been founded by Edward A. Cazalet in 1893 to encourage the study of Russian language and literature, and which continued for four decades to publish *Proceedings* and to organize activities. It had many members in Russia, and it provided a centre and a library for the army and naval officers who had qualified in Russian.[76] Arthur Sykes, declares in an article[77] that Russian in schools is impossible, as schoolmasters cannot be shifted from their obsession with Latin and Greek. The *Proceedings*, however, reported in 1893 that an Institute of Mercantile Education had been set up at Streatham, where Russian was offered. In 1897 a small flurry of correspondence in the *Morning Post*, started by Cazalet and Kinloch, deplored the fact that Russian could not be learned in schools (it could in Germany, it was said); the commercial argument is used very forcibly. These were the very first ever examples of pressure in the newspapers for Russian in the *school* system. On 25 February 1898 the *Manchester Guardian* devoted a witty leader to the activities of the ARLS, which finished: 'In sober earnest, however, the new Society will do real service if it is at all successful in diminishing the too general neglect of Slav studies at the universities and amongst the educated people of this country generally.'

Reference to Russian in schools is absent from the contemporary professional journals of modern language teachers: *Modern Language Quarterly* (from 1897) and *Modern Language Teaching* (from 1905). Reference to Russian is made exclusively to universities until 1914; notices of a very few Russian textbooks appear, and all of them are of primary interest to specialist and adult students. In the *Russian Review*, an excellent academic journal produced for less than three years between 1912 and 1914 by Bernard Pares at Liverpool, lists of teachers and institutions where Russian might be studied appeared regularly, but there is no

---

[75] Quoted by Susan Bayley, 'Modern language teaching and the Bryce Commission of 1895', *Journal of Educational Administration and History*, vol. 21, 1989, no. 2, pp. 28-34; quotation on pp. 32-33. Bayley has published a series of informative papers on modern languages in the Victorian age and early twentieth century, and this paragraph draws liberally on her research: 'Gender, modern languages and the curriculum in Victorian England', *History of Education*, (with D. Y. Ronish) vol. 21, 1992, no. 4, pp. 363-382; 'Modern languages: an "ideal of humane learning", *Journal of Educational Administration and History*, vol. 23, 1991, no. 2, pp. 11-24; 'Modern languages as emerging curricular subjects in England, 1864-1918', *History of Education Society Bulletin*, no. 47, 1991, pp. 23-31; '"Life is too short to learn German": modern languages in English elementary education, 1872-1904', *History of Education*, vol. 18, 1989, no. 1, pp. 57-70.

[76] Galton, p. 273. The library at SSEES holds the few surviving papers of the ARLS; of particular interest is a book of newspaper cuttings charting the work of the Society.

[77] See note 66.

specific mention of schoolchildren studying Russian. An article in *Modern Language Teaching* for 1911 entitled 'Practical Teaching in Russian' by M. V. Trofimov declared that the article was compiled in answer to inquiries received at Liverpool University from individuals who wished to learn by themselves.

It may reasonably be supposed, however, that there were cases of schoolmasters encouraging promising pupils to take up Russian. Morfill was encouraged to take an interest in Russian at school in the late 1840s: maybe that teacher also gave him some formal guidance. Mr Schnurmann was at Cheltenham College for 22 years: surely he must have given similar encouragement to the occasional boy in his boarding house? Indeed he *offered* to do so: from 1892 Russian was offered at Cheltenham as an extra on a basis of private tuition, but the school is unable to say whether anyone took up the offer. At Leigh Grammar School (then in Lancashire), Russian was taught by a Mr R. R. Edge from 1917, who worked there from 1906 and had some eminent pupils.[78] He is unlikely to have taught Russian formally at the school before 1914, but he may have encouraged interested pupils to study alone, in view of the Lancashire cotton industry's strong and long-standing links with Russia. However, Board of Education statistics record no state secondary schools as teaching Russian before 1914. Oundle had initiated plans for Russian teaching just before the First World War broke out.[79] It has proved impossible as yet to find any evidence to suggest that Russian was taught within the formal curriculum of any school before 1914.

School pupils who picked up Russian informally or as an extra probably owe this to the enthusiasm of individual teachers for the language, literature and culture of Russia. In the commercial colleges the motivation was to expand trade with that country. The Board of Education's *Statistics of Public Education in England and Wales* for 1906-08 report four 'schools and classes for further education' (all in England) in which Russian was taught; by the 1911-12 report the figures distinguished between 'schools' and 'classes', and there were nine schools with a total of 22 classes in Russian.[80] There were three commercial and technical colleges teaching Russian known to Pares's *Russian Review* in 1912-1914: the City of London College, Manchester School of Commerce, and Liverpool School of Commerce. The teacher at Manchester was David Bondar, author of the 'Method' already mentioned, and a prolific provider of textbooks, journals, and supporting materials for both teachers and learners. In 1914 the teacher at

---

[78]Private information from Eric Miller, whose father was taught by Edge before 1923. See also Board of Education: Study of Russian in secondary schools etc., 1916-1935. National Archives ED 12/228.

[79]or so the MLA believed (see *Modern Language Teaching*, 1917). W. G. Walker, *A History of the Oundle Schools,* London: Grocers' Company, 1956, p. 535, ascribes the introduction of Russian at Oundle, however, to the outbreak of war.

[80]The Board of Education was perhaps a little haphazard in the way it collected statistics in its earliest years, and successive volumes of the *Statistics* differ as to what they actually published. Figures relevant to our study did not appear in every annual volume. Figures for Scotland do not seem to be available.

Liverpool was Trofimov; his was the lectureship established jointly with the University by Pares. There were Berlitz schools where Russian was offered in eight cities by 1914. These included Dublin, Edinburgh and Glasgow. Mark Siev or Sieff was teaching at the Gouin School of Languages in London and at the Central YMCA. A list of about 15 apparently freelance Russian teachers is given in the *Review,* many of them offering private lessons to individuals and/or claiming to be well experienced as teachers of Russian; some also offered translation services.

The Society for the Encouragement of the Arts, Manufactures and Commerce, later to become known as the Royal Society of Arts (RSA), began offering examinations in Russian in 1889. The Society's interests were wide-ranging, and they were particularly concerned to foster the education of the working classes through nineteenth-century organizations such as the mechanics' institutes. Its work in examinations began in the 1850s, and by 1881 the main focus was on commercial examinations. There were only two candidates in the first year of 1889, one of whom passed. It was a decade before other candidates came forward—seven, of whom only one passed—and in the years before the First World War there were never very many of them; but there were *some*: an average of perhaps ten per year. In addition, the London Chamber of Commerce was by 1898 encouraging the study of business Russian by offering two prizes for proficiency.[81]

By the end of the nineteenth and beginning of the twentieth centuries it can clearly be said that Russian should no longer have been seen as a recondite subject, or a joke—as to the senescent dons at Oxford—or beyond the capabilities of British people to tackle. There was a not insignificant number of travellers and businessmen, expatriates, military and naval men, teachers and academics, and others who had come to grips with the language, sometimes to a very competent level. When the situation arose, as it did in 1914, where a great need for linguistic ability in Russian was perceived, some preparation of the ground had taken place. The weaknesses in the response to the challenge, and the successes of many who participated will be examined in the next chapter.

---

[81]*Proceedings of the ARLS,* no. 23, 1898, p. 5. Under what auspices proficiency was assessed is not stated.

Chapter 3

The 'Boom' in Russian Studies and its Rise and Fall from 1914

> *Russia, when she came into her own, like Italy, instinctively attracted the best of English minds.*
> BERNARD PARES

IN his *Autobiography* Neville Cardus, writing of the early years of the twentieth century, states that H. G. Wells was 'running around bursting into notions'. Wells expressed one of these notions shortly after war broke out in 1914 in a letter to the *Times Educational Supplement*. By that time he was extremely well known as a novelist, for his liberal egalitarian social and political views, and for scandal in his personal life. He wrote:

> Sir,—I happen to be a parent whose sons are just going to school, and this accident has brought before me a very striking deficiency in our national equipment at the present time. I want my boys to learn Russian. I have wanted that for some time, but my personal reasons are enormously reinforced by the existing situation. It is clear that this war will make Russia a land of unprecedented opportunity for enterprising young Englishmen in business, in engineering, mining, and all sorts of practical openings. Next, on a rather higher ground, it is politically of the utmost importance to increase the mutual understanding of our two countries and to have a man of our educated class at least as able to understand a Russian newspaper as he is now to read a German one. And thirdly, as the best reason of all, Russian opens to an Englishman a whole world of intellectual and moral stimulation such as no other language except French can offer. Yet, so far as I can ascertain, there is not one British public school with a Russian teacher at the present time, and quite a considerable number of English boys, from the families settled in Petrograd and from the English colonies in Russia, are not even keeping up such knowledge of Russian as they have already acquired. I am doing what I can to remedy this state of affairs, so far as the public school to which my boys go is concerned, but I feel that this is a matter for the attention of abler and more influential people than myself and for treatment on a large scale.[1]

---

[1] *Times Educational Supplement*, 6 October 1914, p. 167. Wells sent his boys to Oundle.

Wells goes on to argue that not only the public independent schools, but also county schools and adult evening classes should be teaching Russian. Russian should be an allowable substitute for Greek in 'various university examinations'. Finance should not be an obstacle. 'A score or so of thousands of pounds spent upon teaching Russian in England and English in Russia now may mean a difference of millions in our trade with Russia in the years to come.' Business opportunities, an increase in mutual and intellectual and moral stimulation—these three arguments for Russian were commonly employed at the time. To them may be added the reason only hinted at by Wells: that Russian presented an intellectual challenge to the student which is comparable to that offered by Greek or other commonly studied languages. After 1920, when Wells visited the new Russia speaking no Russian and relying on the good English common sense he valued highly, and when he wrote a book based on a fifteen-day visit, there were many Russian émigrés who felt it was *he* who exemplified the need for mutual understanding. The commercial argument was a very powerful one for learning Russian at least until 1918, but there were many who could see that this alone would never assure the future of Russian studies: what if the political and military situation were to change? And it did, very sharply and very soon.

Other voices joined the chorus. A parliamentary answer reported in *The Times* (18 February 1915, p. 14) stated that the Boards of Trade and Education were considering steps to extend the teaching of Russian in commercial schools and to encourage its study in other types of educational institution. Max Beerbohm was later to write, 'There was, at the outbreak of the War, a great impulse towards Russian. All sorts of people wanted their children to be taught Russian without a moment's delay.'[2] We shall in due course return to Beerbohm and read his account of the eventual change in this public attitude.

For the moment Russian was in great demand. Friendship societies intensified their activities and new ones were set up. The Anglo-Russian Literary Society (ARLS), which had been in existence and had been publishing *Transactions* since 1893, and was to go on doing so long after the War, was one of them. Thirty-four academics (including Forbes and Goudy) and literary figures (including J. M. Barrie, Constance Garnett, Henry James, Arnold Bennett, Galsworthy, Wells, and many others) signed an 'address to our colleagues in Russia', confessing boundless admiration for Russian literature. The terms in which this is expressed, patriotic and sentimental as they are, make one wonder who the author was and how it could be that *all* these men and women could subscribe totally to it. Two extracts convey the spirit:

> It is not only because of your valour in war and your achievements in art, science, and letters that we rejoice to have you for Allies and friends; it is for some quality in Russia herself, something both profound and humane, of which these achievements are the outcome and the expression.

---

[2] Beerbohm, 'On Speaking French', in his *And Even Now*, London: Heinemann, 1920, pp. 289-299.

The final peroration runs:

> When the end comes and we can breathe again, we will help one another to remember the spirit in which our allied nations took up arms, and thus work together in a changed Europe to protect the weak, to liberate the oppressed, and to bring eventual healing to the wounds inflicted on suffering mankind both by ourselves and our enemies.[3]

Many of the signatories of the 'address' knew perfectly well, and had often enough said in the past, that the Russian autocratic monarchical régime was quite unsuited to this noble mission. But it was wartime, and cold reason had been replaced by exaggerated hopes for a bright future.

A parliamentary group, the Anglo-Russian Friendship Committee, had been set up after exchanges of parliamentarians in 1909 (from Russia) and 1912 (to Russia). Very active for a brief period was the Russia Society. This group was open to all interested, though it was formed at a meeting in Speaker's House, and the Speaker of the House of Commons was its President. It held its inaugural meeting on 11 March 1915, and it was very active indeed in fostering Russian language teaching. A parallel Russo-Scottish Society (later Russia Society of Scotland) was formed in Glasgow, and it started branches in Edinburgh and elsewhere. It declared its intention to act in cooperation with the Russia Society.[4] Murray Frame has discovered newspaper evidence of the activities of the Dundee Branch: lectures, concerts, meetings on cultural and political topics by all shades of opinion:[5] it may be assumed that such programmes were typical of branches in both Scotland and England. The Society's contribution to Russian teaching was to keep a register of ninety teachers and lecturers, including 'well-qualified native teachers of Russian (ladies and gentlemen)' 'in London, the Midlands, South, Glasgow and elsewhere' and offering them to heads of schools; to arrange Russian classes in London (and doubtless elsewhere); to compile in conjunction with *The Times* Book Club lists of suitable textbooks; to run a prize essay competition on Russia for schoolchildren; to provide interpreters to the front; and to grant certificates of proficiency in Russian. The Society claimed in 1916 to have been directly concerned in teaching Russian to over two thousand people. A library was being formed; books by members were presented to the King; a 'movement to send Russian boys to English schools' was being encouraged.[6]

The Russia Society later amalgamated with a body named the Anglo-Russian Friendship Society on 5 March 1917. This may well have been the same group as the Friendship *Committee* mentioned previously; the new organization was said to be acting in cooperation with the Russia Company, and was called the United

---

[3] 'Russia in Literature. Tribute by British men of letters,' *The Times*, 23 December 1914, p. 10.

[4] *The Times*, 23 Jan. 1915, p. 6; 11 Mar. 1915, p. 7; 24 Mar 1915, p. 4; *The Scotsman,* 11 Mar. 1915, p. 7; 22 Mar. 1916, p. 6, 22 Nov. 1916, p. 5.

[5] Frame, 'Dundee and the "Grand Purveyor"'.

[6] *The Times* (Russian Supplement), 29 April 1916, p. 6.

Russia Societies. I have found it impossible to trace formal records of the major activities of any of these groups other than the ARLS,[7] though the activities of the Russia Society were well publicised at the time in national papers, particularly *The Times* and *The Scotsman*. The United Association has left no mark in *The Times*, or anywhere else I can see. Equally invisible in Britain, at least, though papers are held in the archive of the Russian Federation—is the *Bratstvo* (Fraternity) Club, though papers on the Russian side are held in the archives of the Russian Federation. On 12 July 1917 *The Times* and *The Scotsman* both reported that a meeting of members of both houses of Parliament and prominent gentlemen passed the following resolution: 'That, in order to celebrate the inauguration of the new era in Russia, and to develop an exchange of ideas [...] between the British and Russian people, the oldest and youngest democracies in Europe, already united on the battlefield in defence of democratic liberty, a club be formed [...] to be known as the Russo-British 1917 Bratstvo (Fraternity)'.[8] A friendly message was received from the Russian Prime Minister, Prince Lvoff, and Lloyd George accepted the presidency. After that little or nothing reaches the press. The formation of the club was part of the unsuccessful propaganda effort to keep Russia in the war against Germany after the Revolution of February 1917; later in its short existence (it closed on 31 December 1921) it supported intervention in the Russian Civil War and organised relief to destitute refugees, not to mention cultural activities. According to Olga Kaznina, the British membership was small (twenty out of 150 in late 1919).[9] I can find no evidence that it fostered the teaching of Russian.

The MLA allowed a Russian Sub-committee to convene, and its activities and deliberations were publicised in *Modern Language Teaching*. Nevertheless, the MLA allotted no more than three pounds for its expenses: a sum so small as to be almost insulting. The few surviving reports indicate that the sub-committee had to fight for space in the journal, and that Neville Forbes, Sir William Mather and Mr Watts, of some of whom more will be heard later, stumped up £80 between them to provide a solid financial basis. The twelve members were mostly university teachers of Russian. *Modern Language Teaching* did report the activities of the group, often sympathetically, but it is possible that there was

---

[7] One file of correspondence relating peripherally to the Friendship Society is preserved at the University of Hull.

[8] *The Times* 12 July 1917, p. 7; *The Scotsman* 25 July 1917, p. 4. Some information is provided by Olga Kaznina, *Russkie v Anglii*, pp. 26-32. Kaznina draws attention to a difference between the English and the Russian statement of the aims of Bratstvo. The Russian text reads: '[Bratstvo] is established with the aim of making permanent the changes which have occurred in the life of the Russian people since the revolution of 1917 and for the sake of creating conditions in which the great democracies of Russia and Britain might enter into close unity and teach each other the best they have and which ought to be taught.' The English version stated the aim of acting as an intermediary between the oldest and the youngest democracy in Europe and of creating cultural and political relations. (pp. 26-27)

[9] Kaznina, p. 28.

some wariness about the emergence of a new language, which may have been seen as a threat to French and German.

Why was it, though, that a sudden great demand for instruction in Russian was experienced? 'Obviously'—we read in many sources—it was the outbreak of war. But this is actually not so obvious as it may seem. There was no more than a modest outburst of popular desire to learn Russian in 1941, when Britain and the Soviet Union became allies. In 1914-1915 more than one factor came into play, which the declaration of war instigated. The first was that the business community saw a great opportunity to steal lucrative export markets from the Germans. A Russo-British Chamber of Commerce had been founded in Russia[10] in 1908. This body was urging local British Chambers to affiliate, and the desire for a healthy trading relationship which it typified also played a significant part in encouraging the learning of Russian. Trade between Britain and Russia had actually been declining in the twenty years before the War.[11] It was finally realised that Britain had allowed Germany to overtake her in commercial activities, it was often repeated that German propagandists had turned British interests against Russia, and it was certainly true that Germans were very much more likely to have a knowledge of Russian that British merchants were.

While the first and third of these matters may be accepted without much question, the second—the propaganda point—is hard to believe. That the British business community was so obtuse as to fall for German psychological warfare of this type seems unlikely, to say the least—and if it is true, it is disgraceful. The argument was none the less trotted out regularly, and not only in the commercial world either. Academics were beginning to say they realized that a dismissive view of Russian literature and culture had been fostered by jaundiced German scholars, and that it was now the duty of British scholars to challenge it. One aim of the formation of the Russia Society was that 'German intrigues should be nullified'.[12] George Hume, a man claiming thirty-five years' experience of business in Russia, wrote of British suspicion of Germany, while frankly admitting Britons had been far less adaptable than the Germans in their approach to the market.[13] In the same issue of the Russian Supplement to *The Times*, M. V. Trofimov deplored what he saw as the German interpretation whereby mankind was divided into 'Die Menschen und die Russen' [humans and Russians—quoting Klinger]; Britain had taken over the notion that Russia

---

[10] There is a slight difficulty of terminology here: the Chamber was often referred to as the 'Anglo-Russian Chamber of Commerce', and it may be that this title was used by the British branch. Press advertisements used 'Russo-British'.

[11] Neilson, pp. 98-99.

[12] *The Times*, 23 Jan 1915, p. 6.

[13] 'Russian commerce. Some German methods', *The Times* (Russian Supplement), 17 Dec. 1915, p. 7.

represented savagery and brutality.[14] Elsewhere Trofimov admitted that the Russian government had been tyrannical and cruel, but 'the warm sense of humanity in the Russian heart is not to be confused with the government.'[15]

In the second place, there was undeniably a rush of emotion towards Russia, which suddenly became, not the savage, threatening 'bear' of previous decades, but our 'glorious ally' along with France in the herculean struggle against Germany. To leaf through both the serious press and the more popular local papers such as the *Nottingham Guardian* is to see that newspaper comment was eulogistic; Russian troops were 'heroic' and 'determined'. Russian staying power was essential to reducing pressure on Allied armies on the Western front, so the public had to believe in it. *The Times* published regularly and gratis the extensive *Russian Supplement*, later renamed *Russian Section*, which reflected the immense interest in Russia at the time. A new and favourable attitude to Russian language and culture consequently emerged.

The *Times Educational Supplement* weighed in on 4 January 1916. p. 6. Under the heading 'The Learning of Russian: Needs of the Future', 'A correspondent' argued:

> To relegate the study of Russian to commercial schools as is so often urged, is only another instance of the pitiable lack of understanding of what education means and of the consequent uncritical attitude which worships specialization while distrusting experts.

The writer attacks ingrained governmental attitudes:

> The government practically closes the civil service to [modern linguists] by penalizing modern languages, while placing a premium upon classics.

and he goes on to deplore the 'lack of preparation in Russian at school', while praising those Cambridge colleges which have offered entrance scholarships for Russian. Further:

> It may be argued that it is impossible [to introduce Russian into the school curriculum]. But it will have to be done all the same.

The academic world saw its chance. Its intentions had little to do with commerce or military advantage. But the 'new and favourable attitude' to Russia was welcomed by them, and by their supporters in the world outside academe, as we shall see, and the introduction of Russian into higher education on a much larger scale than previously, was the consequence. However, Ronald Burrows of the School of Slavonic Studies at King's College, London, wrote as early as 1915:

---

[14] Trofimov, 'Russian language: political and economic importance', *The Times* (Russian Supplement), 17 Dec. 1915, p. 11. It is interesting to see that as late as 1951, Elizabeth Hill in her inaugural lecture at Cambridge declared that German Slavonic scholarship [of the period under discussion] was 'often set in a prejudicial false perspective, tinged with contempt.' (Hill, p. 33).

[15] 'Teuton and Slav', *Modern Language Teaching*, XI(3), May 1915.

'The teaching of commercial Russian will be of little political use unless the more literary and scholarly side of the matter is *also* developed.'[16] Sir Robert Blair, an education officer at the London County Council, wrote to the Board of Education in similar mood in 1916: 'In the interests of education we ought to seize the present condition of the public mind—an emotional condition—which will pass and may be long in returning.'[17] These are astute remarks, and the survival of Russian in the universities, if not to so great an extent in other sectors of education, is due to the fact that the view of Burrows and Blair prevailed.

A very practical matter was the increased need for diplomats and officers in the armed services who could communicate with the Russian ally in his own language. As we have seen in the previous chapter, the civil and the armed services did not in the nineteenth century rely on the universities for the training of linguists; they were in no position to offer much help, at least until the end of the 1890s, when Schnurmann taught diplomats at Cambridge. However, in 1916 the War Office asked the School of Slavonic Studies to provide intensive three-month courses in a number of languages, including Russian, and this teaching continued after the war, as long as Britain was involved in the intervention in the Russian Civil War and longer.[18] There are occasional press reports of officers taking courses, including correspondence courses, in Russian.[19] Towards the end of 1918 The Queen's College, Oxford, again advertised its Laming Scholarship for Russian, making it clear that the College had not at that very late stage in the war lost sight of an important objective. 'This Scholarship is founded with a view [...] for the better understanding of the Economic and other Relations of this Country [...] especially with Russia; and for the provision of a University Training for those Persons who intend to enter upon a business career [...] or into the Diplomatic or Consular Service, or other kindred Service of the Crown.'

Yet another issue of general policy is of great importance to the study of Russian in 1914-1918. This was not obvious at the outbreak, but it became a very sore point indeed as the War progressed. There emerged in the country strong criticism of the education system. The need to wage a technologically advanced war had revealed many inadequacies particularly in the scientific and technical knowledge of the nation. Young public-school educated officers were immensely courageous in leading their men 'over the top'. However, their study of Latin and Greek and the exclusion of almost any science from their schooling left them lamentably ignorant of even quite simple scientific concepts, and,

---

[16]*Times Educational Supplement*, 4 May 1915, p. 64, emphasis mine—JM.

[17]National Archives ED/24/1173 4079.

[18]Roberts, p. 11.

[19]For example, 'Teaching of Russian: the qualifications of tutors' *The Times*, 31 August 1916, p. 5., mentions 500 army officers having taken up the language (under what auspices is not stated) and 100 naval officers following a correspondence course. It is stated that financial rewards were offered to the officers.

worse, they had difficulty in assimilating such new knowledge as would have enabled them, for example, to help their men face poison-gas attacks on the battlefield. It was even stated that the majority of casualties from gas attacks would have been avoided if both men and officers had had some elementary understanding of science. Now, a knowledge of Russian would scarcely have helped them in this respect. But at last the faith in a classical education as the one and only, the indisputably best, way of training the mind, was shaken. There was immense public concern, and a 'Neglect of Science Committee' was formed to lobby for change.[20] We shall return to this matter later, but it seems more than likely that Russian as a school, college, or university subject benefited from the new scepticism towards the traditional curriculum.

It is not easy to separate the three sectors of education in which Russian language teaching flourished during the First World War. To avoid undue confusion, we shall none the less try to do so while acknowledging their interdependence. University Russian departments would have liked there to be numerous secondary and public schools to send up undergraduates with a knowledge of the language. Universities arranged non-graduating and extra-mural classes for any who wished to present themselves. There was a considerable degree of collaboration between universities and the technical and commercial colleges. Teachers of Russian were often shared between higher, further, and secondary education. We shall examine each sector separately while attempting to indicate the connections between them.

Commercial and Technical Colleges

The most spectacular blossoming of Russian teaching after 1914 occurred in the commercial institutions. As we have seen, Russian had been taught in a few evening, technical, and commercial colleges before the war; Chambers of Commerce in many major cities were the main instigators of the great increase in Russian teaching in these colleges after 1914. Their motivation was the desire to appropriate those markets which the Germans had dominated until war broke out.

The MLA published the results of a survey taken in mid-1916. The Russian Sub-committee had sought information from schools, education committees, and universities or university colleges in England, Wales and Scotland. Even at this distance in time it proves possible to show that their survey is not complete, but it is informative none the less.

Punching far above its weight comes Scotland, where 557 students were known to be learning Russian—the cities here mentioned specifically are Glasgow, Dundee and Aberdeen; 391 students were studying in 'classes at 18

---

[20] The matter is concisely described in E. W. Jenkins, *From Armstrong to Nuffield*. London: John Murray, 1979, esp. p 53.

centres under the Continuation Class Code.' Aberdeen in particular had an imaginative scheme for sharing Russian teachers between schools and for making Russian instruction available to the public, particularly to 'business houses', and by October 1916 sixty students were enrolled in two classes.[21] But even Scotland is beaten proportionally by the City of Bradford (population at that time well under 300,000), where 281 were studying Russian; 434 others outside London, and 704 in London itself were enrolled in Russian classes.[22]

The staggering figure in Bradford invites further investigation. A report in *The Times Russian Section*, 30 September 1916, p. 11, provides details: leaders of the textile industry had sought to improve trading relations with Russia for after the war. 'A study of the Russian language and of the habits and business methods of the people of Russia by young men [in the textile industries] is regarded as one of the essential conditions of this development.' The Director of Education (A. C. Coffin) had devised a scheme of instruction in Russian language, life, and business conditions which had been warmly praised by Board of Education inspectors and by visiting university professors. It was proposed to send students to Russia for up to a year to live in Russian families. Bradford industrialists, in particular the Dyers' Association, were intending to contribute to the expenses of the students. Russian educational authorities had expressed warm enthusiasm for the scheme, about the realization of which we have no information at all. However, it was undoubtedly imaginative; if political upheavals had not overtaken it, it would certainly have been of great commercial benefit to the Bradford woollen industry.

The conditions in the East Midlands are perhaps more typical, but no less interesting. Chambers of Commerce in Leicester, Loughborough, Derby and Nottingham had all set about establishing Russian classes in local institutions. In Leicester this meant the greatly respected Municipal Technical and Art Schools[23] and in Derby the Technical College, which was no less highly thought of.[24] The Nottingham Chamber, however, approached the University College, not at that time a university in its own right. The College appointed a lecturer, Basil Slepchenko, a Russian academic with business experience who had been stranded in England in 1914 by the outbreak of war, and classes began in the autumn of 1915. Leicester also employed Slepchenko from 1915, and from November 1917 Derby too made use of his services. In a *curriculum vitae* Slepchenko later claimed to have been teaching 150 students at his peak, and this may not be too much of an exaggeration.[25] Of the three cities, it was Leicester

---

[21] 'Educational' [news]. *The Scotsman*, 27 May 1916, p. 12.

[22] Bullough, *The Teaching of Russian*.

[23] *Kelly's Leicestershire and Rutland Directory*, 1916, p. 530.

[24] Tolley, B. H. *The History of the University of Nottingham*, I, p. 9. Named the Derby Municipal Technical College, this institution was formed in 1891 from the former School of Art and the former School of Science.

[25] Basil Slepchenko: curriculum vitae of 1931 (typescript, 1 p.)

which showed the most imagination in the employment of Slepchenko: the Chamber of Commerce asked him to tour the city's industries with a view to 'familiarizing him with trade terms to be translated into Russian for the benefit of the students and their employers.' [The President of the Chamber] also spoke of the possibilities of conducting a short exhibition in Russia of Leicester goods, to be accompanied by some of the pupils for the purpose of establishing and enlarging Leicester trade in that country.''[26]

Classes at the Nottingham University College were rather smaller in number (around 40) than in the Leicester Technical School (73 in 1916), and this may be because the lower middle classes of Nottingham found the 'university' cachet somewhat intimidating. The Russian classes there were not of degree standard, of course, and probably differed in no way from those in Derby and Leicester. By good fortune we have a breakdown of the social provenance of the 42 members of the two Nottingham classes in May 1917. The day students consisted of: 2 lace manufacturers, 5 no occupation, 3 students, (six of these ten were women); evening students were: 1 lace manufacturer, 1 hosiery manufacturer, 1 solicitor, 4 teachers, 1 clerk of works, 3 no occupation, 2 managers, 3 warehousemen, 14 clerks, 1 agent, 1 apprentice hosier. In the face of this, the reaction of the Chamber of Commerce seems disproportionate:

> The Chamber of Commerce had supported the initiative as a means to extending the trade between Nottingham and Russia at the end of the war. They had no interest in providing with tuition ladies intending to travel, foreigners and gentlemen of position. The majority of the young men whom the Chamber desired to assist have joined the army, whilst certain aliens are learning the language with the avowed intent of capturing the trade with Russia at the end of the war.[27]

The Chamber had been allowing the College fifty pounds a year towards the expenses of teaching Russian. This they promptly withdrew, while granting one guinea for every student 'approved by the Foreign Trade Committee.' It is very hard to see why they felt they were not getting value for money in return for their nugatory fifty pounds! Nowhere else at the time did local business try to manipulate the behaviour of an educational institution, even where incomparably greater sums of money had been donated.

The sharing of teaching staff between universities and technical colleges—and indeed between secondary schools and universities—was not uncommon; it continued for two or more decades. We have seen that Liverpool University and the Commercial College had had a joint lectureship since 1908. Remuneration in all these establishments was not princely, and it was clearly expected that teachers would hold multiple appointments. H. J. W. Tillyard, later briefly to be professor

---

[26]Leicester Chamber of Commerce Minutes, 5 Feb. 1917. Record Office for Leicester, Leicestershire and Rutland.
[27]Nottingham Chamber of Commerce Council Minutes, 1 May 1917.

of Russian at Birmingham, ran a 'non-graduation course of elementary instruction' in Russian at Edinburgh University, and also taught at Hawick Technical Institute.'[28] Hawick was 52 miles by rail from Edinburgh, and the journey can scarcely have been easy. It is greatly to the credit of this small border town of fewer than 17,000 inhabitants at the time that it should have had the enterprise to set up Russian classes to further the export prospects of the local industry in woollen cloth, carpets and hosiery. A news item in *The Scotsman* of 25 May 1916, p. 6, stated that there were 47 students (some of them, one imagines, from Galashiels and Selkirk)[29] enrolled in the class, and that 'a gentleman' (unnamed) had offered to give each student £50 to enable him to go to Petrograd to perfect his command of the language. There were probably other such small towns not named in the MLA survey where the study of Russian was encouraged.

English and Welsh towns and cities not already mentioned known to have run Russian classes in their technical and commercial colleges during the War were: Birmingham, Brighton, Cardiff, Hull (probably the first city to institute such new courses after the declaration of war, in September 1914), Leamington, Leeds, Newport, Northampton, Sheffield, and Middlesborough. In addition, special classes were set up specifically for businessmen in Huddersfield; journalists and businessmen were studying Russian in Fleet Street, London; Bradford too had its special businessman's class. It may be assumed that the existence of such classes was designed to protect mature people from the supposed indignity of sitting in the same classroom as teenagers. Another aspect of adult education which deserves mention is that British prisoners of war and internees, especially when confined in the same camps as Russians, were learning the language. Study materials were provided by the British Prisoners of War Book Scheme.[30]

One part of Britain remained immune to the enthusiasm for the study of Russian: Ireland. The *Times Educational Supplement* of 16 October 1916, p. 182, asserted that nothing had yet been done in Irish universities to promote Russian. The anonymous 'correspondent' declared that there was no reason to include Russian in the school curriculum. 'The ordinary pupil will certainly not drop German to take up Russian [...] Nothing short of a revolution in our curricula is likely to make the admission of Russian into our schools.'

The Royal Society of Arts, which had a strong interest in vocational and commercial education and was a pioneer in the provision of examinations for students in continuation classes and colleges, examined a total of 550 candidates in its three grades in Russian between 1916 and 1919. While this does not compete

---

[28]*The Times* Russian Supplement, 26 August 1916, p. 11. An advertisement in *The Scotsman* of 4 December 1915 announces Tillyard's Edinburgh University class, which was to begin in January 1916. The fee for this course at the University, it may be interesting to note, was £1. 11s. 6d (a guinea and a half), with a five-shilling entrace fee in the case of non-matriculated students.

[29]'South of Scotland Chamber of Commerce', *The Scotsman*, 2 Sept. 1916, p. 1.

[30]*Modern Language Teaching*, XII(7), 1916, p. 193. The Royal Society of Arts Annual Reports indicate involvement in examinations for such prisoners.

with the nine thousand examined in French at the same time and even the 869 in German, it represents a significant interest in the language. However, this energetic activity in Russian teaching diminished markedly almost as suddenly as it began. The stupendous upheavals in Russia in 1917 and the consequences for the war effort in the following years were not understood in Britain. In the late winter of 1917 British policy was to keep Russia in the war against Germany at all costs. It was not in the interests of the Provisional Government to continue the struggle, but they did so; the Bolshevik October Revolution followed, which Britain failed to perceive as a consequence she had contributed to. Russia now had a government which was to impose a social and economic structure which was quite unexpected by those whose aim was trade and commerce. Soon eleven nations including Britain were intervening unsuccessfully in the Russian Civil War and building up resentment which persisted for many decades. What point was there in learning Russian for commercial purposes? There were, of course, other good reasons, but it did not seem so to many at the time. Public interest and enthusiasm evaporated. Britain's glorious ally had apparently ratted on us.

It may be thought that Scotland was an exception to the distaste the British public felt towards the October Revolution and to events in Russia. 'Red' Clydeside has entered the folklore of the left, and it is argued that Aberdeen and possibly Dundee were even more enthusiastic for political developments in Russia at that time than was Glasgow. Clydeside workers crammed into classes to learn about the revolutionary struggle in Russia and about Marx, Lenin, and Trotsky; meanwhile their middle-class contemporaries were enrolling for courses in classics of Russian literature at the University.[31] Support for the Russian Revolution in Scotland was, however, much more apparent than real: when it came to elections moderate Labour won decisively.[32]

The British public and government were unable to see the broader picture and sympathize with the infant democracy, when all they were interested in was beating the Germans. Russian language continued to be available in some commercial colleges—press advertisements in 1918 confirm this. Teaching, however, was on a much smaller scale. Entries for RSA examinations dropped from a peak of 266 in 1917 to 56 in 1920, and only 17 (the lowest point) in 1927, before recovering slightly to reach 43 in 1937. Meanwhile German had recovered from its wartime unpopularity (which, however, never threatened its fairly strong position)—there were 583 candidates in 1927. The MLA had very wisely foreseen the problem early in 1917:

> We have no assurance that [enthusiasm for the language] will last in its present strength. It is probable that it will decline [...] and steps should be

---

[31] Kirkwood, 'The University and the Wider World', p. 2.

[32] Kenefick, 'Aberdeen was more red than Glasgow', and Frame, 'Dundee and the "Grand Purveyor"'.

taken without delay to substitute for the actual uninstructed enthusiasm *a permanent and enlightened interest* [...][33] (my emphasis—JM)

By late 1917 the profuse flow of press articles had dried up completely. The survival of Russian language studies now depended on institutions other than the commercial colleges.

Russian in schools: 'Off the beaten track of common knowledge and ideas'

The Sub-committee for Russian Studies of the MLA coined this phrase in their 'Memorandum on the Teaching of Russian', which was published in February 1917 just as the first of the Russian revolutions toppled the Tsar.

However, shortly before the war the Board of Education had issued its Circular 797 on modern languages, the first such statement by a government institution on the subject. Nothing could have been further from the educationists' minds in 1912 than Russian; the word is not mentioned. Modern languages at that time still meant French plus German. Thirteen lines in fifty pages recognize the 'claims of Italian and Spanish' (p. 13); Latin is the only other language mentioned. Nevertheless, the Circular is not irrelevant to establishing the context of the introduction of Russian. We learn, for example, that 'The Board would favourably consider any proposal for the introduction of [Italian or Spanish] into the curriculum under suitable conditions.' So the Board at this time sought at least to guide or encourage curricular innovation in the language field. We learn also that modern language teachers had been more poorly paid than other teachers until recently, and that some language teachers were not well qualified particularly in relation to the need to teach the spoken language, a requirement that was seen as an innovation to be encouraged. The Circular also bewails a marked decline in German teaching, which was explained by the crowded timetable and by the requirement for Latin in many university arts faculties. What pupils were asked to do by public examinations showed a gross mismatch with the welcome change in the aims and methods of teaching. Some of these problems continued for decades to dog modern languages, especially 'second' foreign languages like German and Russian.

The MLA Russian sub-committee recognized that

> The War has greatly influenced the attitude of the public and of educationalists towards the question of Russian studies. Considerable enthusiasm has been roused for the language and for the necessity of a closer understanding between the two countries. To this extent an attempt to introduce Russian into schools has probably become easier. But in justice to the language and the people of Russia *it must be said that the study of Russian is not any more desirable now than it was, in fact, before the War.* Apart from certain practical considerations brought to the fore by the present situation, but also

---

[33]Bullough, p. 26.

easily overstated, the claim made here for its consideration derives its weight by no means directly from the actual political relations between the two countries.[34] (emphasis mine—JM)

An acerbic comment is to be found in the *Memorandum*, and it will strike a chord with many teachers who have sought in later years to urge that Russian should be taught more widely in schools. Writing of the fact that Russian lies off the beaten track of common knowledge, we read: 'This "exoticism" may act as a stimulant to the venturesome; but it acts equally as a repellant to the cautious and indolent, and affects the status assigned to Russian in popular estimation more powerfully almost than the practical difficulty of introducing it in schools.'

Two or three dozen schools were not 'repelled'. Cheltenham College, Mr Schnurmann's old stomping ground (he retired in 1914), introduced Russian to the general curriculum; a Mr Henley was now in charge. Among other independent schools which introduced Russian at this time were the City of London School, Dulwich College, Eton College, Holt School (Liverpool), the Leys (Cambridge), Manchester High School for Girls, Oundle (possibly partly in response to H. G. Wells's pressure), Repton, Princess Helena College, George Watson's College (Edinburgh), St Paul's (London) and Tonbridge. Other possibly less famous establishments did advertise Russian in their curriculum: Stanley House, Bridge of Allan, was one of them.[35] Maybe they saw it as a good selling point at that time. Of the schools listed, Cheltenham, Dulwich, Repton, and the Leys had three or fewer learners. Cheltenham, however, was planning expansion of Russian into the general curriculum. It was not universally popular. Whilst Eton reported that the boys were keen, Dulwich noted a 'lack of response'. Nevertheless, Brighton College, Clifton College, Harrow, Highgate, King Edward's Birmingham, Radley, and the Perse (Cambridge) declared they were either intending to introduce Russian or were actively considering doing so. Clifton College certainly took the plunge in 1916, as did Sherborne.[36]

The MLA Russian sub-committee assembled this information with great energy, but with considerable difficulty. A circular seeking the views of one hundred schools on the possibilities of teaching Russian at first received not one single answer. Later personal approaches by sub-committee members received a better response. 'In the majority of cases schools have failed to rise to the occasion, or to appreciate the need for a study of Russian.' It had been hoped to institute a register of teachers of Russian, but since the schools proved so uncooperative, this was only achieved after considerable effort.[37]

---

[34]Bullough, p. 2.

[35]Advertisement in *The Scotsman*, 11 April 1917, p. 9.

[36]Information in this paragraph has been gleaned from various sources: Bullough, *Memorandum...*, news items in *The Times*, 30.9.16, *Modern Language Teaching*, XIII, October 1917, and elsewhere.

[37]Macgowan, p. 93.

In the first decade of the twentieth century, following the Bryce Report on secondary education of 1895 and education acts in 1899 and particularly 1902, state secondary education was only beginning to develop and cannot be regarded as a fully fledged 'system'. Regulations for secondary schools promulgated in 1904 provided that the curriculum for twelve- to sixteen-year-olds was to be non-vocational and was to include modern languages. The Board of Education, which had been set up by the 1899 Act as the central supervisory authority, included in its 1907-08 *Statistics of Education* the numbers of schools in England teaching Latin, Greek, French, German, Spanish and Italian; there were no more than one or two schools offering Spanish and Italian, and Russian is not mentioned, so it may be safely assumed that it was taught nowhere in state secondary education. This situation was to change in the 1914 War.

There is in the National Archives at Kew a fascinating file, which is probably the only official record of what went on in the classrooms where Russian was taught in 1914-18 which has survived.[38] The documents are mostly rough notes penned by HM inspectors on scraps of paper as they attended Russian lessons in various schools, mostly under the auspices of local education authorities. In addition to these schools, the inspectors mention a number of others where evidence suggests Russian was taught at the time. The schools are (the exact names are not always clear, and, of course, schools change their names):— Northampton County Borough Town and County School for Boys, Northampton Technical and Commercial School, Kettering Grammar School, Weston Favell School, Wilson's Grammar School (where the teacher was a French colonel who had worked in a Russian military academy for twelve years), Holloway County School, Hanson Boys' Secondary School (Bradford), Bristol Merchant Venturers Secondary School, Leigh Grammar School, Hackney Downs School, Lewisham Catford St Dunstan's College, Pitsmoor Secondary School (Sheffield, later to become Firth Park Grammar School), Coalville Grammar School, Walsall Grammar School, the independent Manchester High School for Girls, and Robert Gordon's Secondary School, Aberdeen.

The inspectors' reports reveal that the main problem, and one which is a constant subject of discussion in the professional press in 1914-1918, is that of the availability of teachers and of their quality. Enthusiasm for Russian in Northampton, for example, was great in both technical and secondary education, but the teacher, a thirty-seven year-old Russian called Dabert was no better than average in ability, to say the least. Though he used no more than 'the method of the textbook', the boys at Northampton Boys' School were 'sticking to the subject well.' At this school, the boys had refused (perhaps on mistaken patriotic grounds!) to continue with German, and the head had demanded guarantees from parents that if boys joined the class, they would continue for at least two years; forty gave this guarantee but the head would allow only twenty of the more able

---

[38] National Archives ED 12/228.

to join the class. The same teacher at Kettering Grammar had not hit it off quite so well with the pupils; he started with 14 boys plus 11 girls from the girls' school. Four of the girls quickly dropped out, and Mr Dabert's knowledge of English was found by the inspector to be so poor that he could not explain difficulties. He had also started a class for eight teachers and one school governor. However, he was then called up for military service in the Russian army. Kettering had further difficulties recruiting suitable teachers. Weston Favell had three teachers in three terms, none of them very good; the inspectorate nevertheless recommended that the 'experiment' should continue, provided a good teacher could be found. The comment of the inspector at Kettering is more negative; 'it should not continue unless conditions can be greatly improved.' By April 1918 the Head at Northampton Boys' School had discontinued Russian because 'the failure of successive teachers has made the subject exceedingly unpopular.' It is scarcely surprising that the President of the Board of Education in a parliamentary answer on 30 March 1917 stated: 'There are grounds for thinking that there is not a sufficient supply of competent teachers of Russian in this country.'

Curious incidents surrounded Russian at Holloway County School. 'Mr Unwick [presumably one of the inspectors] has just found out that Russian has been started at the Holloway County School, but the LEA has heard of it and is considering whether to stop it or not.'[39] One is reminded of the classic Punch cartoon of 1871: 'Go directly and see what [baby]'s doing and tell her she mustn't.' But this was not the end of it. A note dated 21 March 1917 reports that a Serbian teacher of Russian, a Mr Tsekerov, had been interviewed by 'the Reader in Russian at King's College' (presumably Trofimov), who decided he was not proficient enough in Russian to teach it. The inspector feels that Mr Tsekerov (who had studied Russian for five years) had been shabbily treated, especially as 'it is a little curious that the Reader [...] having weeded out the Russian teachers in London has started a class at King's for would-be Russian teachers [...] The case has interesting features.' It has indeed.

At the same time it is good to report that the inspectors found Miss Adamson at Manchester High School for Girls to be getting 'excellent results'; at Hanson School boys aged 15 were studying Russian as their *fourth* foreign language, but the lessons were going 'very well', despite the inspector's thought that four foreign languages was an excessive load. Here, it may be apposite to note, the teacher was an unnamed English master who had discovered an enthusiasm for Russian, and who sought regular contact with Russian residents in Bradford. Trade between Russia and Bradford was strong. An inspector reported that 'the school should for the present be allowed a free hand'.

Despite some of these disappointing reports, the inspectors make anything but negative statements about most of the schools. (Their findings are very briefly

---

[39] Memo dated 20 Dec. 1916.

summed up in *Education in England and Wales, being the report of the Board of Education for the Year 1917-18*, p. 25: 'Several experiments have been made in the teaching of Russian, and the results in some cases are stated to be promising.') The inspectors comment in their notes on the enthusiasm for the subject in Bradford evening schools and the intention of the Bradford authorities to offer travelling scholarships to Russia. Likewise, local demand for Russian in Leigh was high in view of the town's long trading relationship with Russia. Dr Lloyd Storr-Best, the charismatic linguist head, first at Coalville and then at Sheffield Firth Park Grammar School, kept the subject going until 1932, but it went into hibernation from his retirement in that year until after the Second World War. Glowing reports, not just from the inspectors, but from Professor Neville Forbes of Oxford, on the work of J. Kolny-Balotsky at Walsall Grammar School are found in the file; Kolny-Balotsky later became professor of Russian at Leeds University.

It is not given great prominence in the reports, but surely a major problem must have been the lack of a Russian course suitable for schoolchildren. We are not told what book the Northampton boys and girls used. The chronological list of Russian courses and grammars in the Bibliography of this volume suggests very little that might be suitable, and many of the books listed for the war period are phrase-books, purely descriptive grammars, self-instruction manuals and the like, while what was needed was a progressive *course* in Russian in a style that might have appealed to young people. No such thing was to appear for thirty years. The one title appearing to promise this, Underwood's *A School Russian Grammar* of 1916, is utterly unsuitable to this or any purpose: a mere 62 pages—and very short pages at that—of descriptive grammar totally lacking *any* connected examples of Russian. There is not one Russian sentence in it, nay, not one phrase of more than two words. How a master at Eton could have imagined it would be of any use in schools defies reason to ascertain. Even as a resource for reference it can have had little purpose.

It is odd to discover the existence of some prejudice against certain teachers of Russian. A news item in *The Scotsman* in 1915[40] ran: 'There is reason to believe that in past years teachers of the Russian language were often (sic!) merely disguised German agents, working against Russia.' This is wartime paranoia, and one must not forget the extent to which anti-German passion rose during the 1914-18 war. That such twaddle could have been taken seriously in Britain is something of a national disgrace.[41] It does appear, however, to have been put about by certain elements in the Russia Society.

The question of the availability, training, and certification of teachers of Russian is raised all this. Who were the teachers working in the field in the war

---

[40] 'The Teaching of Russian', Tuesday 7 September, p. 6.

[41] Teachers who had naturalized as British citizens for as long as thirty years were sometimes dismissed because they were 'Germans'. A particularly unpleasant example may be seen in *The Scotsman,* 27 May 1916, p. 12.

period? Some of their names and a little about their personalities have been mentioned here. Three conferences of teachers of Russian were held at Kings College, London, in 1916-1917; for the first of them we have a list of 24 participants. Seven of these are members of the MLA Russian Sub-committee. The other seventeen include Dr Storr-Best, Kolny-Balotsky, Slepchenko (all of whom have been mentioned already in these pages), four ladies (from Cardiff, the London County Council, and Manchester), seven male teachers from the LCC, one from Bradford, Mr Khromchenko from Derby Technical College, and teachers from Harrow, Birmingham and London. Eleven of the 24 have what can be interpreted as Russian or Slavonic names. Some of them became well-known as teachers or authors of textbooks (Sieff, Kolny-Balotsky, Segal, Raffi, Timotheieff). Only four of them are positively known to have had school teaching experience. The conference, to judge by the published summary of proceedings,[42] was a thoroughly stimulating and lively occasion in which both Slavs and British took active part. It was therefore a precursor of the many memorable conferences of the Association of Teachers of Russian which took place in much later years, after 1958. It is interesting to note the first emergence of the complaint made often in later years that teachers of Russian experienced a sense of isolation. The attenders at this first conference clearly sought to overcome that sense by lively social and professional intercourse.

Participants debated the qualifications of teachers. It is entertaining to look at a slightly earlier exchange in the press on the subject. In August 1916 the Russia Society was doing its utmost to facilitate the supply of teachers to schools. We have already noted that this was accompanied by a certain anti-German attitude. The virtue of the Society's intentions, however misguided, could not be doubted. It sent round a circular about the qualifications of teachers of Russian. It admitted that some with the 'slightest' qualifications were well able to teach. However, some 'have no business to do so [...such as] certain Russian and Polish Jews having only an imperfect knowledge of the language [...] also [...] revolutionary exiles and political adventurers contact with whom may be undesirable for persons intending to take up positions in Russia.'[43]

Well now, it is true that some Russian Jewish families used Yiddish in the home—but scarcely outside it. It is undeniably true that Russian teaching may sometimes suffer from Poles who think they can speak better Russian than the Russians. The anti-semitic tinge in the circular is unpleasant—though typical, unfortunately, of the historical period we are considering, as any reader of the press of the time will confirm. It was the other remarks which outraged that Russian political exile and later professor Michael V. Trofimov, and which

---

[42] Report of Conference of Teachers of Russian, *Modern Language Teaching*, XIII(6), 1917, pp. 158-169.
[43] *The Times*, 7.9.15, p. 10.

provoked him to a restrained, dignified, humorous and ironic response in the correspondence columns of *The Times*:

> Sir, I have read with great surprise some of the statements in a circular letter by the Education Sub-committee of the Russia Society. I am afraid that the Russia Society were misled in their strong faith in a Russian passport as a test of the political status of a Russian person. Unfortunately for the Russia Society, a Russian has a soul as well as a passport, and a soul is too delicate a thing to be described even by a most shrewd police-officer. Besides, it often happens that the spiritual outlook of a person is entirely different from that suggested by his or her outward appearance including political status testified by a passport. I think we had a bitter experience with the Germans and we ought to use a better standard than a passport for qualifying Russian teachers. Now, there is only one test for passing a person as a tutor, and that is his or her good social or academical standing. I don't know what educational authority—beside the implicit faith in a Russian passport—have the Russia Society for directing the teaching of Russian in this country, but it seems to me that some guidance is necessary. I wonder if the Modern Language Association or the British Teachers' Union would consider the urgent question of supplying Russian teachers for British schools.
>
> Michael V Trofimod [sic]
King's Coll., Strand, Aug 31

The Russian flavour in both the language and the sentiment of the letter enhances its pungency. Trofimov was a refugee who had in some way offended the Russian government. He was therefore one of those 'contact with whom may be undesirable for persons intending to take up positions in Russia.' Indeed, though Bernard Pares later negotiated a safe conduct for him to return if he wished, he never felt it was safe to do so. His rebuke to the Russia Society was justified, but to be fair to them, their attitude exemplifies the difficulties for a cultural organization of dealing with a nation whose social and political structure, and whose approach to international relations, differs markedly from one's own. One hopes that the leaders of the Russia Society learned from this.

At the King's College Conference of Russian teachers, after some constructive debate, the qualifications for a teacher were formulated as follows:

The candidate should be in possession—

1. Of the standard spoken Russian of the country.
2. Of an academic standing not lower than that of a secondary school.
3. Of a knowledge of English and general experience of teaching modern languages.

The Russia Society had also played a part in the certification of students of Russian by setting up a board of examiners. The topic of public examinations is of some importance, in that the way a subject is taught and learned is strongly influenced by the way students know it will be tested. We may therefore at this point go back a few years and interpolate a brief account of the examinations many of the younger students took at this time. The Society of Arts, from 1908 *Royal* Society of Arts (RSA), had long since (1889) been offering examinations in Russian; the London Chamber of Commerce and the London Matriculation Board now set up examinations in Russian, while Oxford was to include Russian in the Higher Certificate examination.[44] It would be fair to say that the RSA had the longest experience in the field, and that it had always been particularly interested in the commercial aspect of language learning. Its earliest syllabuses demanded theoretical knowledge of grammar, translation from and into Russian, the writing of an essay on a technical, scientific or commercial subject, and the ability to transcribe a manuscript text. The examiner at this time was the Very Rev. Eugene Smirnoff, Chaplain to the Russian Embassy in London. His report ran: 'I am very far from being satisfied [...] I should like to see much wider knowledge of the grammar, much greater ability in expressing the Russian sentences, and more care in working the whole examination paper.'

On reading the 1889 paper it obvious that the reverend gentleman had not the remotest idea of what could reasonably be expected of an English-speaking student after two or three years of part-time study. Moreover, young Mr Charles Moncur of Sheffield, aged 17, the first and only successful candidate, deserved much less grudging praise for having survived the ordeal. He was called upon to translate into Russian a passage including the words, 'At some remote period of which very little is known with certainty, but when, it may be supposed, what are now the various Slavonic peoples spoke the same tongue and worshipped the same gods, some kind of mythological system, in all probability, prevailed among them.' It is scarcely surprising that no candidates came forward for ten years after this, or that in 1899 only one out of seven passed.

By 1916 Trofimov was in charge; there were three grades of examination, and the highest was not so tough as the single grade in 1889. The lowest grade was much more down-to-earth and realistic in what it required of relative beginners. There was an oral exam and a dictation; it seems these were optional extras.

The School Certificate was introduced around this time, and papers were first taken in 1919. Russian was mentioned in its own right (not as an 'authorized other language') in the 1919 syllabuses. Papers set by the Joint Matriculation Board in 1921 (Higher) and 1923 (School Certificate) have survived:[45] they are very demanding, even the School Certificate ('First examination') requiring translation from prescribed texts by Dostoevsky, Gogol', Pushkin, and various lyric poets. Other evidence suggests that these examinations were intended to matriculate Russian émigrés seeking entry to British universities, rather than home candidates, and it became necessary later to adjust standards. In any case, the statistical sections of the annual Reports of the Board of Education indicate that there were few entrants. In 1919 twelve entered the First Examination and

---

[44] Announcement by Neville Forbes at the Conference: see Report of Conference, p. 163.

[45] I am grateful to Alan West, formerly of the JMB, for tracing these papers.

nine passed with credit; in 1922 there were 36 entrants, in 1924: 35, in 1926: 42 and 1927: 33. the 'pass with credit' rate varied from 28% to 57%. No figures were published for 1920, 1921, 1923 or 1925. No figures were published for Highers except between 1926 and 1929: they amounted to no more than 5, 3, 5 and 1 candidate respectively.

These small numbers need to be interpreted with caution. The School certificate was not a single-subject, but a 'group' examination, and some school pupils may have studied Russian without offering it as one of the limited number chosen for certification. It may also be that the RSA or Chamber of Commerce examinations were more suitable for, or more attractive to, certain types of student. An average of 46 students per year entered the RSA examinations in Russian between 1930 and 1939. It was then and it remains the case now that, although the School Certificate examination is mainly intended for sixteen-year-old school pupils, entrants may be much older: eighty years ago this was a route to university matriculation for more mature pupils.

We have jumped ahead of the First World War period in this account of examinations. To return to the Conference of teachers at King's College, we find that Basil Slepchenko's contribution to the proceedings of the Conference was on the subject of examinations:[46] speaking in Russian, he argued that English students were daunted by written examinations, and that the teacher's job was to support their enthusiasm for the subject by ensuring total fairness in the assessment process. We see in his short paper the way a Russian who is conditioned to expect examinations from childhood to university which are *oral* combats the British assumption that *written* papers are the acid test of knowledge. He was, however, astute enough to press the argument that oral tests as a corrective to unfair and false assessment were essential. After discussion, the meeting unanimously recommended 'that the system of Oral Examinations be strengthened and its scope enlarged.'

Russian in Higher Education: remedying the 'abysmal lack of knowledge of things Russian'

'[I] met with a certain amount of opposition [...] perhaps it would be more correct to say criticism as to the possibility of English students acquiring the Russian language.'[47] This was one reaction when the Chairman of the Nottingham Chamber of Commerce took soundings in 1915 on behalf of the Principal of University College, Nottingham, to seek support for the introduction of the language to the commercial section of the College. The 'critics' of the idea were badly informed: by 1914 there was clear evidence that students whose native language was English were well able to make a fair attempt at Russian.

---

[46]Slepchenko, 'Garantii pravil'noi otsenki...'

[47]Minutes of the Nottingham Chamber of Commerce Council Meeting, 13 April 1915, pp. 19-21.

When war broke out there had been five universities in Britain where Russian might be studied.[48] To compare this with other intellectually advanced countries: in Germany at the same time there were four chairs of Slavonic languages, three of them in Berlin, though German academic attitudes ensured that close study of the languages and of the 'best literature' worked to exclude any more practical considerations.[49] Otto Hoetzsch had begun his life's work of trying to foster the study of Russia in Germany, which was rendered 'futile' by the War, by the rise of Nazism two decades later, and by Stalinist attitudes in Eastern Germany at the end of his life.[50] In the USA Russian was taught by 1913-14 in Harvard, the University of California, Michigan, Yale, Wisconsin and Chicago.[51] Two chairs of Russian existed in France: Lille (founded 1892) and the Sorbonne (1902).[52]

The five British universities, all English, (there may have been others where occasional classes were held) were Oxford, Manchester, Liverpool, London (King's College) and Cambridge. The four Laming Scholarships were set up at Queen's College, Oxford, in 1916. At four of these universities (all but Liverpool) the teaching of Russian, however enthusiastically espoused, could scarcely be described as a major enterprise in terms of the numbers of teaching staff (one in each) or of students involved.

In 1916 J. P. Scott wrote:

> Let us hope that the introduction of Russian into our universities, our colleges and our schools will be made with intelligence, insight, sympathy, and thoroughness [...] Let it not suffer as French, Italian, Spanish, and German have too often suffered in this country from bad teaching, indifference, neglect, and, above all, from unsympathetic treatment.'

In the eight to ten years from 1914 this challenge of Scott's was taken up by six institutions of higher education which started teaching Russian: University College, Nottingham, and the Universities of Sheffield, Leeds, Birmingham, Glasgow, along with Armstrong College, Newcastle upon Tyne (then a college of Durham University). The substantial strengthening of Russian implied in the foundation of the School of Slavonic Studies in 1915 at King's College, London (where Russian had been taught on a small scale since 1889 in the School of

---

[48] See p. 47, and also Stone, 'The History of Slavonic Studies in Great Britain'. The main secondary sources of information are the histories published for specific universities (Roberts, and R. E. F. Smith), and general histories of particular universities, not all of which are models of communication. Fortunately, it has been something of a tradition for new professors of Russian to begin their inaugural lectures by outlining the origins of the subject in their university, and I have been able to use offprints and typescripts of their papers.

[49] Palme, pp. 133-134.

[50] Schlögel, 'The Futility of one professor's life...'

[51] Meader, 'Russian Studies in America'. Meader was in charge at Michigan. See also Edgerton, 'The History of Slavistic scholarship in the United States'. Edgerton regards only Harvard and California as 'significant' departments at this time.

[52] Veyrenc, 'Histoire de la slavistique française'.

Oriental and Colonial Languages), and the establishment of a chair at Manchester in 1919 (where Russian had been taught in the English Department) may be seen as a consequence of the War. In addition, there were sporadic classes for non-degree students at Bristol, Southampton, and Edinburgh; it was considered at St Andrews.[53] The Senate of the National University of Ireland in 1917 admitted Russian as a language for matriculation; classes were begun at University College, Cork. (This is despite the scepticism reported in *The Times Educational Supplement* in the previous year.) Each of these universities and colleges has a story of its own, but there is a great deal of convergence between them as regards the motivation for the founding of departments, the organization and funding, the appointment and encouragement of staff, the curriculum, and the extra-curricular activities of teaching staff and their impact upon the public in their cities. It is impossible to do more than sketch these elements, but a picture emerges of purposeful activity which—in most cases— outlasted the end of the Russian Empire and of the War.

How was the subject to be funded? Commerce was very often the source. As we have seen, a lectureship at Cambridge was being supported financially by the Worshipful Company of Fishmongers.[54] At Liverpool before the War Russian benefited from a bequest by John Lord Bowes and by funding from a noted benefactor of the University, John Rankin.[55] William Lever, the soap magnate, later Lord Leverhulme, used money gained from successful litigation for libel to endow a travelling fellowship. In 1917 the Board of Education reported that the Birmingham Chamber of Commerce had raised £9,000 for a chair of Russian at the University, and that £10,000 had been donated to Leeds University by Sir James Roberts, for the same purpose.[56] The chairs at Manchester and Sheffield were liberally supported by Sir William Mather and Douglas Vickers, both leading figures in the industry of their respective cities. The Principal of Glasgow University, Sir Douglas Macalister, showed true entrepreneurial spirit in raising funds: he was publicly complimented on his self-taught Russian by a visiting delegation of the Russian Duma, and took the opportunity to harangue the local notabilities on the need for a Russian lectureship and to pass round the hat. Sir William Weir immediately stumped up £2,500 and others followed suit. (The only condition was that the lecturer should devote 'a proportion' of his time to the Commercial College work on Russian.)[57] These endowments totally eclipse

---

[53] Modern Language Association, 'Memorandum...' A. Logan Turner, *History of the University of Edinburgh*, p. 192. *Modern Language Teaching*, XIII (3 & 4), 1917.

[54] Giles, 'Russian Studies at Cambridge'.

[55] Kelly, Thomas. *For Advancement of Learning. The University of Liverpool 1881-1981*. Liverpool: University of Liverpool Press, 1981, p. 148.

[56] *Report of the Board of Education for 1915-1916*. London: HMSO, 1917. Command Paper Cd 8594, p. 72, paras 196 and 197.

[57] Moss, Michael, J. Forbes Munro and Richard H. Trainor. *University, City and State: the University of Glasgow since 1870*. Edinburgh: Edinburgh University Press, 2000) p. 140.

the trifling sum of fifty pounds per annum which the Nottingham Chamber of Commerce had offered (and later withdrawn) to the University College—yet even fifty pounds was enough, as we shall see, to get the subject established there.

It should nevertheless be emphasised that the many very generous endowments were not motivated purely by the hope of commercial gain. It is perhaps difficult in the early years of the twenty-first century to understand—in Britain, at least—that beneficence by the commercial sector a hundred years ago often represented a large degree of altruism. The oft-repeated remark of the Nobel-prizewinning economist, the late Milton Friedman, 'There is no such thing as a free lunch' is now so much part of our folklore, that we forget the great amount of civic pride which business firms felt in supporting higher education in their own city. In the end it may well have benefited commerce by raising local morale; this benefit was often indirect, and many of the benefactors were genuinely concerned to foster higher education. Pares wrote that such benefactors took 'a wider outlook of business statesmanship.'[58] James Roberts was a Bradford millionaire businessman of considerable experience in Russia, and who spoke Russian fluently. Among his other altruistic benefactions he bought and presented Haworth Parsonage to the Nation and to the Brontë Society. William Mather had been a long-term resident of Russia, which, we are told,[59] he regarded as his second home. It may therefore be assumed that motivation in putting up the money for Russian at many of these universities was not purely directed to the increase of profit, any more than the organs presented by Sir Jesse Boot to more than one Nottingham church were designed to improve the sales of aspirin tablets and Andrew's Liver Salts at Boot's the Chemist.

Such endowments established the subject on a firm basis. The Chair at Birmingham was indeed to be named the 'Birmingham Chamber of Commerce Chair'.[60] But there, unlike Nottingham College, there was little attempt to call the tune in regard to how the money was to be spent. The Birmingham Chamber, indeed, made it quite clear when certain discordant voices in the University were raised to deplore what they saw as mercantile aims (and this, believe it or not, in the Faculty of Commerce!) that they had no intention of trying to manipulate the University.[61] On the other hand, at King's College it surprisingly and untypically proved well-nigh impossible to raise funding for the School of Slavonic Studies from business sources (in the capital city!) during the War.[62] King's

---

[58] Pares, *A Wandering Student*, pp. 94-95.

[59] Pares, 'Forty years on', p. 56.

[60] Smith, pp. 12-13.

[61] Smith, p. 7.

[62] Roberts, p. 7.

College was assisted by the Treasury, the London County Council, which paid a professor's salary,[63] and by £100 from the Serbian Embassy.[64]

In assessing the forces behind the establishment of Russian in higher education we should not neglect the influence of friendly elements inside the establishments concerned. Most of the financial backers of Russian studies were also, as we have seen, enthusiasts for the country and its culture. Usually there were university leaders who protected the subject in lean years and who had argued strongly for its establishment in the first place. (Donald Burrows, the Principal of King's College at London, and the historian and parliamentarian H. A. L. Fisher at Sheffield were notable but not isolated examples.) There were often peers of the Russian staff in other departments who supported the subject: without such help Russian would have had more difficulty in surviving.

The appointment of staff at the various establishments was tackled in different ways. The initiators and leaders were often British: Pares at Liverpool and later London, Bruce Boswell jointly at Liverpool and Leeds, R. W. Seton-Watson at London, G. A. Birkett at Sheffield, Hugh Brennan (actually an Irishman who had been attached to the British Legation in Petrograd) at Glasgow. In earlier years the older universities had appointed exclusively British teachers: William Morfill and Neville Forbes at Oxford, A. P. Goudy at Cambridge; W. J. Sedgefield at Manchester. After 1915 a number of the new appointments were of Slavonic origin, several of them were or became well-known scholars in due course: D. S. Mirsky at London till 1932, M. V. Trofimov at Manchester, and J. Kolni-Balozky at Leeds. Birmingham apparently took leave of its senses and appointed to the Chair of Russian a classicist with a strong research record in Byzantine music, an interest which he did not relinquish after his appointment. If there was a good reason for this, the historian of the Department can suggest only that the successful candidate was a nephew of the professor of commercial law.[65] He did not stay long, and when he left for a chair of classics, he was succeeded by Sergei Konovalov, whose later reputation as a Slavist was respectable. In fairness to Julius Tillyard, the man in question, he had been teaching Russian at Edinburgh and Hawick, as we have seen, and he did, it appears, fight his corner for the subject with reasonable if not total success; his personal relationship may in fact have been an advantage.

Salaries paid to staff varied greatly between institutions, and clearly some of the remuneration was intended as part-time reward only. Trofimov was paid a mere £120 per annum at London, but received £700 when he took the chair at Manchester in 1919.[66] At Birmingham Louis Segal received £200 a year as head

---

[63]*Board of Education Annual Report for 1916-1917*. London: HMSO, 1918. Command Paper Cd 9045.

[64]Roberts, pp. 6-7 and 9-10.

[65]Smith, pp. 13-14.

[66]Private information from Professor John Elsworth. While at London Trofimov taught at two schools, indicating that his small remuneration at King's College was seen as a part-time salary.

of department.[67] Pares was awarded £600 p.a. at London in 1917,[68] though he was still on war service and did not take it at once. The Leathes Committee (of which more later) reported that the average annual salary for modern language professors and lecturers at Oxford in 1913-14 was £282. This 'indicates the inferior esteem in which the subjects are still held.'[69] It should be mentioned that it was customary at the time for university teachers to collect a proportion of the fees earned from their students; thus at Liverpool in 1908 a professor's salary was £500 plus one third of the fees up to a maximum of £1,000.[70] At Oxford, one may assume that college posts offered the opportunity to augment the bare teaching salary, and in fact in 1910 a readership in Russian had been advertised at a salary of £300 per annum, plus a maximum of two pounds per term for each student taught by the person appointed.[71]

It may be considered that the presence in Britain of qualified—and indeed gifted—teachers who were native speakers of Russian was a direct result of the War and the Revolutions of 1917. Slepchenko, for example, was left high and dry by the outbreak of war, Trofimov was unwilling to return to Russia for fear of imprisonment both before and after the change of régime.[72] Others did not return to Russia after the October Revolution, because they would doubtless have found conditions there uncongenial. Their presence here was of great benefit to Russian teaching in Britain.

The nationality and status of the head of department are, of course, only one element in the success of the subject. Many of the prime movers had profound motivation in their belief in the subject, which may be seen in various forms, many of them combining: political, publicistic, patriotic, intellectual, cultural, even emotional. Bernard Pares confesses to having had 'a scheme for a more systematic organisation of Russian studies in England.' This he saw as a 'contribution to national service.'[73] It was not merely a question of holding down a job for several of these men. The School of Slavonic Studies at London University, which Pares joined after war service in 1919 had the political aim of furthering the cause of the small Slavonic and Eastern European nations in the European context. The Slovene Janko Lavrin, who succeeded Basil Slepchenko at Nottingham in 1918, was motivated to some extent at least by his Pan-Slavist ideals. The wealthy business people who supported the new departments were some of them speakers of the language and connoisseurs of the culture. There

---

[67] Smith, p. 9.

[68] Roberts, p. 10.

[69] Leathes, p. 42.

[70] *Reports from those Universities and Colleges in Great Britain which Participate in the Parliamentary Grant 1907*. London: HMSO, 1908. Command Paper Cd 3885, p. 51.

[71] *Modern Language Teaching*, VI, 1910, p, 92.

[72] Pares, *My Russian Memoirs*, p. 249.

[73] Pares, 'Forty years on', p. 56.

were also knowledgeable journalists—Harold Williams—and men of letters—Arthur Ransome, Aylmer Maude, D. S. Mirsky—who were in some cases considered for senior teaching positions, and who at the very least were available to appear as guest lecturers on public occasions, adding lustre to the activities of the university concerned. The importance of public lectures should not be underestimated: during the War and afterwards it was seen as a duty to mount public lectures on Russia. Apart from public service, it may well have been perceived that the survival of Russian studies depended upon maintaining a high profile outside the undergraduate lecture room.

As for the Russian curriculum which higher education institutions followed, it did not slavishly follow the traditional language, philology and 'the best' literature, which other university foreign languages courses had adopted to assure their academic respectability in the face of the Classics. Pares's great project fostered his philosophy of 'Nation Study'. The term echoes the German notion of *Landeskunde*, taken over in later years by the Russians as *stranovedenie*. It emphasizes that language study must be wedded not just to theoretical philology and literature, but to the history, thought, life, and institutions of the country where the language is spoken. Pares outlines the curriculum he constructed for the School of Slavonic Studies.[74] The alternatives offered to traditional language and literature courses included history, economic history and theory, law and institutions, and an economic option (agriculture, industry, trade or finance). Surviving records at other institutions do not always show the details of the curriculum pursued in the establishments discussed here, but many of them followed this principle. At London there was the linking of academic and political fields;[75] Liverpool, Nottingham, Birmingham, Leeds and Sheffield were strong in commerce. History, current affairs, institutions and literature were present within and without the official curriculum in most places. This established a tradition in university Russian studies which placed the subject ahead of other languages in this respect.

After the War

This account of the wartime development of the teaching and learning of Russian in three sectors—higher, secondary, and further vocational education—shows many features in common between the three. Motivation—the desire for friendship with a wartime ally, the need to develop trade, the realization that Russia had an important culture which deserved study, and the need for critical understanding of the nation with which friendship was sought—was shared at different levels of intensity and understanding across the educational spectrum. The implications of the year of revolutions, 1917, was not fully comprehended by the British public. Politicians and everyone else were preoccupied with the armed

---

[74]Pares, *A Wandering Student*, pp. 277-278 and 282-283.

[75]Roberts, p. 13.

struggle, which they wanted to continue at all costs. The régime in Russia after October did not want this at any price. We return to Max Beerbohm and his words quoted above. He had referred to the desire many people had when war broke out that their children should learn Russian. The flippancy of his remarks conceals an essential truth:

> I do not remember that [parents] wanted to learn [Russian] themselves; but they felt an extreme need that their offspring should hereafter be able to converse with moujiks about ikons and the Little Father and anything else—if there were anything else—that moujiks cared about. This need, however, is not felt now. When, so soon after his début in high politics, M. Kerensky was superseded by M. Lenin, Russian was forthwith deemed a not quite nice language, even for children. Russia's alphabet was withdrawn from the nurseries as abruptly as it had been brought in, and le chapeau de la cousine du jardinier was re-indued with its old importance.[76]

To attempt exegesis of this passage which it was never intended to bear, but which can surely be sustained: the message is that the popular mood had no clear idea why Russian was wanted in schools (certainly not to converse about ikons); moreover, a change in the political climate has proved crucial in removing Russian from the curriculum. The abruptness of both introduction and removal, commented on by Beerbohm, should indeed make people reconsider the underlying reasons for such moves.

The following two decades, which will be covered in the next chapter, were not a total disaster for Russian studies. The 'boom' turned to 'bust' in the commercial sector, and while Russian did not completely disappear, it was no longer prominent. Russian virtually died out in the schools in the 1920s and 1930s; it none the less survived in a few independent schools, and when it did eventually re-emerge as a school subject, that emergence was made easier by the fact that it had once been part of the curriculum.

Positive factors were to be seen in the university sector. The First World War had given great impetus to Russian Studies in the universities by jolting the complacency of the British public with regard to language study and by reminding them that Russia, to which the nation was then allied in war, had a language and a culture which was worthy of study. Academics and intellectuals had known this for years, and took the opportunity to press the case. Chambers of Commerce and individual businessmen found funds to encourage universities to establish Russian teaching and in some cases whole departments. The fortuitous presence in Britain of visiting, émigré or refugee Russians provided a reservoir of teaching talent to add to the corpus of native British scholars, and universities made good use of both. Russian teaching was consequently started in eight higher education establishments. There was fairly wide support from colleagues within the institutions concerned for setting up the subject. Despite the many lean years which

---

[76] See note 2.

ensued, the argument for the study of Russian in higher education had been won, quite apart from the political, economic and military motivation which gave rise to Russian departments in the first place.

The disillusionment with our once 'glorious ally' when it was clear that we had lost this ally did not undermine the establishment of Russian Studies in British higher education. This is a credit to the teachers and professors who tirelessly promoted the subject. One writer commented at the time of the October Revolution: 'The test of their ability [that is, of teachers of Russian] will be their success or failure in maintaining the newly founded study of Russian in spite of the complete collapse of popular enthusiasm for the subject.'[77] Popular attitudes may have assisted the establishment of these departments, but the change did not bring about their immediate demise. The argument that Russia was a vitally important country and civilization and should be studied seriously in Britain—this argument had been won during the War and was not to be lost in the immediate aftermath. Most university departments mentioned in this chapter survived for decades after the First World War. There were some exceptions. Sheffield closed its department in 1943, but re-opened it in 1965. Russian at Edinburgh ran for a few years only, starting again thirty years later; at Armstrong College, Newcastle, it survived from 1915 no further than the early 1920s.[78] Liverpool, one of the first and best, survived until 1987. An interesting oddity was Queen's University, Belfast, where a local business donor, Henry Musgrave, gave £10,000 for a department of Russian language and literature in 1918, but agreed to its being allocated to Spanish when the Russian Civil War and the ensuing turmoil appeared to make normal commercial relations between Northern Ireland and Russia impossible.[79] The others—Oxford, Cambridge, London, Leeds, Manchester, Nottingham, Glasgow, and Birmingham—survive in one form or other without a break to the present time.

---

[77] Waterhouse, G., 'The Place of Russian'. *Modern Language Teaching,* XIII (7 & 8), 1917, pp. 219-221.

[78] I am indebted to Ms Elaine Archbold of the Universiy of Newcastle for information on Russian at Armstrong.

[79] 'Russian at Queen's University, Belfast', typescript dated 14.11.1997, provided by Professor Marcus Wheeler.

Chapter 4
Russian Between the Wars. Treading Water, but Still Afloat

> *The spirit of our land is interwoven with its language to the highest imaginable extent.*
> N. JARINTZOV

THE two decades following the decline in the wartime enthusiasm for Russian life and language may on the face of it look like a bleak period for the subject. Reference to Russian language learning disappears not entirely, but to a large extent, from the daily press, the Russian Sub-committee of the MLA ceases to meet and indeed to exist. Nevertheless, in 1921 a Conference of University Teachers of Russian and other Slavonic Languages, chaired by Neville Forbes and later by A. P. Goudy, was set up. Annual meetings or conferences were held, following those which took place during the First World War, and the word 'university' in the title did not mean that school teachers were unwelcome. Pares claimed some success in influencing the introduction of Russian to 'a number of leading secondary schools', and stated that the annual meetings continued into the Second World War.[1] While this body unquestionably did fight for the subject, as we shall see, it was greatly concerned with such matters as the correct spelling and transliteration of Russian, and–perhaps more importantly for the teaching profession–the provision of dictionaries. It must also be reported that the Conference showed active concern for the plight of students of Russian nationality marooned in Britain after the Revolution, and set up a 'Russian Relief and Reconstruction Fund' to meet individual cases of need.[2]

At this period we again see that relations between Britain and the Soviet state affected the popularity of Russian and the character of those who studied it. Government and public were divided in their attitudes. Accounts of diplomatic and related activities describe British and, for that matter, other nations' attempts to intervene in Russia without any very consistent or clearly expressed aims. When in the early 1920s this intervention ceased, somewhat desultory attempts were made to re-establish trading links between Britain and Russia. British officials in Moscow, now the seat of Soviet Government, reported famine, deprivation, squalor, terror by the Cheka directed at various classes in society,

---

[1] Pares, *Russia and the Peace*, p. 180; see also Roberts, p. 37 (and photo between pp. 60-61).
[2] *The Scotsman*, 15 August 1921, p. 6.

oppression, Party intrigues and a struggle for power before and after the death of Lenin in 1924. British representatives were discriminated against, subjected to all sorts of restrictions particularly on travel, forced to live in extremely cramped accommodation, and found that any persons they were able to contact were persecuted by the Soviet police. Their ability to report accurately on events, social conditions, and political moves in Russia, which had never been particularly good, was extremely limited. The few British journalists stationed in Russia were vital in providing a flow of information which was superior to that which came to the Foreign Office from official representatives.[3]

Teachers of Russian again became an object of paranoid suspicion. In an address to the MLA in 1921, Lord Askwith was reported as saying: 'The Russians had emissaries in England now imparting the Russian language to the English people and inducing them to go as missionaries of Bolshevism in different parts of the world.'[4] On top of British intervention in the Russian Civil War, and unease over the rise of Stalin, there was the 'Zinoviev letter' affair, when an attempt to influence crucially a British general election in 1924 was made by an apparently forged letter from a Soviet politician.[5] In 1927 the British police raided the premises in London of ARCOS, the Soviet trading organization; the government had imagined that the police would find a stolen War Office document as well as evidence of meddling in India by the Communists. Two hundred police over four days failed to discover the missing document or irrefutable evidence of Soviet wrongdoing; however, they removed 250,000 other documents confirming Soviet interference in British domestic affairs, but not really anything very surprising or 'publishable' enough to vindicate the partial violation of diplomatic immunity. A divided Cabinet dithered over whether a break in diplomatic relations could be justified, then 'to cover up their blunder' the British Government severed relations with the Soviet Union until 1929.[6] The public was tending once more to see Russia as the 'bear' whose hug was to avoided at all costs.

While anti-Soviet feeling was probably the dominant emotion, and while there were others who saw the Soviet state through rose-coloured spectacles, there were some who could consider the position dispassionately and confess to British ignorance of Russia. Lord Robert Cecil proposed an enquiry by the League of Nations 'into Russian conditions' to clarify the situation. Hamilton Fyfe, in an

---

[3] For a full account, on which this paragraph is based, see Hughes, Chapters 6 and 7.

[4] *The Scotsman*, 5 January 1921.

[5] See A. J. P. Taylor, *English History 1914-1945*, London: Book Club Associates, 1977, pp. 225-226. Hughes (p. 208) gives an account of the possible or likely provenance of the letter.

[6] A. J. P. Taylor, the author of the phrase quoted (p. 255), is particularly scathing about the Cabinet's behaviour. Wright, in *Spycatcher*, on the other hand, asserts that evidence was found to 'smash a large part of the Russian espionage apparatus'. (p. 226) For details of the raid and its consequences, see Harriette Flory, 'The Arcos raid and the rupture of Anglo-Soviet relations, 1927', *Journal of Contemporary History*, 12, 1977, pp. 707-723

article entitled 'The Russian riddle', declared in relation to British policy towards Russia: 'All through we have suffered from action taken without knowledge [...] If those who were in charge of British interests in Russia had known more, they would not have predicted so confidently that "Lenin could not last".' British support for reactionary Russian generals (Kolchak, Yudenich, Denikin)—Churchill's 'gamble in Russians'—had proved a costly humiliation. Fyfe derides those Tories who liked Lenin because 'there was no damned nonsense about democracy' with him. The Cecil proposal was to be supported, Fyfe wrote:

> If [the proposed enquiry] begins its life by explaining so intricate a puzzle as Russia is to nearly everybody, and by clearing the way for that general peace which cannot be made till Russia's arms are laid down, and for re-opening to British manufactures a market which will keep our factories and workshops busily employed [...] it will have proved its worth.'[7]

Fyfe now appears to have been far too optimistic, but at least he was balanced. Throughout the 1920s and 1930s there were people, including many prominent men and women, not all of them of a strongly left-leaning political persuasion, who did not share the feeling of antipathy reflected and encouraged by the press. It is very difficult to write dispassionately about these people. The activities of such intellectuals as Sidney and Beatrice Webb, Bernard Shaw, H. G. Wells, Harold Laski, John Strachey, Walter Duranty (a Briton working for the *New York Times*), Victor Gollancz, and Hewlett Johnson, have been the subject–along with many more French, German, and other European writers and artists–of several academic studies, most recently a chilling book by Ludmila Stern, who had the advantage of access to the confidential files held by Soviet security and propaganda organizations on these people. We pause briefly to mention the disparate views of these intellectuals.

Several uncomfortable facts emerge. There is no doubt that several of the people in question ignored or even denied facts which should have been obvious to them, such as the extent of the famine in Russia around 1930, the brutality with which the 'kulaks' were dispossessed,[8] the unexplained disappearance of large numbers of people, and the real nature of the show trials of the 1930s. Duranty in his published articles stated firmly that there was no famine in Russia, while informing the British Foreign Office that perhaps ten million had starved to death.[9] Some, even pacifists, condoned Soviet government terror and violence or justified it as political necessity. When their fellow-artists and writers, and the interpreters and 'minders' who had accompanied them on tours of Russia, disappeared to the prison camps or to execution, they asked—with certain honourable exceptions—no questions, but even then they asked them in private. Stern

---

[7] Fyfe, *The League* (1920), reprinted in *Modern Languages,* I(4), 1920, p. 102.
[8] Olga Litvinenko and James Riordan, *Memories of the Dispossessed*, Nottingham: Bramcote, 1998.
[9] Stern, pp. 26 and 27.

remarks that the 'organizations that dealt with foreigners were probably the most affected by the purges.'[10] Why did the famous people behave like this? It is suggested that they were reluctant to lose their status as left-wing writers; they were fêted and generously received; their books were translated and they received royalties on large numbers of copies (to that extent they were corrupted). If they did express serious doubts, they were virulently abused by leftists and by the Russians alike. And some of them were undoubtedly thoroughly duped. There were more than a few who decalared that the old Bolsheviks accused and condemned in the show trials must be guilty as charged.

Soviet agencies targeted specific artists whom they regarded as sympathetic; they tried to suborn friendship societies. Happily, the British Society for Cultural Relations with the USSR (SCR) proved very hard to break.[11] An individual who gave the Soviets many problems was the publisher Victor Gollancz, whose Left Book Club (LBC) was from 1936 enormously popular: it had 57,000 members by 1939 (though this number declined to 15,000 by 1942.)[12] Gollancz, however, was far from tractable, and published very little indeed of the propaganda materials the Soviets sent to him in hope of publication.[13] Perhaps most disturbing is the fact that, when Stern spoke to a conference in France about these events as recently as 1997, her remarks were received frigidly by the aged deniers who were still even then prominent in French intellectual life.

This is more than a little relevant to our subject. In the 1920s and 30s the British nation was divided over Russia; even potentially favourably inclined people, such as members of the LBC, were split, as John Lewis's history of it clearly demonstrates. A widespread knowledge of Russian might at least have informed the controversy; parties of highly-placed fact-finders were apt to visit the country with no Russian-speaker among them. Many regarded Soviet Russia with abhorrence: democracy had been removed, the Emperor murdered, the property-owning classes dispossessed, and many, many people executed, exiled and imprisoned. And yet, when one reads the autobiographical chapters of *The Socialist Sixth of the World*, by Hewlett Johnson, the famous 'Red Dean' of Canterbury (the LBC Monthly Choice for December 1939), it is not hard to see why men of principle such as Johnson, Christian principle in his case, deplored the way capitalist society enriched the few and left many in desperate poverty— this Johnson knew from his time as an engineering apprentice and later as parish minister; one sees why they deplored the way Britain abandoned the Spanish people to Franco while the Soviets actively supported the republicans, the failure

---

[10] p. 206.

[11] Stern, pp. 133-138. A Soviet article of 1966 complains that the SCR did not adopt a 'clear political position' on Anglo-Soviet relations over the ARCOS affair: Kuz'min, p. 205. The SCR insisted that it was a non-political organization, a concept which the Soviets were unable to understand.

[12] Lewis, *The Left Book Club*. For membership figures see p. 132.

[13] Stern, 158-162.

to confront fascism, and the way sectors of the British press resolutely ignored their point of view.

We are then presented for the second time in the century with a situation in which Russia is detested in some quarters, while in others it is a beacon of enlightenment. Reasonable people tried to bridge this gap; some of them wished to learn Russian. It is hard to know how many would-be Russian linguists there were. The SCR (of which more later) was founded in 1924, and teaching the language was important to it: learners were put in touch with private teachers, Russian courses and conversation groups were organized, and Russian and English-speaking members helped each other with their respective language. By the Second World War the Russian evenings in London were crowded; classes were run under SCR auspices in other cities too. There were numerous small advertisements for private Russian lessons in the press; language schools such as Berlitz advertised regularly. The Institute of Linguists' magazine *The Linguist* (52 pages for sixpence) advertised Russian content. The LBC, which was not simply a reading circle operating by mail order, but which had many local groups which held meetings, and which even organized study visits to Russia until it encountered regular refusal of visas in 1938, published some twenty books out of over 250 in its twelve-year existence with titles relating directly to Soviet Russia. Some of the 57,000 members in 1939 must surely have been interested enough to make some attempt to learn Russian. Perhaps the many 'occasional students' at various universities in the 1920s and 1930s and the numerous enrolments in evening classes instanced later in this chapter included some of them.

While all this was going on, the Russian émigré community in Britain was organizing itself. Files survive of a fortnightly newspaper called *Russkii v Anglii* which appeared between January 1936 and the outbreak of war in 1939. It was published (subscription price two-and-sixpence a year) by a group with the curious name of *Obshchestvo Severian v Velikobritanii*, the Society of Northerners in Great Britain. From its pages an impression of the life and work of Russian emigrants can be learned: support for the destitute, church life and activity, theatre and musical shows, Russian shops, restaurants, even a Russian shoemaker, a printer, a Russian economic association, a library. The aim of the paper was 'to stress what unites us as Russian emigrants'; there was even criticism from some readers that they stressed the negative elements of Soviet life back home. The publishers estimated that there were as many as 33,000 Russians living in London. Happily, the feeling was expressed that Russians were accepted in Britain, whereas in some countries they were not. Some of the 33,000, it must be supposed, were eventually to become teachers of Russian.

Government interest in Modern Languages. The Leathes Report (1918)

We go back in time and return to the end of the First World War to place the later learning of Russian in a wider context. Discussion of the fate of the language between the wars must be placed against the background of a fresh element in the educational scene: the intervention of government in modern studies. This will take us far beyond the study of Russian, or even of modern languages in general, and into much broader issues of the curriculum in both secondary and higher education. At the same time, it should be remembered that the influence on education of government policy is easy to overestimate. Governments can be crucial in shaping the education system of a nation, but at the same time the law of unexpected consequences often enough comes into operation. Politicians may ignore the findings of the commissions they set up—in fact, they usually do—and they may act according to what they believe to be politically possible or pleasing to the electorate. The curriculum, including the teaching of Russian in both schools and higher education, was the subject of a fair number of reports in the twentieth century which sometimes did and sometimes did not result in administrative decisions. These reports include the work of government, parliamentary, or ministerial committees, and commissions. These, along with documents prepared by voluntary and professional groups will figure in later chapters. The first major report commissioned by government on modern languages was the Leathes Report of 1918.

In writing of government policy, it is important to remember the separate status of Scotland, where public attitudes and policies may differ. However, it was not until 1885 that the Scotch (later renamed 'Scottish') Education Department (SED) was separated from England; it began a gradual removal to Edinburgh in 1922, completed in 1939, and is now, in the twenty-first century, under the control of the Scottish Executive. The shape of modern British education was determined by education acts of 1870, 1902, 1918, and 1944 for England, and 1872, 1908, 1918, and 1945 for Scotland. While this looks as if Scotland was usually a year or two behind England, in some ways the opposite is true: Scotland had compulsory school attendance, free tuition in state schools, and a higher leaving age before England did—in the last case, seventeen years before.[14] It is certainly true that both nations have kept a close, interested, and sometimes even envious eye on the opposite side of the border. The Leathes Report, however, was set up by the Prime Minister in 1916 (Herbert Asquith) and was meant to cover the whole of the United Kingdom.

Modern linguists have tended to take this Report of the Committee chaired by Sir Stanley Leathes, Head of the Civil Service Commission for government examinations and an editor of the *Cambridge Modern History*, at its face value. That value is, in fact, considerable: the Report was diligently compiled, evidence was earnestly taken, the final document was extremely well written and argued, and it still reads coherently to this day. But the notion that government or civil service were particularly interested in the committee which compiled it, or that they cared a fig for its findings, is mistaken. To substantiate this judgement, it is necessary to examine the conditions in which the Leathes Committee was set up and to look at what happened after the civil servants received the completed

---

[14]James Scotland, *The History of Scottish Education, Volume II*, pp. 16-17.

report. Those conditions relate to wartime alarm about the education which had been received by British soldiers and officers alike, to persisting traditionalist attitudes to the school curriculum (such as it was), to the existence of the vested interests of teachers of other subjects, and to the need for certain civil servants to preserve their own prerogatives.

The real problem was not modern languages, but science education. In the previous chapter it was stated that many inadequacies had been revealed by the war in the scientific and technical knowledge of the nation. Government scientists went so far as to use the word 'clodhopper' to describe the level of scientific concepts of servicemen on the battlefield; one said 'heroism had become a substitute for intelligence'.[15] It was not just the war. It was felt that as long before as 1867 and 1878 the two Paris Exhibitions had been a 'humiliation' for Britain, and Gladstone had set up the Samuelson Commission on technical education, which led to changes in the United Kingdom. But now men were being slaughtered in tens of thousands, not because they could not speak foreign languages, but because the technology of warfare was beyond the comprehension of most of them. A Neglect of Science Committee was established, and a memorandum on the subject was signed by many Fellows of the Royal Society, and by schoolmasters and others.

A frantic reaction followed from proponents of subjects other than science. Sir Richard Livingstone's arguments in his *Defence of Classical Education* were strongly refuted by H. G. Wells.[16] Modern linguists, it is humiliating to have to admit, joined in a campaign with teachers of history, classics, English and geography to confound the science lobby, but made fools of themselves after much in-fighting by arriving at a position over the school curriculum which scarcely differed from that of the scientists.[17] Observers with a sardonic sense of humour must have enjoyed observing this pointless and demeaning scrap. Meanwhile, *The Times* called stridently for a Royal Commission on education.

On 18 April 1916 the prominent educationist, Sir Philip Magnus wrote to the Prime Minister making suggestions (at Asquith's invitation) on the composition of such a Commission.[18] (Magnus had served on the Royal Commission chaired by Samuelson in the 1880s.) Liverpool Education Committee was also prominent in the campaign for a Royal Commission, and it enlisted other education committees in support. Such a Commission could actually have recommended drastic changes to or even the abolition of the Board of Education, as Sir Robert Blair, Education Officer of the London County Council, hints in a letter marked 'Private and unofficial' to Sir Lewis Selby-Bigge, Secretary to the Board of

---

[15] Quoted by Jenkins, p. 53.

[16] London: Macmillan, 1916. For the controversy with Wells, see Jenkins, p. 54, and for Wells's review: *Nature*, 1 Mar 1917 and 10 May 1917.

[17] Jenkins, p. 55.

[18] National Archives: ED/24/1173.

Education.[19] The Board was desperate to prevent it. Internal papers[20] belittle the demands of Liverpool, find imagined chinks in the arguments of the *Times* articles and call the paper's ideas 'revolutionary'—realising correctly that they call for a radical reformation, not merely development on present lines. A Royal Commission is 'unthinkable' by reason of its likely complexity and the length of time it would inevitably take. The need for a review of education is recognized, 'however badly and inappropriately it may be expressed'.[21] A printed document labelled 'Strictly confidential' declares it to be 'very undesirable on many grounds that a Royal Commission should be established.' Complacency asserts, while grudgingly allowing some ground: 'Although there is no reason to believe that generally speaking the war has revealed anything like a failure of the educational system, there is a general feeling that its improvement is required.'[22]

Fortunately for the Board of Education, their resistance to the idea of a Royal Commission was successful. The compromise was to appoint in the first instance two committees to examine science and modern languages; later two more were established, on classics and English. Three of them were set up in the name of the Prime Minister and should therefore relate to the whole United Kingdom. Selby-Bigge urged testily but unsuccessfully against including Scotland in the deliberations, claiming to fear that the work of the committees would become unwieldy.[23] However, while an official of the SED was assigned to each of the science and modern languages committees, neither of these seems to have had a member resident or professionally active in Scotland. Witnesses who gave evidence to Leathes included two members of the SED, three principals of Scottish schools or colleges, and the proprietor of *The Scotsman*. The Committee on the teaching of English concerned England alone.

Early in the Leathes report there is a broadside against the classics lobby, and an ironic welcome is given to the newly compulsory oral examination in the Cambridge Modern and Medieval Languages Tripos. The modern side of the 'great and wealthy' schools is too often regarded as 'the refuge of the intellectually destitute.' The influence of outside examinations was 'directly harmful. Their methods are based on the Classical tradition.' The War, however, has given an impetus to day and evening classes, especially in Spanish and Russian. It is high time, since, 'If the foundations of our strength and wealth were being insidiously weakened by our own complacency and by foreign energy, the process was only evident to close and vigilant observers.'[24]

---

[19]ED 24/1173 4079.
[20]ED 24/1173.
[21]ED 24/1173, p. 8.
[22]RECON 1/14 2948.
[23]RECON 1/19 2948.
[24]Leathes, pp. 1-5.

Under the heading 'Neglect of Modern Studies' the Report considers the various arguments for 'modern studies', as it decides to call its subject rather than 'modern languages' alone: their business value (pp. 9-11), modern studies and the increase of knowledge (by this it means that 'all the civilized countries of the world collaborate' to seek knowledge and therefore languages are necessary to share that knowledge) (p. 11); the value of knowledge concerning foreign countries and peoples (p.11); the value of modern studies for the public service (diplomacy, education, agriculture, fighting services) (pp.12-15); and the value of modern studies as a means to general education and culture. (p.15) C. V. James has—perhaps rather unfairly—described these arguments as 'a nice blend of the aesthetic and the mercenary'![25] As for the public, the Committee found in a letter from professors and lecturers at universities and colleges a unanimous view that instruction should be provided not merely in the languages and literature, [...] but also in the history and broad outline, the customs and institutions and the social conditions of the foreign peoples concerned. (p. 17)

'We believe that the War has aroused more than a fleeting interest in modern studies [...] shown by the foundation [...] of chairs in modern languages, by attendance at evening classes in languages hitherto neglected, by experiments in the teaching of Spanish and Russian in schools, by the tone of the public press.'

As to the role of Russian specifically in education, the view of the Committee is interesting and rational in parts, but bizarre in others. Paragraphs 67 and 68, page 20, run:

[67] Apart from those political and national considerations which may demand a preference for German; we should be inclined to say that the place given to German in schools and Universities, though inadequate before the war, was still unduly superior to that allowed to Italian, Spanish, and Russian...

Of Russia and Russian the national ignorance was almost complete, though in the last ten years before the war some interest had been awakened. Here there were great opportunities for industrial enterprise, but we left the country too much to the Germans. The future of Russia is even more uncertain than that of Germany, but unless the worst should happen Russia should offer a great opening which can only be used by a nation which has studied, as well as the language of Russia, her social anatomy, the character of her people, her geography, and her economic conditions and capacities. Russian is a difficult language, though the evidence we have heard leads us to believe that its difficulties are often exaggerated. The need of grammars and other aids to study is being gradually supplied; but a satisfactory dictionary is not yet available. Though Russian literature of late years has attracted great interest and exercised some influence, we shall probably be right in conceding

---

[25]James, 'Shag vpered i dva nazad' [One step forward, two steps back. Title in Russian, text in English], p. 1.

to it little educational value; nor is Russian history a subject to be recommended for study in schools. At present it appears as amorphous, obscure, unaccented, and uninspiring. Perhaps when it has been worked up for use some of these features may turn out to be superficial; they may rub off in the handling, and the true structure and contours may come to light. Such work is work for the Universities; until it has been accomplished, schoolmasters cannot be expected to make much of it. Finally, each and all of these countries make contributions to knowledge. Judged by this last criterion, Germany and France stand first, Italy third, and Russia and Spain last.

[68] We conclude that, after France, all these four countries–Germany, Italy, Spain, and Russia–deserve a first-class place in the Modern Studies of our Universities [...] In schools where a second language is taken, we see no reason why any one or all of the four languages should not be on the list of optional languages. provided resources are available and good teachers are forthcoming.

How salutary to be told: Russian literature has 'little educational value'; Russian history is 'uninspiring'! Mere schoolmasters 'cannot be expected to make much of it.' Who advised the distinguished committee to that effect? There is, none the less, a recognition of the importance of Russia in the world and of the value of studying her people, her society, and her economy. Stripped of the value of her literature, history, and culture, however, what is really left of educational value in the study of the language and life of the country? If trading opportunities are all that it amounts to, study of the subject has a very insecure base. This was a conclusion we reached in relation to commercial colleges in a previous chapter.

The Leathes Report had 53 recommendations. In general it represented a most enlightened and forward-looking attitude both to education in general and to modern studies in particular. There was encouragement to business, the Foreign Office, the civil service, and the armed services to take modern languages seriously; also, the talents of women and their availability should be used. The Government should legislate for 175 new teaching posts in universities for modern studies, and the curriculum should allow for language, literature, philology, economics and history, with choice for students. Spanish, Italian, and Russian should be raised to the level of German. The notion that Russian should be taught on a level with German was to persist for many years in government reports; it originated with the Russia Society in its circular of 1915.

Facilities for Spanish, Italian and Russian in schools should be arranged; classes should not be too large. Evening, part-time and adult education classes should be expanded. Assistance for the initial and in-service training of language teachers should be given. Exams at all levels should be improved, and oral tests used whenever possible. Science, mathematics and classical students at Higher School Certificate should be encouraged to take a translation paper in modern languages, and their certificates should be appropriately endorsed.

What were the consequences for the education system of the Leathes Report and its three fellows? They were not actually suppressed so much as deliberately clothed in obscurity. They were, of course, published by HM Stationery Office as Command Papers, the Science and Modern Languages reports in 1918, the Classics and English in 1921. On 8 May 1922, four years after Leathes had reported, the Board of Education signed its response. Marked 'Confidential. For the use of the Office and Inspectorate only', a typescript Office Memorandum no. 55 entitled *Board of Education. Office Committee on the 'Four Reports' (Natural Science, Modern Languages, English, Classics)*[26] running to 44 pages contains a full, and it must be said thoughtful, discussion of the reports. But that is all it is. In the four years which had passed, the brouhaha had died down, *The Times*, whose writers doubtless possessed a memory no longer than that of most journalists, had ceased to trumpet revolution, the universities were no longer part of the remit of the Board (the University Grants Committee was set up in 1919) and Sir Philip Magnus had reached the age of 80 (though he had another nine years in him yet) and might be thought to have had other priorities. The Office Committee was able to play down the importance of the motivation for the Reports by saying they represented a wartime 'mood of national self-criticism'; their main influence was seen as being on teachers and the Board's contribution was to 'draw attention' to certain points. Any proposal with financial implications is rejected for reasons of stringency. The conclusions of the Office Memorandum are insipid to a degree: minor tinkering with regulations, issuing circulars to 'draw attention' as noted, and a decision that no change was necessary in school examinations. The one slight positive step was to issue a circular on the English Committee's 'conception of the place and function of English', and to the need to establish the teaching of modern languages and classics 'on a broad base of history and literature'; science teachers were to be warned against confining all their teaching to experimental work. Those who had hoped for the incisive and decisive action a Royal Commission was more likely to have precipitated were surely vindicated—and must have been bitterly disappointed by the victory of the likes of Selby-Bigge.

At the same time the Office Document contains many progressive and encouraging features: it praises the 'wider recognition of humanistic ideals' of all four reports, including science, it recognizes the central importance of English and that 'all teachers are teachers of English', it accepts the argument that university entrants should be able to offer combinations of subjects across the curriculum in a way that became common only many years later. It promises to encourage schools to exchange pupils after the age of 16 to remedy complaints about limited curricular choice. In general it praises the breadth of vision of the four reports; all see the wider educative benefits of their subjects and can articulate them. They comment with approval on the stress on oral English, modern languages, and even classics. The Memorandum lacks reference to any specific language

---

[26] The copy of this document lent to me bears no file or catalogue number. I am unable to give any details of it other than those mentioned in the text.

except—and then only in passing—French and Latin. Leathes's recommendations on adjusting the balance between languages in the education system are ignored. In any case, this is a 'confidential' document, it remained and was always intended to remain unpublished, and was therefore to have no impact on government policy.

The Report itself, however, did much to stimulate morale in the modern language teaching profession, and it was discussed and referred to throughout the 1920s and 1930s in professional journals. But if we turn specifically to Russian, its effect was minimal. In charting the history of the subject at this time, it is necessary to become, like Autolycus, a 'snapper-up of unconsidered trifles', since the volume of evidence on the progress of Russian is small and fragmentary in comparison with both the earlier and the later twentieth century. Fortunately, the 'trifles', when carefully assembled, add up to a fairly informative picture.

Technical, Commercial and Evening Schools

The study of Russian did not die out totally in vocational colleges and evening institutes, at least in the seven years after the war. However, a steady decline set in. Advertisements inviting students to enrol may be found in the press. The Board of Education *Statistics of Public Education in England and Wales* number 66 Russian classes in 27 schools in 1919-20. In 1922-23 this had dipped to 24 classes in 9 schools: a figure comparable with the 1911-12 position. In 1925-26 there were 46 classes in 14 schools; after this statistics do not seem to have been published. For comparison, it may be noted that in 1926 there were 141 such establishments teaching Spanish, 530 French and 41 Italian. German enjoyed a slow, but steady recovery after the war from 204 classes in 78 schools in 1919-20 to 376 classes in 116 schools in 1924-25.

Comparable figures for Scotland are not available, but the news columns of *The Scotsman* print occasional items: one recurrent theme is the energetic attempts made in the mid-1920s to keep Russian going at the Heriot-Watt College. An eloquent appeal to the young men of Edinburgh from the Principal not to neglect a line of study which everyone else was neglecting, and to prepare for the time when Russia would again become a great commercial country, doubtless exporting its goods into Leith. This provoked one pseudonymous 'Anxious Parent' to protest that a knowledge of Russian and other languages had not guaranteed his three children employment. Less that two years later the Principal indicated that only three students were attending the Russian class; yet the Governors were to try again to popularize the class and recruit more students.[27] We do not know if the attempts were successful; the impression is rather that public enthusiasm was distinctly on the wane by 1925-27.

Waning, but still not completely disappearing. The business world was not entirely oblivious of opportunities in the Soviet Union: Hugh Brennan of the

---

[27]*The Scotsman*, 5 October 1925, p. 5, 16 October 1925, p. 10, 10 May 1927, p. 5.

Russian department at Glasgow University addressed the Institute of Bankers in Scotland in 1930, speaking both of the 'enigma of the Soviet' and the 'limitless possibilities' of the Russian market. In 1931 Edinburgh was announcing the opening of six technical institutes, and Russian was among the languages offered 'arrangements being made to carry on these to an advanced stage.' Glasgow and West of Scotland Commercial College in 1933 was offering special courses including Russian in training for business.[28] The RSA continued to offer commercially-based examinations in Russian with an average entry of 27 between 1925 and 1939 (as opposed to five thousand odd for French and a steady improvement of the position of German from 410 entries in 1926 to 850 in 1939). This is considerably less than the peak of 266 achieved in 1917, and less than half the number for 1920 (56),[29] but it does not represent *total* annihilation. The basis remained for later recovery.

Secondary Schools

The file in the National Archives described in the previous chapter contains accounts of meetings at the Board of Education about the state of Russian teaching in schools with Pares and Forbes, representing the Conference of University Teachers. They were seeking a regular flow of undergraduates, and in 1926 were quoting Firth Park Grammar School, Sheffield (where Russian had started in 1921 under G. H. Birkett, who taught also at Sheffield University, and who was later lecturer at Glasgow), and Leigh Grammar School as reliable providers of such students.[30]

> The results of Firth Park School are the more significant that Sheffield is the one university which has not found it possible to continue the maintenance of its Russian department, and yet the university lecturer [G. A. Birkett], who continues as holding an honorary post, writes that he has some 60 students [...] It would be the greatest mistake if the teaching of Russian were now to decline in this country, as we have no doubt whatever that the arbitrary circumstances which have hindered commercial intercourse, will on their removal, be followed by a greater need of trained specialists, particularly in technical subjects, with a knowledge of Russian than ever before.[31]

Leigh boys had won four open scholarships in Russian to Oxford. In 1926 a hundred boys were learning the language there; there were forty-two at Firth Park.

An attached memo reports a meeting between Board of Education officials and Pares and Forbes. The civil servants gave the inevitable answer that the

---

[28]*The Scotsman*, 30 October 1930, p. 11; 9 September 1931, p. 8; 28 August 1933, p. 14.

[29]Figures provided by Claire Batley, from the RSA's records.

[30]The *Slavonic and East European Review* contains a short news item, 'Two English Schools', vol. VI, 1926-27, p. iv. about Firth Park and Leigh G. S.

[31]ED 12/228 S 452/7.

Board had no power to issue circulars furthering specific subjects. The recommendation was that Pares and Forbes should approach sympathetic heads to 'try the experiment' of teaching Russian. Independent schools were suggested, if only because of their higher leaving age.

The same National Archive file contains a number of other significant documents. A letter from Pares of 1930 raises again the matter of Russian in schools. It also emerges that London University had been imposing matriculation requirements for students of Russian which were geared for native Russian speakers (who were scarcely likely to study Russian anyway) and made it difficult for British applicants to achieve acceptance; Pares had these removed. Clearly, he should have done so before this.[32] The intense difficulty of many examinations in Russian may be explained by the feeling that they were or might be for native speakers. How sympathetic the civil servants were to the notion of Russian in schools may be judged by some of the notes they jotted on these papers. They can scarcely have helped the cause of Russian. One document contains the words: 'A widely held belief seems to be [sic! On such evidence is national educational policy based] that the Russians are used to carry on their commercial transactions in German and French.' Further, a memo signed 'HBW' states 'I have certainly heard it said that much at any rate of Russian literature can be equally well studied in French'. To read this nonsense makes one wonder how the education received by public servants led them uncritically to accept these notions and to allow them to influence policy.

A letter dated 1932 from Pares and Goudy (Forbes had died by this time) laments the closure of Russian at Firth Park. Leigh no longer figures. Pares covered the same ground in a lengthy letter to *The Times*, published on 28 September 1932, p. 8. Happily, after the Second World War, Firth Park was to become and remain for many years, a bastion of school Russian learning.[33] But for the 1930s, Russian was left to a few independent schools. Entry statistics for School Certificate tell the sorry story: between 1929 and 1934 the figures for entries were 39, 10, 14, 26, 23, and 22. Pass rates were appalling: an average of about 45 percent, and in 1932 only four of the 26 entrants passed. There is no record of any entries for Higher School Certificate from 1930 to 1946, and figures for Scotland are not available for this period. From 1935 to 1938 (the last year for which figures were published before the war) there were only 13 entries, of whom ten passed.

---

[32] Until the 1960s and 1970s there were still some university Russian departments that demanded qualifications in Latin for entry, choosing to ignore the fact that secondary schools, under considerable curricular pressure, would have had to provide Russian, another language, *and* Latin, along with every other arts, science and mathematical subject in the curriculum. Pares was uncharacteristically slow to pick up on the unreasonable demands of his own university.

[33] This is regrettably no longer true. See Haywood for an account of happier times at Firth Park.

Universities

The endpapers of the *Slavonic and East European Review*[34] for 1929-30 contain information about the ten university-level departments where Russian could then be studied, with outlines of the courses which might be followed, and with the names of academic staff. The School of Slavonic Studies, still at King's College, London, showed seven members of staff; eight others had one each: Oxford (professorship vacant after the death of Forbes), Cambridge (A. P. Goudy, Reader), Glasgow (Brennan), Manchester (Trofimov), Birmingham (Konovalov, 'independent Lecturer'), Leeds (Kolni-Balotsky, Lecturer), Sheffield (Birkett, Lecturer), University College Nottingham (Lavrin, Professor); Liverpool, once the leader, had two (Boswell, Professor, and Slepchenko, Lecturer). Of these, Slepchenko was unfortunately shortly to lose his job owing to financial stringency following the impending economic collapse—and 'to no other reason', as Boswell asserted in a reference written for him at the time, declaring his dismissal as 'disastrous for Russian studies and for me personally';[35] Lavrin held the title but not the salary of a professor; Birkett's post, as we learn from Pares's letter in the National Archives papers quoted above, was honorary, though a published history of Sheffield University does not admit it. Konovalov was elected professor at Birmingham, presumably just after this issue of the *Slavonic Review* was published, and at the same time was made a lecturer at Oxford. Stone describes his chair at Birmingham as 'part-time',[36] a fact not confirmed by R. E. F. Smith, but from Smith's account of the activities Konovalov undertook in Birmingham, he crammed an immense amount into the time he spent there. Nevertheless, he held the two posts simultaneously until 1945, when he was made a professor at Oxford.

Holding part-time posts in plurality was not uncommon in the Slavonic field. Before taking up the chair in Manchester, Trofimov had taught in at least two schools at the same time as at the School of Slavonic Studies. From 1917 to 1919 Bruce Boswell had been in charge of Russian at both Leeds and Liverpool universities; Slepchenko had taught in more than one institution both when he was in Nottingham and in Liverpool; Birkett taught at Firth Park School and at Sheffield University; Lavrin was an honorary lecturer at King's College, London; and Konovalov, as well as his two official jobs, was also an honorary lecturer at King's, and he taught evening classes at the Midland Centre in Birmingham until the mid-1930s. These men all clearly felt it their duty to foster the study of Russian in secondary and further education as well as in the universities. At the same time, it must be remembered that numbers of students reading for degrees in Russian were very small indeed: there were only ten first degrees awarded in Russian at the School of Slavonic Studies between 1920 and 1939, there was one

---

[34] vol. VIII, for 1929-30, pp. i-iv.

[35] Slepchenko, typescript curriculum vitae and testimonial by Boswell.

[36] *Slavonic Studies at Oxford*, p. 17.

student in each part of the Tripos at Cambridge in 1933 and an average of fewer than one a year at Oxford, and it was nearly two decades into the history of the Nottingham department before anyone was awarded a degree in Russian—and the first was a post-graduate rather than an undergraduate degree.

What, then, were university Russian teachers doing with their time? In many places they do not seem to have been short of students—but they were not degree candidates. Some were studying for civil service examinations; there seems to have been a continuing, but reduced demand for technical and commercial Russian. Birkett, as we have seen, was said to be teaching sixty students in Sheffield. The School of Slavonic and East European Studies (it had added 'and East European' to its title definitively by 1931, and we shall henceforth refer to it by its usual abbreviation of SSEES) had over a hundred external students, many of them in evening classes, in various Slavonic languages in 1937 (a figure which reached 200 late in the War), and this institution taught a steady flow of students from the armed services,[37] a sideline which must have done a good deal to assure the future and the financial security of the School. Elizabeth Hill mentions having two Tripos students in 1937.[38] Two years later she mounted a dramatic production in Russian with a cast of 36, so presumably whoever else was being taught at Cambridge at the time must have been involved. In nearly all universities academic staff gave considerable numbers of public lectures on Russia and the Soviet Union, and they often taught courses on aspects of Soviet society or politics for non-language students, or for the public. They worked for the eventual establishment of their departments with a tradition comparable with that of other languages. To some extent they engaged in propaganda for the subject, though it must be said that neither the professional periodicals nor the news media made more than perfunctory mention of Russian in any sector of education in the 1930s.

One exception to this is a whole page in the *Times Educational Supplement* for 24 June 1939, p. 251, given up to several anonymous contributions: a short book review article, a note on 'Progress at Cambridge', news of the play performed there, and a more substantial article: 'Careers for students of Russian: what universities can offer'. It is not too difficult to spot that the author of the review article is Elizabeth Hill, since it resembles more than closely a signed review she wrote for the *Slavonic Review* a year or so previously. Since 'Progress at Cambridge' and the account of a student production of Gogol's *Revizor* ('the first full-length play ever produced in Russian in Cambridge') are something of an advertisement for Slavonic Studies there, the conclusion seems inescapable that she wrote these too. One might guess Pares to be the author of the main article, but in terms of the relative emphasis given to the arguments, it does not read quite like one of his efforts, and could well also be by Hill. It puts

---

[37] Roberts, pp. 39, 46 and 51.

[38] Jean Stafford Smith (ed.), p. 192.

the case for Russian as being of growing international importance, and significant in learning and in cultural life. Russian is of obvious relevance to journalism, librarianship and the public service; it is useful in comparative linguistics, to historians, economists, geographers and scientists, especially in biology. 'With the present and pending changes in the political relations between Russia and this country, pressure in the direction of teaching Russian may shortly come from parents.' This, of course, was written just before the Soviet-German Treaty of August 1939, and illustrates the danger for supporters of Russian of putting forward political arguments based too closely on current events.

The article closes with a reference to the need for the staff of Russian departments to engage in research and publication, a field, however, in which Hill herself did not excel. The author considers British output in the field to be small in comparison with France, Germany and the USA. Nevertheless, the School of Slavonic Studies had begun in 1921 to publish the *Slavonic Review* (later named *Slavonic and East European Review*), which was the only specialist journal in the field, and swiftly became a major instrument for the publication of Slavonic scholarship. America could not match this; in fact, when the Second World War broke out, the journal was passed to the United States for the duration of hostilities; wartime conditions of paper rationing in particular made this step necessary.

Not all of the people mentioned above established great reputations for research; several of them made a distinguished beginning, while devoting most of their time to the firm establishment of the departments which they headed or within which they worked. The Second World War was to put an end to much academic research, while the public service took on a higher priority: some staff were called up for military or other war service, three very senior members of SSEES joined the Royal Institute of International Affairs, Hill herself worked in the Balkans section of the Ministry of Information, and Lavrin served at the BBC External Services.

We have already noted that Russian was established in British universities largely by British scholars in the first place, and that people of Slavonic origin emerged slightly later, the First World War having created a situation where some outstanding Slavs were stranded in Britain and wished to stay. The names in the *Slavonic Review* roster indicate that partnership between Slavs and non-Slavs continued on a basis of equality. While there must surely have been occasional personal irritations, there is little serious evidence of professional animosity between Slavs and British. In *A Novelty* R. E. F. Smith gives an entertaining account of disputes at Birmingham *between* Slavs, all in the best tradition of British academic manoeuvring. This contrasts sharply with the situation in other languages at the time. The journal *Modern Languages* in the 1930s ran a long and bitter polemic about the appointment of foreign scholars to professorial chairs in British universities, arguing that young scholars would not take up modern studies if they suspected they were being blocked for promotion by foreigners, sometimes–it was said–of dubious qualification. Angry letters were balanced with acid responses from those who had made the appointments; both sides remained adamant.[39] Such disputes do not seem to have arisen to the same extent in Russian studies. At the same time it may be remembered that Russians such as Konovalov and Trofimov were permanent residents in Britain, who had identified themselves with the country and dedicated themselves to academe here before promotion to senior positions. They were not 'parachuted in' over the heads of deserving Britons.

The question of the role of expatriate teachers in foreign language teaching is affected by the relations between Britain and their country of origin and to the status of such teachers in that country. In the 1930s the problem here was not so much with Russian, as with German, but controversy over Germany illuminates some issues which became important in later years with regard to the USSR and Russian. A very sharp exchange of correspondence was published in *Modern Languages* in 1936. A master at a famous public school had upbraided H. J. Chayter, Master of St Catherine's College, Cambridge, for attacking Nazi racial doctrines of 'Aryanism': *Modern Languages*, he asserted, was no place for 'politics' and such remarks would damage good relations with Germany. The Master's response was swift, acid and devastating. Nazi racial doctrines were not a political matter, they were plain factual 'balderdash'. 'I do not propose to suppress or distort facts in order to spare the susceptibilities of the invertebrate type of internationalism preached by Mr C—.'[40] Just occasionally in later years there have been proponents of Russian teaching who have verged on an 'invertebrate type of internationalism'. This issue, to which we shall return, is important not only because it concerns imparting perspectives to students which may be partial in one direction or another, but because potential teachers of German (Jewish refugees from Hitler, for example) and of Russian (asylum seekers from Stalin's purges) might be blackballed on the grounds of political unacceptability. We have seen that during the First World War the wrath of Trofimov (a refugee from tsarism) was aroused by the desire of the Russia Society to make 'a Russian passport' an essential qualification for teachers of the language. We shall see in a following chapter that a Foreign Office committee narrowly avoided the same monstrous error.

The Armed Services: the Royal Air Force

The Royal Air Force (RAF) was founded in 1918, and certain persons at the Air Ministry were keen to foster the training of interpreters in a range of languages.

---

[39] See *Modern Languages*, vol. XIII(3 & 4), 1932, p. 1, XIII(5), pp. 129-130, XIII(6), pp. 159-160, 161-164, and 189-191.

[40] *Modern Languages*, XVII(2), 1935, p. 60. The late writer and actor, Peter Ustinov, was a pupil at the school where Mr C— taught at this very time. In his entertaining, but fairly obviously most unreliable, autobiography, *Dear Me* (London, 1977) Chapter 5, he hints at the genuine difficulties the school had in adopting appropriate attitudes for coping with German pupils (including himself, as at that time he was still sporting a 'von' before his surname).

Files surviving in the National Archives from as early as 1920 and the Air Ministry Weekly Orders (AMWO) issued throughout the 1920s show that leaders of the new service kept a very close eye on what the Navy and the Army were doing in this field, and at the same time had some ideas of their own.[41] We shall return to the Army and Navy in due course, while looking at what the RAF had in mind at a time before it became prominent in military Russian.

A proposal in 1920 to make modern languages compulsory for RAF cadets at Cranwell did not find universal favour. Languages would be 'beyond' most of the cadets; however, a reasonably generous allowance of time and finance was made for those few who wished to take up or continue with a language on their own. It was realized that languages were no less important to the RAF than to the other services; the time to consider serious linguistic training was felt to be when cadets were commissioned. The language of immediate concern was Arabic, in view of the presence of the RAF in Iraq and the likelihood that this would continue. Others which figure in the discussions were French, German, Spanish, Italian, Roumanian, 'Czechoslovakian' (the persons concerned seemed unaware of the difference between Czech and Slovak), Persian, Turkish and 'all the Balkan dialects'. This was an ambitious programme indeed; in 1924 the RAF had serving officers with interpretership qualifications in French (3), German (3), Italian, Spanish, and Japanese (one each), and Russian also only one,[42] a second class certificate at that, which was held by some to be of little use. A senior Indian Army officer, Colonel Wilkinson Dent, had, however, been serving as a Russian interpreter on attachment to the RAF Iraq Command since October 1922, stationed at HQ Baghdad.[43]

Pressure for Russian was building up by 1924. A lively internal debate is reflected in the papers. There was scepticism about the need for *interpreters:* these could either be recruited 'locally' or would emerge in time of war, as they had done in 1914. *Intelligence gathering* was, however, another matter. The Soviets were 'interfering' in Iraq and the RAF needed to keep a wary eye open. Another reason was the close cooperation between Germany and Soviet Russia instanced by the Rapallo Treaty of 1922. Now, there is little evidence that RAF officers volunteered in more than tiny numbers for training as interpreters in Russian; one suggestion in the papers was that one per year should be trained, and this nugatory figure was confirmed in later Air Ministry Orders (AMO) long after this in 1934. Fears of wasting public money were expressed: only carefully selected men holding permanent commissions should be allowed to train, while at the same time the grant for such training was higher than that allowed for other languages. A difficulty for Russian was the near-impossibility of residence

---

[41] AIR 2/140: 'Observation on studies of modern languages at RAF Cadet College'; AIR 2/251: 'Revision of scheme for foreign language interpreterships.'

[42] AIR 2/251: revision of scheme for foreign language interpreterships, minute 15, dated 16.6.24.

[43] Monthly Air Force List, July 1924, p. 61.

in Russia. The Soviets themselves advised against it, saying—interestingly—that even before the First World War the presence of British officers in St Petersburg had aroused the suspicions of certain elements in the Government that their real purpose was to collect intelligence 'and might provoke unpleasant incidents.' This was reported to Ramsay Macdonald, at the time both Prime Minister and Foreign Secretary, as coming from Georgii Chicherin, Soviet Commissar for Foreign Affairs.

The 1924 papers, King's Regulations of 1928, and the 1934 AMO (A 165/34) show that London University (King's College) was closely involved in the preliminary training that RAF officers received in Slavonic languages. Mr Raffi at King's was the linking person: he advised the RAF to seek residential facilities for trainee interpreters in Riga and Libau (now Liepaja). The College was hardly making a fortune out of the services: it charged thirty pounds a month for eighteen hours instruction for five officers or fewer, plus five pounds for each additional officer. The RAF at that time could certainly not have found five officers to train, but any candidates could have joined the army and navy students at King's. Applicants who passed a preliminary exam in Russian were rewarded with ten pounds; one only would be sent to King's College, but might have to repay the College's fee if he failed his exams at the end of the course.[44]

The RAF has never kept lists of officers and men qualified as interpreters; careful trawling of AMWOs, AMOs, and the RAF List is necessary to trace the very modest progress made before the end of the 1940s. By 1949-50 there were 48 serving airmen with some knowledge of Russian, Polish, Czech, and Rumanian.[45] This figure surely reflects the RAF Kidbrooke enterprise, which will be described in the next chapter.

In view of the infinitesimal number of RAF officers qualifying in Russian in the 1920s, it may seem that excessive space has been devoted to the matter here. The debate so energetically carried on in the Air Ministry is none the less of significance for future developments, as we shall see in a later chapter.

The 1920s and 1930s were, therefore, a quiet time as regards Russian studies. A statement of policy by the MLA, which, it will be remembered, had a Russian Sub-committee during the First World War, makes no direct mention of Russian. The Association

> urges on local education authorities, and the governors and heads of schools the necessity of securing a wider field of study for German, Spanish, Italian and European languages other than French; and suggests that wherever

---

[44] *The King's Regulations and Air Council Instructions for the RAF*, HMSO: Air Publication 958, paragraphs 416 and 421, p. 115.

[45] AIR 2/10818, quoted by Jackson, p. 321.

Sir Jerome Horsey, c. 1550-1626, as imagined by the nineteenth-century painter, A. Litovchenko

Sir George Buck states that the Muscovian and Sclavonian languages were spoken in London in 1615, but were they *taught*?

Of Languages:

Cap. 37.

Besides the Latine and Greeke tongues which are taught in these Schooles before named. There be also in this Cittie Teachers and Professors of the holy or Hebrew Language, of the Caldean, Syriak, & Arabike, or Larbey Languages, of the Italian, Spanish, French, Dutch, and Polish Tongues. And here bee they which can speake the Persian and the Morisco, and the Turkish, & the Mulcovian Language, and also the Sclavonian tongue, which passeth through 17. Nations. And in briefe divers other Languages fit for Embassadors and Orators, and Agents for Marchants, and for Travaylors, and necessarie for all Commerce or Negotiation whatsoever.

Oooo   Of

James Heard's respectful dedication to the Russian Empress, 1827.

To Her Majesty
Alexandra Feodorovna,
Empress of Russia

The following attempt to facilitate the acquirement of the Russian language to a nation whose friendly and mutually advantageous intercourse with this Empire has been uninterruptedly maintained since the sixteenth century, is by permission and with the deepest reverence dedicated by

Her Imperial Majesty's

most humble
and most devoted Servant,
James Heard.

Ivan Nestor-Schnurmann

Anna H.Semeonoff

Sir Bernard Pares

Dr Lloyd Storr-Best

Fred G. Gregory

Pioneers and activists

Harry Milne

David J. Rix

Alan A. Haywood

Teachers, activists and authors of textbooks

Professor Terence L. B. Wade

Above and below: Russian students at work at JSSL Crail, c. 1956

RAF Sigint operators in Berlin
off duty, 1957

Their place of work

Ukrainian visitors confer with sixth-year pupils at Leith Academy, c1959.

Tea-time Russian. Alan Richards coaches volunteer learners in an after-school session at Bilborough College, Nottingham, 1980.

A thoughtful moment at a MAPRYaL congress, 1980: Dr Daphne West and Professor Gareth Jones

International Russian-speaking olympiada 1978.

A Scottish competitor faces the judges. Steven McQueen of Liberton High School, Edinburgh

Participants of all nations enjoy a social event.

Olympiada contestants visit a Young Pioneers' camp and make friends with the campers.

The home of the
Muscovy merchants
as it is today.

JSSL Bodmin
in 1956

British exchange teachers meet
Valentin Bulgakov, Lev Tolstoy's
last secretary, at Iasnaia poliana
in 1961.

Above: Dr Elizabeth Hill addresses her department, Cambridge, 1949.

Below: Nottingham University students rehearse Bulgakov's Zoikina kvartira, 1990.

possible a freer choice should be offered as to the first modern language to be learnt.[46]

This could scarcely be regarded as ringing support for the study of Russian. This 'policy' left much to be desired, though it was, one supposes, better than nothing.

It would not be true to say that no-one cared about Russian. We have seen that students came to university Russian classes, maybe not for degrees, but for other reasons—and we do not always know for certain what these reasons were. There have always been Britons who acquired a fascination for Russian life and culture: the wealthy businessmen in earlier years who endowed professorial chairs of Russian; an acquaintance of my own worked at a lathe in a factory for thirty years with Semeonoff's Russian grammar propped up before him, until in retirement he went on a course and became a teacher.[47] Others spoke up for Russian in the 1930s. I give two examples, as I cannot find many more.

In 1931 Sir Francis Goodenough published a report on *Modern Languages and Modern Commerce*. When he spoke to the MLA, the vote of thanks was proposed by Sir Kenyon Vaughan Morgan, who said someone had asked him what foreign language he should study. He 'advised him to study Russian, which was destined one day to become very important again.'[48]

In 1933 the Earl of Onslow, who had served in the British Embassy in St Petersburg, and who had been Paymaster General and Deputy Speaker of the House of Lords, became Chairman of the council of SSEES. In 1936 he wrote to *The Times*:

> The encouragement given by the Foreign Office and the activities of the Director of the School of Slavonic Studies in the University of London, Professor Sir Bernard Pares, have been instrumental in securing a revival of the study of Russian in our schools. Eton, Harrow, Westminster, and Marlborough have led the way, and other great public schools are likely soon to follow. Eton already has twelve boys learning the language. Now that the great public schools have set the example, may we hope that the local education authorities will follow? The East and the West of Europe must enter into closer relations as time goes on and communications improve. For many years Eastern Europeans have had the advantage of those in the West by being far more familiar with Western conditions than we Westerners were of conditions in Eastern Europe. Knowledge is power, and it is important that we

---

[46]'A Policy', in *Modern Languages*, XV(6), 1934, p. 205.

[47]For the record, he was a Mr Beningfield, he was 75 years old when I met him in 1975, and he was even at that age teaching at the Ursuline Convent School, Brentwood, where he was mentoring one of my teacher-training students. I know no more about him than this, but I respect and admire his persistence and dedication, and that of other such enthusiasts. Russian in Britain owes a lot to such people.

[48]*Modern Languages*, XII(3 & 4), 1931, p. 82.

should be as fully equipped with knowledge of the East of Europe as the East is with knowledge of the West.[49]

Again, this is less than a scintillating prospectus for the study of Russian. The letter does, however, make—once again—the point, so often, doubtless, accepted, but not resulting in much action, that Britain ought to learn to know the East of Europe. Britain in the 1930s should have been, but was not yet, ready to understand that the Soviet Union was going to demand attention from us sooner or later, and many in Britain had forgotten the cultural reasons for the study of Russian. The importance of the Russian language in diplomatic activity was well understood by British representatives in Russia at this very time. Embassy staff had only one official translator throughout most of the 1930s, and had to rely on second-hand information about what was going on in this most secretive country. Lord Chilston, Ambassador on 1934, urged the Foreign Office 'to establish a special training scheme under which members of the Consular Service could be seconded for a year to a university or college, where they could learn Russian before being sent to Moscow to help Embassy officials in the mammoth task of reviewing the Soviet Press. This apparently sensible scheme was scotched by the Foreign Office, ostensibly on the grounds that it would be difficult to organize, though in reality it seems certain that the expense was the real reason.'[50] At the same time, the FO in the person of Lord Stanhope on 15 February 1936 wrote to Bernard Pares at SSEES 'urging that Russian should more frequently be studied and stating that additional importance was now being given to it in the examinations for the Diplomatic Service.'

The contents of this letter were revealed by Pares in a letter to *The Times* of 11 June 1937. He reported what must seem to us like only very slight progress in regard to Russian in schools, but it was at least a start. To Onslow's list of schools he adds Winchester and Rugby; Harrow and Marlborough had seconded teachers to the USSR to learn the language; Wellington, Bryanston and Oundle were considering introducing or re-introducing Russian. In the maintained sector the London County Council was seconding eight of its teachers to SSEES to study Russian with a view to teaching it in London schools. The 1937 conference of university teachers of Russian was to invite teachers from all these schools to discuss the organization of assistance from the universities, and to consider teaching materials, library stocks, correspondence courses and a summer school.

The events of 1939 to 1941 were about to shock the nation and revise attitudes yet again. One is tempted to write that a world war again brought about an opening of minds. Or was it that? Have British minds ever really opened to Russia? Or has the country only noticed Russia when dire emergencies occurred or striking, even frightening, challenges were perceived?

---

[49] Reprinted in *Modern Languages*, XVII(6), 1935, p. 82.
[50] Hughes, p. 237.

Chapter 5
Wartime Again. A Slow Revival

This country is now more receptive to Russian ideas and more united in admiration of her character and deeds than ever before in our mutual history. Perhaps we are inclined to overdo that admiration, and the danger of exaggerated obeisance is the consequent reaction. There is no place in the twentieth century for such a synthesis of unalloyed virtue, wisdom and nobility as the prosaic letters USSR seem to stand for in too many starry eyes.

EDWARD CRANKSHAW, 1944

A READING of *Modern Languages* for the late 1930s and early 1940s might lead to the conclusion that Russian had been abandoned by the 'trade' journal of the language-teaching profession. There is very occasionally an entry in the 'Bibliography' section: the odd grammar, reader, edited text or dictionary, and even more rarely is there a review of any length or degree of thoughtfulness. In one issue, indeed, there are entries for Hottentot and Norwegian, but nothing for Russian. An article entitled 'A Plea for Swedish' appeared. Spanish figures regularly and in detail; teachers of this language maintained a high profile. As late as 1938 editorial comment is looking back with admiration at the Leathes Report of 1918, clearly indicating that public policy had not moved on much since then; the 1938 Spens Report, which discussed the secondary curriculum in the light of proposals to introduce technical and modern secondary education alongside what today we would call the grammar schools, had relatively little to say about modern languages. Spens was the first official discussion of some of the issues relating to the tripartite system of secondary education which was to follow the Butler Education Act of 1944 (which did not actually establish it), and led later to much thought by the teaching profession, not least the MLA in their desire to face the problems of language teaching in new types of school. On Russian affairs *Modern Languages* had little or nothing to say.

Nevertheless, evidence of the existence of an iceberg of Russian below the surface may be derived from the world of publishing. Though *Modern Languages* was paying little attention to Russian-language books, important contributions to the store of available teaching material for the subject were certainly appearing, or re-appearing. The oldest of these, David Bondar's *Simplified Russian Method* of 1911, with its invaluable commercial section, was revised or reprinted in 1931, 1932, 1934 and 1937, and reached its sixth edition in 1954; the same author issued readers and editions of classic stories in the 1930s, as at other times. The

Linguaphone Institute issued recorded materials in 1935. University teachers weighed in: G. A. Birkett produced the first edition of his *Modern Russian Course* in 1937: it stayed in print until at least 1963. J. Kolni-Balozky (or I. Kolny-Balotsky–his name and initial are spelt variously) issued *A Progressive Russian Grammar* in 1938, 1944 and 1946. M. V. Trofimov produced what is to the mind of the author of these lines the best and most thorough reference grammar for its time and for years to come, *Handbook of Russian*, in 1939.[1] S. K. Boyanus (who had collaborated and continued to do so with V. K. Myuller on dictionaries published in Moscow) began publishing Russian manuals in 1935: his best-known is *Spoken Russian* (1939).

Less overtly academic works also appeared. Charles Duff's *The Basis and Essentials of Russian* appeared in 1937; Russian was only one of the many languages in which this author claimed expertise. Charles Hugo, another language-teaching entrepreneur with a penchant for self-instructional material, had published his *First Lessons in Russian Without a Master* (1915); other titles by him such as *Russian Grammar Simplified* and *Russian Reading Made Easy* appeared throughout the 1920s and 1930s. Louis Segal was the most prolific of all these authors: from 1915 to 1962 he issued a staggering list of titles: a dictionary which was very successful in terms of the number of editions it ran to, though not felt by academics to meet the need for a really reliable work, courses with titles like *The Self-educator in Russian*, annotated editions for students of Chekhov and Tolstoy, *A Commercial Year Book of the Soviet Union* (1925), historical and literary surveys–as well as revising the sixth edition of Bondar. Three editions of his grammar appeared in the 1930s. Segal's Russian-English Dictionary was the standard work issued to services students in the 1950s.

Not quite the most prolific, but certainly the grammar-book writer with the greatest impact upon the Russian-learning public was Anna Evgenievna Goering-Semenova (1883-1965), known on the title page of her books as Anna H. Semeonoff and remembered by generations of students of Russian for her *New Russian Grammar*. The success of this book places her among pioneer Russian teachers of the twentieth century. Her story is that of an immigrant who set out to make her mark on British society with determination and vigour: not for nothing do her family refer to her as a 'tartar'.[2] She was attending a course in Edinburgh for teachers of languages in 1914 when war broke out and decided not to return to Russia, making her home in Scotland with her two children for the rest of her life. To earn a living, and taking advantage of the 'boom' in interest

---

[1] The book itself bears this date, but the British Library catalogue lists the identical title under Trofimov's name in relation to a work twenty years earlier. It may be that Trofimov wished to disown an earlier publication.

[2] For the biographical details here I am greatly indebted to the Rev. Robert Semeonoff, who has talked to me at length about his grandmother 'Anya' and shown me surviving family papers. He plans eventually to publish details of them and make them available in a public archive.

in Russia and Russian, she set herself up as a teacher of Russian. Over a hundred small advertisements in *The Scotsman* over the years 1914 to 1950 announce her services as class teacher, individual coach, and correspondence tutor; at different times in her life she taught in at least three Edinburgh schools: the Royal High, George Watson's and much later Daniel Stewart's Colleges, retiring from the latter as late as 1959 after seventeen years of part-time service. Resisting family pressure to return permanently to her husband in Russia, she nevertheless took out a Soviet passport in 1925 and renewed it regularly (with permission to reside in Britain) all her life. She made regular visits to Russia and seemed to have no trouble obtaining visas. Her philosophical views were distinctly in favour of the ethos of the Soviet régime, as some of the contents of her books imply;[3] her ease of travel to and fro is surprising, to say the least. But it is her books which concern us here. The very first dates from 1917, a *Russian Poetry Reader* in collaboration with Julius Tillyard, followed by an edition of three Pushkin stories in 1919. *Brush up Your Russian* was followed by the Grammar: between 1934 and 1960 this went through eleven editions, three of them in the 1930s. It has been both cursed and praised; the weight of judgement is favourable: many are grateful for the guidance it gives through the labyrinth of Russian grammar.

The fact that no fewer than ten authors were publishing in the field and that all these Russian courses were published and regularly reprinted in the 1930s surely indicates that—no matter how few schools, colleges, or universities were teaching the language, or how few students had enrolled in such institutions—there was serious interest in Russian at the time. But that interest was not by any means necessarily in formal institutions. Several of the books mentioned here were explicitly for self-instruction. Some that were intended for use with a teacher, Semeonova, Kolni-Balozky and Birkett, issued keys to the exercises for independent learners. The frequency with which nearly all of these books were revised or reprinted indicates that there must have been many learners around: someone was clearly buying these books, and doing so in large numbers. Moreover, the calibre of their authors and the quality of what they produced, old-fashioned, dry, and academic as it must seem today, were high; these books lasted for decades and are not all entirely forgotten in the twenty-first century.

Russia and the Russian language, despite appearances, then, were not thoroughly out of favour by 1940. As one looks through and reads newspapers and journals such as the *Times Educational Supplement* (*TES*), the *Journal of Education*, *The Times* itself, *The Scotsman,* and others, it becomes clear that ground prepared in earlier years had not been left derelict. There are in the press numerous small advertisements for Russian lessons and occasional news items about classes. Private language colleges such as Berlitz, Gouin, and other tutorial

---

[3] Particularly revealing is this exchange from *Brush up Your Russian* (London/Toronto: Dent, 1933, pp. 30-31). '*Mr S:* Look at this charming young couple. They seem to be discussing something very earnestly. I bet it's the Five Year Plan. Someone told me yesterday that even young lovers speak of nothing else. *Mrs S:* How characteristic of Russian youth to be so devoted to their cause.'

establishments made lessons available. SCR—a most interesting, perhaps misunderstood (sometimes wilfully), but energetic organization—was prominent in encouraging anyone who cared to learn Russian and running fortnightly meetings in London for Russian conversation practice. The provincial branches, which sprang up and died down with surprising rapidity—they had declined from a dozen and a half to four only in 1939, but thirty-three existed in 1943—often followed a similar policy.[4]

And it was not only teachers of Russian who were beating the big drum. An extraordinary letter to the Editor of *The Scotsman* from Charles Sarolea, explaining why he was resigning from the professorship of French at the University of Edinburgh, appealed for 'better teaching and more teaching' of foreign languages. He attacked the appalling standards in the teaching of French and the 'total neglect of Russian' (a language which he knew well).[5] J. Boyd, Professor of German at Oxford, spoke up for 'The post-war linguist: his training and national importance' in March 1941, pointing out the need in a future Europe to gain the friendship of nations by knowing their languages, cultures and life. It is another plea for diversity in language teaching, but he does not underestimate the difficulties of introducing new languages.[6]

In 1941 *Modern Languages* carried an advertisement for the first SSEES summer school, offering intensive courses at Oxford (where most of the School was evacuated) in eight Slavonic and East European languages, including Russian. Participants numbered about a hundred, and the courses continued until 1950, changing their location every year: Aberystwyth, Durham, Exeter,

---

[4] The SCR suffered from the widely-held belief that it was a 'fellow-travelling' or 'front' organization, devoted to converting unwitting British people to communism, and acting as a subversive element in British-Soviet relations. SCR declared itself to be non-political. The list of distinguished people who became vice-presidents in the twenties and thirties—Ashley Dukes, Leonard Woolf, Virginia Woolf, E. M. Forster, Bernard Pares, A. Smith Woodward, Aldous and Julian Huxley, Ivor Montague, John Maynard Keynes, Kingsley Martin, Philip Noel Baker, Elizabeth Hill, Sir Ernest Barker, Edward J. Dent, R. H. Tawney, H. G. Wells, Lord Haldane, Bertrand Russell, Laurence Housman, and a score of others—surely represents a wide variety of political standpoint. Many respectable educators were members: Professor Sedgefield, Dr Storr-Best among them—the latter used a radio talk in 1925 to urge people to join! The *Encyclopaedia Britannica* enlisted SCR help with articles on Russian science, philosophy, literature, art, economics and education. However, such organs as the *Morning Post*, and particularly a scurrilous journal called *The Patriot* poured ridicule on the notion that it was possible to carry on cultural relations with the Soviet state, and they published numerous foolish and intemperate items. These may be read in the SCR's archive of press cuttings; they now provoke a wry smile. It is certainly true that the Soviets tried to manipulate SCR—and that they often failed, as M. Kuz'min's article referred to above clearly demonstrates. It is also true that communist sympathisers joined SCR (among other respectable organizations). Britain is, after all, a free country. It is also true that SCR appealed to left-leaning people, and that some of the figures justly excoriated by Ludmila Stern belonged to it. However, SCR deserves credit for keeping open channels of communication with the Soviet Union, and the Society was invited to send a representative to the Foreign Office Committee on Russian Studies during the Second World War.

[5] *The Scotsman*, 19 March 1931, p. 8: 'To the Editor of *The Scotsman*'.

[6] *Modern Languages*, XXII(3), 1939, pp. 73-82.

Nottingham, and Paris. The Editor of *Modern Languages* refers to this as 'a definitely new move in the study of modern languages in Britain'. A letter from a Lt-Col. Robbins, dated 23.7.41, in Cambridge University Library, seeks advice: 'We have under consideration a political, military and language course designed to train officers for possible attachment to Missions in the USSR, and I should much appreciate an opportunity of consulting you [Elizabeth Hill] on this matter.' A syllabus for a four-week course is appended, consisting of language tuition and background lectures, which were given by some very eminent speakers. Further, the *Daily Telegraph* in 1941 reports that members of the armed services were attending 3,200 classes run by local education authorities in languages; though French and German are the most popular, Russian, Norwegian, Dutch and Polish are also represented. The Army List for April 1942 names 64 officers qualified as Russian interpreters, 38 first class and 26 second. This is, of course, only half the number just before the First World War. Only nineteen naval officers were qualified in 1939. The RAF, which did not publish figures which can easily be retrieved, encouraged both officers and airmen to become qualified as interpreters, and while Russian is not specifically mentioned in *King's Regulations* until 1928, the AMWOs as early as 28 October 1920 announce (p. 6) that personnel who qualify as first-class interpreters in Russian in the Civil Service examinations will be rewarded with eighty pounds: considerably more than for any other European language. This is not to say that anyone actually presented himself for the exam. As late as 1935 (the only list to which I have had access: Air Ministry Order AMO N.556) no RAF officer or airman was listed as having passed the exam.[7]

Lest it be thought that these relatively small developments arose from Hitler's invasion of the USSR, it should be emphasized that some of them were afoot *before* this major military and political shock was received. 'A naive admiration for Russia as a workers' state had persisted in spite of everything among the British working class'.[8] When the invasion came and when in 1942 the British-Soviet Alliance was signed, editorial comment in *Modern Languages* runs: 'No doubt a great impetus to the study of the Russian language will follow the new interest in Russia arising from our alliance with her, and not least from the glorious and heroic resistance of the Russian armies in their Titanic defensive battle on the Eastern Front.' Calder remarks: 'The recoil of public opinion from its belief that the Russians were poor fighters took it swiftly to the opposite extreme, so that every sign of resistance was greeted like a major offensive.'[9] One cannot by any means deny the heroism of the Soviet Army in 1941-45, but the argument for Russian studies cannot survive if it depends purely on an

---

[7]I am grateful to Mr Clive Richards of the Ministry of Defence Air Historical Branch (RAF) for supplying information and photocopies of certain relevant AMWOs and AMOs.

[8]Calder, *The People's War*, p. 260.

[9]*Modern Languages*, XXIII(2), 1942, p. 37; Calder, p. 261.

emotional foundation. 'Our glorious ally' in 1914 was perceived to have feet of clay in 1918, and the learning of Russian suffered in consequence.

Historians and eyewitnesses have chronicled the labyrinthine twists and turns of British-Soviet diplomatic relations from 1939 to 1941 and the attitudes of the public.[10] Governments strove manfully to remain sitting on the fence in case Hitler should attack Russia, as many—but not by any means all—politicians and diplomats expected he would. Those old enough to remember 1941 do indeed recall a strong increase in public interest in matters Russian among the public when the conflict came, but while SSEES reported a 'considerable increase' in the numbers of external students for Russian, the enthusiasm scarcely amounted to a stampede. While University College, Nottingham, noted a significant increase in students and staff who would learn Russian between 1940 and 1943, Sheffield University in fact closed its Russian Department in 1943, and Birmingham reported only one or two students a year reading Russian. Leeds, Liverpool and Manchester were similarly sparsely provided with students. 'Glasgow post-war numbers never matched those of the pre-war period.'[11] For several years after the entry of the USSR into the war *The Times* made no mention of the study of the Russian language, in contrast with the attention given to it by that newspaper during the First World War. On 22 August 1941 a very brief announcement appears of an attempt by one James Malcolm to revive the Russia Society, of which he had been a founder in 1915, and which, as will be recalled, was a great support to Russian-teaching ventures at that time. And that is the last we hear of it. Occasional short news items mention receptions held in London by the SCR, an Anglo-Soviet week in 'a South coast town' (wartime security prevented the town even being named), and the announcement by R. A. Butler, President of the Board of Education, of a four-day course for teachers in 1942 'to give an objective view of the USSR, its life, culture and achievements'. More sinister was a question asked in Parliament by the member for Newcastle West, who declared that certain elements in society encouraged by 'men of the cloth', including an organization calling itself the Russia Today Society, were engaging in intimidatory activities against any expression of support for delaying the second front in the war against Germany. The Minister concerned claimed that 'so far as he knew' these remarks were 'grossly untrue' and an abuse of parliamentary privilege by the MP.

The Minister was not telling the truth. The Russia Today Society was Communist-controlled and was one of a number of flourishing organizations; their activities were 'blessed by bishops, financed by the government and given

---

[10] Keeble's account, *Britain and the Soviet Union, 1917-89,* centres almost exclusively on diplomatic activity, while Kitchen's, *British Policy Towards the Soviet Union During the Second World War,* fleshes the story out with detail and sketches of the personalities involved; he also does not neglect public and popular attitudes to Russia. These are focused upon particularly by Calder.

[11] Kirkwood, 'The University and the Wider World', p. 5 fn.

musical accompaniment by Guards' bands.'[12] As for intimidation, there were reports of it. The 'Second Front Now' movement, which plastered graffiti on walls everywhere was a nuisance to Churchill[13] and his government, but its moral support for the Soviet struggle must have been welcome to others. Our question must be, did such agitation foster the cause of the teaching of Russian? While there was undoubtedly an increase of interest, it does not seem that there was a great burst of enthusiasm for the study of the Russian *language*, at least not on the scale of the First World War.

One reason for this slight reluctance may be that admiration for Soviet military prowess and the desire to support the USSR in the war were strongly tinged with mistrust and dislike for communism. Right-wing Conservatives feared that support for the USSR could be used by the unscrupulous to encourage Communist activities in this country.[14] But it was not only Conservatives: correspondence in the *Left News* clearly demonstrated that many people on the political left, even the very left, were uneasy: for example Leonard Woolf in *Barbarians at the Gate*, 'saw in Russian politics much that he regarded as totalitarian and immoral.'[15] It may also be that the impressions of those British soldiers and diplomats who had gone to work in the USSR from 1941 were filtering home. Alan Haywood, who spent a year at Archangel and Murmansk in connection with the aid convoys, writes of an atmosphere at that time of 'suspicion and fear' on the part of the Russians, and of a deliberate policy to limit communication between the British and the better-educated among the Russian population. It is scarcely a recipe for good relations, whether cultural, military, social or diplomatic.[16]

On 26 May 1943 *The Times* published a two-column article reviewing Anglo-Soviet cultural relations during the one year since the signing of the Anglo-Soviet Alliance. The item makes no mention at all of the study of the Russian language. However, interest in Russian was increasing, and some of the textbooks which remained standard for twenty or so years appeared: Hill's revision of Forbes's Grammar (1943; Mark Sieff's *Colloquial Russian* (1943), Natalie Duddington's readers (1943, 1949), Elizaveta Fen's readers and conversation books (1942, 1944, 1946).[17] The *Journal of Education* too reviewed ten new or revised publications in 1944.[18] An article of 1947 by a distinguished Slavonic

---

[12] Kitchen, p. 103.

[13] Churchill, IV, pp. 60 and 757.

[14] Ruth Dudley Edwards, *Victor Gollancz, a Biography*. London: Gollancz, 1987, pp. 352-353.

[15] Lewis p. 118., who briefly summarizes the differences of opinion (pp. 116ff.)

[16] A. Haywood, 'Wartime experiences in Russia', *ATR Newsletter*, 1983, no. 2, pp. 20-23.

[17] Fen was a child psychotherapist of Russian origin. She published stories, novels, and two volumes of memoirs. She is probably best remembered for her translations of Chekhov plays.

[18] May 1944, pp. 260-262.

linguist[19] reviews the whole range of Russian teaching materials then available concisely and informatively. The Rt Hon. Leslie Burgin, MP, writing in the *Daily Mail Yearbook for 1944*, p. 39, hoped for a '*very great interest in the study of the Russian language* on the part of peoples of all nations' [Burgin's emphasis]. Cyril Osbourne asked in the House of Commons on 6 December 1945 whether the Minister would consider making compulsory the teaching of the Russian language in secondary schools and also arrange for an exchange of teachers between this country and the USSR. This disingenuous question received the expected answer that the Minister (Ellen Wilkinson) did not prescribe languages to be taught; she none the less intended to issue a circular to local education authorities and governing bodies 'recommending [...] a development in the teaching of Russian' Exchanges were also in her mind 'when conditions make this practicable.' It was many years before conditions did; a later minister, James Callaghan, was to give a long parliamentary answer in 1946 on Soviet non-co-operation on the subject.

The Norwood (1943) and Thomson (1947) Reports

When it became clear that the Allies were not going to lose the military conflict of the Second World War, the nation turned to thoughts of education. The 1944 Education Act for England and Wales and the 1947 Education (Scotland) Act set the scene for twenty or thirty years of schooling. Their consequences, including some unintended, included the establishment of a *Ministry* (not Board) of Education south of the Border whose minister was to 'secure the effective execution [...] of the national policy' on education, the raising of the leaving age to 15 and the intention to raise it further, organization of schools into primary, secondary and further, abolition of fees in state schools, and other measures. Prior to the 1944 Act, a Committee chaired by Sir Cyril Norwood, President of St John's College, Oxford, had reported on *Curriculum and Examinations in Secondary Schools* in relation to England and Wales. Norwood had something to say about Russian in schools:

> 'In the immediate future the balance [between one foreign language in the curriculum and another] may be substantially altered. We enter this caution because, though no-one can as yet estimate with accuracy the range and the depth of the impact which Russia will make on the post-war era, it is probable that it will be real and deep, and a live education must concern itself with what is significant for the future. There is intense interest among the young in all things Russian, the literature, the art, the music, the ballet, as well as the political system. Yet it is not at present a matter of practical politics that Russian should become one of the languages studied in the early years of the Secondary Grammar School: it is possible that the language is in any case too difficult for this stage. But there is a good case, in London and the larger

---

[19] W. K. Matthews, 'East European Studies 1941-46', *Modern Languages,* XXVIII (3), pp. 100-104.

> urban centres, for starting the experiment of two-year intensive courses in Russian in the VI form: for the rest it is fortunate that much of what is best in the literature and thought of Russia is available in good English translations, and can be used by the teacher in many other types of lessons than those of modern languages. In saying that at present not much can be done in the teaching of Russian at school, because of the present dearth of teachers, if for no other reason, we are speaking of the present only. But even now we think it incumbent on all schools which keep their pupils to the age of 18 to make them acquainted with the ideals and achievements which have changed the face of human society over a great area of Russia and Asia, and cannot be without significance to the coming generation; to be rightly and properly understood they must be studied in the unprejudiced atmosphere which should be characteristic of a good school.
>
> Courses of foreign languages beginning in the VI form should become much more common than at present. [...] We would suggest that under favourable conditions Russian should be included.[20]

For the time at which it was published, this is unquestionably a wise statement. The Committee were right to foresee the importance of Russian studies, they were clearly aware of the perceptions of young people with regard to Russia. One cannot help warming to their feeling about 'a live education'. They were wrong, as later experience proved, that Russian was too difficult for the early years of secondary education: if schoolchildren were expected to learn Latin, the Committee should perhaps have realized that Russian would be no more of a problem. They were right to be cautious about the availability of teachers—one might stress *good* teachers. We must respect and praise their note of caution: 'we are speaking of the present only'.

If there is one element in this statement which makes one feel a little uneasy, it is the remark about 'the ideals and achievements which have changed the face of human society over a great area of Russia and Asia.' This was written during the Second World War. Stalin was in full control of that part of the Soviet Union which had at the time been left to him by Hitler. While the achievements of the Soviet Union could in many cases be pointed to with pride, the ideals Stalin embodied were controversial, to say the least, and the Norwood Committee should maybe have been enlightened enough to recognize that. We are perhaps again back in a world where our 'glorious ally' could do little wrong. Some very good journalists wrote somewhat sycophantic articles and books at the time; at least one of these later made amends by more measured assessment of the Russian wartime experience.[21]

The Committee chaired by J. Mackay Thomson reported in a document with similar subject matter and of comparable scope in 1947, 'To review the

---

[20] Norwood Report, pp. 116-117

[21] I refer to Alexander Werth, whose two wartime books positively turn the stomach, but whose 1967 reconsideration *Russia at War* is a very different kettle of fish.

educational provision in Scotland for young people who have completed their primary education and have not attained the age of 18 years or discontinued full-time attendance at school...' Thomson, however, did not display the same breadth of vision as Norwood. His Report wrote:

> In a memorandum issued in 1907 the SED made this remarkable pronouncement:
>
> 'The knowledge of a language other than the mother tongue is not a necessary part of the equipment of an educated mind.'

'Remarkable', indeed; perhaps little short of astounding:

> In Chapter V we made clear our unqualified acceptance of this view and our equally strong conviction that it does not detract in the least from the great value of language learning for those who are able to profit by it.

The attitude that only some were bright enough to benefit from learning foreign languages was shortly to become very unfashionable, being seen as élitist. Three more extracts—the only remaining points at which Russian is mentioned by name or implication—run as follows:

> We could as a nation ensure one thing—that over the country as a whole each main language [including Russian] was understood and spoken by considerable groups of our people. (p. 86)
>
> On cultural grounds French would secure a high, but not an exclusive place. But even its strongest advocates hardly contend that it matches Spanish and Italian in ease of acquisition, or Russian and Spanish in utility. (p. 87)
>
> Great as are the claims of Russian on cultural and practical grounds, our evidence is definite that the language is difficult and that younger secondary pupils would make little progress in it. (p. 87)

The 'utility' of Russian is accepted, not argued. Its cultural value is relegated to a subordinate clause. 'Definite' evidence from goodness knows where is quoted to its detriment as a school subject before the age of 16. (The list of witnesses to the Committee and of bodies which submitted memoranda, do not appear to include an exponent of Russian language teaching, though, of course, there may have been one.) It is fortunate that Scots teachers were not put off by this view; the success of Russian teaching to younger school pupils, for over twenty years from 1960 at least, outdid in terms of proportionate numbers the good work done south of the border. Thomson put in a word for Russian after the age of 16:

> What was impossible with ordinary pupils of 12 and 13 because of the difficulty of the language becomes relatively easy with selected boys and girls of 16 or more; and unless we ensure that a due proportion of our able senior pupils, destined for commerce, technology or administration, are given a working knowledge of the principal language of the USSR, we shall be guilty of inexcusable blindness to the realities of the world situation.

Commerce, technology, administration. Is that all Thomson could advance as reasons for Russian? He was badly advised: there were plenty of people in Scotland who could provided much better counsel.

A contemporary critique of the Norwood Report

The Norwood Report at least offered the prospect of change, in contrast with Thomson's somewhat inadequate response to modern conditions. However, more or less as soon as Norwood appeared, a most refreshing and provocative response was published: *Language Studies and International Relations*, by J. O. Roach, London (etc.): Harrap, 1944. Roach was a prolific writer on languages (including English), especially as regards the testing of proficiency. He attacked the very basis of Britain's provision in schools for language tuition. If we teach everyone only French and German, believing them to be basic to our understanding of Europe, we distort the national perception of European conditions, culture— everything, he argued. At the same time, we sanitize French and German studies: we give a false idea of modern Germany and France: 'a Germany where Bismarck was not known and where Frederick the Great was a phenomenon to be lightly brushed aside by the littérateur, just as Pétain would lead us back soothingly to Louis XIV.'

What about Norwegian, Swedish, Dutch, Danish—and other languages? asked Roach. We cling to the notion that French and German culture are basic to our understanding of Europe; we are imprisoned by this notion. 'The Norwood Committee swing over to commerce and salesmanship and the massive "impact" of Russia.'

The notion that some schools should teach 'minor' European languages like Norwegian or Flemish (the latter on the sound grounds that the Dutch-speaking population of Belgium could never be fully understood through the medium of French—as events in recent decades have surely amply proved)—must have been too much for the traditionalists. *Modern Languages* brushed his arguments aside: 'we all know Mr Roach's views'. Roach's argument is hard to counter, but there was never any chance that his opinions would have been found politically acceptable. He appears at one point to go so far as to lay down his preferences (p. 15) for the distribution of language knowledge among School Certificate candidates in the future, by 1953. He supposes that it might be conceivable that 15,000 might enter in German, 10,000 in Spanish, 6,000 in Russian, 4,000 in Italian, and 6,000 in the 'new languages'. French would have as many as all the others put together. He clearly did not care to challenge the supremacy of French.

Enthusiasm for languages other than French and German may have caused some unease in the MLA, which has traditionally pressed for diversification of provision, but then the interests of teachers of the various tongues may conflict. It is hard to know whether in the 1940s and 1950s school teachers of Russian, Spanish, or Italian were *also* teachers of French or German; it may be supposed that a class of pupils learning Russian or Spanish meant one class fewer of German or French pupils. In any case, the Editor of *Modern Languages*, a barrister-at-law and perhaps not a teacher, A. H. Sleight, poured scorn on Russian in the school curriculum:

> After reading what the author [Bodmer, in *The Loom of Language*] says of the complexities of Russian, one is more than ever sure of the futility of including it in the school curriculum.[22]

In the same issue of *Modern Languages*, the Headmaster of Sedbergh was reported in summary:

> Russian might have the virtue of difficulty but probably too much of it. It was unlikely that any but the ablest of boys would achieve enough facility ever to read much. Besides, who was to teach it? Real understanding and enthusiasm on the part of the teacher were essential, and where were the teachers who had lived in Russia or who had been allowed to see anything there or to get any understanding? We did not want smatterings taught by three-week conducted tourists.
>
> The time was not yet ripe for raising Russian to the status of a normal second language, though that might come before long. In the meantime a beginning might be made in big schools as a post-certificate subject for boys who had not two other languages to study, provided we remember that smatterings were always poor education, and particularly for the young modern linguist at all costs to be avoided.[23]

While these views are coloured by the false notion of the excessive difficulty of Russian, there are some fair points here. Who, indeed, was to teach Russian? Were teachers available, were they trained, were they able, were they enthusiastic, were they *teachers* as well as enthusiasts? Was Russian so important to them that they would stick with the job and perhaps sacrifice other aspects of a career in teaching in order to perpetuate the subject? J. H. Bruce Lockhart, the headmaster in question, and brother of Robert, the 'British agent' whom we have mentioned already in these pages, is right to be cautious. However, in 1945 there was no solution to the problem of travel and tourism (and this long remained a problem). This is not the place to dispute his opinion that smatterings are *always* poor education; depending what he meant by 'smatterings', the view can be questioned. As for the imagined 'difficulty' of Russian, a chance reference in an entirely unrelated article in *Modern Languages* from this period refers to French as 'a very difficult language'.

The Editor of *Modern Languages* did not survive: perhaps his unfortunate comments led to his resignation. He was obviously misled by Bodmer's ill-

---

[22]*Modern Languages*, XXVI (1), Dec. 1944, p. 1.

[23]The same, p. 47.

informed statements,[24] and was unwise to prefer them to the experience of his Association's Slavonic Committee. His response to being 'mildly taken to task' by them (why only 'mildly', one wonders?) is supercilious and evasive.[25]

This was the first mention in *Modern Languages* of an MLA Slavonic Committee. It must be said that they appear to have been somewhat pusillanimous. Only occasionally did they submit a report to the AGM, and one of these indicates poor attendance at meetings. Still, they existed, and apparently held annual day conferences; a report of one such for 1949 appeared in the *Times Educational Supplement*,[26] the last paragraph of which returns to Bruce Lockhart's point: the lack of 'free and friendly interchange of linguists, and the genuine desire to establish understanding, good will and respect is deliberately frustrated by hostility and political prejudice.' Not until several years after the death of Stalin were country-to-country exchanges even remotely possible for teachers and learners of Russian; for Russian learners of English they were virtually impossible for many decades after that.

In the first issue of *Modern Languages* edited by the group which succeeded the previous editor a helpful editorial comment is made:

> The recent controversy on the inherent difficulty in learning Russian will probably be roused once again by the statement [in *Ministry of Education Circular 81*, which is described below]:- 'Pupils of good linguistic ability (and Russian would hardly be taught to any others)'. There is much room for research into this question of difficulty of languages. Does a different style of alphabet at once render a language difficult? Is Greek more difficult than Latin? What constitutes difficulty in the acquisition of vocabulary? Is it helpful, for example, for students to study a cognate language rather than a completely different one? Do grammatical difficulties provide stumbling blocks of first magnitude?[27]

In 1946 *Modern Languages* published the abstract of a conference address by the indefatigable Dr Storr-Best, who was now 82 and who had still another eleven years to live: his subject was 'Russian as a school subject'. No-one reading or listening to this can have had any excuse for continuing to believe Russian was entirely remote from English, that it was immensely difficult, or that the verbal system, accidence or syntax should give pupils inordinate difficulty: as a former council member of the Classical Association as well as a former President of the

---

[24] F. Bodmer (ed. Hogben), *The Loom of Language*, London: George Allen & Unwin, 1943, pp. 415-416. Bodmer's remarks in a chapter headed 'The Diseases of language' are hostile and written in surprisingly emotive language. They show that Bodmer had no more than a tenuous knowledge of Russian (a 'smattering', perhaps.) At least two of the four statements on which he bases his conclusion that Russian presents serious difficulties to the learner can easily be shown to be false.

[25] XXVII (1), December 1945, p. 2.

[26] 'Unity through languages. The Study of Russian', 16 September 1949, p. 635.

[27] *Modern Languages* XXVII (2), 1946, pp. 38-39.

Institute of Linguists, and as a former head with eight languages taught in his school, he gave a masterly account of the contrasts and comparisons between Russian and languages from Sanskrit onwards, and a realistic account of what the difficulties are which face the learner of Russian. Such reasoned argument from a leading educator was welcome. The tide was going his way, but it may not have appeared so at the time.

The editorial and news columns of *Modern Languages* refer to the educational controversies of the age, such as the first experiments in comprehensive education, which were first noted in 1948. They do not mention Russian very often. A pamphlet produced by the students at SSEES was given some prominence: *The Case for the Teaching of Russian in Schools* [1949: the date is assumed, as the publication bears no date]. This eleven-page pamphlet is of considerable interest: the mature post-war students (it must be remembered that ex-servicemen in the years after 1945 were encouraged with financial inducements to study at universities) put forward a moderate and cogent argument, based on the Scarbrough Report, which we shall examine shortly. The document begins by declaring that Russian should not be taught solely as preparation for a degree course. 'The need is for a large number of people having at least a good reading knowledge of Russian combined with high qualifications in other fields of study, and for a limited number of students who will become teachers and lecturers in Russian. They argue for Russian as 'a vehicle for humane education' and go on to deal with questions such as 'is Russian too difficult?', 'is there a literature worth reading?', the advantages of Russian as a subsidiary, and 'the social importance of the study of Russian in schools'. The students 'ask for [the] careful consideration [of Russian] by headmasters, headmistresses and others concerned.' (p. 4) In 1948 Nicolas Sollohub had published an article in the *Times Educational Supplement*, specifically on one of these themes: 'Is Russian too difficult?' reporting on the experience of teaching young cadets aged about 15 to 17 at the Royal Naval College, Dartmouth, concluding that it can be taught at school with success—by Englishmen. Eight years later 'A Plea for Russian in grammar schools'[28] appeared. But the needs and interests of teachers of French (in particular) and German were paramount. For ten or more years, the primary journal for teachers of modern languages had very little indeed to say about Russian, even when it began its resurgence. Then in 1959 they appointed Sir William Hayter, former British Ambassador in Moscow and Chair of the Hayter Committee, as their President. His presidential lecture[29] is not a plea for Russian, though it makes many references to his experience in the USSR. No, if one must be critical of the MLA, it is of the Russian teachers among its membership. They made a minimal contribution to the work of the Association and kept a very low profile. Not in the articles, nor the book reviews and listings,

---

[28] by T. W. Edwards, *Modern Languages* XXXVIII (1), March 1957.

[29] 'Modern languages and modern politics', *Modern Languages* XLI (1), March 1960, pp. 4-8.

news items, correspondence, branch reports, committee activities—in none of these areas did Russianists produce much impact. It could not have been clearer that a new agency seeking to promote Russian particularly in schools was needed. This agency soon emerged.

Let us return to the 'iceberg below the surface', since for the period under examination it is actually very difficult to establish how many secondary or public schools were teaching Russian and which they were. The Scarbrough Report believed about fifteen public schools had taught Russian 'at one time or another' between 1920 and 1947, and the Earl of Onslow's letter to *The Times* mentioned four of them, to which we can add George Watson's College, where Anna Semeonova had been teaching since 1917, and Winchester College, which began Russian in the 1930s. An incidental remark in a publication of 1949 by Dr Eric James, at that time High Master of Manchester Grammar School, runs: 'Surely Russian has a claim, and the Ministry [of Education] duly urges upon the schools the desirability of some provision for Russian teaching.'[30] This remark of a headmaster in post indicates clearly that central government *was* taking a hand in advocating Russian, and it gives the lie to later protestations in the 1960s that the Ministry could not intervene to support specific subjects, including Russian. Some state schools which had dropped Russian were poised to resume: Firth Park re-started Russian after the war under the leadership of a notable teacher, Alan A. Haywood, who had been a pupil there in the 1930s. Moreover, there is further evidence here of active encouragement by the Ministry of Education: Haywood reports that they intervened with the head in 1946 to urge the reintroduction of Russian.[31] As for universities: the Scarbrough Commission reported nine in 1947, at which a little under 150 students had been reading for degrees in 1945-46. The largest departments were Oxford (24 students), Cambridge (30), Glasgow (about 20), and University College, Nottingham (28—but not all of these were degree students.) London (SSEES), Birmingham, Leeds, Liverpool and Manchester could muster only 42 between them.[32]

One of the partly hidden sectors was the technical colleges and adult education institutions. Statistics for the School Certificate examinations from 1947 (the first year they were published after the war) do show a significant increase from the single figures in the 1930s, but it took until 1958 for entries for Russian, by this time the General Certificate of Education Ordinary Level (GCE O), to exceed 100. School Certificate or O level, however, were not the exams which technical or commercial college students would have taken at that time. Ministry of Education Circular 81 of 15 January 1946 which is discussed in Chapter 6 drew attention to the statistics of the Royal Society of Arts. As we

---

[30] Eric James, *An Essay on the Content of Education,* London: Harrap, 1949, p. 38. Later in the book (pp. 109-110), in another direct reference to Russian, James clarifies the point: 'Changes... are never commanded; it is merely requested that certain possibilities should be borne in mind.'

[31] See Haywood, 'Russian at Firth Park...'

[32] Scarbrough, pp. 122-123

have noted, the RSA had first set a Russian examination as long ago as 1889. While 34 candidates had entered RSA Russian in 1938, this had risen to 205 in 1945, and the examiners' report indicated satisfactory standards 'with room for improvement.' (The figure for German in 1945 was 466, a drop from the 850 who sat in 1939.)[33] The Circular reported that enrolments of 300 or so had been recorded in London colleges offering Russian 'for some years.' The students attended classes for two hours weekly for 30 to 36 weeks in the year. 'Many continue their studies over three years and reach a standard which would enable them to take part in daily life in Russia without embarrassment.' (p. 1.) It cannot be said too often that not by any means every learner wishes to gain a certificate; keen students were studying independently in many places. The SCR in the 1940s and 50s reports increasing attendance at classes known to and sponsored by them, and at their conversation groups.

The other partly hidden sector was that of Russian for military and diplomatic purposes. We have seen that hundreds of army and navy officers and diplomats acquired Russian for Civil Service Interpreters' examination up to and even during the First World War. After the war there were military students at Cambridge, King's London and Oxford; King's had from its very inception offered teaching to the services, in the first instance to avoid having its premises requisitioned by the Government. The by now well-established pattern of study followed by residence abroad was often followed. In the 1920s and 1930s, as the Foreign Office were later to complain, there were not enough of them to fulfil the needs of the services, and this not only in Russian, but in Western European languages and Japanese as well.[34] Navy Lists identify 19 interpreters for Russian among about 350 officers qualified in various languages at the outbreak of the Second World War, five more than there had been in 1935. Their dates of qualification indicate very small numbers of men training—one or two a year, allowing for retirements from the service. A good half were senior officers: Lieutenant Commander or above, and more than half obtained a 'higher' grade of qualification.[35] In these decades SSEES prepared officers with basic Russian, after which they were despatched to such destinations as the Baltic States. Commander Anthony Courtney, on the other hand, was largely self-taught before he lived with a Russian family in Kishinev, Bessarabia, at that time under Romanian control.[36]

---

[33] Statistics supplied to me by Ms Claire Batley of the RSA Archives, 2007. The Annual report for 1945 of the RSA contains the examiners' report.

[34] 'Naval Interpreters: insufficient numbers', *The Scotsman*, 23 Jan. 1933, p. 14.

[35] *Navy List*, 1935 pp. 317-319, and 1939 pp. 382-384.

[36] Courtney, pp. 1-23. The Commander's account of the development of his love of the Russian language is of the greatest interest: it began as a small child when his father brought back wooden toys and books of Russian stories from a business trip and translated them to him, creating a determination to learn to read them for himself. At school he toiled over Hugo's Russian course, gaining great prestige among his fellows: 'I found... that an assumption of expertise in an uncommon

Little documentary evidence survives of the work of universities in training service personnel in Russian in the 1930s. It was if not exactly haphazard, then left very much to the initiative of individuals. A letter to a former army student from Elizabeth Hill[37] in 1938 reads: 'I have 30 students here this year, but I am sorry to say not one of them is an army officer, though I changed the time of my elementary Russian lecture to 6 p.m. in the hope that it might draw some of the engineers.' Even if military men were not enrolling, it is good to read that thirty people, mostly reading other subjects for the Tripos, turned up voluntarily. There is evidence that other universities—Sheffield, Nottingham, London—kept up the tradition started by Messrs Schnurmann and Goudy at Cambridge and Liverpool at the end of the nineteenth century of offering Russian as an extra-curricular subject. What may be thought strange about this is that the university departments concerned appeared somewhat dismissive of non-degree courses, whether for military men or anyone else, even though the existence of such students must have been crucial in keeping their departments alive. In the late 1930s Cambridge, as noted above, mounted a play with a far larger Russian-speaking cast than degree students could have supplied.

It is not easy to discover just when the armed services realized that men (and sometimes women) of *non-commissioned* status were eminently employable as interpreters. The earliest references which can be traced are AMOs of 1942, 1944, and 1945: A574/42, A514/44, A753/45 and A 754/45, which announce the introduction of new RAF trades of Interpreter (technical) Group II and Interpreter Group IV. It was wartime, and the RAF clearly envisaged certificating conscripts on entry or after a short refresher course, implying that some recruits had a knowledge of Russian: more evidence of the 'iceberg'. It is not known how many—if any— Russian-speakers were thus recruited.

Courses run at universities for service personnel were to become a crucial influence in the development of Russian language studies. Courses at SSEES lasted for six months and there were 36 hours per week of class contact. An alumnus of a course which ran in 1944-45, John Ingram, gave the following details of his experience. He recalls ten or fifteen army and RAF students on the course, mostly NCOs, and only one or two commissioned officers. He was aware that there was 'a whole lot of confusion at that time' about many things in the conduct of the war; the students were unable to detect any real purpose in their training. One widely believed hypothesis was that General Eisenhower foresaw a need for interpreters in cooperating with the Soviet Army in Germany in the last stages of and after the war, but Mr Ingram said that his training—which brought him and his fellows up to a high standard of practical interpretership—was totally wasted by the RAF, though in his later life and career it was very

---

language is very seldom challenged.' (p. 15.) The scandal which ensued after he was compromised by the KGB in an attempt to unseat him from the House of Commons is more sensational, but to our theme less interesting.

[37]Cambridge University: Elizabeth Hill Papers, file C2 (b).

valuable to him. He expressed admiration and affection for his teachers, especially Arshak Raffi, whom he must have caught at the very end of his career at SSEES, which ran from 1915 to 1944. A fellow-student was later to become a distinguished professor of Russian. Another he described as a hitherto uneducated working-class man of astounding linguistic talent—who also did very well in later life. A slightly later course was attended by Squadron Leader B. A. 'Jimmy' James, the legendary escaper from one Stalag Luft after another; in between episodes of tunnelling he had learned Russian, and after release went to SSEES to train formally. He then returned to Germany until 1953 for intelligence duties. A similar career was followed by Sir John Harvey-Jones, a naval officer at the end of the war who studied Russian and German at Cambridge and worked for a few years thereafter in liaison and naval intelligence, before achieving considerable fame as an industrialist.[38]

Cambridge was where the spy George Blake learned his Russian: in *No Other Choice* he paints a perhaps surprisingly warm picture of Elizabeth Hill and her teaching.[39] He was in the Special Intelligence Service at the time and not a military officer. Commander Courtney states in his memoir that he collaborated with the Foreign Office by giving naval 'cover' to nominees of theirs; Blake was one such.[40] Blake went on to gain further experience of the spoken language by living with a Russian émigré family, in his case in Dublin.

The courses at Cambridge began in 1945, and were run for officers and men of all three services. Surviving records show two cohorts of about 75 men of all ranks mainly in the army and navy beginning their studies in 1945; the names include several who became well-known and long-serving teachers of Russian. The courses were to last six to eight months; 75% of the students were total beginners working to become competent translators, the rest were intended as interpreters for the Allied Control Commission. Sixteen or seventeen of each cohort failed the final test, but Hill energetically urged that a second chance should be given to some able men who had failed through bad luck: 'Perhaps this extra grace will enlarge their capacity for learning Russian at our dizzy pace.'[41] Most of those who failed were of commissioned rank. It may well be that there is a sociological reason for this: the Second World War had a notable democratizing effect. It became clear in the services that there were many of relatively low 'station' in life who possessed considerable talent which would be of benefit to the nation as well as to the armed services. It is clear that some of these men of working and lower middle class origin who were recruited from the 'other ranks' onto the Russian course and had no problems in competing on equal terms

---

[38] James and Harvey-Jones died within a few days of each other in January 2008. Their Russian training figures in their obituaries: of James in the *The Independent*, 21.1.08, pp. 10-11, and *Daily Telegraph*, 22.1.08, p. 35, and of Jones: (by Nicholas Faith) in *The Independent*, 14.1.08, p. 36.

[39] London: Cape, 1990, pp. 104-105.

[40] Courtney, p. 52.

[41] Cambridge University Archives SLAV I/B10.

with the public-school-educated officers. It should also perhaps be remembered that in those days city grammar schools, however long established or academically excellent, were regarded by the 'establishment' as 'not much class.'

Records show Hill's interest in educational technology for language learning: gramophone records, radio broadcasts from both BBC and Moscow Radio, and film. Military authorities, the electronics firm Pye of Cambridge and the Cambridge Arts Theatre were all enlisted to provide or install equipment, or to offer a venue for film showings. It takes nothing from Hill's energy and enterprise to say that she used the existence and importance of these courses to urge the Faculty of Modern and Medieval Languages to increase the staffing for Russian by one professor, one reader, two or three lecturers and three or two faculty assistant lecturers or lectors. At the time she was the sole lecturer in charge.[42] She also had an eye to life after the war and the survival of Russian: when they returned to civilian life 'they should be encouraged to complete their degrees in Russian [...] and this should help to solve the problem of providing teachers of Russian, research workers, Slavonic scholars and public servants.'[43]

One of the 200 servicemen trained in Russian at this time at Cambridge University was Peter Meades, an artilleryman who learned Russian on one of the first six-month courses in 1945. Six more months' training in technical Russian at Bad Saltzuffen gained him promotion to the dizzy heights of sergeant and a three-month stint interpreting in Hamburg for a team of Soviet officers who were overseeing the dismantling of a tractor factory which was to be sent to the USSR as reparations. He writes: 'By the end the Russians admitted I was fairly fluent.'[44] After this his experience replicates Ingram's: a great deal of time spent hanging around waiting for interpreting tasks, but none materialized. Again, Meades after demobilization made Russian his career, as a teacher at JSSL and later in higher education.

These stories illustrate two features of service life for linguists which call for comment. The first is that highly gifted, trained and qualified linguists were often rewarded by promotion no better than the level of a competent drill instructor. The Government could scarcely have attracted non-conscripts on this basis. Secondly, the failure to connect training with consequences will strike a chord with many who have served in HM Forces. The dislocation is not always so crass as it is in the case of Ingram and to a lesser extent Meades: the later services Russian courses had clear aims in terms of the job trainees were eventually to do, even if the teachers were not always allowed to know what they were exactly, and the students only discovered it when the training was nearly complete. But a happy feature of the Russian courses was that many intellectually gifted young men, whose gifts had never previously been noticed or who came from a class

---

[42]SLAV I/A1/1-107.
[43]SLAV A1/48. The memo is unsigned, but Hill's authorship can safely be assumed.
[44]Personal communicaton.

of society where education was thought to be not for the likes of them, were 'discovered'. It was demonstrated that men from the most diverse backgrounds were capable of intellectual achievements some of them had never dreamed of; and a not insignificant number who had before military service not considered going to university did so and eventually became distinguished professionals in various fields of endeavour. In 1984 B. F. Skinner wrote: 'Education is what survives when what has been learnt has been forgotten.' The services Russian courses discovered many who have forgotten all their Russian by now, but who received an induction into scholarship through the process of learning it. In a review of Elliott and Shukman's *Secret Classrooms* Catherine Andreyev expresses it exactly: 'Able people can be stretched and will enjoy the experience [...] When new areas of knowledge beckon, we meet on equal terms and [...] educational background and social standing are not important. If this could be properly applied in the current educational world we could drop much of the politically correct baggage with which we are saddled and get on with teaching our students the enjoyment of getting immersed in knowledge.'[45]

One may gain some wry amusement from a footnote to the Cambridge courses provided by that paranoid self-styled 'Spycatcher', Peter Wright. He had it in for the Cambridge course: it was 'a recruiting ground for the KGB'. Later Wright asserts that several MI5 employees who had learned Russian in the JSLS classes at Cambridge 'chose to leave', when unable to 'account for discrepancies in their backgrounds'; he continues that 'in the end we [presumably MI5] decided that the only safe thing to do was to close the school down.' A security problem was presumably to be dealt with by depriving the country of the opportunity to learn the very thing that might allow it to combat the treachery so feared. Needless to say, there was no question of these courses closing down. Wright's singular belief that the services Russian courses spawned spies was matched by a possibly apocryphal attack on them attributed to Andrei Vyshinsky, the chief Soviet representative at the United Nations, as 'spy schools'.[46] It has been assumed that Vyshinsky, if he ever really did make this remark, meant that they trained men to spy *against* the USSR. But one wonders if he was capable of irony: *The Times* commented in its issue of 1.12.51 (p. 6), 'To students of Russian Mr Vyshinsky's scorn is rarely inelegant.' Wright, in view of his obsession with the conflict between appearance and reality, would perhaps

---

[45]*Oxford Magazine*, Michaelmas Term 2002, p. 20.

[46]No-one who repeats this statement about Vyshinsky has been able to give chapter and verse; *The Times* digital archive carries no trace of the remark; I have spent far more time than is good reading Vyshinsky's UN speeches to spot it, without success; no-one I have contacted from JSSL has any recollection of hearing of it. Soviet diplomats of the period said many pretty foolish things, but it seems unlikely that Vyshinsky, living in a glasshouse of the fragility he did, would have thrown such a stone. None of this proves that Vyshinsky never said what is claimed, but I am forced to conclude that the story is simply an 'urban myth': an oft-repeated tale of no substance which gives satisfaction to those who repeat it. It reflects the paranoia of the post-war years, and it makes a good story.

imagine that Vyshinsky was acknowledging the assistance given to the KGB by these courses.

Immediately after the war several universities appointed as lecturers servicemen who had learned Russian or been active as interpreters during the war: Edward Sands and Peter Squire at Cambridge, John Fennell at Cambridge, Nottingham and later Oxford, Richard Freeborn at Manchester and SSEES and Frank Borras (who had taught himself Russian during idle moments while on not-very-active service) at Glasgow and later Leeds.

We have reached the stage—the decade of the 1950s—when Russian was poised for a leap forward in British education. Seeds sown in the first half of the century bore fruit, at least for a while. Though the scale of Russian teaching has significantly diminished more recently, we shall see that the present situation results both in its strengths and its weaknesses from the groundwork done by the pioneers whose activities we have seen before 1950.

Chapter 6

Poised for Expansion. Russian from the Late 1940s to the Early 1960s

The position of Russian language studies in Britain is steadily improving, though not yet nearly up to the standard which national requirements demand. Until Russian is widely taught in schools, progress must be inadequate.
    'A SPECIAL CORRESPONDENT' IN THE *MANCHESTER GUARDIAN*, 1958

IN December 1944 a significant exchange took place in the House of Commons in the debate on the King's Speech. The attitude of leading public figures to foreign language study was to change. Speaking on intellectual relations between Britain and the rest of Europe, the Foreign Secretary, Sir Anthony Eden, revealed that the matter had been discussed at the highest international level:

> Both the Prime Minister [Winston Churchill] and I discussed [the matter of languages] at Moscow with Marshal Stalin and Monsieur [V. M.] Molotov [Soviet Foreign Minister], [... and] the question of contacts between our two countries on a literary and language basis. There is no doubt that a very great effort is being made in Russia today in the teaching of English, and we have to get going to see that we do not drop far behind in a comparable effort on our part. [...] It is difficult to exaggerate the limitations which exist today owing to the language barrier. It is also difficult to over-estimate the importance of meeting them. One is apt only too easily to be old-fashioned and to think that particular languages which were taught in the nineteenth century still hold their position today. But all that is changed and certainly, as far as the Foreign Office examinations are concerned, [...] there is to be a readjustment in the languages which we propose to set for the examination.[1]

It is clear that Russian was the language of primary concern in the circumstances. Eden's priority was apparently not universities or secondary schools, but the Civil Service examinations. Educational institutions of all types, however, inevitably fed their former students into the diplomatic and political system.

Somewhat sinister developments were behind the motivation for Eden's speech. While it was not generally known to the public, a distinct cooling of

---

[1]Hansard, December 1944. 406 HC DEB.5.s., columns 291-293.

relations was beginning to be perceived in London. General Burrows, the head of the British Military Mission, had complained that the Soviets were increasingly reluctant to answer his questions, and in Autumn 1944 Stalin had personally demanded his recall to London. 'As the war in Europe drew to its close, the British FO was gradually forced to begin reappraising its policy towards Russia.'[2] Enquiry was not welcomed by the Soviets. The more Russian we knew, the less need we would have for direct questioning.

A more general concern was expressed on 9 March 1945 in a lengthy letter to *The Times* from W. J. Sedgefield, who had been active in university Russian for forty years. He proposed an approach to the teaching of the Russian language, by which should be established 'an organization for securing a body of students to serve as pioneers in the process of bringing together into a closer understanding the British and the Russian peoples.' Sedgefield regarded cultural and economic matters as interdependent, and sought a 'Central Institute' to oversee university studies in Russian, academic relations with such institutions in Russia and the Soviet Republics, to superintend exchanges of students, and to collect and disseminate information about Russia. In the political conditions which were shortly to establish themselves, much of this was to become unattainable. None the less, the optimism about Russian studies which the letter typifies and the awareness of the national need for knowledge of the field are significant.

The most vigorous response to the need for Russian came from the armed services, as we saw in Chapter 5. For two decades from 1945, services Russian, now including the Royal Air Force, was the backbone of the Russian-speaking profession in Britain, on which the universities and schools fed until they were in a position themselves to contribute to the pool of experts. The *Manchester Guardian* correspondent quoted here was right to point out that stability for Russian in higher education and consequently the value to the nation of knowledge of Russia would have eventually to be based on a firmer foundation than the armed services could provide. But for the moment the services did immense good to the study of the Russian language.

At Cambridge University there is a typescript 'Report on a visit to Germany by Dr Elizabeth Hill [...] in connexion with Russian language training, Nov. 10-18, 1946.'[3] The visit was at the invitation of the RAF. Hill attended a four-power meeting of the Control Authority, and found the Soviets 'formal and non-committal'. It contains much of interest, including some remarks on the nature of interpretership and the character of a good interpreter. Six months' intensive training, she reckoned, would produce a translator, but oral fluency and 100 percent accuracy required much longer. Hill encountered interpreters at the Allied Control Commission: while the British and French were smart, efficient and accurate, the Russians—after four years' training at the Language Institute in

---

[2]Glees, pp. 55-56.
[3]SLAV B10.

Moscow—possessed poor English pronunciation, and were inaccurate and slipshod through lack of knowledge of words and idioms. They interpolated remarks of their own and were not checked. 'I did not find any enthusiasm [among Russian officers] over the fact that so many more British were now able to understand and speak their language. [It] means one more line of Soviet defence broken down. They still repeat the old slogan that Russian is an impossible language for British people to learn, whereas my own experience has shown that this is a fallacy. If the British had the four years' training the Russian had, the results would be spectacular.'

This raises the general issue of language as politics. From the end of the war to the death of Stalin relations between East and West were fraught. Hill puts her finger firmly on the language issue: knowledge of Russian is a weapon in this conflict, and many more of the Soviets were expert in English than vice versa. When the US Ambassador to Moscow, George F. Kennan, was declared *persona non grata* and expelled in 1952, *The Times* (7 October 1952, p. 6) commented: 'Whatever else may be behind the Soviet attack on Ambassador Kennan, it is abundantly clear that his wide knowledge of [...] the Russian language worries and disturbs the Soviet rulers.' When Stalin died and diplomatic relations began to thaw, it was analysts at the United Nations whose linguistic study of Vyshinsky's speeches confirmed the new spirit. *The Times* again (9 April 1953, p. 6): 'Russian linguists again remarked on the distinct change in Mr Vyshinsky's vocabulary, which in its conciliation and positiveness, certainly seemed to accord with the new mood of the Kremlin.' Within a few years the USSR was on a different tack, much to the advantage of Russian language teaching.

Army, Navy and Air Force

For the moment, however, Britain was assembling a corpus of Russian linguists to break down the line of defence to which Hill referred. For about fifteen years after the Second World War a strong feature of British society was the existence of military service for males aged from 18. The term of service varied, but for much of the time it was of two years' duration. Modern journalists with a poor sense of the meaning of words sometimes refer to this as a 'draft': this word was never used in Britain, and it was in any case emphatically *not* a draft (in the dictionary definition of a 'drawing off of a party from some larger body for some special purpose [such as] military use') it was *universal* and compulsory for young men. Society had to take it into account: universities were required to defer entry for students, and employers were obliged to treat servicemen fairly when they were eventually demobilized. The country, particularly the transport system, swarmed with servicemen in uniform and civilian clothes; the burden on the Exchequer of maintaining the training, housing, feeding, transporting, and employment of these men–even though pay was nugatory–was phenomenal. But the State had at its disposal, or even at its mercy, an immense pool of manpower from all classes in society, everyone from the most to the least able. There was also, of course, a sizeable regular army, navy, and air force, which recruited abundantly from national servicemen: the bait was greatly enhanced pay and promotion for men who would 'sign on'. Some able men did just that. Russian was taught to both regulars and conscripts.

Chapter 5 noted some failure of the services to make use of the men who completed the courses in the 1940s. However, when the Soviet Union again became a bugbear to the Western powers, a need was perceived for military intelligence; no-one (on either side) knew what the future held or what the intentions of the Cold War opponents were. The Government realized that a pool of good Russian linguists should be created, and that they should be used. Training interpreters to sit around waiting for something to interpret was not going to suffice. The services were to set up and organize courses of their own, but the universities of London and Cambridge would still continue to be closely involved. During basic training potential linguists were found; sometimes officers approached likely candidates, and at other times volunteers were sought, interviewed and if found suitable despatched to the training schools. Some naval conscripts were destined for the Russian course even before enlistment.

The story of these Joint Services Schools for Linguists (JSSL) is told by Elliott and Shukman in *Secret Classrooms*; Hawkins provides an equally informative account particularly of later developments up to 1989 in *Russian Language Training in the Services*.[4] These writers trace the conception of the new services' Russian courses back to the FO Committee whose work was described in Chapter 5. They report that an Admiralty Russian course was operating at Mount Pleasant in London, and probably an Army course at Camberley, but the most ambitious venture was the RAF Russian-language school set up in 1949 at Kidbrooke, South-East London, with a British instructor (or perhaps two) and several Slav teachers of oral Russian. (At this stage the RAF counted trained interpreters in Slavonic languages as follows: serving airmen 25, released airmen 9, passed the Russian course 8, attending Russian course 17. Total: all languages Russian, Polish, Czech, and Rumanian, 59.[5]) Following Hill's work at Cambridge University on their behalf, the RAF took thirty students a year for training in Russian,[6] not all of them from the Air Force. They were both NCOs and officers, who took a twelve-month course.[7] This was in several ways an

---

[4] The late Brian Hawkins's book, excellent in the way it combines hard fact with illuminating and entertaining anecdote, is marred by having no proper title page and verso, no ISBN, no date, no publisher, and no place of publication. No discredit to Mr Hawkins, but as such one may see it as a typical Army cock-up. I am grateful to Mr R. Avery for information about Russian at Beaconsfield more recently, where he is Officer Commanding the Slavonic Languages Wing. Other publications giving accounts long or short of services Russian are those by Wade ('Eyes right...') and Woodhead. I have also drawn on the personal recollections of many other men and on my own experiences.

[5] AIR 2/10818, quoted by Jackson, p. 321.

[6] One trainee remembers more than this by 1951: forty or more.

[7] Elliott and Shukman, pp. 28-29; Hawkins p. 4.

experimental operation. David Haysom, who has researched the operation, writes in a private communication:[8]

> The course was made up of airmen and soldiers from all parts of the globe. two trainees were Merchant Navy during the war and had learned some Russian in Murmansk and Archangel on the North Atlantic convoys. Another had been a prisoner of war in Hong Kong, and yet another had fought with Tito's partisans.

A recruit onto the third cohort at Kidbrooke, Trevor Lloyd, a regular airman, has recalled in another private communication that it comprised a few naval trainees, a handful of army men, and the majority of airmen of all ranks.

The RAF called in their old friend Elizabeth Hill in 1949 to advise them, and her rigorous and detailed report survives: she praised the industry of the students, but criticized selection procedures (which had admitted some unsuitable students), the slow pace of progress (after six months the airmen were showing a level of achievement she felt should have been reached after four), and the failure to use Russian and English native speakers rationally. The slow progress she felt was due to the inability of the Russians to analyse the language and explain grammar to British students; they should be used exclusively for colloquial work. This division of labour was certainly a strong feature of the courses as they developed.[9] Hill was called in regularly for consultation, and invited to take part in the selection procedure. Mr Lloyd recalls being interviewed in 1950 by a board which included Hill; he was called upon to read aloud in German, a language in which he was knowledgeable, and translate what he had read extempore. The board was apparently satisfied.

The RAF was particularly anxious about the perceived threat from the USSR; a lightning air attack on NATO was to be prevented at all costs. Thirty linguists a year were not going to be enough. By 1949 the joint Intelligence Committee had accepted that a much larger operation was needed. Planning was undertaken (Elliott and Shukman give an account of this, pp. 29-38) and two JSSLs started operations in September 1951 at Coulsdon and Bodmin.

What was the real purpose of these newly established courses? The new 'push' for Russian (and some other languages too on a lesser scale) in the services was directly concerned with 'Sigint'—signals intelligence. The importance of the interception and decoding of radio traffic had been well understood long before the 1950s. It is said that orders were given—by whom is not clear, but in view of the importance of the matter it may have been Churchill himself—when Hitler attacked Russia that wireless intercepts were not be used as a source of intelligence about the Soviet Union. It is also said by some that such intercepts

---

[8] and also in his unpublished typescript 'Linguists, Languages and Schools.'
[9] Cambridge University Library, Elizabeth Hill Papers SLAVI/B 10.

could not be decoded; others say the opposite.[10] Serious signals intelligence by the RAF probably began in 1949 at Obernkirchen near Bückeburg.[11]

In the last three decades there has been a great expansion of academic research into this activity. Scholars report that immense efforts were made by British authorities to keep the history of intelligence secret. Not until decades after the War did the story of the decrypting of German and Japanese codes become known; in the 1980s the Thatcher administration still refused to admit (though everyone knew it) that GCHQ at Cheltenham had anything to do with military or diplomatic intelligence. The story of wartime intelligence was quicker to emerge than accounts of peacetime activities. Scholars now refer to the story of intelligence as the 'missing dimension' in the history of the Second World War and assert that Allied successes in the field were so far ahead of the Germans' that the War was shortened by three years. The literature of this relatively new subject is immensely interesting.[12] Great importance is attached to the work, even the mundane daily drudgery done by the linguists trained in Russian at JSSL. The duty of the 'translators' was to monitor radio traffic by Soviet forces and record it in writing for later analysis.

Over the relatively few years of the existence of the JSSLs, the courses varied in their organization. In outline, however, there were two distinct courses, which began together and bifurcated at an early stage. The methodology was progressive for its time and certainly effective. Educational psychology had not at that time–and probably has not since–really established how people learn foreign languages. Teachers follow their instincts. The system used at Bodmin was that students were taught grammar in large classes of around 40 and then in the following hour despatched to small groups (6 students in the early stages) for oral practice. Next session—grammar again; then groups, and so on. Interspersed once a day came military activities, intended as a change from intellectual work: physical training, rifle shooting, drill, cross-country runs—what the military mind conceives as a way of cultivating *mens sana in corpore sano*. I have no doubt it was very good for everyone.[13]

An inevitable weakness, not of the course, but of its basis, was the lack of appropriate teaching materials. A much-used course book was that by Anna H. Semeonoff which gave a thorough if dry and overwhelming account of the grammar of Russian. Accompanying this was Elizaveta Fen's *Beginner's Russian Reader*, and a weekly supply of—it must be said—not very inspiring ancillary material. Nevertheless, the great strengths of the training were the thoroughness of the grammatical approach, and the insistence by some, but not all, of the Slav

---

[10] The pros and cons are discussed by Glees, pp. 247ff.

[11] Jackson, p. 319.

[12] See items in Bibliography by Aldrich, Aid and Wiebs, Andrew and Dilks, Gaddis.

[13] The author of this account is writing from personal memories, and the reminiscences may not be entirely dispassionate.

teachers of the need to speak Russian in the classroom. Russian was employed sufficiently to overcome the psychological barrier of using it for everyday transactions. In later life I met one of the Russian native teachers. He commented from experience of meeting supposed linguists: 'If he went to JSSL, he'll speak Russian; if he didn't, he won't.' The Slavs might have been more consistent if more closely supervised: I have no recollection of a senior member of staff ever visiting a lesson in an advisory or supervisory capacity.

There were around twenty-four hours of language instruction a week and the expectation that students would do some homework. A feature of the courses was the regular assessment of progress. Whoever failed a major exam was sent back to some naval, army or air force unit and would probably find himself stoking up on a battleship or on 'general duties.' (This was the RAF euphemism for menial tasks.) Having failed the course there was no second chance for a national serviceman to train in another field. After about two months of the basic course there was usually a 'major' examination. Those who achieved a certain mark might be transferred to an advanced 'interpreters' course at Cambridge or London Universities—but only 'might': the conditions varied. In January 1956 all those in the army who passed the 'first major' were transferred to the university course, those in the navy and RAF were interviewed and it was decided whether or not they were of 'officer-like quality'. Some very good linguists (including the man who came top of the whole intake) were rejected.

After this watershed, the courses differed markedly. The 'university' men were made officer cadets and transferred to Cambridge or London universities for highly intensive courses. The purpose of this was not the radio monitoring, but simply to create a pool of excellent linguists for use in a future military emergency. There the cadets remained for twelve months. Course members at London remember five or six hours of instruction five days a week. There was grammar instruction based not on a published textbook, but on materials compiled by the teachers (which went beyond what any published grammar at the time contained); a good deal of 'extempore' translation from Russian was practised, and prose translation into Russian too: passages were not the 'gossamer wings' type of examination prose, but narrative and current affairs. Long lists of vocabulary, meticulously classified by gender and stress patterns, were set to be learned. One or more pages of a Soviet novel were set every day to be ploughed through in the students' own time and huge lists of vocabulary compiled; at first much of the grammar was beyond the students and comprehension was difficult; none the less, it was learning by immersion; the content had to be paraphrased in Russian in class. Oral proficiency was stressed. There were interpreting role-plays usually with a military scenario. Monthly tests were held, and to fail two consecutively was to be sent back to the translators' course.

A *kursant*[14] on the Cambridge course in 1953-54 reports:

> In the Cambridge course there was the same relentless ethos of the Forth Bridge being painted over and over again by Stakhanovites: grammar, translation, word lists and tests. There were also essays and lecturettes. The grammar was taught through the pellucid lectures of Dr Alexis Vlasto and the continued use of Semeonoff under motherly Mrs Hackel. We were thrown in at the deep end where we encountered nightmare monsters called participles long before they told us how to master them. The word lists—thirty words each day tested every Saturday morning—suggested that the Roget family had possessed a hitherto undivulged fluency in Russian. Afterwards we would troop off to the old Arts Cinema to watch Soviet film classics.[15]

After these twelve months the cadets returned to JSSL for six months' further military training. The aim was to add competence in technical language. A student on an early course reports that the desire of the military mind to instil a knowledge of 'real military life'—particularly that of the parade ground—led to a feeling among the cadets 'that we were in fact regressing.' A visit from George Bolsover, Director of SSEES, had a clear result: 'Shortly after his visit major changes were instituted.'[16] Some high jinks took place: once the Rag Queen at St Andrews University was kidnapped and held to ransom for charity. (A prominent participant in this escapade was later knighted and became Master of a Cambridge College.) At the end of the course the cadets were examined, and received a Joint Services Schools for Linguists certificate stating that they had 'qualified as a service interpreter' in an examination conducted by the Civil Service Commission. Forty percent in both written and oral sections was necessary to pass; 60% was considered second class, and 80% earned a first class award—but this mark was extremely difficult to achieve. To pass at any level was probably to have reached a standard at least as good as that of final degree standard in Russian language.[17] Successful students were either promoted to junior commissioned rank in the Reserve on completion of training or, if not thought suitable officer material, demoted to private for the last few weeks. The two years' national service period was then within sight of its conclusion: they were no more use to the services and their time was occupied by military trivia. Their function was merely to be added to the pool of linguists who would be useful in time of war.

Those who had not got onto the university courses, however, continued for about seven further months (this period was reduced in 1957 to five months) and

---

[14] The Russian word *kursant*, plural: *kursanty*, was regularly used to denote a student/participant on services Russian courses and it will henceforth be used here in this sense.

[15] Dr John Dunstan: personal communication.

[16] J. C. Q. Roberts, 'Marked for life', *Rusistika*, no. 25, 2002, pp. 3-4.

[17] I am grateful to George Avis and Dr Alan Suggate, both *kursanty* at London in 1955-6 or thereabouts for this description. See also Elliott and Shukman, pp. 148-167.

qualified as a 'service translator', a euphemistically expressed qualification which, in language terms, was above the standard of GCE A level. The certificates bear on the back a brief list of the tasks expected of the candidate: translation to and from Russian, essay in Russian, reading and conversation, dictation, 'written interpretership' (taking down in English a passage dictated in Russian). They then had three more months of training in signals intelligence at another military station, to enable them to work as radio monitors, tracking the activities of the Soviet army, navy or air force and recording it for analysis by those who knew more about it than they did. The training included much intensive work on listening skills: a regular method was to listen to tape-recordings of *tsyfry*—numerals read more and more quickly as the course progressed. This was an excellent way of making the recognition of numbers second nature; a vital skill in radio monitoring. However, one tutor decided to make the exercise even more difficult by introducing somewhat dissonant background music, which had the unintended effect of making one student throw down his pencil to wallow in Bartók, his favourite composer at the time.

Trevor Lloyd reports that the earliest Kidbrooke trainees received no such signals training; they were thrown in at the deep end in Germany and had to discover how to do the job for themselves. This must have been extremely difficult. He was shortly given the task of compiling teaching materials for use in the signals training at RAF Wythall.

Standards of assessment in these more practical skills were perhaps not so stringent as they had been on the language course. One former trainee remembers a sergeant announcing: 'You lot are having an exam next week, and, by the way, you've all passed!'[18] Promotion on completion of training was in the RAF to the rank of Junior Technician (below that of corporal).[19] The work which the linguists did when posted was moderately boring and infinitely repetitive. The boredom was relieved for some by the fact that it was done in a city, such as Berlin, where off-duty time, which was abundant, could be spent in a stimulating cultural environment. Not all were fortunate enough to serve in places like Berlin, however. Yet even elsewhere life could be enjoyed, as Peter Jackson's recent history of RAF Uetersen amply records.

What was the value to the country of this boring and repetitive work done by the linguists? Many had the impression that it was pointless; what could have been the purpose of writing down over and over again, 'one, two three four five; how do you receive me?', 'permission to take off', 'am approaching landing', 'undercarriage down' along with all the coded call signs? Professor Richard Aldrich has no doubts: he is quoted by Leslie Woodhead: 'That monitoring of

---

[18] Woodhead, p. 85.

[19] No further certificate was provided to servicemen on completion of training. My own certificate of discharge from the RAF bears the following laughably mendacious description of the work of a Linguist: 'Records the language in which qualified, and after suitable training, translates and assists in the preparation of summaries.' This nonsense raises the issue of secrecy, to which we shall return.

Soviet pilots was absolutely critical for East-West reassurance [...] Any large animal makes a noise when it moves, and the Soviet armed forces [were] a very large animal. Essentially what you were doing was listening out for any unusual rustling in the jungle as this animal begins to assume an attack posture.' He sums it up: 'The intelligence services were the cutting edge of the Cold War.'[20]

The *esprit de corps* which developed on these courses—though the participants might well have denied it at the time—was strong. Many reunions of groups of *kursanty* take place to this day; there is an RAF Linguists' Association which along with former RAF Gatow (Berlin) Sigint operators maintain websites. A naval equivalent group existed until recently. It is an interesting example of the way an intensive educational and professional experience induces 'bonding' in a way that many men found positive.

Certain of the facts recounted in the paragraphs above in theory contravene the infamous Official Secrets Act. Because they have been recounted by Elliott and Shukman, by Leslie Woodhead's television documentary *My Life as a Spy* and his book with the same title, and because they have become a subject for serious academic research, even the regular appearance of scholarly journals devoted to the subject, it is unlikely now that the author of this book will be carried off to prison for relating them. This fate awaited certain undergraduates at Oxford in 1958, who were unwise enough to mention these matters in print in the student journal *Isis* of 26 February 1958, and—to the disgrace of public justice—were briefly jailed for so doing. The article mentioned further facts about British 'ferreting' operations: sending out aircraft or ships to provoke Soviet response in order to test their capabilities, and so on. The Lord Chief Justice of England presided at their trial, which perhaps further indicates that the 'system' at that time was unhealthily obsessed with secrecy and had not yet experienced modern desire for openness. Oddly, what was revealed by the student authors was reprinted in the news columns of *The Times* on 22 May 1958, p. 6, and amounted to little that reasonably aware people did not know already. The students' aim as supporters of nuclear disarmament was to highlight the dangers of a conflict arising from provocation by British agencies. Some might think this an exaggerated fear, but its expression in *Isis* led to a serious question in the House of Commons on 19 March which was given a reply by the Secretary of State for Air which can only be described as evasive. A pantomime was acted out in which certain evidence was heard in camera (what this can have been—other than an admission by the authorities that the statements in the article were true—is left to the imagination). It is a sorry tale, and it is to be hoped that all those involved have long since repented their part in it. The Chief Justice, it must be said, fell over backwards to impose a mild sentence in conditions not too

---

[20] Quoted by Woodhead, pp. 242-243. Professor Aldrich has confirmed to me this account of his remarks, but in view of later research, he considers that he would have added that the fruits of the intercepts were by no means always passed on to those that needed the information. Those who have ever been in the armed services will recognise this symptom of institutional inefficiency.

uncomfortable for the students. He felt that a custodial sentence was necessary in order to avoid 'making a farce of the Official Secrets Act'.[21] The Act was made a thorough farce of in more recent years when the authorities omitted even to prosecute a woman who was known to have spied actively for Russia for fifty years, not to mention the notorious Mr Blunt.[22]

The incident illustrates that the military mind and academic attitudes do not necessarily mix, but there are aspects of service life which benefit learning. Schoolchildren and undergraduates are not paraded at 8.15 every morning and marched to classes; soldier students are. Classes could not be missed, students could not stay in bed however little they fancied getting up. While conduct of classes by the civilian teachers was invariably gentlemanly, students were subject to military discipline, and if they failed to learn, it was not due to a dilatory approach to attendance and punctuality. However, the services and the academics did come into conflict. One senior teacher writes of 'the hell of teaching academically in the teeth of unsympathetic military management.' A dispute over unreasonable punishments led to the acting Principal of the JSSL at Crail being ordered off the camp by the acting Commandant, only to be reinstated when the actual Commandant returned from leave and had his deputy posted.[23]

A feature of the organization of the courses which bore on the nature of the teaching was their staffing, in particular the use of émigré Eastern Europeans, for the most part fairly elderly ones. Some were not Russians; most of those who were had fled the country thirty years previously; they actually imparted the Russian of the early 1900s, and it had changed, both in pronunciation and

---

[21] The story may be read in *The Times* for 1958: 20 March, p. 5, 18 July, p. 5, 19 July, p. 4. The Navy exerted pressure on the defendants by calling them them up as reservists, an action *The Times* sardonically called an 'unfortunate coincidence' (5 May, pp. 7 and 11, 6 May, p. 7.)

[22] The whole issue of secrecy is of great interest, and deserves a footnote to the work of service intelligence collectors who used the Russian language to carry out the task. The Official Secrets Act demands total silence from all who sign it about absolutely anything learned from official sources. This is both ludicrous and unenforceable. More seriously, it actually hinders worthwhile intelligence work. National servicemen had no choice: they must do as they are told, but intelligent civilians employed by GCHQ apparently dropped out of the work in large numbers because they were not informed of the value to the state of the work they were required to do, and consequently had little job satisfaction. The most telling incident, which reveals official attitudes in the 1980s at least, is recounted by Detective Chief Superintendent David Cole in the excellent popular book in which he recounts his investigation into the crimes of the spy and sexual offender Geoffrey Prime, who had trained as a Russian linguist and who worked at RAF Gatow, Berlin. When preparing the case for the prosecution of Prime, Cole reports that he received total cooperation from everyone, with one exception: the top management of GCHQ, the body which Prime had betrayed to the Soviets. These guardians of national security issued a 'point-blank refusal' of cooperation, and gave Cole the distinct impression that he and his investigation were nothing but a 'thorough bloody nuisance' and a threat to the secrecy which they so jealously guarded—above even national security. He describes them as 'reluctant, obstructive or obtuse'. It took the intervention of the Director of Public Prosecutions, Sir Thomas Hetherington, to remind these highly placed persons that their duty to society and to the state was of greater importance than maintaining GCHQ as a secret garden. (Cole, pp. 157-158.)

[23] Private information from George Bird, the Principal concerned.

vocabulary. They did not teach the linguistic register sometimes needed by military translators; colloquial youth slang and some obscenity would have been useful in deciphering the occasional tantrums of Soviet tank and air crew. The British teachers were not allowed to visit Russia for security reasons and consequently were totally reliant on their Russian colleagues for oral support. Nevertheless, many of them had a phenomenally good command of the language. Politically speaking, the situation was interesting: it was neutral. Any reference to politics was, in my experience, tangential, and students were not indoctrinated. The native speakers might have been expected to be hostile to the USSR; they probably were, but on the whole they did not peddle such notions in class. In any case, intelligent young men discount propaganda, so that any attempt at political influence would have been resisted. Doubtless all shared a strong wariness towards the Soviet Union: the 1950s were, after all, the decade of Stalin's death and of the very slow emergence of the USSR from isolation under Khrushchev. Moreover, one met very few of the starry-eyed enthusiasts, teachers or students, who took the *Daily Worker* as gospel, who denied the excesses of Stalin, and who imagined the USSR was a workers' paradise.

The consequences of the JSSL courses have still not been fully assessed. It is calculated that around 5,000 men successfully completed instruction at JSSL either as interpreters (the 'university' courses) or as so-called 'translators'. Systematic research has not tried to establish exactly what happened to all alumni of both courses. But a climate of opinion favourable to Russian studies, Russian culture, and Russian affairs was created in all sorts of areas. Historians, theatre directors, scientists and technologists, business people, media pundits, novelists and dramatists, civil servants, and teachers of other subjects had all undergone thorough training in Russian in the services. The massive expansion of area studies in universities and other research establishments since 1960 is in large part due to this corpus of expertise which in its turn was due to the JSSLs.

JSSL, then, both rescued and enabled the expansion of Russian studies. Without the JSSLs, numbers of students in the 1950s and early 1960s would have been minuscule, recruits to the school-teaching profession would have been fewer, and university departments would have lacked some of their best and most respected lecturers and professors. Without this ready-made body of men the subject might well have quickly faded from the scene.

By 1959, with national service in process of abolition, the university courses were closing down, and the translators' courses were contracting. JSSLs had often been situated in very small towns: that at Bodmin (5,500 inhabitants) had been moved bodily to Crail, a Fifeshire town of little more than 1,500, at Easter 1956. The camp alone almost equalled this, with 718 students and 30 civilian teaching staff, not counting the military establishment.[24] It was considered by

---

[24]Figures supplied by Crail Museum Trust. The leaflet *Crail Airfield*, 2004, reports that, in addition, as many as 500 reservists each year were recalled to Crail for refresher courses.

the authorities that Russian language training in the services should continue after 1959, but that the camp at Crail was unsuitable; costs of running the courses had increased astronomically.[25] The separate services went their own way. The teaching of Russian continued, but it was no longer the mass operation it had been in the 1950s. Nevertheless, many of the ex-students of the JSSLs were positioned to make a major contribution to Russian, Slavonic and Soviet studies.

HIGHER EDUCATION. The Scarbrough (1947) and Hayter (1961) Reports

The work of these committees and of the Annan Commission (1962) spreads over fifteen years. They were all closely linked in the furtherance of Russian studies. Scarbrough and Hayter dealt also with Oriental, East European and African Studies. Sir William Hayter's Sub-Committee was set up specifically to review developments consequent on the recommendations made in 1947 by the Earl of Scarbrough's Committee; frequent reference is made in the Hayter report to work being done concurrently by the committee chaired by Noel Annan on Russian in schools.[26]

Scarbrough and Hayter are both emphatic that the teaching of languages is not their prime concern: it is 'the interpretation to the British people of the whole way of life of these peoples.' (p. 6) The 1947 Report arose out of the post-war concern that Britain should not remain ignorant of important regions of the world; language was a means to ending this ignorance. The Scarbrough Committee was not to confine its investigation to universities, but recognized that it was only Russian which was taught to any extent outside higher education. Their broad conclusion was that existing provision was 'unworthy of our country and people.' Further, 'it would be harmful to the national interest to allow the present state of affairs to continue.' (p.8)

The current situation had been researched for Scarbrough by a Foreign Office (FO) Committee on Russian Studies. It had been considering the future of relations with the USSR ever since the signing of the Anglo-Soviet Treaty of Alliance on 25 May 1942. The Committee was set up with inter-departmental agreement; it first met in 1944, was chaired by Sir Orme Sargent, and among its members were several invited academics. Its findings do not appear to have been published in full, but they saw the light of day as *Russian Studies*, Circular 81 of the Ministry of Education.[27] (The authors of Appendix E of the Scarbrough Report base many of their remarks upon this.) Circular 81 is a mere three pages

---

[25] Elliott and Shukman give an account of the need for change, pp. 204-205.

[26] Sir William Hayter was a former British ambassador in the USSR, Lord Scarbrough was a former Parliamentary Private Secretary to Anthony Eden, had been Governor of Bombay, and a serving officer in both world wars. Mr N. G. Annan was Provost of King's College, Cambridge.

[27] R. E. F. Smith appears to have seen the full report (*A Novelty*); I. W. Roberts, pp. 47-48, gives some information which is not in the Circular and which may be found in the 'Foreign Office Committee on Russian Studies' archive (see below).

long, but is very much to the point. It devotes equal attention to Russian in technical and commercial colleges on the one hand and schools on the other. Three hundred students were estimated to be studying Russian in technical colleges in London alone and to be reaching a useful standard of proficiency, but few of these were doing so with much encouragement from employers. Soviet trade being a state monopoly, commercial contact was limited, but firms needed economic analysts who could read Russian; technicians 'who may spend short periods in Russia erecting plant should again lead firms to wish to encourage the study of the Russian language'. (p. 2) The Circular regrets the tendency to close down courses at advanced stages when support dwindles, arguing that this penalizes those students who are keenest. It was seen as important to bridge the gap between pure language work and 'the broader knowledge of Russian culture'. As for schools: 'development of the teaching of Russian in schools is the basis for an advance of Russian studies in all spheres.' Teachers were therefore needed; pupils should not be discouraged from taking up Russian at school by examination standards which are far too high (aimed at native speakers, it is said) for those who have only had very limited opportunity at school to study the language. (pp. 2-3)

The work of the FO Committee on Russian Studies is largely concealed from public view, except for two fairly substantial files which survive in the National Archives. This material[28] fleshes out the picture of government concern to foster Russian studies in the mid-1940s. Considerable efforts were made over student and teacher exchanges, library facilities, administration of higher education, the purchase of books in the USSR for British libraries; a serious attempt was made to compile a union catalogue of Russian-language holdings in British libraries.[29] A civil servant, a Miss Tripp, was sent to Moscow and Leningrad to find out about Russian libraries. For some reason which is not clear there was great interest in the Soviet handbook for entrants to higher education; a translation of it was made, and Miss Tripp was asked to look out for further copies when in Moscow. Foreign Office employees formed a FO Russian Language Society with printed notepaper, and began to explore the notion of a study visit to the Soviet Union. The British Embassy, claiming to be too busy and citing the shortage of hotel rooms in Moscow, thought the idea was 'not to be encouraged at the moment'. They also feared the Soviets would not agree to such a trip unless they saw some propaganda advantage to themselves; moreover, doubtless from personal experience, they foresaw the dangerous effect of vodka on the civil servants. They 'might talk freely under the influence of Soviet hospitality about the workings of the [Foreign] Office.'[30]

---

[28] FO 371/56827 and 56828.

[29] I have been unable to discover what became of this catalogue; the papers in the National Archives (Documents N 1059 and N 6231) show that it was financed by the National Central Library.

[30] Document N 3791.

Civil servants kept a close eye on the national press. Energetic attempts were made to persuade the Soviets to allow exchanges of students—totally without success, owing to Soviet intransigence and obstruction. Numerous promises had been made by eminent people, but no results were ever forthcoming. There is disagreement among civil servants on occasion, as we shall see, and it is clear that the Scarbrough Report was seen not merely as an educational issue, but a matter of foreign policy concern. It must be said that some papers rather seem to show that some officials lacked a firm desire to make progress and were very good at seeing the objections to any course of action. The Books and Periodicals Sub-Committee were unable to make any recommendation for the procedure for acquiring books from the Soviet Union—it surely should not have been beyond their wit to devise something. The file in the National Archives contains a document summing up the work of the Committee on Russian Studies up to mid-1946: disappointment with failure over exchanges, moderate satisfaction with some good work on books and libraries, and satisfaction that support of the Scarbrough Commission had been worthwhile.

The different perspectives of education and foreign policy personnel can be spotted in one or two revealing extracts. There is, for example, a short cutting from the *Daily Express* reporting in telegram-style brevity a talk by Storr-Best at the Conference of Educational Associations. The *Express* cannot always be relied on for complete accuracy, but the Doctor is quoted as urging the government to renew attempts to set up exchanges with the USSR which had been abandoned in 1924, to establish training courses for Russian teachers at Sheffield University (as had been urged by Pares in the 1930s), and to persuade the London County Council to set up Russian classes in evening institutes; this would all contribute, said Storr-Best, to 'clear away much of the fog of mistrust between Britain and the Soviet.' This is contemptuously dismissed by the author of a memorandum attached to the cutting; the final remark is described as rubbish, the first two suggestions are ignored and the third is said to be due to ignorance, since the LCC did in fact run such courses. Dr Storr-Best can safely be ignored, is the conclusion. It is a pity that there were FO officials at this time who regarded Russian studies as unlikely to do much to 'clear away [...] the fog of mistrust'; the FO has not always taken this view.

According to R. E. F. Smith, an early draft of this FO report contained a certain recommendation, which he quotes thus:

> Whilst recognizing the valuable services rendered in the past by teachers of Russian origin (but not Soviet citizens), the Sub-Committee feels that their employment in future (except possibly in junior language and literature posts) would not be in the best interests of Anglo-Soviet co-operation or indeed of the development of Russian studies in this country. Poles who, after the conclusion of hostilities, are unable or unwilling to return to Poland should also not normally be employed as teachers of Russian.

Smith's conclusions are that these remarks 'demonstrate how desperately short the country was of competent teachers and scholars in the Russian field. [...] Not all Russian émigrés were as competent as Konovalov—there were [...] some adventurers.'[31] However, the spirit of the quoted remarks is both distasteful and sinister, returning to the notion of a 'Russian passport' (or in this case a Soviet passport) as a necessary qualification for teaching, the very idea which was ridiculed by Trofimov in 1916, and which no university teacher of principle could possibly support. It is hard also not to see it as 'invertebrate internationalism', in H. J. Chayter's words quoted in a previous chapter: for goodness' sake let us not do anything which might conceivably offend the Soviets! Professor Ewart of Oxford deplored the idea that a person teaching Russian should have to be *persona grata* with the Soviet Union. 'It would be a menace to academic freedom.'[32] However, clearly not all FO civil servants deserved Hugh Dalton's epithet: 'the palsied pansies of the FO'.[33] It is refreshing to read a typed comment with an illegible signature gummed to one paper: 'I am relieved to note that the malicious [sic] recommendation urging a ban on the teaching of Russian by émigré Russians has not been reproduced in the Ministry of Education Circular [...] This entirely unjustifiable political gesture could only result in a still greater lowering of Russian standards in a country where very few natives speak the Russian language even relatively well.'

The explanation of the inclusion of these regrettable remarks in the FO report lies in the personality of a civil servant crucial to the deliberations of the committee: Christopher Hill. Hill, in later life an academic historian, was at that time a member of the Communist Party, a fact he had never concealed, but which the FO apparently knew not or cared not about. The suggestion was that Russian in British educational institutions should be in many cases in the hands of teachers recommended by Soviet authorities; émigrés should be dismissed. Hill's position of strong influence within the FO may not in other ways have conflicted with his communist convictions. His own answers to these contradictions are reported, and demolished, by Glees. (pp. 279-288)

The Scarbrough Report remains totally silent on the role in the development of Russian studies of expatriate Russians resident in Britain. That contribution was enormous, and moreover one of the members of the Russian sub-group (Konovalov himself) was precisely such an expatriate.

The Scarbrough committee recognized that numbers of undergraduates might not increase very much, and at the same time urged that this fact should not be allowed to hinder development of research and teaching. It is obvious that the twenty-first century notion—that study should be carried out by academics only if they could prove 'value for money' and earn funds for their universities by collecting fees from students to cover their costs—was not to take hold for many years. The wider teaching of Russian (and other languages and subjects within

---

[31] Smith, *A Novelty*, p. 32; he quotes certain archive papers which I have not been able to trace.

[32] I stumbled on a copy of Professor Ewart's letter in Cambridge University Archives SLAV I/A.

[33] Kitchen. p. 31.

the Committee's remit) in schools was supported, not only as a means of stimulating the supply of undergraduates, but to contribute to wider knowledge of the country in the general population. Following the appearance of the Report, a conference of university Russian teachers chaired by Elizabeth Hill in May 1948 urged heads of secondary schools 'to become aware of the importance of Russian and consider its value as a second modern language.'[34] The oft-quoted recommendation, originating even before the Leathes Report of 1918, resurrected by the FO Committee and published in Ministry of Education Circular 81, that Russian in secondary education should reach the same extent 'as German is taught today', (p. 128) was to be repeated in the Annan Report and, of course, never realized.

The first principal recommendation of the Report was for the 'building up of an academic tradition comparable in quality and in continuity with those of the major humanities and sciences.' (p. 69) This was to be achieved by strengthening departments, by maintaining a balance between languages and related subjects, by closer integration with the humanities and sciences as a whole, by providing more opportunities for graduate research in Britain and abroad, by increasing library stock, by encouraging visits abroad by staff (no easy matter in 1947) and by welcoming exchange teachers from abroad.

As a means to achieving the strengthening of university departments of Russian, the Committee was in a dilemma, and came close to wanting to eat its cake and have it. While Russian at the time was being taught in twelve universities, it recommended that Russian should be concentrated in five of them: Cambridge, Oxford, SSEES, another English university, and Glasgow. The trouble was that it did not wish to discourage Russian elsewhere, and in fact it would have been very difficult and embarrassing for the persons involved in making the recommendation to do so, since they were the heads of department at Oxford, Cambridge and Glasgow. By the time the Hayter Sub-Committee reported, there were thirteen university departments teaching Russian, only three of them of any size, and eight more institutions seeking to start departments. The Scarbrough recommendation of concentration had been—and continued to be— widely disregarded, not least by government, which had spread the grants more thinly, so that the 'wide dispersal of effort in relation to the number of students being taught' was already being seen as a danger sign for the future. Hayter agreed in principle that 'a university is not a university unless it can offer its students the opportunity to learn Russian', but felt that this notion 'conflicted with the practical possibilities.' (p. 89) Indeed the report stated directly that 21 was too many. (p. 91) This bird came home to roost in 1979, when demand for places to study Russian fell so far short of supply that closures of departments and retirements and re-deployment of staff occurred, leaving a trail of bitterness and disappointment which survives to this day.

---

[34]'Study of Russian', *The Times*, 8 May 1948, p. 3.

In the second place Scarbrough recommended 'the provision of appropriate training for careers in the countries concerned', and in the third, 'the satisfaction and development of the growing interest in these regions among the general public.' (p. 69) There were suggestions as to how these aims might be achieved. The proposals were costed, and it was recommended that in ten years interested departments of state should hold a joint review to assess progress. (p. 72)

The Scarbrough Report was an immense encouragement to the Slavonic Studies profession both in terms of finance and of morale among academics. The Hayter and, indirectly, the Annan Reports reinforced this feeling at an interval of a decade and a half. The recommendation: 'For an initial period, financial assistance should take the form of special earmarked grants' (p. 72) was accepted, but rescinded in 1952, to the dismay of departments of Oriental as well as Slavonic studies. (Hayter, p. 22) By 1961 Hayter had a number of other reservations. 'The overall pattern of development of Oriental and Slavonic studies [is] disappointing.' 'The British education system is still centred on western Europe, with an occasional bow to North America and the Commonwealth. This seems to the Sub-Committee anachronistic.' (p. 3) Disappointment was expressed that money for new posts had gone disproportionately to language departments, when the intention had been to encourage area studies. Too many universities were entering the field. Not enough research was being done on Slav countries, and the number of students outside of language departments who come into contact with the ideas, history and problems of the non-western world should be increased. Despite all this the tone of Hayter is optimistic, particularly as regards what was at the time seen as the likelihood of Russian in schools increasing.

In the 1930s, Bernard Pares had argued for Russian in schools on the grounds that university studies were very difficult for students without Higher School Certificate. The notion of Russian being taught *ab initio* at university was at that time strange to the university teacher—at least as regards those students with a degree as their aim. Hayter too took this line. The National Service Russian courses ended around 1960, and universities were no longer being fed by young men (they were exclusively men) well trained in Russian; the universities had to teach from scratch. Hayter propounds the argument that for a university teacher to have to sink to the level of 'routine' language teaching is totally inappropriate, nay, even 'frustrating' and 'stultifying'. (p. 93) In the intervening years, many university teachers have come to see that there is intellectual challenge and stimulation in *ab initio* language teaching; they have written teaching materials and devised courses. They have, in fact, had no choice: input from the schools has never provided the undergraduates to make their departments fully viable.

Not all university Russian departments supported Russian in schools. In response to the FO Report the University of Birmingham noted: 'We do not feel that Russian ever can or should be a main subject for school teaching. The most that schools should do is provide such teaching in Russian as may make it easy for students to take Russian as a subsidiary or main subject at university.'[35]

University expansion

Though the Scarbrough Commission had been uneasy about uncontrolled expansion of Russian departments, the fact that the subject did expand clearly reflects a widespread awareness in the academic community that Russian was vital to the national interest.

The *Universities Quarterly* contained three articles on Russian in 1953. George Bolsover provided an overview and used familiar arguments on trade and international relations. He also remarked that 'in a few extremist quarters' anyone who learns Russian is regarded as a communist. Bolsover closes with these words: 'The sooner the universities and schools advance together in establishing Russian studies on a broader and firmer basis, the better equipped Britain will be to face the many problems which Soviet Russia has created for the world in which we live.' (p. 232)

Hugh Seton-Watson moves away from the idea of Russian being a niche for the specialist towards its role as an important part of the background of many a professional person in other fields: 'it may even be argued that, for a British administrator or teacher in Nigeria, the careers of Dmitri Tolstoy and Stolypin are more revealing than those of Peel and Gladstone.' (p. 237) H. M. Hayward, then Head of Russian at Leeds, urges for more time to be given to language work and proposes four-year degree courses to cope with the necessity of teaching Russian *ab initio*. In this connection it may be significant that a few years later another university teacher, Ronald Hingley, commented publicly on the inadequacy of university language teaching. He declared that when he was running one of the military Russian courses at London University, they 'had sent to them graduates whose Russian was not equal to that of servicemen who had started from scratch three months previously.' He concluded that universities did not teach Russian, they assumed a knowledge of it.[36] He also deprecated the stress placed on airy-fairy prose composition tests, which were sometimes so difficult that it was impossible to place the students' attempts in order of merit.

It was therefore again the JSSL methods which created expectations of what intensive courses in higher education should be like. These issues soon came to the forefront of attention: new departments appointed teaching staff who had been gifted schoolteachers and who did not see routine language teaching merely as a 'frustrating' activity.

This was not the only element in the life and work of university departments of Russian and Slavonic studies in the 1950s which was changing. Many univer-

---

[35] Cambridge University Archives: Elizabeth Hill Papers, SLAV I.

[36] 'Varsity Russian not adequate', by a Reporter, *Sunday Times*, cutting undated; internal evidence suggests January 1960.

sities were employing younger staff: for example, John Fennell was only 34 when appointed to head the Nottingham department in 1952. While this department had for many years taught Russian to quite large numbers of non-degree students, it and others were moving towards 100 percent candidates for degrees. At Nottingham in 1952 there were only two such students; by 1957 it had become eleven. This picture was replicated in many universities: recruitment was to a large extent from former JSSL students, and it was almost exclusively male. Statistics of numbers of university students across the United Kingdom were collected and published in desultory fashion by central government at this time, and it is often hard to know how to interpret them. The way the figures are presented varies from year to year. For the years 1957/58 to 1964/65 the table is entitled *'Estimated* numbers of students obtaining university first degrees... Central and East European languages and studies.' (italics added) It seems more than likely that about 80-85% of the numbers given are for Russian, as the ratio of Russian to other E. European languages in 1965 onwards is about 5: 1. However, we have no easy way of knowing how many graduates had studied two languages, Russian and another, for their degree. This table shows 49 students in the academic year 1957/58 rising steadily to 93 in 1964/65.[37]

In 1960 there were thirteen British universities teaching Russian, seven of which received earmarked grants (following the Scarbrough Report) for building up strong Slavonic departments: Birmingham, Cambridge, Glasgow, London, Manchester, Nottingham, and Oxford. The others were Liverpool, Edinburgh, Bangor, Exeter, Keele, and Leeds. Around 80 teaching staff were employed in Russian studies, a figure which was to rise to about one hundred by 1965, and about 70 honours degrees in Slavonic Studies, mainly Russian, were awarded. The services courses had wound down, but meanwhile 1958-59 had marked an increase in Russian in schools, though it would take a few years for pupils to work up to Advanced Level GCE, the relatively new qualification for university entry. In 1959 sixty-six candidates had passed A levels in England and Wales, by 1963, 293 were successful. Figures in Scotland are not published. However, fourteen more universities had started, or were planning to start Russian departments by 1964: Aberdeen, Aberystwyth, Lancaster, East Anglia, Bristol, Durham, Hull, St Andrews, Swansea, Sussex, Reading, Southampton, and York. The Hayter Report rightly feared that the slow increase in schools Russian would not support this expansion: it represented 'an increased vitality, but a decreased virtuosity'.[38] Birmingham, Leeds, and Liverpool were meeting this problem by admitting students to study Russian *ab initio* onto four-year courses. The Hayter Report had pressed for non-literary studies, and had pressed for new posts: Oxford and SSEES had acceded to this recommendation. Cambridge had always taught Russian history to undergraduates. Birmingham, Glasgow, and Oxford

---

[37]*Statistics of Education Part 3, 1965*, London: HMSO, 1967: Table 57.

[38]Hayter, p. 31.

were offering courses principally centring on Soviet affairs, but the last two of these universities were doing so to post-graduate students only. By October 1964 twenty universities were offering courses where Russian language was essential. Five hundred new students were expected at subsidiary or primary level, 150 of these would be reading for honours degrees.[39]

As a footnote to the specifically British situation, it may be noted that Trinity College, Dublin had introduced Russian in 1959. As for government policy, the Republic of Ireland inevitably ploughs its own furrow. However, on the academic front there was cooperation and exchange of staff and ideas. An Irish Association of Slavists was founded in 1975 and straddled the border, embracing from the Republic Trinity College, the National University, and the National Institute of Higher Education in Limerick, along with the two Ulster departments which existed at the time: the New University of Ulster and Queen's University at Belfast.[40] Jumping ahead in time, by the end of the century, only Trinity College survived in the whole of Ireland; the situation in schools in the Republic, however, may now in 2008 be a little more promising.

Many of the departments in British universities were small. There was a fair amount of travelling by lecturers from university to university, without which a rounded curriculum could not have been offered. Language teaching, despite Hingley's strictures, was improving, and in many departments it reached a very high standard. Opportunities for students to visit the Soviet Union and extend their knowledge of Russian there were still limited. Hopes had been raised in 1954, when a Labour Party delegation led by Clement Attlee visited the Soviet Union; the Rector of Moscow University indicated that exchanges with foreign countries would be welcomed. A flurry of correspondence in the press and a leading article in *The Times* followed in an attempt to encourage the notion. However, the most percipient contribution to this correspondence was by John Clews, International Vice-President of the National Union of Students. He wrote:

> It goes without saying that the Soviet student in this country will be treated just as any other visitor, free to go where he likes [...] If reciprocity is to mean anything, then the British student in the USSR should have the same freedoms. If he wants to hitch-hike to the Baltic States from Leningrad, then he should be able to do this [...] If scholarship is to mean anything, then the British student must be able to refer to all editions of Soviet publications, to all source material, not just that currently in favour. [...] The British student in Russia can only achieve what Professor Atkinson has in mind [...] if he has all the necessary material made available to him.[41]

---

[39] For a fuller account, see Richards, 'Russian in the Universities, 1964.'

[40] See Bannister; and Wheeler, 'Irlandskaia assotsiatsiia slavistov'.

[41] *The Times*, 18 August 1954, p. 7. The rest of the correspondence may be read in *The Times*, 12.8.54 p. 6, 17.8.54 p. 7, 19.8.54 p. 7, and 20.8.54 p. 7.

Just so! But there was little hope of this. It was only at the end of the decade and in the early 1960s that systematic student exchanges were instituted. British students in Russia were subject to supervision and control, even if is was erratic and inefficient. As for teachers, most of them had never visited Russia, except for a few of a slightly older generation who had served there during the war. By 1958 an annual four-week visit by 25 or 30 (it varied from year to year) school and university teachers was introduced. These continued for many years, and apart from allowing teachers to improve their language skills, they provided a forum for them to meet. School teachers almost invariably worked alone in a school, and contact with colleagues was greatly valued. By 1960 a small number of postgraduate students, some in Russian studies, the rest in other subjects, were being exchanged for a year at a time. Extended periods in Russia for undergraduates came a few years later.

There were, however, occasional expeditions by students to the USSR. Harold Shukman recalls as an undergraduate taking part in a three-week delegation on the invitation of the Anti-Fascist Committee for Soviet Youth in 1954.[42] Some young people recall with pleasure a massive youth congress in Moscow in 1957. The propaganda purpose of such events was obvious and many of the meetings (as with the teacher exchanges referred to above) were somewhat false and even a little embarrassing, but nevertheless it allowed interchange to take place. University departments which sent their undergraduates abroad to improve their spoken Russian still tended to do so by despatching them to Russian émigré families in France or other western countries.

Resurgence of the subject in schools

An early sign that the modern language teaching profession and indeed the teaching profession in general were both open to the idea of Russian in schools was the first edition of *The Teaching of Modern Languages*, published by the Incorporated Association of Assistant Masters in Secondary Schools IAAM) in 1949. The only paragraph devoted to Russian in this first edition is very brief, but strongly expressed: '[Russian] ranks [...] as a "world-language", and, though its essential difficulty makes it unlikely that it will be taught as a full school subject, we should be well advised to augment the small facilities that exist for the study of this language, as well as of the literature, history and social organization of the country with which we have made a twenty-year alliance.'[43]

Important steps forward in the development of Russian in schools took place in the 1950s. Both the Scottish Education Department and the Board (later Ministry) of Education in England and Wales had issued circulars or letters in the mid 1940s recommending Russian to schools and education authorities.[44] Though

---

[42] Privately communicated information.

[43] pp. 355-356. Considerable space was devoted to Russian in later editions of this book.

[44] The Scottish circular was dated 11 February 1946.

from 1951 to 1955 only six schools newly introduced Russian to the curriculum, between 1956 and 1960 159 schools did so, according to Nicolas Sollohub's Nuffield Survey.[45] The ground was prepared by changes in public attitudes towards Russian, which may be partly explained by the services courses and by events in the wider world. After all, with five thousand young men being trained in the language, many in the population must have been acquainted with one or other of these former servicemen and have concluded that to learn Russian was possible, interesting, and most significantly—normal. In the area of government education policy, in 1956 there appeared from the Ministry of Education, *Modern Languages. Pamphlet no. 29*. Over a hundred pages long, this 'pamphlet' reflects the changing circumstances in world politics and, for that matter, British educational conditions. It is anonymous, but clearly compiled by HM Inspectorate of Schools. The introduction proclaims the death of the notion that only the classics were the route to a true education, and includes the words:

> Public opinion has changed and none would be likely to deny that the study of modern languages, in common with the study of English and the ancient classical languages, has not only a logical and intellectual value: it can also—if it is conceived as broadly and liberally as the traditional study of Latin and Greek—provide the artistic and aesthetic training which mark the truly educated and cultured person.

Further arguments for modern languages are put;

> To the practical and intellectual advantages to be gained from learning modern languages there has recently been added the broadening influence which, during the past 20 years or so, has probably helped to make many thousands of our pupils less insular and prejudiced in outlook than they might otherwise have been.

A fair amount of space is devoted to Russian. It is noted that entries in public examinations for Russian are small, but that Russian is increasing proportionately more than French. A report of 1950 on Russian teaching is cited.[46] Twenty-nine schools were said to be teaching the subject in England, fifteen of them independent schools. Twenty-four evening institutes and commercial colleges were known to be running Russian courses. Russian was being taught mainly by self-taught teachers of English origin, only two of whom had spent any time in Russia. Only five schools taught Russian before the sixth form. Time allocated to Russian varied considerably.

---

[45] Sollohub, p. 4. This table of Sollohub's is a unique contribution to information on the introduction of Russian in schools between 1946 and 1965.

[46] I have not been able to locate a published version of this survey. Maybe the authors are referring to the 1946 Circular no. 81 described above. It must be said that all these pamphlets, and even major reports signed by academics are lamentably haphazard in the way they refer to earlier work.

Russian is supported in the secondary school curriculum, but the usual scepticism about the subject is reported. Of 200 schools surveyed in 1947 ninety-six had deemed Russian

> too difficult, and it was found that suitable books were often hard to come by. Russian stood apart from the course of western civilization and to introduce it into an already overloaded curriculum at the expense of Latin or German or Spanish was inadvisable. Russian isolation, the alleged poverty of contemporary Russian literary output and the fact that what is worth while in past achievement has been made accessible in translations were cited as reasons for not introducing the subject. (p.15)

The Pamphlet rejects this line of argument:

> Admittedly Russian presents difficulties for the average Englishman, but not more than do the ancient classical languages. For the pupil with some linguistic ability the value of Russian as a discipline is very great, resembling even more closely than German the discipline of Greek. Literary Russian is remarkable both for its subtlety and its flexibility. And although the contemporary output—so far as we are able to judge—may not be of high quality, the nation which produced Pushkin, Turgenev, Dostoievsky, Tolstoy, Chekhov and Gorky will surely give birth to other great writers in the future.
> (p. 16)

The latter part of the year in which this pamphlet appeared was, however, a black one for relations between the West and the Soviet Union. The brutal suppression of the Hungarian revolution in October-November 1956 changed the atmosphere created by Nikita Khrushchev's visit to Britain earlier in the year. But in October 1957 a new element emerged: space exploration began with the launching of the first artificial earth satellite, Sputnik-1. Though this was but a few weeks before the United States sent up a satellite, it created the impression of massive Soviet superiority in scientific research. The Americans especially perceived important failings in their education system. The Soviet Union became again a vital subject for study and research. Public interest in space exploration, culminating in the first manned space flight by Yurii Gagarin in 1961, fuelled a desire for Russian studies. The subject was poised for a major advance.

The anonymous Special Correspondent in the *Manchester Guardian* on 9 August 1958, quoted at the head of this chapter, was clearly pretty well informed, but equally clearly had the same problem as we have in finding the exact facts. He (if it was a 'he') quotes a parliamentary answer by an education minister to the effect that about 60 schools—presumably in England and Wales—were teaching Russian. A parliamentary answer reported in *The Times* on 16 December 1958 gives 'nearly 70' as the figure for schools, and 'about 40' further education establishments. In any other country this would settle the matter, but in England education ministers and their departments do not keep systematic figures and in fact do not know the exact answers to such questions.[47] The Minister's figure may possibly have been something of an underestimate: the Incorporated Association of Assistant Masters reported that 8 schools *started* Russian in 1957, 50 in 1958 and 74 in 1959; the Association of Teachers of Russian listed 101 schools and 92 further education establishments in mid-1959, and the Incorporated Association of Head Masters believed there were 300 schools teaching Russian in 1961.[48] It is not clear whether some of these estimated figures apply to the whole United Kingdom.

The United Kingdom was in the mid-1950s ahead of the United States in terms of the number of schools where Russian was taught. In 1955-56 only nine American secondary schools were known to be offering Russian, and around this time there were four experiments with pre-school and elementary school children. However, by the autumn of 1959 there were 400, and by 1960-61 over 500,[49] and Britain had been well overtaken. While certain British educators in the Russian field were by the mid-1960s expressing caution, fearing that a vast increase in schools was not what the situation really needed, the reaction in America was much more outspoken and the disagreement sharper. William Edgerton of Indiana University described the leap from fewer than a dozen schools to 500 as 'an unhealthily rapid spurt' which could lead to disaster: there were not that many good high school teachers in America able to teach the language well enough, and some of the 'eager souls' were guilty of the 'very kind of narrow-minded empire building they so justly attribute to the teachers of French, Spanish, German, and Latin.' Edgerton feared that unsympathetic school administrators were waiting for the opportunity to reward failure of Russian courses with its removal from the curriculum.[50]

Conditions in Britain may not have been exactly comparable, but while Britain had the JSSL trainees who might be recruited into Russian teaching, the United States had students from the Army Specialized Training Program and the Navy Language School, which had been very active during the War, and had developed teaching methods which were both controversial and effective.[51] One hundred and twelve army personnel were training on twelve month courses in the Russian language in 1947-48. A feature of the development of Russian in America which was absent from Britain was the financial support provided by the charitable foundations, which, according to Walter Laqueur, made the

---

[47] I can vouch for this personally: on two occasions in the 1980s the English Department for Education (under whatever name it was working at the time) passed on enquirers to me, stating that surveys carried out on behalf of the ATR provided information not collected by the Department.

[48] I.A.A.M, *The Teaching of Modern Languages,* p. 287; I.A.H.M., *Modern Languages in the Grammar School,* 1966 edition, p. 21.

[49] Parry, pp. 134-138.

[50] Edgerton's view was expressed in conversation and is is quoted by Parry, pp. 160-161.

[51] Parry, pp. 107-110.

development of Russian Studies possible.[52] But the American figures showed the same instability as the British ones were very quickly to exemplify too: even the very first, those nine schools in 1956, were accompanied by six others which had started, but dropped the subject. In both countries the respective professions were delighted when numbers of schools increased: in the United Kingdom it may be true, as Vaughan James suggested later, that fewer schools but with the language more firmly established would have worked to the benefit of the subject and the national interest. Charges of 'empire-building' are easy to level, but the suspicion must be scrupulously avoided.

As for UK examination entries, 55 candidates took Ordinary level GCE in 1952, 83 in 1955, and 133 in 1958. The *Manchester Guardian* correspondent was impressed by a huge increase in Advanced level entries, being apparently unaware that servicemen on the JSSL courses were allowed and indeed encouraged to take this exam, at least until 1956, a fact which must have distorted the statistics. Figures in Scotland were available to the Annan Committee, but otherwise not published. They were: Leaving Certificate entries (Lower grade) in 1951, 1959, 1960 and 1961—1, 16, 39, and 80 respectively. Higher grade entries were 1, 16, 15, and 31 in the same years.[53] Although the numbers are still small, this illustrates a striking percentage increase.

The Foundation and Early Activity of the Association of Teachers of Russian

The end of the 1950s was marked by an event of considerable significance for the development of Russian teaching in Britain. This arose out of a landmark cultural agreement between Britain and the Soviet Union, which was referred to in the sole Annex to an Anglo-Soviet Communiqué signed by Harold Macmillan and Nikita Khrushchev after their meeting in Moscow, 21 February to 3 March 1959.[54] An earlier series of parliamentary questions put in 1957-58 had extracted the story from ministers: in 1955 the British Council had set up a Soviet Relations Committee with government encouragement, and a Joint Declaration on the subject had been issued in 1956. By 1959 a formal agreement was signed, which typifies the shape of the series which followed for many years.[55]

---

[52]Parry, p. 119; Laqueur, p. 7.

[53]Annan, p. 11.

[54]*Anglo-Soviet Communiqué on the discussions of the Prime Minister ... and the Foreign Secretary ... with the Chairman of the Council of Ministers of the USSR ...*, Soviet Union No. 1 (1959), London: HMSO, March 1959.

[55]*Parliamentary Debates (Hansard)*, 1957-58, p. 23, reports a question asked on 28 April 1958. The MP concerned had been pressing the Government to negotiate a formal inter-governmental agreement; the Minister resisted the notion with growing irritation, on the grounds that the British Council was fulfilling this function perfectly well. The 'Joint Declaration' may be seen as Command Paper Cmd. 9753: 'Soviet Union No, 1 (1956)', HMSO. Despite the Minister's reluctance to consider a formal cultural agreement, the first of a long annual series was concluded and presented to Parliament on 1 December 1959: see *Agreement ... on Relations in the Scientific, Technological, Educational and*

Article V 'Educational Exchanges' provided for reciprocal visits by university staff, postgraduate students, teacher-training students, teachers of English in the USSR and Russian in Britain, exchanges of pedagogical literature, and the establishment of summer schools.

Under the British Council's auspices, in 1958 the first month-long course for teachers of Russian took place in the Soviet Union. There were 26 participants, five or six from universities and higher education, the rest from secondary schools; all parts of the United Kingdom were represented. Few had been to the USSR previously, even senior university teachers, and not only on this course, but for several years to come to visit that country induced a considerable degree of what we have come to call culture shock. Nevertheless, the experience was memorable, and for many teachers it was the first time they had had much of a chance to get to know their fellow-workers in the field. Inspired perhaps by the formation in December 1956 of a Provisional National Committee of British Slavists, the body which later became BUAS (the British Universities' Association of Slavists), they decided to keep in touch.

While the people concerned were considering how best to do this, quite coincidentally *The Times* instituted a correspondence on the study of Russian in schools, which figured in thirteen issues of the paper. In those days *The Times* was an organ which attracted a very great deal of respect among what it referred to in its advertising material as the 'top people'. This correspondence, headed 'Who learns Russian?', is significant as a pointer to attitudes at that time.[56] The letter which set it all going was from A. D. C. Peterson, head of the Education Department of Oxford University. It may or may not have had anything to do with the *Manchester Guardian* article; maybe Peterson was the unnamed special correspondent. The line he took was in some ways a little unfortunate, as it seemed to over-stress the importance of Russian as a language for scientific research while wishing that scientists might take Russian Advanced level in the sixth form. R. J. Morda Evans of the Royal Naval College at Greenwich (who had been on the Moscow teachers' course) attacked the dominance of French; he also expressed the need for opportunities to visit Russia if teachers were to teach with confidence. Two headmasters expressed their support for Russian, but outlined the organizational difficulties when scientists had such a heavy programme and when Latin was still required for entry to Oxford and Cambridge (and elsewhere). Another writer urged schools to start Russian two years below the sixth form. A graduate in Russian deplored the fact that her daughter, who had wanted to start Russian from scratch at university had been actively discouraged by three universities on the grounds that Russian was far too difficult (Arabic was offered instead at one!), that it was 'not suitable for girls', and there were 'no jobs for Russian graduates.' This provoked two responses: one writer

---

Cultural Fields.

[56] See *The Times* for 23-30 September 1958: 23; p. 11; 24; p.11; 25; p. 11; 26; p. 13; 27; p. 7; 29; p. 11; 30; p. 11; and for 1-11 October: 1; p. 11; 2; p. 11; 3; p. 11. 4; p. 7. 6; p. 11; and 11, p. 3.

advised the girl to try again, as universities were not the most consistent of institutions and might think better of it, and Frank Borras wrote to say that his department at Leeds would have accepted her on a *four*-year *ab initio* course in Russian. Mrs Eva Strauss put in a plea for evening classes to be better supported by local authorities: she deplored it when the 'eagerness and tenacity' of the relatively small numbers of students was rewarded by class cancellation.

Exam syllabuses were criticized for their preoccupation with nineteenth-century literature and their lack of any concept of the contemporary language. A correspondent cites unsuitable textbooks, lack of travel opportunities and the erroneous view of the difficulty of Russian—'is it surprising no one will study it?' The predictable Scottish headmaster wrote to praise the progress made in schools in Scotland; an English head anxious to start Russian reported she had failed to appoint a suitable teacher despite many contacts in the profession. A master at Winchester College attacked the notion of the special mental-training value of Latin. Two scientists recommended non-literary Russian syllabuses for science students. There were two letters hostile to any retreat from the special position of French and Latin: 'To abandon one of the languages which carry the tradition of our civilization is to close yet another of the roads which lead to a culture wider than that of the laboratory.' Another scientist says that Russian is not necessary, as essential articles are available in translation; two others retort that this is rubbish—translations if they exist are often poor and always very expensive to buy or commission.

We have here in these twenty letters a refreshing new mood in the debate. Hostility is minimal. Difficulties are listed, but the overall sense is of optimism: these difficulties can and should be removed. On 6 October 1958 *The Times* summed up in a leading article entitled 'A Language worth knowing', which is very knowledgeable and quite poetically written—by whom, it would be interesting to know.

> 'Russian has a shamefully and dangerously low place in British schools and colleges [...] The difficulties [...] are widely overrated and the rewards are great [...] Two hundred years ago, when Lomonosov [wrote of its grandeur, liveliness, strength, tenderness and richness, Russian] was like an organ which had not been properly played. Anyone thinking of taking up a language [...] should at least consider the instrument which Tolstoy and Pushkin touched to heights of clear and simple beauty.'

C. Vaughan James, a participant in the first exchange course in Moscow, who was then teaching at Tottenham Grammar School, grasped the moment and wrote to the paper on 2 October suggesting the formation of an Association of Teachers of Russian (ATR).[57] Peterson (who became President of ATR) offered to organ-

---

[57] Vaughan James deserves major recognition in the history of Russian teaching in Britain. His energy and drive were instrumental for twenty years and more in inspiring others to further the cause of Russian in the entire education system.

ize a conference at New College, Oxford. This took place in January 1959, when 75 teachers of Russian, 'more than we realized existed', gathered for what turned out to be the inaugural meeting.[58] They are listed in a cyclostyled document which survives: all of these have addresses in England, but teachers from other parts of the United Kingdom soon joined the Association, and membership doubled in four months. A circular typed by James includes the words: 'At business meetings on the Monday [5 Jan. 1959] it was decided to form an Association of Teachers of Russian'.[59] Minutes of this meeting have been lost, but surviving paperwork clearly indicates the way discussion went.[60]

The ATR was to have a marked effect on Russian teaching in British schools. It was clear that the spirit of the time required an injection of passionate enthusiasm, which—as we have seen—was largely lacking in the Modern Language Association, as far as Russian was concerned. ATR turned out to be the ideal channel for this enthusiasm. It produced and circulated its first duplicated *ATR Broadsheet* in May 1959; from issue number 3 it was printed, and from no. 8 renamed *ATR Journal*. It was again renamed *Journal of Russian Studies* from no. 18 (1969). These periodicals all contained a brief but comprehensive statement of aims:

> 1. To exchange information and experience concerning methods of teaching Russian.
> 2. To exchange information concerning textbooks and teaching aids and, where necessary, to compile new ones designed expressly for use with modern teaching techniques.
> 3. To provide information for education authorities, heads of schools and heads of departments interested in beginning Russian.
> 4. To review existing examinations and suggest improvements.
> 5. To encourage the establishing of Russian with a regular place in the curriculum of secondary schools.
> 6. To press for more frequent and widespread interchange of teachers, students and materials with Russia.

These aims were pursued partly through the establishment of sub-committees. Leading members of ATR were crucial in producing new teaching materials, in monitoring and reforming the examination system, in advising teachers, experienced and inexperienced alike, on the suitability of materials and on teaching methods. This was done through articles in the journal, by occasional publications, by private correspondence, and at the annual conference, which quickly became an exercise in in-service training of very high quality indeed.

---

[58]This account of the founding of ATR is taken from C. V. James, 'Otkuda vy?' *Journal of Russian Studies*, no. 18, 1969, p.3,

[59]Leeds Russian Archive, Association of Teachers of Russian MS 1403: ATR Administrative, Correspondence, etc files.

[60]Muckle, 'The Archives of the ATR' p. 3.

Enterprises to which the ATR devoted particular energy from the start included pressure for exchanges with the USSR, and primarily the provision of teaching materials for use in schools. The membership was invited to respond to questionnaires, and a hundred responses (an amazingly high rate of response, as any educational researcher will confirm) established that a textbook to GCE O level in two years was what was required. It was noted in *ATR Broadsheet* 2 (1959) that four textbooks of various sorts had been submitted to publishers. A particular and recurrent theme is the need, in view of the relative difficulty of assimilating Russian vocabulary, to compile a defined list of words that beginners might concentrate on. Work on this idea continued for several years, and an examination board agreed eventually to the compilation of a suitable defined vocabulary. Another early enquiry carried out by the Association was to establish teachers' opinions on existing published material; brief assessments of the books concerned were published in the *Broadsheet*. The high number of responses to these enquiries is surely an indication of the level of enthusiasm for the subject and of perceptions of the urgency of the situation.

A feature of the ATR was the partnership between secondary and higher education teachers, and between Slavs and British native teachers. To examine the lists of members published in the early journals is instructive, if inconclusive. Though new members were always asked to give professional details, these details have not survived. We have no idea how many had academic qualifications in Russian and at what level. There is a strong representation of former JSSL students. About nine percent have unmistakeably Slavonic surnames, but there may have been many more Russian women married to British men who took their names. By the beginning of 1960 ATR had grown to 200 members, and by end of the year there were 290. A list of 170 schools where Russian was taught was given: 2 in Northern Ireland, 2 in Wales, 23 in Scotland and 143 in England. Evening institutes, commercial and technical colleges amounted to 124. Needless to say, this does not represent the results of a systematic survey, but probably comprised little more than the names of the institutions where the members taught. Further education is a particularly difficult sector to chronicle, as evening classes start and collapse very quickly if numbers of students decline; a survey carried out in September might be radically altered by November. Here examination entries are little guide, as many part-time students see learning as a leisure activity are not in the least interested in obtaining qualifications.

The 1960s were the time when the provision of appropriate teaching materials took an exponential leap forward. The ATR, as we have indicated, took a hand in actively encouraging the writing and publication of school textbooks. To interest commercial publishers in textbooks for a subject that was only very precariously established in a few schools was easier than one might suppose, since well-known firms saw it as a point of prestige to have Russian books in their catalogues, even if they lost money on them. Some school Russian teachers in the very early days were persuaded to put up some money for shares in a new small publisher in order to further publication in the field; profits were never sufficient for them to be paid any interest, apparently, but at least the publisher concerned issued many books, particularly student editions of Russian literary works, which were of great value to the profession. One mistake made by ATR was soon rectified. The Association tried working with specific authors and instituted a stamp of approval for new textbooks, but agreement was not always possible to reach. On one occasion an author, who had been working in tandem with ATR members found himself unable to meet their contradictory requirements and used his own best judgement. Surviving minutes of an early committee meeting report an apparently interminable discussion about the relatively trivial matter of the order of cases in noun declension paradigms; in the end no conclusion was reached, and it was left to the author to decide. Very soon ATR decided to abolish its stamp of approval and to influence practice through reviews in its periodical publications and by demonstrations and discussions at conferences and local meetings.

The main, but certainly not the only, problem had been suitable materials for younger school pupils. Now that schools were introducing Russian at age thirteen or younger, the academic grammars of Forbes, Semeonoff, Birkett, and the like, which were conceived for serious adult students, began to be replaced by courses likely to interest and appeal to younger learners. Earlier work by Moore and Struve had moved tentatively in this direction, and there had been at least one American progressive course for children, but the first really successful school textbook appeared in 1960 by a former pupil and later teacher of Storr-Best's school: it was A. A. Haywood's *A First Russian Book*, which took the familiar form of a series of chapters beginning with a text or story, usually of the 'soap-opera' variety, followed by grammar analysis, exercises and translation. It could be handled by the teacher in various ways, and was suitable for oral approaches. The book and its successor *Second Russian Book* were a godsend to teachers of the younger school age-group, and one or two other similar courses (by Seeley, Duff and Makaroff, and Harding) followed it. Many books produced by British teachers were heavily criticized for the quality of the Russian: it seems that, however simple the language, an English person cannot produce a register of Russian which sounds really authentic. Exactly the same applies the other way about: Soviet school textbooks of English never got the style quite right either.

The shape of school language-teaching materials was soon to change. The 1960s were the decade in which tape recording and other electronic devices started to develop to a standard which made their use in the classroom easy and effective. Methods of teaching based on audio-visual and audio-lingual materials entered the field, and teachers of Russian were as eager as any to experiment with them. At the same time, cooperation between British and Soviet experts in the production of teaching materials became possible. These two matters came together in the Nuffield Foreign Languages Teaching Materials Project, which began at Leeds in the mid-1960s and soon transferred to the Language Teaching Centre at the University of York. Its aim was to produce an audio-visual course in each of several languages for younger school pupils; Russian was one of the languages, and the course *Vpered!* [Forward!] was written by a team headed by David Rix; it was tried out in a number of schools, the teachers sending in reports, suggestions and ideas. Later in the 1960s Soviet publishing houses, especially *Russkii iazyk*, became very active in the production of invaluable materials for both young pupils and older students. Rix and Robert Pullin were two of the British writers who later collaborated with Soviet educators on projects published in Russia.

There is no doubt that courses which used recorded sound were a step forward, which noticeably improved the pronunciation of learners. The teacher, after all, could introduce a variety of voices into the classroom, male and female, young and old, and was freed from the fact that prior to this he or she could never teach a better Russian pronunciation than his or her own. Furthermore, the variety of materials published in the USSR was far beyond anything which British publishers could manage. These included long-playing discs of Russian poetry, plays and prose. The ATR assembled a library of recorded sound and made it available on loan to members. Even if the Soviet courses never quite matched British examination syllabuses, they could be adapted. The boom in teaching materials at this time facilitated the development of Russian in all types of educational establishments, particularly in secondary education.

Changes in the style of the materials used for the teaching of modern languages was not merely a question of adding *son et lumière* to traditional grammar courses. The feeling had been growing for years by the mid-1960s that understanding of the meaning of 'grammar' was incomplete in many ways. For decades there had been language teachers who sought to stress oral proficiency and the ability to communicate with native speakers, but at the same time notions of the benefits of 'grammar-grind' died hard. While most linguists stressed that communication could not be attained without some understanding of grammar, it was argued that a fresh approach should now be adopted.[61] 'Communicative' methodology has in more recent years become the oft-repeated motto, and by the twenty-first century, teaching materials have gradually come to typify many of the new ideas. However, recent descriptive grammars of Russian continue to display implicit assumptions based on the traditional approach.

Great interest was expressed in the principles at stake among the teaching profession in the 1960s and 70s. Of great interest was the work undertaken by Language Centre at the University of Essex: the Contemporary Russian Language Analysis Project, known as CRLAP. With unheard-of levels of funding for the time, £30,700 from the Nuffield Foundation, the Project was reckoned to have occupied over twenty man-years in its preparation; without the participation of a computer, a relatively new feature of research in language, it would have been impossible. A vast corpus of tape-recorded material was assembled, transcribed

---

[61] It is not possible to expatiate on this topic here; a helpful guide to the points at issue may be found in papers in a recent publication by Davie, *et al.* (eds).

and analysed. The importance of this was declared to be that, at the time, there was a great need for teaching materials for Russian in many specialisms, in both the arts and the sciences, and to discover exactly what Russians said and wrote in these disciplines (and in general conversation, of course), as opposed to what grammarians *said* they said, or wanted them to say, was an important and very large step forward. Moreover, Russian teaching was at the time dominated by émigrés and by others who had been taught by émigrés, and all of our Russian was to some extent outmoded; prolonged residence in Russia in order to 'authenticate' one's Russian was, at that time, still out of the question for most people. (We have seen that teaching materials written by British people were often criticized for their unidiomatic Russian.) The Russian language had been in a fluid state in the eighteenth and nineteenth centuries; in the twentieth it continued to develop in very interesting respects.[62] It may be added that Soviet linguists expressed great interest in the CRLAP project and did what they could to facilitate the research carried on in the USSR.

The Report, published in 1972, was issued in a form which must be considered rather indigestible for all but dedicated linguists.[63] However, its influence on the work of the profession may be estimated in other ways. It helped to create an atmosphere in which a new concern with language as it really is used became a high priority. Several of the co-workers on the project went on to write Russian grammars and course materials. An archive of recorded materials was assembled and kept for record purposes at the University.

The Annan Report (1962)

The background to this activity was the climate of opinion created by a third report commissioned by the Government. The Committee chaired by Noel Annan, Provost of King's College, Cambridge, was to 'investigate the possibility of improving and extending the teaching of Russian in schools and in the establishments of further education in the United Kingdom and to make recommendations.' The Committee had seventeen members including the Chairman. Four HM Inspectors of schools served as assessors, and there was a secretary. A majority consisted of teachers of Russian, heads of schools where Russian was taught and other known supporters of the subject. Its recommendations greatly stimulated the morale of teachers of Russian at the time, though it was possible in later years for opponents to describe the Committee as a pressure group, or to see it as representing vested interests.

---

[62] See Comrie *et al*, and Ryazanova-Clarke and Wade which give an extensive account of these changes and indicate the size of the problem for teachers.

[63] See: Language Centre, University of Essex. A brief but informative short account is by Ken Russell, 'The Contemporary Russian Language Analysis Project: Results and prospects', *ATR Occasional Papers*, IV (i) 1970, pp. 14-16.

Annan argued for an increase in Russian teaching on grounds of national need: to read scientific and technical literature, to establish trading relations, to enable better understanding by civil servants of Soviet affairs. Cultural relations at the time were burgeoning; the USSR was becoming more accessible to tourists. The educational value of Russian literature is stressed for its own sake and as a means to understanding the country; the language is essential to any profound study of Russian history and culture. These arguments are very familiar. But the Committee goes further to argue that 'a few expert linguists will not suffice', and that 'Russian needs to be known by those in "line" as well as in "staff" in business.' How much expansion is recommended? Annan asked for Russian to be expanded to 'the present extent of German'; this it held to be 'both justifiable and realistic', and they see it as an immediate objective. (pp. 6-7) This was exactly what Leathes had recommended in 1918, and others before him.

The authors of the Report assembled some partial statistical evidence of the number of schools and further education establishments where Russian was taught at the time, and some details of examination entries. There had been a striking increase in the number of schools teaching Russian between 1945 and 1960. At the same time about 250 further education establishments were known to be offering Russian in about 450 classes, but industry and business were making very little use of these facilities, as all but 29 of the classes were said to be 'general in character'. As to the subject itself, it was declared that the perceived difficulty of Russian could be surmounted when enlightened teaching methods were used. A problem for schools was finding a place for Russian in the curriculum; since French and Latin *both* held a favoured position, Russian could only advance at the expense of Spanish or German—both of them important languages which had advanced much more slowly than their importance warrants. The widespread demand for Latin as an entry requirement by universities was preventing pupils specializing in both science and arts from taking Russian at school. Annan does not say this, but it is surely significant that Latin was an entry requirement even for some university Russian departments: as late as 1970 six of them were still requiring Latin. The reluctance with which this requirement was dropped contributed to Russian departments cutting their own throats.

Annan estimated that more than half those teaching Russian in schools had no degree in Russian, though some were native speakers and others had certificates gained in the armed services. Russian teaching could clearly not be expanded without training more teachers. To increase Russian to the level of German would require a total of 1,500, and it was reckoned that 120 new teachers each year for fifteen years would be needed to augment the pool and to replace those retiring. Intensive Russian courses for teachers were proposed. It was further suggested that the introduction of Russian should be eased by schools being granted 'additional teaching strength up to the equivalent of one teacher's work'. (p. 26)

The Report contained substantial passages on teaching methods, examinations, textbooks and teaching materials, visits to the USSR, and the work of the ATR.

But what effect did all this have on the schools? Ministers agreed to set up intensive courses for would-be teachers of Russian, and these ran for several years. However, the curriculum of schools had long been entirely the responsibility of the governors. HM Inspectorate could and did encourage ventures into Russian, but moral support was all they were able to give. The main result of the Annan Report was to encourage enthusiasts for Russian and provide them with ammunition, and there is no doubt that for nine or ten years after its appearance the number of schools where the language was taught increased to its peak in 1971. The Report could be brandished and quoted to head teachers and governing bodies. But the aim of increasing Russian to the level of German was never attainable in the context of British schooling, given all the constraints, not least the force of tradition.

The response of the Department of Education and Science (DES, as the Ministry became in the early 1960s) to the Annan Report and the failure of that Department to take more than minimal decisive action may be judged from documents in the National Archives and from an article by C. V. James.[64] Like all such reports, it was never to be taken as a statement of intent on the part of the Government. Certain recommendations of the Commission were not accepted by the DES, and the only concrete result of the publication of Annan was the establishment of intensive courses for teachers already qualified in other subjects who wished to be able to teach Russian. The DES asserted that it could do no more than encourage, advise, and recommend action on the part of local education authorities and heads of schools. It would seem to have been reluctant to do even that. While Annan stated that an increase in the amount of Russian taught was 'vital to the economic and political life of the country', the DES did not see the matter as particularly urgent. The 'crash' courses to provide new teachers of Russian were held at Holborn College, Liverpool College of Commerce,[65] Birmingham, and Glasgow. In the English colleges eighty places were created and 71 were filled. In Glasgow the course was similarly undersubscribed. It is possible that the failure to recruit students was due to the reluctance of local education authorities to release teachers and the refusal of the DES and SED to advertise the courses widely for fear of being thought to 'influence' LEAs. James was optimistic about moves in examination syllabuses towards more oral assessment, and modern literary set books in Advanced and Higher examinations; he similarly was hopeful that teacher exchanges would soon be established, and that some way of accrediting Slav teachers who were at present unable to teach in schools as qualified staff. James's conclusion was that 'any further progress will

---

[64] ED 181/103. Typed notes recording Association of Teachers of Russian discussions with DES following Annan, 16.6.64. C. V. James published his account of the meeting: 'Annan and After', *ATR Journal*, no. 12, 1965, pp. 15-21.

[65] An account of the Liverpool course was given in V. A. Mealor, 'The Intensive course for teachers at Liverpool College of Commerce, *ATR Journal*, no. 11, 1964, pp. 36-37.

depend on our own efforts.' (p. 21) Significant changes would depend on constant pressure.

It is interesting, having read Vaughan James's account of the meeting, to see the records kept by the DES. The file in the National Archives confirms James's account of the meeting in every respect; it adds information, however, which is of interest here.

The DES were at first disdainful about ATR. Who the devil were they? Their inspectors were quite assertive: Dr E. A. Greatwood HMI (a member and loyal supporter) declared, 'ATR has the best right of any association to interest itself in the Annan Report and a rebuff to it would be unfortunate.' The requested meeting went ahead on 16 June. Points raised were: though teachers had paid leave of absence to attend the intensive courses, they had to bear their own living expenses if away from home. The DES would create no precedent by subsidizing these costs. ATR sought more places on such courses: the DES pointed out they were undersubscribed and that jobs were not necessarily forthcoming for people who had successfully qualified. Greatwood noted that 'promotion prospects were not substantially improved because of completing the course in Russian.' The Annan proposal for a language institute to be set up had been abandoned after much discussion, but a Committee for Research and Development in Modern Languages was established instead.

Two years later a further flurry of concern briefly occurred in the press: a short but prominent news item in *The Times* instigated by a journalist by name Roy MacGregor-Hastie protested at the failure to implement the Annan Report, contrasted interest in the English language in Russia with our provision for Russian, and declared that 'ministerial action is required to dispel the apathy among local education authorities, universities and schools.' The call for ministerial action, as we have seen many times, was doomed not to be answered. The only published response was a rather inconsequential and not particularly well-informed letter from a professor of Russian querying some of MacGregor-Hastie's facts and expressing scepticism about his opinions. While teachers of Russian continued to quote the Annan Report in the years that followed, this was the last time that the press gave it any attention.[66]

The introduction of French into primary education was at this time much in favour. The DES were at first of the opinion that this measure would facilitate diversification of other modern languages in secondary education. In the event this proved to be a fallacy. The Inspectorate came quickly to the conclusion that it strengthened the position of French in the system.

An issue of particular relevance to Russian was the qualification of teachers of Russian origin without British certificates. There were mature students' courses offered by teacher-training institutions, but men and women of Slavonic

---

[66] See *The Times*, 'Plea to Minister for more teaching of Russian: Report recommendations "almost ignored"' 5 April 1966, p. 7; 'Teaching of Russian', 12 April 1966, p. 9.

origin could not necessarily meet their formal entrance requirements. The DES would not press these institutions 'for the benefit of any particular group'. Admission to such courses was a matter for the colleges concerned, who were subject to the regulations of the Area Training Organizations (ATOs). It was suggested that ATR should take up particular cases with the ATOs.

The refusal of the DES to recommend anything much to schools or local authorities must have been discouraging to the ATR delegation. They would not even actively encourage LEAs to send teachers on the intensive courses. This reluctance was, apparently, accepted by ATR, but the papers show that at least one civil servant commented that the Secretary of State *does* have some responsibility, but only if things go seriously wrong.[67] We repeat Vaughan James's conclusion: 'any further progress will depend on our own efforts.' Those efforts will be recounted in the following chapters.

---

[67] A memory personal to the author of this book seems to illustrate that the DES, through HM Inspectorate, *did* try to press schools, though not openly. In 1962, as the Annan report appeared, I was a young teacher of Russian at a local authority grammar school in Sussex. The aforementioned Dr Greatwood arrived at the school, ostensibly to scrutinize my proficiency as a teacher. As an inspection it was thoroughly and professionally carried out. It is obvious, however, that the 80 minutes the Inspector spent with the Headmaster *before* he appeared in my classroom cannot have been occupied with a discussion of my professional competence. I imagined and hoped that he was encouraging the Head to persist with Russian in the school and to help create the conditions for its survival. In fact the Head did not need persuading, but support from the Inspector was welcome.

Chapter 7

After Annan. The Road to Atkinson. The 1960s and 1970s

It makes little sense to spend the country's wealth on weapons of mass destruction which, as deterrents, it is hoped never to use, while simultaneously trying to economize by reducing the educational budget for Russian studies or cutting the external services of the BBC. Education about the Soviet system and information about its impact on world events form a vital part of our defence and are cheap in comparison with tanks and missiles.

THE TIMES, 1983

THE period from 1960 to the early 1970s was probably the most stimulating and challenging time for teachers of Russian in Britain. For ten years numbers of schools and higher education establishments where the subject was taught increased exponentially. Teaching materials burgeoned, exchanges with Russia became easier than they had been within living memory, scholarly activity increased in language, literature, and area studies to the extent that the 'scholarly tradition' spoken of in the Scarbrough Report was clearly establishing itself.

These were years when there was a great deal of optimism, but little complacency, as the position was universally recognized to be precarious. In a Foreword in *ATR Journal* 13, 1965, p. 7, Vaughan James goes so far as to say that the future of Russian studies 'looks blacker than ever before'. James was ever energetic and forceful in his advocacy of Russian in both secondary and higher education, but he was never a man to appear over-optimistic. When one looks at the drive and enthusiasm with which school and university teachers were promoting their subject at this time, 'blacker than ever before' may seem unduly negative. As it turned out, the judgement was not without substance. It was quite a few years before the reasoning behind it was justified by events. Meanwhile, there was a great deal of positive achievement to report.

The sectors of education in which Russian figured—secondary, further, and higher—were at this period even more interdependent than in earlier decades, and it is not entirely appropriate to divide up our account of Russian teaching and learning over the various types of institution. Much of what one says about universities and polytechnics at this time relates to what was going on in the schools, which in turn relied for support on moves in higher education. This should be borne in mind in the discussion which follows.

There were several reasons for Vaughan James's wariness. One was that a new Labour government had in 1965 issued a circular calling upon local education authorities to submit plans for the abolition of examinations at age 11 for entry to secondary education and to reorganize their schools on 'comprehensive' lines. While many teachers shared the politicians' desire to democratize or to remove the injustice inherent in the system, teachers of Russian did not know whether to fear that Russian would get lost in the inevitable upheaval, or whether the subject would benefit from the formation of larger schools with—possibly—more curricular choice. Experience in the profession of teaching Russian to average or less able children was scant; at an ATR conference in the mid 1960s it proved difficult to find enough participants with sufficient experience from among those present to make up a panel on the topic. Secondly, the government was not going to implement the Annan recommendations; and without strong central backing for Russian, and without co-ordination of the supply of teachers and the matching of them to schools which wished to introduce or continue with the subject, it became hardly any easier to persuade the real power-brokers, school heads and governing bodies, that it was possible, desirable, and educationally beneficial to offer Russian in their school. Then, as the 1960s moved into the 1970s, Britain was again applying to join the European Community; there were fears that its languages, at the time confined to the west and lacking any links with the Eastern part of the continent, would come to dominate the curriculum.

Nevertheless, if there were challenges for teachers, there was much to show that they were capable of rising to them. British teachers of Russian were, in addition, helped by the gradual thawing of relations between Britain and the Soviet Union. The thaw facilitated exchanges and visits to Russia, and perhaps more important than that, they enabled cooperation between Russian and British authors of teaching material. Moreover, books which would never have been a viable commercial proposition in the United Kingdom could be published in the USSR. Despite political sensitivities and failures in cultural understanding, some courses appeared which British schoolteachers found extremely useful. Soviet gramophone recordings of the classics of poetry, drama, and prose were also of considerable use to British teachers. Of particular importance was the fact that Soviet books were, by British standards, extremely cheap; they were also pretty efficiently provided by a book supplier which had had excellent links with the USSR since the 1930s. This firm, Collet's, was even able to publish the work of British Russian teachers with subsidy from the USSR.

Russian in Secondary Education

The development of Russian in schools was carefully monitored by the ATR in a survey dated 1963/64[1] and by the Nuffield Foundation in 1966/67.[2] The ATR's journals until 1965 also contained lists of members and of schools and colleges where Russian was taught, from which some statistical evidence may be gleaned, though these data cannot be regarded as exhaustive. A 1961 *Broadsheet* lists about 180 schools, 26 of them in Scotland. These lists are usually simply records of the names of the Association's members and of the schools where they taught, and not until the 1963/64 survey was there a serious attempt at near-complete coverage. The compilers of these surveys were always appropriately modest about their completeness, since schools cannot be forced to reply to questionnaires. The ATR survey found 309 schools in 1963 where Russian was taught, but promptly admitted this was probably an underestimate; 8,580 pupils were known to be learning Russian in these schools. They consisted of 41 in Scotland, 8 in Wales, none in Ireland, the rest in England. When updated in 1965, the numbers were 320 in total, 39 in Scotland, 9 in Wales, 5 in Northern Ireland (four of them in Belfast).[3] The Nuffield survey listed 454 schools (including 63 in Scotland, 15 in Wales, 5 in Northern Ireland, and one British school abroad) with 10,984 pupils learning the subject. Of these, 120 schools were introducing Russian at the age of 11, 12, or 13. Twenty-six of these schools were comprehensive, 14 of which were introducing Russian at 11, 12, or 13.

While these figures looked encouraging at the time, the place of Russian when compared with other languages was tiny. For every sixteen-year-old school pupil offering Russian at GCE Ordinary level there were 150 offering French, 55 Latin, and 25 German. Russian tended also to be taught for a much shorter period, usually two years to O level.[4]

Teachers of Russian were active in attempts to reform the methods of testing modern languages in the public examination system, and indeed in advocating a re-thinking of the language curriculum in general. As early as 1959, the AGM of ATR had resolved to make an 'official expression of dissatisfaction' with the most recent O level examination from the Joint Matriculation Board. Moves were afoot which eventually resulted in massive changes when the General Certificate of Secondary Education (GCSE) was instituted; the 1960s and 1970s were a time of discussion and experiment, along with some research. The pages of teachers' newsletters and journals reflect this. There was much interest in two issues in particular: raising the profile of oral skills, and reducing—if not abolishing—translation from English into Russian. At post-sixteen level there were moves to introduce alternatives to literature; following Bernard Pares's tradition of 'nation

---

[1] R. A. Peace, 'ATR Survey, 1963-64'.
[2] Sollohub, *A Survey...* This is summarized in Chamberlain, 'The Past, present and future of Russian'.
[3] 'List of schools where Russian is taught', *ATR Journal*, no. 13, 1965, pp. 80-83.
[4] C. V. James, 'The Case for Russian'.

study', it was argued that Russian could lead the way in broadening the modern languages curriculum.[5] The profession was now inclined to look at examination testing of language achievement in terms of 'discrete' skills: receptive and productive, or expressed otherwise as aural comprehension, reading comprehension, speaking and writing. Some doubted how discrete these skills actually were. The relatively new discipline of applied linguistics was of great interest to teachers, and the importance of research in testing was recognized. The point the discussions had reached in 1966 was reported in an article by P. T. Culhane in that year.[6] While teachers of Russian were prominent in the negotiations for new syllabuses, the issues were equally applicable to all modern languages. Culhane outlined these issues: examinations boards could not dictate classroom practice, merely reflect it. They had to provide tests which would provide evidence year-to-year which would enable standards to be compared. There were questions to be resolved of reliability, aims, and comparability, and there was a need for research to establish standards in general. There was considerable support among teachers of Russian for the use of dictionaries in examinations for students studying Russian for scientific purposes.

By 1964 the Associated Examination Board was offering a GCE Ordinary Level examination with 25% of the marks allocated to the oral test, and with no English to Russian translation. It claimed 'an emphasis throughout on modern colloquial speech and on knowledge of the country whose language is being studied.' In Scotland by 1967 an SCE Alternative Ordinary grade examination in modern languages had been introduced with the aim of improving the aural/oral aspect of language teaching. In England and Wales a significant innovation in 1965 was the institution of the Certificate of Secondary Education (CSE). Previous public examinations at age 16 were intended solely for the more able young person; the CSE was intended to cater for children in the top 60% of the ability range. It was often taken as a backup to O level: to obtain grade 1 was considered equivalent to an O level pass. There was no equivalent to this in Scotland, and some Scottish schools entered pupils.[7] The really innovative feature of this certificate was that teachers were able to compile their own syllabuses and mark the papers, subject to moderation by the examinations board.[8] Some schools made a particular point of insisting that their teachers of all subjects took on this option. As far as Russian was concerned, not a great many candidates entered: the peak was reached in 1974, when there were 376 entries. In the same year 2,579 candidates took GCE O level Russian.

The ATR's *Journal* and *Occasional Papers* are a colourful source of information on the very wide range of activities engaged in by teachers at this time. The

---

[5]Richards, 'Russian and the aims...'

[6]Culhane, 'Research in "O" level examinations'.

[7]J. B. C. Davidson, p. 49.

[8]Enthusiastic support for this approach may be read in Tennant, 'Teaching Russian...'

Association was a lively self-support group; there was collaboration between schools to enhance teaching by out-of-school activities; local groups, known as *kruzhki* (circles), constituted themselves and met for discussion and informal in-service training. The local groups had, in fact, been introduced almost at the very start of ATR, when it was realized—quite rightly—that they could be a real source of strength to the profession. The Association's sub-committees provided information and guidance to those who sought it; the main Committee made representations to other bodies when appropriate. We shall return to specific examples of all this in due course.

Exchanges

It was perhaps in the area of exchanges with the Soviet Union that the 1960s were most refreshing for teachers and learners of Russian. We saw that in the mid-1940s the British Foreign Office found their Soviet counterpart impossible to deal with as far as cultural exchanges were concerned. Following the first Cultural Agreement in the late 1950s, the long-awaited *ottepel'* or thaw which slowly emerged after the death of Stalin, as more enlightened policies developed, led to a greater willingness on the part of the Soviets to admit foreigners, carefully controlled though that admission was.

The first of the annual courses for about 25 teachers was the seed which led to the foundation of ATR. From the point of view of the British participants in these courses, they were splendid. There was good colloquial teaching provided. There were opportunities to visit literary and historical museums and galleries, to see the sights, such as the Moscow Kremlin, to go to theatres, cinemas, and operas, to shop for books, and to see Russian city life at first hand. There were visits to lessons in Soviet schools in both Moscow and Leningrad. Relatively trivial events seemed full of significance. Those were the days when foreigners were forever being stopped in the street by wide boys seeking to buy the clothes off their back: ordinary Marks and Spencer products were held to be luxuries, and the most unexceptional garments were regarded as great prizes. One woman on a 1961 trip was begged by the floor warden in her hotel to sell her a simple plastic mackintosh which looked like a leopardskin; a friend for life was made when she simply gave it to her at the end of the visit. One man gave 20 kopecks to a beggar outside a church, and the woman prostrated herself on the ground in gratitude. Such things were not encountered in Britain. Participants also discovered that the customer in the USSR was not always right; on trying to order coffee after a meal, the response was, 'Why do you want coffee? You started with soup!' And all came to regard almost with affection the ubiquitous notices saying *Zakryt na remont* (closed for renovation). Little did we suspect that one day in 1991-92 the whole Soviet Union would be *zakryt na remont*.

If teachers on their first visit suffered considerable culture shock, so did schoolchildren, but they usually showed that they could cope with it perfectly well. Pupils went occasionally in the early 1960s on tourist visits from specific schools. A number of visits organized on an inter-school basis took place, sometimes organized through town twinning arrangements. Some of these offered opportunities for the development of language skills as well as knowledge of the country. Particularly successful twinnings were those between the two steel towns of Sheffield and Donetsk and the Leningrad-Manchester connection, which led to at least one notable stay for Manchester schoolchildren in a Pioneer camp on the Gulf of Finland. There were also ATR-led visits by coach on several occasions. With the Soviet Pioneers (the youth movement for young teenagers) the British children reacted interestingly. While they tended to avoid *utrenniaia zariadka*, the customary morning physical jerks which seemed at the time to be almost a religious obligation to the Soviets, they actually said they enjoyed the parades with flags which accompanied roll-call. Living conditions in the camps were spartan, but bearable, with rudimentary dormitories and communal open lavatories with old copies of *Pravda* for toilet paper. One pupil who went on one of these trips said the food was so good he did not mind such minor hardship. An insurmountable cultural problem was the afternoon nap for up to 90 minutes taken by Soviet children. This the Manchester teachers replaced by impromptu Russian lessons. A major benefit of these visits was the opportunity to form friendships with youngsters of their own age, which many of the boys and girls did. Harry Milne, at a later period in charge of a group of Edinburgh pupils at a camp in Kiev, was impressed with the way it was run: 'The relative influence of the adult leadership and the elected [children's council] leads, I think, to an interesting experiment in guided democracy.'[9]

The difficulty of making more than superficial contact with Soviet citizens was a recurrent problem with adults. On the early teachers' courses, contact even with professional colleagues was subtly controlled. *Vstrechi*, formal-informal gatherings, tended to be rather artificial with Russians and British standing in two lines or semicircles interacting as two groups rather than as individuals. To some extent this represented Soviet philosophy, whereby the 'collective' was superior to the individual, but it did in fact control personal relations and prevent 'undesirable' contacts with western people getting out of control. Teachers on these short visits did, of course, often succeed in making friendships with Russians through chance contacts, but it was certainly in spite of the system rather than thanks to it. This problem disappeared for post-graduate, and later undergraduate, students who studied for an extended period in the Soviet Union, living in student accommodation alongside Russian young people.

It should not be forgotten that many of these visits to the Soviet Union (not tourist or the pioneer-camp visits) were organized under reciprocal arrangements. This had a consequence which it is easy to forget. Twenty-five British teachers of Russian or thirty postgraduates represent a recognizable percentage of the

---

[9] For accounts of these pupil visits, see M. Hart, 'Holidays in Russia', *ATR Broadsheet* no. 6, 1961, pp. 37-40; Gabrielle Wilson, 'ATR Trip to Moscow', *ATR Journal* no. 10, pp. 7-9; J. K. Blackadder, 'Visit of Manchester schoolchildren to Leningrad July 1964', *ATR Journal* no. 12, 1965, pp. 43-46; H. Milne, 'Scottish pioneers', ATR Newsletter, Sept. 1973, pp. 1-3.

British Russian-speaking workforce. The same number of Russian teachers of English is a minute proportion; the Russian participants on the equivalent courses in Britain had in effect won the lottery when they earned or somehow acquired a place. In 1961 at a meeting with colleagues a university teacher of English was asked, 'What organization does your department have for visiting English-speaking countries?' and was told: *'Organizatsiia blestiashchaia; nikto ne edet.'* (The organization is brilliant: no-one goes.) Doubtless the Soviet bureaucracy had calculated that small numbers of British visitors could do little political harm to anyone they met; the Russian travellers abroad, though an infinitesimal proportion of the profession, needed to be watched. In relation to one teacher exchange, one of the British participants was obliged to pull out at the last minute because of his wife's illness. When it was noticed that the British party in Moscow was one short, nothing was said, but one of the Russians in London was required to return home at once. The principle of reciprocity had been infringed.

Until near the end of the Soviet era this reciprocity and the 'collective' attitude, along with the warnings Russian participants received to maintain a wary attitude, tended to blight contacts with Russian individuals and groups visiting Britain. Several universities have a story of a visiting Soviet lecturer who was summarily removed back to the USSR for no apparent reason, except that he or she appeared to be enjoying themselves too much or was getting too close to British colleagues. Parties of visiting youth, workers, trade unionists and the like were sometimes led by martinets who tried hard to prevent contacts between individuals, allowing them only with the whole group, and then on formal occasions. *Bditel'nost'*, vigilance, was dinned into Soviet travellers abroad: they were to be extremely wary of attempts by the capitalists to corrupt them. One typical party of young people arrived in a provincial city. Its leader protested angrily that his group were staying in private homes, and demanded they should be placed in a hotel; the lack of funds (which the Soviets could neither understand nor believe) meant he lost this argument. A more understandable problem was encountered when a group of Russian students staying at a teacher-training college became frantic when they were assigned private rooms: they had never slept in a room alone in their lives. All these confrontations and misunderstandings were eminently instructive to the British. On the one hand they illustrate why contact with Soviet reality was so educative; on the other, some of them left a nasty taste in the mouth and detracted from good relations.

Despite all this, most universities regularly employed colloquial language assistants in Russian departments, who often made a significant contribution to the teaching of the language, and who comprised a living link with Russia. The opportunity for them to come to Britain was often a reward for good political behaviour, and sometimes the teachers concerned were of a much higher status than one might imagine was strictly necessary for what the job entailed. This was a bonus for the university concerned. In schools the presence of a 'Russian assistant' was very much less common; a mere handful spread over the country was all that could be seen, though Scotland in 1975 boasted six.[10] The post-to-post schoolteacher exchanges provided for in the inter-governmental cultural agreements and overseen by the Central Bureau for Educational Visits and Exchanges allowed a very few practising British teachers of Russian to teach in Moscow and Leningrad (hardly ever anywhere else) and schools used their Soviet partners in the classroom. These arrangements were often of considerable value in raising the profile of the subject, but numbers involved were small.

In-service training, intensive and 'refresher' courses at home and abroad

In the 1960s there was much activity by colleges, universities, schools and groups of teachers in the field of refresher courses for teachers and others, intensive training for anyone wishing to learn some Russian (quite apart from the one-year Annan courses for would-be Russian teachers), revision or coaching courses for sixth-formers about to take Advanced level examinations, Russian-speaking clubs for teachers, students, pupils or anyone interested, and Russian 'days' partly for enjoyment, for practice in speaking and listening to Russian, or for engaging in cultural activities, films and so on. Birmingham University ran day courses on Russian studies (literature, politics, history) and the teaching of Russian for a decade or more. Other intensive, often residential, courses owed something of their methodology to the services Russian courses which were still prominently at the forefront of the minds of many providers. Courses for senior school pupils had a particular advantage, in that classes in schools preparing boys and girls for A level GCE were likely to be small, and contact with students from other schools brought awareness of the strengths of others, which might well be a challenge and a stimulus to further work. One pair of sixth-formers on such a course were staggered by the knowledge some of their fellow-participants had of recondite Russian vocabulary: for some reason it was the fact that one girl knew the Russian for 'sewage' which impressed them most! One young teacher with a degree in French and German, but with a JSSL translator's certificate in Russian obtained nine years previously, was appointed to teach his main languages in a grammar school, but was invited to teach some Russian too. Keen to do this, to revive his extremely rusty Russian, he enrolled on a university intensive vacation course open to all comers, only to find that a fellow-student was one of the sixth-formers he would be teaching the next term. It could have been very embarrassing in the highly competitive atmosphere of the course. Honour was, however, satisfied when our hero gained the gold medal, beating his future pupil into second place by a short head.

A feature of teacher—particularly schoolteacher—activity in the 1960s, which continued for many years, was the regular meetings of local groups. These were mainly the *kruzhki* of the ATR, set up by an early decision of the Association, but often enough working in collaboration with other enthusiasts for the Russian

---

[10]Sinclair, 'Modern Languages in Scotland', p. 113.

language. Birmingham and Liverpool were among cities with Russian-speaking clubs which met frequently. Many other centres organized regular meetings to hear talks in Russian, to discuss teaching issues, to exchange views on how to approach the set books at A level GCE, or to hear accounts of visits to the USSR. One *kruzhok* was briefly in danger of becoming a club for elderly émigrés (or more exactly émigrées) until a coup mounted by certain members broadened its scope. Probably the most determinedly active *kruzhok* (later divided into two) was that in Scotland, which did all of these things. Under the convenorship of the tireless and energetic Harry Milne (later justly rewarded with the MBE and the Pushkin Medal), it was rigorous in scrutinizing the Scottish public examination papers every year only a few days after the exam had been taken, and in making representations to the Board. The Scots also had prior warning of changes in the examination system, such as the introduction of the Certificate of Sixth Year Studies (CSYS) in the mid-1960s, and were formally and informally consulted by HM Inspectorate. Though the SED would not agree to meet any but official bodies (and ATR did not count as such), they dared not ignore the ATR Scottish Branch; Mr Milne's position as a Fellow of the Educational Institute for Scotland certainly helped the voice of Russian to be heard.[11]

As the 1960s progressed, agencies in the USSR were coming to realize that the teaching of Russian abroad was something they should foster, as a means to education, to good international relations, and (as they also doubtless thought) to the extension of Soviet influence in the world. The name of Professor V. G. Kostomarov became well-known in the West as a proponent of Russian teaching, and in 1968 he was invited to participate in a committee meeting of ATR in York. In 1966 he had announced the foundation of a research and methodological centre *(Nauchno-metodicheskii tsentr russkogo iazyka)* affiliated to Moscow State University. The aim of this was to offer 'all-round assistance to organizations and persons studying Russian outside the USSR'. In 1967 the journal *Russkii iazyk za rubezhom* (the Russian Language Abroad) was started and an international association of teachers of Russian language and literature, MAPRYaL *(Mezhdunarodnaia assotsiatsiia prepodavatelei russkogo iazyka i literatury)*, was founded.[12] While national differences in attitudes to school teaching and examinations meant a certain degree of mismatch between the aims of the materials and activities of these bodies, they were none the less of immense value to teachers of Russian, not least the textbooks and teaching aids which were produced, in particular by the offshoot of the Centre and the Association, the publishing house Russkii iazyk.

---

[11] Space does not permit us to pay tribute to all leading figures in the more recent history of Russian teaching; Harry Milne was one of the truly striking characters in its development in Scotland, and not only there. He was a frequent attender and speaker at conferences in Britain and abroad, the mainstay of the East of Scotland ATR circle for many years, a regular contributor to Russian-teaching journals, an author of teaching materials, and an immense support to colleagues old and young.

[12] V. Kostomarov, 'Tsentr... ; 'Sozdanie...'

At the same time, the close involvement of Soviet agencies in the teaching of Russian abroad, and the—necessarily—welcoming attitude of British teachers to this development led to certain slight political difficulties. There were attempts—clumsy ones—on the part of the Soviets to influence the content of the *stranovedenie* (information about the country) which was taught to British children. Conference papers were read by Soviet educators attempting to lay down a 'typical' content for the information about Russia which was imparted. There was no way that British teachers were going to take the slightest notice of this. However, there were numerous occasions on which the Soviets dictated, or tried to dictate, which Soviet activists the ATR should be allowed to entertain at its annual conference; ATR, whether through naivety or exasperation, tended to go along with this, in the hope that *someone* at least would come. There was one occasion when Soviet guests as a conference so far forgot themselves as to heckle a speaker, and another when they self-righteously 'reported to the Embassy' that a certain émigré publisher was allowed to hold a display in the book exhibition. A disturbing incident, however, was instigated by an office-bearer of the Association: an article (on a totally innocuous subject with no political bearing) had been scheduled for publication in the journal; the imagined problem was that the author of the article had earlier got himself into trouble with the Soviets, and the Editor was instructed to cut out the contribution. 'Invertebrate internationalism' again. Not offending the Soviets (if indeed they would have been offended) was preferred to academic freedom. The incident led to at least one resignation.

The qualifications and training of teachers of Russian is a recurrent theme in the development of the teaching of Russian in Britain. Language teachers, of course, need a very good knowledge of the tongue they are to teach. They may be native speakers or not; if they are, the problems they face are quite different from those a non-native speaker has: can they comprehend the difficulties a learner has? Perhaps because everyone has in their circle of acquaintance someone totally unqualified and untrained, but who is an excellent teacher, initial training is seen as desirable, but in the English system, at least, not essential, and it was not compulsory until 1974. This pendulum has swung back slightly in recent years, when 'school-based teacher education' or learning the job *on* the job have become fashionable again. This practice is sometimes dismissively referred to as 'sitting next to Nellie', and it can indeed— but should not and need not—mean slavishly modelling one's teaching style on a 'master-teacher'. In the 1960s, if Russian teachers sought initial training, they trained to teach their other language (most did in fact have another language to teach, or they would not find a full-time appointment) and applied the principles they thus learned to Russian. In the mid-1960s specialist training became available at the University of York; Nottingham College of Education (now part of Nottingham Trent University) offered a BEd degree in Russian. Birmingham University had a Russian linguist on the staff of its School of Education; Sheffield and Nottingham Universities later appointed specialists in the field.

But as for the in-service education of teachers of Russian, the most significant contribution was made from the late 1950s until the late 1980s by the ATR through its annual conferences. These were unfailingly regular: a year was never missed in three decades. They were residential and lasted two or three days. They were an opportunity to learn of new developments of all sorts, to debate with fellow teachers, to speak and listen to Russian, and to participate in cultural events. The December 1965 Conference gives a flavour of the type of occasion these were. There was a lecture on the background to current trends in Soviet economics, one on Russian music, a forum on advanced oral work in sixth forms and universities, and lectures on 'how to read Pushkin' and on Maxim Gorky. A discussion on radio and television Russian courses was led by two authors of programmes, and a producer. Topics covered were Russian in technical colleges, the role of written language in the early stages, and school parties in the USSR. A lecture on alternatives to literary studies at school and university was held jointly with all the other language-teaching associations which were meeting in the same city (Leeds).

A virtue of the conferences was, as with all such meetings, the chance to meet colleagues in other schools, in other types of institution, and from different backgrounds. Russians and non-Russians met socially and professionally. Formal discussions after lectures were often illuminating and instructive in unexpected ways. Once a senior professor of Russian descent bewailed the fact that English students were so prone to error: 'They are learning Russian already two or three years, and they make such elementary mistakes.' No-one flickered. For the rest of my career I used the professor's 'elementary mistake' as a mnemonic for my students to help them remember how Russians construct the 'have been doing... for...some length of time.' We are therefore grateful to her.

A hilarious session at the 1964-65 Conference concerned the changes in Russian orthography proposed by a Commission for the Improvement of Russian Spelling, headed by Academician Vinogradov.[13] When the able chairman for the session, Michael Beresford of Manchester University, introduced the topic, he remarked that the proposed changes were very conservative, in that, for example, the genitive adjective endings written -*ogo*, but always pronounced -*ovo*, were not to be changed. At this, one respected member, affectionately known behind her back as 'the Queen of Spades' because of her favoured hair-style, emitted a titanic snort of disgust: 'The very idea!' One immediately thought: this discussion is going to get us nowhere—and so it proved. But it was an animated and lively debate.[14] The presence of the eminent Soviet professor of language, B. V. Bratus, fuelled the flames. Members eagerly fought over such issues as whether огурцы (*ogurtsy* 'cucumbers') should be spelt thus, or огурци (*ogurtsi*). One

---

[13]Comrie *et al.*, pp. 298-303.

[14]Michael Beresford, 'Report on the proposed changes in Russian orthography', *ATR Journal* 13, Autumn 1965, pp. 12-13.

famous Soviet writer, we were told, had declared he would never eat *ogurtsi* if they were offered to him. Should жены (*zheny,* wives) be spelt thus or 'жоны' (*zhony*) as pronounced? Should *kto-nibud'* (anyone) be written with or without a hyphen? Votes were taken. Was the Soviet Academy of Sciences at all likely to pay any attention to the views of a few dozen British teachers of Russian as opposed to the 180 million Russians in the USSR? We were assured that they were concerned to have the views of foreign teachers of the Russian language. Not long afterwards the Russians rejected the proposals *in toto,* and they were happily forgotten. But it was one of the most entertaining debates ever held at these conferences—and certainly the most pointless.

Further and adult education

Probably the most difficult area of Russian teaching to trace in any accurate detail is the work done in adult and further education (FE): what in more recent times than the 1960s we have come to call 'continuing education'. Chapter 3 showed what a powerful effect this sector of the education service had, temporarily, on interest in the Russian language during the First World War. The ATR published a list in 1961 of around 130 technical colleges, evening institutes, and colleges of further education where Russian was taught.[15] A report from Scotland recorded 304 students taking Russian in FE in 1968-69, as opposed to 5,076 for French and 3,754 for German.[16] The whole matter of learning 'for leisure' as opposed to the achievement of academic or professional qualifications is something of an issue: on the face of it leisure may legitimately be seen as less vital than the serious business of gaining examination certificates with career advancement in mind; on the other hand, leisure and 'personal development' are very important indeed to people. Who is to say that they are less important than the other? It can truly be said that there was a certain group of teachers within ATR in the 1960s and later who were strongly committed to teaching their adult and evening class students (Mrs Eva Strauss, Dr Tanya Rutkowska, Mrs Vivien Pixner), and who fought for their right to be encouraged by the education system, and not to have classes closed over their heads. The amount of Russian taught in further education may have been difficult to estimate, but it has never been insignificant.

The broadcasting media, moreover, began in the late 1950s to play a significant part in further education in Russian, and to contribute to the subject through adult and schools broadcasts. While Moscow Radio was broadcasting language lessons, the first manifestation of British enterprise in this direction was a series of forty sound broadcasts devised by Ronald Hingley and transmitted from 2 November 1959 on Network 3, the BBC further education channel. *Radio Times* published a 'pamphlet' (actually a substantial booklet) to accompany this

---

[15]*ATR Broadsheet* 5, May 1961, pp. 31-32. All but three listed were in England.

[16]SED, *Modern Languages in Further Education,* p. 37.

and provide supporting linguistic material. (The *Radio Times* was not in 1960 the vapid celebrity-obsessed down-market gossip-sheet which it has become.) A problem with educational broadcasting in those days, however, was that producers and teachers perceived such programmes differently: the teachers saw them as instructional material, the broadcasters as entertainment. It took several series before these two laudable aims were successfully combined. Another sound radio series, 'Starting Russian', ran for 41 programmes from 25 November 1962. An early broadcast series by L. M. O'Toole and P. T. Culhane was specifically compiled to be used by teachers with adult and evening classes. It was popular, effective and successful, and the textbook and recorded material underwent several revisions and remained on sale for many years under the eventual title *Passport to Moscow* and *Passport to Odessa*. Other radio programmes followed, including the schools programme *V put'* by C. V. James (1966), the further education series *Ochen'priyatno* and its continuation *Svidanie v Moskve* by Michael Frewin and Alla Braithwaite (early 1970s) which remained in print for a good long period, and *Zdravstvuite, druz'ia* by B. P. Pockney in the early 1980s.

The Independent Television company Tyne-Tees was the first to put out a televised course, entitled *Say it in Russian*, which ran for sixty short programmes in all between 1965 and 1967. It was written by Professor William Harrison and Dr Stephen le Fleming of Durham University; other Durham and Teesside teachers were involved in writing and presentation, and the series was accompanied by booklets and gramophone records. Schools broadcasts followed, as did more adult education-oriented series, and perhaps the most lavish television venture was the BBC's *Russian Language and People*, by P. T. Culhane and R. Bivon, which began in 1980. This typified the entertainment/learning dichotomy by being very entertaining while at the same time providing materials (such as a simple 'soap opera') which could be used for productive study with adults in evening classes. The programmes were made with the cooperation of Moscow Television; this was less straightforward than it might seem. They featured short conversations with citizens in the street; these had apparently aroused in the Soviet officials fears of subversion. The presenters wanted to ask questions like: 'Who are you?', 'How old are you?' 'What do you like doing?' 'How do you like the cold weather?' Soviet minders feared they might ask, 'How do you like the Soviet political system?'—scarcely likely in an elementary course.[17] The accompanying materials for these programmes were most recently re-edited and re-issued in 2006.

HIGHER EDUCATION and its relationship with the secondary sector

After the Scarbrough Report, it seemed that every university wanted to open a Russian department. By 1972 the number of universities offering degree courses in Russian or with Russian as a major component had reached 35; more correc-

---

[17]The story is entertainingly told in Doyle, 'Filming in the Soviet Union...'

tly, 37, as there were three institutions of the University of London involved. Four more universities and one polytechnic were offering minor courses. Eight polytechnics prepared students for the degrees validated by the Council for National Academic Awards (CNAA). Of the 45 degree-based institutions, three were in Wales, six in Scotland and two in Northern Ireland. This is a substantial increase from the 13 universities active in the field in 1960, and it inevitably raises the question as to whether the provision was sustainable. At the same time it must be recognized that there had been a good deal of expansion in the numbers of young people in general applying to university. By the end of the decade Russian and Slavonic departments had to face the Atkinson Report and the threat of closure or assimilation into other institutions. For the moment, however, the picture was not uniformly gloomy.

Many universities, especially but not exclusively the newer ones, had constructed innovative courses which centred on aspects of Russian studies other than traditional language and literature or language and history degrees. Some offered wide-ranging European Studies courses; Soviet Studies, sociology, economics, politics, international relations, and philosophy were studied with Russian. Some departments placed particular stress on the language with interpretership in mind. And nearly all sooner or later made clear provision for *ab initio* courses in Russian and promoted the idea of starting Russian at university.

At the same time there was interest among the university teaching profession in Russian for scientists and social scientists, and ancillary courses were offered in many institutions. This was reflected in a number of publications of teaching material, often based on systematic research of the linguistic register concerned. This type of research was exemplified also by work on more entertaining aspects of Russian lexis: one or two university teachers with professional involvement in sport published lists of footballing vocabulary, for example. I know of no course in higher education focusing on *this* particular topic, however.

Some Russian departments in the 1960s and 1970s devoted the major part of their energy to setting their departments on a firm footing as teaching institutions, leaving the establishment of a research tradition till later. A great deal of effort was devoted to the production of teaching materials by university staff, even books for schoolchildren. This may be seen as a sacrifice of research time, but it was in fact an investment for the future of the subject. There were some departments where research predominated. In all departments *ab initio* work, being demanding of teaching time, was still seen as a burden. Intensive language teaching in the armed services should ideally have provided a model for *ab initio* work, but university conditions allow no more than a pale shadow of such courses, and students cannot be treated like soldiers. It was not until the mid-1980s that research was formally assessed externally; teaching quality was not externally assessed until the 1990s. University departments had always been required to engage in both teaching *and* research; staff had always to share in administration. While there have always been teachers who are strong in all three areas, there had been lecturers who claimed to be committed strongly to teaching rather than research; the price they usually paid for this commitment was lack of promotion. We shall see that when assessment of the two fields eventually became established, Russian departments no less than those of other subjects were strongly affected by the new régime.

The results of policies of curricular innovation were various. Where, within Russian departments and closely associated with them, there were experts in the different aspects of area studies, research output in these fields took on a more varied complexion than in the past. The diverse expertise of staff probably attracted students with a wide variety of academic interests into the study of Russian, along with another discipline and perhaps another language also. It did not, for the most part, attract them in vast numbers, and even excellent departments found recruitment difficult. Basically, this went back to the situation in schools: the notion that the stability of the subject in higher education depended on a good base in secondary education proved to be true, as everyone expected it would. A second consequence is related to *ab initio* courses. Some school teachers were of the opinion that this damaged Russian in schools, because some school principals used the argument against Russian that it could always be started at university if desired. It is very hard to know the extent to which this had an effect. In any case, what was a professor of Russian to do—allow his staff to be put out on the street rather than run an *ab initio* course? The essence of university teaching is that lecturers are employed who are dedicated to scholarship and they build up expertise which often cannot be used in other ways; 'diversification' is possible, but may be very difficult.

Since the publication of the Annan Report, the hope, if not the assumption, had been that schools would eventually provide sufficient undergraduates to supply Russian departments. But... 43 Russian departments? That was more than there were French departments, with nearly every school in the country producing pupils with good A level passes in French. How had this situation been allowed to arise?

One hypothesis is that it was due to misguided enthusiasm. Ever so many universities and polytechnics simply felt that it would be good to have a Russian department. The UGC, the universities' funding authority, did not at the time earmark its finance for particular subjects, and it could therefore not control the behaviour of individual universities in this respect. The warnings of Scarbrough and Hayter would have been heeded by a central authority, but carried little weight with individual institutions. They doubtless thought that *they* would survive and defeat the competition. There was no central monitoring body with statutory power, and this remained the situation.

It may also have been that universities and polytechnics believed that the British government would not allow Russian to go under, on the grounds of state security and intelligence, the need for people who understood the Soviet Union, trade, diplomacy and the like. There is no direct evidence for this suggestion, except that the general line of argument is what proponents of Russian systematically argued in the mid to late twentieth century. It may be thought, therefore, that this represents complacency; at least it was misguided optimism.

What was the situation in schools in the 1970s? The ATR mounted a 'Survey of supply, demand and utilization of teachers of Russian in secondary schools' in 1970-71.[18] The results of all such surveys are to be read with caution, and the compilers of this one warn that schools were in the throes of reorganization at the time. (The Labour Government of 1964-1970 had required local education authorities to submit plans for reorganization on comprehensive lines, while the Conservatives, who took power in 1970, revoked this requirement, and this was the situation until Labour regained power in 1974.) The highest figure ever might therefore be an under-estimate: 802 schools were found to be teaching Russian. As many as 212 were found to have once offered Russian, but were no longer doing so. The survey concludes in consequence that there was considerable 'instability' in the provision of Russian. This word recurs again and again in discussions of the situation over the decades.

It may therefore have seemed to universities in 1971 that Russian in schools was in the ascendant, even if the Annan Report's target was not met. But this was hardly the case. The ATR noted a decline in popularity of Russian as a subject; also, an overcrowded timetable was a serious problem.[19] In a report on Russian in the North Midlands, HM Inspectorate noted that the supply of teachers of Russian 'appears to be adequate.'[20] The danger points the inspectors raised were: 'courses with ten or less pupils in each year still constitute over half the total'. When financial stringency arises, Russian was therefore targeted for removal. The inspectors comment that grammar schools, when reorganized into comprehensives, will lose their 'rather privileged staffing ratio' and may have to abandon Russian which is taught to small groups'. The quality of work was 'very varied, being distinctly good in a number of schools but weak owing to poor teaching in about one school in six.' This was no worse than the performance of teachers in German and Spanish, as reported by the inspectors. They commented also that Russian, 'regarded as a difficult language, is... most at risk if the "academic" intake to a school is reduced as a result of reorganization. It may well disappear from a few of [the] schools [inspected] for this reason.'

The notion that primary school French might foster diversity in second foreign languages at secondary level and an earlier start for such languages is demolished by the inspectors' last conclusion:

> In the present survey no case was found where the teaching of French in primary schools was the clear cause of changes in the position of Russian, but in three schools where German had shared the position of first foreign lan-

---

[18]'Survey of supply, demand and utilization of teachers of Russian in secondary schools', *Journal of Russian Studies*, no. 21, 1971, pp. 56-68.

[19]ATR, 'Survey of supply...', p. 67.

[20]DES, *Report by HM Inspectors on... the Teaching of Russian...*

guage with French it no longer does so. There was no example of the earlier start on French leading to the earlier introduction of 'second' languages.

A Scottish report had made the same finding, and it was a theme of an article by C.V. James.[21] Assuming that the North Midlands were typical of the country as a whole, there are other signs here which are ominous. It is not the sixth of the teaching force who are not very competent: that could have been worse. But the approach of comprehensive education, the likelihood of smaller numbers of 'academic' pupils, and most of all the necessity for schools to have full classrooms whatever the subject—these elements were challenges which would arise in the near future. Universities may have been no more than dimly aware of these likely problems, though within a decade or two they would be facing their own version of this problem, particularly the demand for 'cost-effectiveness', and a much more acute version it turned out to be.

The conclusions of the ATR 'Survey of Supply, Demand and Utilization...' were written by that prominent enthusiast and activist for the teaching of Russian, John Davidson. These conclusions resemble some of those of the HM Inspectors. In a section entitled 'The Instability of Russian Teaching' Davidson commented that the 212 schools which had once offered Russian but no longer did so represented a very high figure alongside the 802 which were teaching it and the 144 which might be 'envisaging' the introduction of Russian. In some schools once prominent as torchbearers for Russian, it had died out, or numbers of pupils recruited had dropped drastically. While the Committee of ATR were less than sanguine about the popularity of Russian as a subject, Davidson reports, heads of departments saw an overcrowded timetable as the problem.[22]

A significant comment of Davidson's relates to teacher supply: while many of the teachers he investigated were qualified to teach Russian, but not actually doing so, 'Data collected do not indicate any great tendency to mobility on the part of such teachers.' (p. 67) In other words, they were for the most part reluctant to change jobs in order to teach more or even some Russian. Davidson suggested that these teachers 'would come best into their own when matched with a second teacher as part of a planned development.' Another much smaller but no less interesting survey of the utilization of teachers of Russian had been made a year or two earlier in 1968-69. It concerned the teachers who had learned Russian in the first five years of the Glasgow intensive courses, which had been set up in the wake of the Annan Report. Out of 35 responses to a questionnaire, 15 of these teachers had taught Russian continuously since training; 18 had taught occasionally, and only 2 had had no opportunity to teach Russian. A matter of great concern to a large majority of these teachers was the need to ensure the continuity of Russian in any given school by not leaving it to one qualified teacher only; this echoes Davidson's remark about 'pairing'. Many of

---

[21] James, 'The State of the Union', esp. p. 2; SED, *Modern Languages in Si and Sii...*

[22] Davidson, ATR 'Survey...', p. 65 fn.

these teachers were also concerned that heads of schools must not be allowed to forget the 'attractions and benefits' of the study of Russian: it would seem that they were uncertain whether they were being offered wholehearted support for the subject. At the same time, the teachers who replied to the enquiry (44 had been approached, so the 35 were a high proportion) indicated a high degree of enthusiasm for their new subject and dedication to and identification with it.[23]

In a survey conducted by myself ten or fifteen years later, it was concluded that three times as much Russian could have been taught by the 54 teachers surveyed without entirely depriving their schools of the use of their skills in other subjects.[24] However, the very versatility of teachers of Russian worked both in favour of and against the subject; while it was discovered they rarely lost their enthusiasm for Russian, they were often happy enough teaching another subject. Moreover, if they gained promotion through their other expertise, Russian might be laid aside. The nature of the first post won by a young newly-qualified teacher of Russian and French was also crucial: such young people might hang around for a while at the end of their teacher-training course, hoping a job with Russian would come up, and when it did not, take a post for French. Time and again a Russian post would then be advertised and remain unfilled. Matching demand and supply is almost impossible to achieve in an education system where no sort of overall monitoring is customary, or even practically feasible, given the constraints of tradition.

Could the government have helped the situation? We have seen that ministry or departmental secretaries have taken different views over the years before the national curriculum became mandatory in the 1980s. In 1975 both Reg Prentice and Fred Mulley, successive secretaries of state for education, took the hard line in answers to letters (both dated 1975) from officers of the Great Britain-USSR Association: they both insisted that curricular decisions 'are determined by local demand' (Prentice) and 'It is at the local level that any renewed demand for Russian must come' (Mulley).[25] Local insularity must be respected at all costs.

The Armed Services

The interdependence of every sector of British education with the others is a recurrent theme of this study. The dramatic effect of the National Service courses of the 1950s upon Russian studies has been highlighted in the previous chapter. However, as compulsory national service for young males ended in the early 1960s, the army, navy and air force still needed linguists qualified in Russian, and continued to train them under the umbrella of the armed services; servicemen were joined by diplomats, and even by foreign diplomats at that. The services courses, to that extent, made a contribution to the country's balance of payments.

---

[23] Wade, 'Strathclyde survey.'

[24] Muckle, 'Teachers of Russian and their careers', p. 215.

[25] reported by James, 'Shag vpered i dva nazad', p. 2.

These courses perhaps stood aside from the mainstream of Russian studies, as they had their own vocational aims and a separate *raison d'être*, while inevitably they provided at least some recruits to university Russian departments as undergraduates or even staff.

Crail in Fife was, to the dismay of the local population, abandoned by JSSL in 1960, while the Principal was delighted, having considered it a camp totally unsuitable for its purpose. After that, a highly successful enterprise was run by the Army at Beaconsfield, and another for the RAF and Navy at Tangmere, near Chichester; later the RAF moved to North Luffenham, Rutland, and in 1997 to Chicksands, Bedfordshire. The Navy transferred its allegiance to Beaconsfield in 1964, later withdrawing to the Royal Naval College, Dartmouth between 1976 and 1984. Liaison between the services continued, despite the divorce in 1960, and links were agreed with colleges such as RMA Sandhurst.[26]

The enterprise at Beaconsfield has been admirably written up by Brian Hawkins, a respected insider within the operation. I can add nothing to his account, except to comment on certain features of the courses. Up to the Second World War, interpreter training had been for officers; as we have seen, NCOs were trained during and after that war, and in the 1950s private soldiers, aircraftmen, and naval coders—all the lowest ranks in the services—were trained, and on completion of training received relatively modest promotion. At Beaconsfield senior NCOs were trained along with officers, but while the 'gentlemen' spent four months in Paris with Russian-speaking families before taking their interpretership examinations, NCOs did not. It is not clear why this apparent class distinction was imposed. At least for officers, the tradition established in the 1880s of study at home followed by study abroad (Russia or elsewhere) was continued.

The courses at Beaconsfield admitted between a dozen and thirty students per annum of all sorts: army, navy, diplomatic, British, foreign. Hawkins mentions students, military and civilian, from Ghana, Switzerland, Malaya, Hong Kong, Australia, Singapore, France (very briefly—a special arrangement), and particularly Japan. Photographs show that the students were overwhelmingly male. He names thirty-nine Japanese who were trained at Beaconsfield, all of whom later occupied important posts in the Japanese diplomatic or consular services, or in international organizations, between 1961 and 1989. Forty-six British diplomatic students ttended courses between 1966 and 1982. Between 1962 and 1988 309 students passed CSC Examinations, 34 of them at first class standard. Navy Lists name 37 serving officers qualified in Russian in 1960, 24 in 1970, and 27 in 1980. It may be that the 1960 figure is somewhat higher because of the residual effect on the statistics of officers trained while on national service, or perhaps a few who held short-service commissions, which some young men did in place

---

[26] I regret that this paragraph is convoluted. The constant migration of military establishments is an unfortunate feature of the armed services in Britain: movement seems to be an essential property inherent in the system.

of ill-paid conscription. The later figures compare with 14 RN officers in 1935 and 19 at the outbreak of war in 1939. While the numbers trained at Beaconsfield are not huge, they certainly indicate a substantial provision of Russian linguists to the armed and diplomatic services of several nations. A student from the Royal Family was Prince Michael of Kent, who entered as a subaltern in 1966. Though a talented linguist, he was obliged to leave his placing in Paris as a result of press harassment, which made his life and that of his Russian-French family intolerable. Recent events, however, show that his knowledge of Russian remains good, though he is modest about his own achievements.[27]

It is appropriate to continue the brief history of services Russian beyond the period covered in the major part of this chapter. A parliamentary answer given on 27 July 1989 stated that there were then 162 serving military personnel qualified as Russian interpreters: 32 in the Navy, 94 in the Army and 36 in the RAF. The Minister said: 'The number of Russian interpreters has increased modestly in recent years,' and gave the annual cost of running the Russian courses at Beaconsfield at £420,000.[28]

British naval interpreters were able to be of service to the Russian navy after the tragic sinking of the submarine *Kursk* in 2000. The Royal Navy was able to find a nuclear-trained submarine engineer who was an excellent Russian-speaker, as well as another Russian-speaking officer, among personnel to assist with the unfortunately abortive rescue attempt.[29]

It is worth adding that to this day the National Defence School of Languages at Beaconsfield maintains its Slavonic Wing after 54 years.[30] This Wing also teaches Serbian, Bosnian, Croatian and Albanian. It may be relocated as part of a Defence Training Review. The RAF North Luffenham enterprise closed down in 1995. Since the closure of Russian courses at the Royal Naval College at Dartmouth (except for 'survival' level), men from all three services have been trained in Russian at Beaconsfield, along with diplomats (until 1978) and other civilian interpreters such as those supporting the Joint Arms Control Implementation Group, usually on an eighteen-month course. (The Foreign and Commonwealth Office language school for diplomats in London closed in 2007, and

---

[27] The Prince gives an informative account of his contacts with Russia and its language in his 'Russian reminiscences' (p. 4), which contains a generous tribute to the teaching at Beaconsfield and to the Russian family with which he stayed in Paris. See also www.princemichael.org.uk/diary/months/july_2001.html.

[28] As this book went to press the Ministry of Defence was able to give the latest figures: as at 22.4.08 there were 445 Russian linguists in the armed sevices (excluding Special Forces): 118 RN, 129 Army, 198 RAF. The qualifications of 300 of these were 'out of date', in that they had been gained more than three years previously. (Private communication from Derek Twigg MP.)

[29] The officer concerned briefly describes his experience in remarks reported by Prince Michael of Kent, pp. 10-11.

[30] For most of the information in this paragraph I am indebted to Mr R. Avery, Officer Commanding the Slavonioc Languages Wing at the Defence School of Languages.

Beaconsfield hopes to reclaim some of this 'trade'. The Russian Department at Chicksands closed in 2005). Students ranged from low non-commissioned rank to officers of Air rank and army and navy equivalents. Beaconsfield trainees in recent years have also spent a month in Moscow for language study; meanwhile the Russian Ministry of Defence reports that foreign military personnel (including some NATO countries) are received in Russia at seventy military academies and schools.[31] Beaconsfield continues to seek to train foreign personnel.

Political and International Currents and their Influence on Russian Studies

The relationship between political events and the interest of the British population in Russian has never been direct. But the outbreak of war in 1914, the revolutions of 1917, the alliance with the Soviet Union in 1941-42 have, as we have seen, influenced the study of the Russian language in Britain to differing extents. The brutal suppression of the Hungarian uprising in 1956-57 aroused loathing, but Britain was occupied with her own problems at the time. There was still hostility in some British quarters. As R. A. Peace put it: 'At the very mention of the word "Russian" they see red... The result paradoxically enough is that education in this country is more at the mercy of politicians than it is in the Soviet Union. There the politicians are at least nationally and internationally conscious: in Britain on the other hand local education has resulted only too often in parochialism.' Teachers of other languages too sometimes resented an 'upstart' language like Russian.[32] The launching of the first sputnik in 1957 and the first manned space flight in 1961 created a favourable climate of serious interest in the USSR which certainly helped Russian studies. Later twentieth-century events had a rather more equivocal effect. The invasion of Czechoslovakia by the Warsaw Pact armies in 1968 was one instance.

The Czechoslovak government was attempting to reform the shape of Communism in the country. It was believed that the fact that the Czechs were allowing both an increase in freedom of expression *and* were exploring new approaches to foreign policy alarmed the Soviets. A demonstration by students in Prague included a parade of young men bearing a huge banner depicting in lurid colour an immense pile of steaming excrement and the caption, 'We're in it again.' And indeed they were: on 20 August 1968 Soviet planes landed, tanks rolled in and repression began. Minimal force was used, unlike events in Hungary in 1956. It was regarded with sardonic disdain by many Czechs. In one central square in Prague a row of eight Soviet tanks was standing before a huge advertisement hoarding, left over from before the invasion, which said 'Free speech for all'; ironically, the tanks appeared to be guarding this poster. Another improvised notice had been set up in front of them reading 'Exhibition of tanks.' It is unlikely the Soviet officers saw the joke; perhaps they misread the Czech.

---

[31] Prince Michael, p. 10; http://milparade.udm.ru/22/64.html, as at 27 March 2007.

[32] R. A. P[eace], 'Now is the time to act', *ATR Broadsheet* 3, pp. 34-36.

The invasion caused outrage throughout the non-communist world, and it is possible that it had an effect on recruitment to Russian classes. The peak in numbers of schools where Russian was taught came in 1971, as we have seen, while public examination entries began a decline from that very date, in England, Wales, and Scotland. It is easy to say that mature people should not allow political considerations to affect their attitudes. However, when one is engaging in propaganda for a subject, public distaste has to be faced. The ATR was in a quandary. The year 1968 was when the International ATR, MAPRYaL, was in process of formation. Certain leading officers of ATR felt that the political crisis made it very difficult to solicit funds from 'various official and private organizations' and from academic bodies for the work of MAPRYaL. They therefore informed the Secretary of MAPRYaL to this effect. When the ATR Committee met in October 1968, there was animated discussion, but this action was approved by 10 votes to 4; it was decided that ATR should join MAPRYaL and pay its subscription; that potential academic member institutions should be circulated, but that no approach be made to non-academic bodies until the AGM had been consulted. In the highly-charged atmosphere of the time, this seemed the best compromise.

Though the end of the next decade brought the Moscow Olympic Games, even that happy event, which might otherwise have increased public interest in Russia and her language, was to be overshadowed. There were two events which soured British-Soviet relations. The first was the expulsion by the British Foreign Office in 1971 of over a hundred Soviet 'diplomats' who were accused of spying—or, at least, intelligence gathering. The second was Soviet policy in Afghanistan, of which Western governments made a great issue. This matter has largely been forgotten, but there must surely be many British and American politicians who now wish they had left the Soviets to get on with that particular war without interference. These events probably did not have much effect in themselves on recruitment to Russian courses. However, the charge of intelligence gathering had repercussions for Russian teachers when it was discovered that a prominent officer of MAPRYaL was rumoured to be an officer in the KGB and was certainly *persona non grata* in Britain. ATR had in all innocence invited this person to their annual conference at one time, but—because of the official British obsession with secrecy—was not frankly informed why the visa had been refused. Soviet authorities with no connection with Russian teaching tried various ruses to slip him past the guards, without success until well into the twenty-first century, by which time any objection had expired. The incident illustrates the nature of some of the political difficulties which might arise to obstruct academic relations. Soviet bureaucracy may seem to have been attempting to manipulate cultural exchanges for political ends; British bureaucracy muddied the waters when they could have received cooperation. British teachers may occasionally have misjudged the situation, but gave no real reason to doubt their political impartiality.

Moves in Educational Policy and their Impact on Russian

The decline in Russian teaching in schools after 1971 may be traced in the statistics for public examination entries at age 16, 17, and 18. In 1971 there were 3145 entries for O level GCE and 331 for O grade SCE; 846 entered A level and 227 Scottish Higher. In 1975 2290 candidates entered O level and 224 O grade, with 659 A level entries and 136 Scottish Highers. By 1979 these numbers had dropped to 1756 entries for O level, 200 for O grade, and 396 A levels (Scottish Highers figure unpublished). The available Scottish figures differentiate between school and FE entries; the latter are very small numbers indeed for these years. The Atkinson Report presents the information to 1977 in graphic form. (See fig 7, and Annex C, Table 5.) In Scotland the best year for highers had been 1968 with 229 candidates, but in 1975 it was 127, and in 1977 96 only. A Scottish HMI, Dr G. M. Sinclair, went so far as to say during a conference presentation in 1977: 'Russian, of course, has been disappointing in the sense that it shot up, reached a plateau and gradually tailed away.'[33]

Other statistics reflect the situation too. In 1971-72 the position of Russian can be seen in the table below, which presents Russian in relation to other modern languages at different levels. Taking Russian as 1 in every case, examination entries appear as:

Sector	Italian	Spanish	German	French
University	5	14	22	39
FE	5	12	23	44
A level	1	3	7	26
O level	1	4	12	48
CSE	1	8	28	236

Except for the university sector, figures apply to England and Wales only.[34]

How is this decline to be explained? Between 1960 and 1980 schools in all parts of Britain were undergoing radical reorganization. At the beginning of this chapter three or four factors affecting the expansion and establishing of Russian teaching were mentioned, some of them having a direct influence and some an indirect one. These included the nationwide introduction of comprehensive schools—an education act of 1976 was intended to compel reluctant local education authorities (LEAs) to do this, though a famous court action brought by one LEA resulting in the 'Tameside Judgement' restricted the powers of central government; the realization that the Annan Report was not having the dramatic effect hoped for; the lack of central management of the introduction of Russian, and Britain's interest in entering what was eventually to become the European Union. Some further associated matters need also to be borne in mind. The school leaving age was raised to 16 in 1972, resulting in the presence in schools of more teenagers, some of them reluctant if not actually mutinous.

---

[33] Sinclair, 'Modern languages in Scotland: a historical review', p. 112.

[34] C. V. James, 'Lies and statistics'.

Comprehensive education brought with it in many places an ideological belief in 'mixed-ability' classes, which were not selected according to ability or aptitude. LEAs had to find ways of reorganizing their schools into comprehensives. Some simply amalgamated existing institutions, even if the buildings were separated by distances too long to be walked between lessons. Others established schools for children aged 11 to 16, followed by sixth-form colleges. Others again went for 'middle schools': age 9 or 10 to 12 or 13, then from that age to 18. Worst of all, there were LEAs which tried one method, and a few years later when it was not working too well, tried another. Organizational problems in the mid-1970s were not helped by falling school rolls, a consequence of a reduced birth rate in earlier years. There was also a trend towards co-education. This one was partly ideological: though research evidence is uncertain as to whether girls or boys benefit academically from being taught in mixed schools, it was simply felt by many to be right to have them. Also, it was partly a matter of convenience, as when location of buildings, numbers of pupils, and availability of teachers seemed to indicate that co-educational schools could be managed well. It was sometimes an issue of finance: LEAs could achieve economies of scale, while independent schools could get more fee-paying pupils by admitting both sexes.

Another matter affecting the independent schools was the ending of the 'direct grant' in the mid-1970s, an arrangement whereby participating schools accepted pupils from their local area whose fees were paid by the LEA, or by their parents on a sliding scale according to ability to pay. During a thirty-year period this system had benefited many girls and boys whose parents could never have afforded to pay full fees. The system was replaced for some years by an 'assisted places' scheme, which was far smaller in scope, and some schools were able to offer bursaries and fee assistance. The ending of the direct grant, however, deprived many independent schools of some ambitious, able pupils. It reinforced the 'élitist' image of the schools, giving a further weapon to the enemies of independent selective education. Since Russian has always figured more prominently in the independent sector than in maintained schools, this may be seen as an element restricting the availability of the language to all.

None of these issues, on the face of it, were likely to do much more harm to Russian than to other subjects: it is no more or less difficult to teach Russian in a mixed-ability class than chemistry or mathematics. Co-education may have worked to the advantage of Russian; reorganization may in some circumstances have benefited Russian (such as the establishment of large sixth-form colleges, though there are different opinions about this). On consideration, however, the dangers for Russian become clearer. Two or three schools amalgamate, one of them with Russian on the curriculum: if the 'wrong' head takes over the new school, years of work persuading the person in charge to support the subject may be lost. This would never have happened with French; it might, however, have been an issue with German—that language being perhaps rather less well established than French in the system—but with Russian it easily happened. In general, when LEAs and schools were dealing with the major problems of secondary reorganization, there were sufficient people around in influential positions who regarded Russian as a minor detail, a dot on the graph which was really a bit of a nuisance. At a time when political considerations within the administration of education were considered as more important than the pursuit of knowledge, educational arguments were likely to be brushed aside.

These reflections are made with the benefit of hindsight, but those concerned at the time were coming to very similar conclusions. An important survey by HM Inspectorate on mathematics, science and modern language teaching published in 1977 raised many of the same issues in relation to languages generally, not only Russian. The HMIs expressed concern about mixed-ability teaching. Insufficiently differentiated teaching had led to 'concern about what is happening to more able pupils as well as to those of average and below average ability'.[35] The dominant position of French, which linguist educators had been wrestling with for years—and still do—was a problem which manifested itself in several ways, many of them as harmful to French as to the other languages. French in primary schools was having 'negative results and also imposing a degree of constraint on subsequent language learning in secondary schools which may have had an adverse effect on languages other than French.' Preference for French as first foreign language 'cannot easily be justified, given Britain's position in Europe and the world.' The balance with other languages 'may only be redressed if some schools offer a language other than French as first foreign language. Teachers better qualified in other languages are spending an increasing amount of their time teaching French.'

The Inspectors raised other issues. Reorganization of secondary education and changes in the age of transfer of pupils from primary or middle schools to secondary institutions was tending to a standardization of language provision—in other words, more dominance of French and often enough a poorly established second language in 11-16 schools. Co-education seemed to be increasing the tendency for languages to be seen as a 'girls" subject. This is in fact a contentious point: though unquestionably more girls than boys opt for languages and girls do better on average than boys, researchers find very few boys who actually give the reason for not choosing a language that it is a subject for girls. They simply have other priorities.

Welsh Education Survey no. 2: *Modern Languages other than French in secondary Schools,* London: HMSO, 1973, outlined the current position in the Principality. Russian was taught (as at July 1973) in twenty-four schools in Wales to 520 pupils. Timetabling arrangements were disadvantageous to the subject, teachers hard to find, courses were short, and the teachers who did exist could not always use the methods they wished because 'the great majority of schools are ill-equipped for effective language teaching.' In speaking up for these

---

[35]DES, *Mathematics, Science and Modern Languages...*, p. 2.

languages, however, the last section, 'The choice of first modern language', is a little more encouraging. It rehearses the reasons for the supremacy of French, gives some of the traditional reasons for studying German, Spanish, Italian, and Russian, and then rejects them all, stating that the main justification for studying any of these languages is that there are many millions who communicate in them 'and with whom the pupil can make contact, thus giving insight into various important European countries.' If the status quo is accepted, that is, the vast majority of pupils 'make contact' and 'gain insight' into the French, 'It must be asked whether we are prepared to accept a situation in which *only with France* shall the majority of pupils have the opportunity to make direct contact.' The Welsh Education Office is wise enough also to reject the argument that French is particularly valuable as a lingua franca. Welsh children, after all, do not need French—they have English, which is far more use as a lingua franca.

Many of these same matters were discussed by Scottish educators: an earlier document from the SED, *Alternatives to French as a first foreign language in Secondary Schools* (1971) made a case for diversification. The SED pamphlet raises the issue of parental wishes; it may well be that the unwillingness of parents to accede to changes in traditional provision is a strong reason why diversification has not been put into practice. As for Russian, the document states that its difficulties have been overstressed, and that it does not need to be offered only to 'selected pupils'. 'Provided reasonable objectives are laid down and the pace is suitably adjusted, many more pupils should be able to derive profit from a study of Russian even in mixed ability classes in the first year.'[36]

However, this positive view was not entirely supported by the Munn Report, a seminal study of the secondary school curriculum from age 14 to 16 in Scotland. 'Munn' was accompanied by the Dunning Report, which sought to reform the examination system. These reports are of the greatest interest for the history of curricular thinking not just in Scotland; in the following decade many of the same issues were taken up in England and Wales when the National Curriculum and the replacement of the GCE O level examination by the General Certificate of Secondary Education (GCSE) were under discussion. Scotland has never had a national curriculum and still does not, but the Munn-Dunning proposals amounted to something very close to a 'substantially compulsory curriculum', in the words of Rosamund Mitchell in her response to the Reports. The influence of Munn and Dunning on modern languages, including of course Russian, in classes S3 and S4 was a contentious matter of great concern to teachers of the subject. Briefly, Munn proposed a 'core plus electives' scheme in which foreign languages were to be non-compulsory electives. Their thinking is explained in paragraph 4.11:

---

[36] SED, *Alternatives to French as a first foreign language in Secondary Schools*, Edinburgh: HMSO, 1971, p. 5.

> ...We recognize the value of a language other than English for the insights it can give to another culture. We also recognize its practical value as an ancillary skill in a variety of occupations, especially at a time when the European dimension of our business and commercial life is becoming more and more important. It can also constitute a valuable tool in the further study of other disciplines. These are strong arguments for including a second language in the curriculum, and we are convinced that it is right to introduce all pupils to foreign language study in S1 and S2. It is more debatable, however, whether it would be more appropriate at present to recommend that all pupils in S3 and S4 should be compelled to take a foreign language. Experience so far in schools leaves some doubt as to whether the advantages we have outlined can be achieved in the time available with pupils of low linguistic ability, who may see little relevance in foreign language study and who may in fact have only a limited degree of competence in English itself. We have also been advised that—mainly because languages were restricted for so long to the ablest pupils—the materials and methodology for less able pupils have not yet been developed to a point where effective learning can readily take place. For these reasons we recommend that all pupils should have the opportunity of studying one or more foreign languages in S3 and S4, if they so wish, but that they should not in the present circumstances be compelled to do so. In the case of pupils of some linguistic ability, however, positive encouragement should be given to them to continue foreign language study in S3 and S4, whether or not they intend to be specialist linguists.

In a conference lecture defending his Committee's proposals,[37] James Munn states that their refusal to make a foreign language compulsory for more able pupils was contrary to the wishes of the Scottish Central Committee on Modern Languages (SCCML). To make a language compulsory for some pupils 'would produce an élitist and divisive curriculum which was undesirable in itself, and would be broadly unacceptable to the teaching-profession as a whole.' 'Encouragement', not compulsion, was the policy recommended.

It is easy to see that the language-teaching profession would be provoked to various reactions. The pages of *Modern Languages in Scotland*, no 15, 1978, exemplify the strength of feeling.[38] One side expresses immense relief that the less able are not to be 'tortured' by being compelled to stay with a language to age 16; the other condemns the denial of language study to the less able. An 'élitist' subject will be created say one side; talk of élitism is straight nonsense, say the others. Keep languages for the more able? Yes, say some; no—look what has happened to the classics on that basis—say the others. The SCCML was commissioned by its parent body, the Committee on Secondary Education, to carry out a survey of teachers' opinions. It reported 'a very marked polarization of views.' Teachers agreed that a modern language was not an essential part of

---

[37] Munn, 'The Implications of the Munn Report...', p. 25.

[38] See the papers by Pincock, E. Rooney, and Linton.

the education of every pupil at S3 and S4. Only 9% agreed with a compulsory language for the less-able at that stage. However, 43% thought modern languages should be compulsory for the more able (the view specifically rejected by Dunning.) Only about half thought all pupils could learn a foreign language to the end of S4, even if appropriate materials and methods were developed.[39]

We do not know whether the opinions of Scottish Russian teachers in this respect differed from those of their colleagues teaching other languages. It will be recalled that the view of the place of foreign languages in education reflects that expressed in the Thomson Report of 1947, quoting and reaffirming the view expressed in an SED 1907 memorandum. The paper on the history of modern languages in Scotland by HM Inspector Sinclair, delivered only a year or two earlier, quotes the same remarks, and by its tone indicates that Sinclair expected teachers would disagree with the sentiments expressed: he was clearly wrong. The Dunning proposals on assessment had general agreement: three levels were recommended, for 'credit' (the most challenging, for about 20% of the cohort), 'general' (the next 60%) and 'foundation' (most of the rest: the simplest). There were reservations, however, on the appropriateness of foundation-level assessment in modern languages—again linguist teachers were sceptical of the possibilities of involving the less able pupil.

This survey was, of course, carried out in 1977. It may be that egalitarian notions of the curriculum had not caught on thirty years ago. While one has every sympathy with the teacher who has to cope with unwilling, unmotivated, and fractious teenagers, it is doubtful whether it is possible—in a climate of opinion where inclusivity, equality, and human rights are paramount—to maintain the position that a subject is only to be available to the cream of the age-group, or that it should be a compulsory part of the general education for some, but not for others. Russian has in fact been made available to a wide range of ability in certain comprehensive schools, both in Scotland and England.

In 1981 it was necessary to argue that such a policy was feasible, and two essays by practising teachers and one by a school principal were published.[40] They showed that one London girls' comprehensive school taught six months each of French, German, Spanish and Russian to all its girls. After two years they were invited to choose one of these for a three-year course to CSE or O level. A year later the gifted could add a second language. At one Edinburgh comprehensive academy pupils might start Russian in S1 and add another language in S2. Results at age 16 showed a respectable pass rate at O grade (73%), H grade (83%) and CSE (75%). A comprehensive school in Birmingham was achieving comparable success.[41] It must be admitted that in some of these schools Russian (or a language in general) could be dropped before the age of

---

[39] Scottish Central Committee..., 'Survey of Scottish Language Teacher Opinion'.

[40] Milne, 'Russian as a first foreign language', Handley, and Tennant.

[41] Susan James, 'Russian in Castle Vale School...'

16, but with results like these the incentive for pupils to stick with it was strong. Perhaps the most striking feature was the character of the London teacher: a Soviet citizen, trained in the achievement-oriented Russian system. After nearly a decade in her selective grammar school it went comprehensive, and it was discovered she had a pronounced gift for handling average and less able children.

The publication under the joint auspices of ATR, BUAS, BASEES and the GB-USSR Association in 1982[42] of *Russian in Schools* was part of a campaign to stop the rot. This booklet was sent free of charge to local education authorities, inspectors, advisors, and anyone else who might have influence. Five years earlier the Slavonic associations had got together to form a Slavonic and East European Joint Consultative Committee to cooperate in such a campaign. The Secretary of State for Education was approached, and gave the familiar answer that she did 'not have and does not seek central control of the schools curriculum', while expressing concern that 'the quality and extent of language provision is less than satisfactory.' In 1978, however, the Department for Education and Science asked ATR for a statement of the case for Russian. A document—yet another 'case for Russian'—was compiled and presented to the National Congress on Languages in Education (NCLE) for forwarding to the DES.[43] Among the rank and file of the Russian-teaching profession there had been evidence of fatigue in promoting Russian; as one teacher put it, 'Complaining about the situation has ceased to be therapeutic.' As early as the beginning of the decade an unsigned editorial in an *ATR Newsletter* regretted that members were not communicating, not using the services of the Association, and so on. Had enthusiasm and morale begun to wane?

The request from the DES via NCLE for such a statement may have been a very early indication, despite the Secretary of State's disclaimer quoted above, that the government was beginning to interest itself in the curriculum: ATR had been asked by NCLE for input into a 'national policy for modern languages.'

An *ATR Newsletter* of 1978 raised international comparisons: it was reported that 53 schools in Austria were teaching Russian to 2,600 pupils; in France 26,000 were learning it in schools, while in the Federal Republic of Germany the number of pupils had declined to 16,000 from 22,000 a year or two previously. There had never been an attempt to estimate the number of pupils learning Russian in Britain, but the 1979 ATR survey listed 395 schools teaching Russian. The roughest estimate—very rough indeed—is that over 13,000 children were studying the language in these schools. The estimate is based on the average number of pupils per school in a much later (1992) survey, and there is no way of verifying the applicability of this average to the 1979 list.

---

[42]Muckle, *Russian in Schools*.

[43]Morley and Muckle, 'The Place of modern languages and of Russian...' The statement was much revised by ATR Executive Committee.

As for the Republic of Ireland, in the mid-1970s there was no school Russian here. Following the establishment for the first time of full diplomatic relations between Ireland and the USSR, an attempt on the part of five secondary schools to introduce the language had been made. It failed for lack of suitably qualified teachers. Four adult education colleges in Dublin were running courses for officials, businessmen, scholars, diplomats, journalists and teachers, and St Patrick's College, an educational institute and Catholic seminary was at the time considering introducing Russian.[44]

The 1978 *ATR Newsletter* reports the situation on the ground in one particular Southern English school, in anonymous notes supplied by the teacher at South Wiltshire Grammar School for Girls. This colleague lists the factors which are conducive to the success of Russian in a school: total support and active policy by the head teacher, avoidance of competition with other languages, selective enrolment and insistence that pupils who sign up for Russian complete the course, a recognition within the school that Russian plays an important part in the curriculum (Russian was integrated with study of geography, history, English and other languages), and the presence of a full-time Russian teacher who can make her or himself indispensable to the general life of the school. If these conditions are met, it becomes very difficult to dislodge Russian from the school. Theory and practice come together admirably in these remarks.[45]

The Atkinson Report of 1979

As for the universities in the 1970s, the prime problem was a decline in numbers of students applying to study Russian. Undergraduates in Russian and Russian Studies with language amounted to 1,490 in the year 1973-74; it declined to 1,391 in 1977-78, but rose again to 1,440 the year after this.[46] This *is* a decline, but that is not the whole point. The University Grants Committee (UGC) had expressed concern in its Annual Survey for 1977-78 at a steady decline in student demand for places to read Russian since the expansion of the early 1960s, but that demand had never matched the potential supply of places. It has been noted repeatedly in this book that uncontrolled increase in the number of Russian and Slavonic Studies departments had been regarded with unease since 1947. The UGC had commented on 'undue proliferation' and 'over-provision' in some 'small subjects' including Russian in 1967-72.[47] There had never been any central management of provision for Russian in universities; the situation in higher education was complicated by the fact that some polytechnics were now offering Russian into the bargain. At last the UGC was trying to take a hand in the management of the situation which had for so long been lacking. But even

---

[44] Bannister.

[45] 'Chto delat'?' [What is to be done? Text in English], *ATR Newsletter,* October 1978, p. 11.

[46] Atkinson Report, Annex G (Table 1).

[47] Atkinson, p. 3.

now, it could only *recommend* action to vice-chancellors. Recommendations came from a sub-committee headed by R. J. C. Atkinson, a professor of archaeology, four professors from other universities (not Russian specialists) and two co-opted academics concerned with Russian studies. Their account of the situation was accurate, their analysis of it unsurprising, and their consequent recommendations personally devastating to all concerned with Russian teaching in universities.

There can have been few people who did not recognize that there *was* a serious problem. The profession itself recognized this a few years before Atkinson came upon the scene. Professor Paddy (L. M.) O'Toole writes:

> In the late 1970s, having glimpsed the writing on the wall, but with no notion of the size of the decimation to follow, I persuaded BUAS to set up a working party to consider some rationalization of, at least, intensive beginners' courses across the 35 universities which had Russian departments. I was chair, and we were broadly representative, and I was not trying to [obtain an advantage for my own university]. We proposed having three centres spread regionally, which would absorb the best of the language-teaching staff and incorporate all the best methods and equipment and, hopefully, do the job more efficiently, with visits to the Soviet Union as a standard component. We even considered the thorny questions about the continuing attachment to the universities of the students' degree choice. This attempt to get the 'union' specialists (with most to lose eventually) initiating a rationalization of one fraction of their trade met with a storm of opposition at our AGM: 'Can we risk putting such ideas into the politicians' heads?' 'Won't this lead to the closing of small departments which depend on their beginners' intensive courses?' etc. Well, it did, and the politicians and their henchmen didn't need any prompts anyway.[48]

The Report regarded the rise in the number of Russian departments as 'from the beginning [...] disproportionate.' Universities had reacted optimistically, hoping all the time for an increase in students coming from the secondary schools. A peak had been reached in 1969-70, but 'at its highest the number of entrants was still modest.' Languages in general were proving less popular with older school pupils, but the decline in Russian was greater here than in other languages. Some academics regarded the 1968 invasion of Czechoslovakia as a factor in bringing about disillusionment, but the Sub-committee saw this as having no more than a short-term effect. The decline in numbers 'must in our view be related to what has been happening in the schools.' (p. 4) It was due to changes in the demand from pupils and their parents, and not to any 'enforced restriction upon the availability of qualified teachers.' Heads had recently been reducing provision for language teaching in schools; 'Russian is particularly vulnerable, and is likely to be the first sacrifice to economy.'[49]

---

[48] Private communication.

[49] All quotations in this paragraph are from Atkinson, p. 4.

Conscious of the national need for linguists in 'second' languages—German, Spanish, and Russian, the report expresses concern at a general trend away from these languages—while French inevitably survives. The imbalance needed to be rectified; 'Education Departments' were recommended to take note of this. It is not quite clear why: perhaps the reasoning is that they might be able, through teacher-training policies, to bring some influence to bear. If so, this was very unlikely to succeed: departments of education did in some cases foster positive attitudes to Russian, but their primary concern was to provide training for those graduates in modern languages who offered themselves to the profession. Those teaching Russian in universities were also advised by Atkinson to establish personal contact with schools.[50] Most departments already did so. The Report sought to encourage intensive *ab initio* courses in universities. Reporting the feeling mentioned above that such courses worked against Russian in the schools, Atkinson remarked that there was no evidence one way or the other.

The authors of the Report set out various reasons which 'in [their] view justify the proposals [they] make for rationalizing the present provision.' Many departments were too small (56% numbered four staff or fewer). Distribution of such small groups over forty universities 'constitutes a wasteful and academically unsatisfactory use of resources.' The oft-repeated opinion that there should be a 'Russian presence' in every university represents an ideal which is 'unrealistic in present circumstances' (this, it may be remembered, was the view of the Scarbrough Committee); moreover, there are many subjects with as much 'academic and public justification' as Russian, but which are offered in far fewer universities. Economies of scale—the reduction of very small teaching groups, duplication of library resources—can be achieved. 'Above all, more satisfactory provision could be made for teaching and research in larger units.' Emphasizing that the decline in student numbers had been confined to language-based studies, the Report praises the development of work in Russian history, politics, sociology and economics, in line with the Hayter proposals.[51]

The recommendations boiled down to two: staff teaching language-based courses and indeed whole departments should be reduced in number. The proposed reductions could not take less than five years from 1979 and would be 'workable only if they are implemented within a planned programme'. The Report's recommendations are addressed to the vice-chancellors and principals concerned: we are still in a world where university autonomy is valued; if Russian had ever been the subject of a 'planned programme' the situation might have been less intractable. The plan Atkinson asked for would have to be implemented with the help of the UGC and with the agreement of university chiefs.

---

[50] Atkinson, paragraphs 45 and 49, p. 9.

[51] Atkinson, pp. 10-11.

An outburst of bitterness and complaint followed the publication of the Report. Not surprisingly, BUAS, NASEES and ATR were highly critical. Anthony Cross called it 'a further sad testament to British officialdom's inability to come to terms with Russia and the Russian language.' One senior member of staff remarked on 'the relish with which some vice-chancellors sought to implement the recommendations.'[52] Many university teachers feared what they saw as 'martyrdom', and saw many years of dedicated work in building up departments called into question. Scholars of all ages had been building up a body of knowledge based on their own expertise, and they now faced possible forced redundancy. Nearly three decades later, the anger survives.

BUAS responded to the Atkinson Report in a blistering six-page document,[53] criticising its failure to cover its terms of reference, its composition, lack of consultation with those who could have provided reliable information, its failure to consider research and the difficulties of undergraduate and post-graduate study in the USSR, a perceived tendency to interpret positive moves in a negative light and to choose negative evidence where positive points could have been made. Departments, it was asserted, are given little or no credit for their efforts to ameliorate the situation and stimulate undergraduate demand for Russian. BUAS deplored the failure of Atkinson to advocate an inquiry into the whole situation of imbalance in modern language provision, while arguing for cuts in Russian studies which would only make matters worse. There were no clear criteria for deciding which departments should close or which amalgamate; some of the proposals for redundancy were 'irresponsible' and would lead to many leading scholars being scrapped. Unacceptable proposals for redeployment are made. BUAS and ATR both deplored the passive acceptance of an unsatisfactory situation for Russian in schools, and ATR pointed out that the Report presented evidence that, even though Russian classes in schools might be small, they are cost-effective in that courses are short, and a higher proportion continue to examination standard and university studies in Russian. The Report's 'consumerist' attitude and simplistic acceptance of notions of supply and demand were found unacceptable.[54]

Particular resentment was felt at the failure of Atkinson to recognize the achievement of the profession in establishing very firmly a new academic tradition in Russian studies, which was exactly what the Scarbrough Commission had asked it to do. It had been agreed in the mid-1940s, as the Foreign Office papers show, that a document on the British contribution to Slavonic Studies should not be issued, because it would appear extremely thin. Yet thirty years later, despite all the time and energy which academics had expended in building up their

---

[52]Cross, 'A banner with a strange device...'p. 3; Kirkwood, 'The University and the Wider World'.
[53]Leeds Russian Archive, ATR Papers, MS 1403/3696.
[54]Leeds Russian Archive, 1403/4704.

departments, a very solid body of research had been written, and British scholars of Russia were more than holding their own in international academic fora.

Faced with the situation of Russian in higher education, what *was* the Committee to recommend? The expansion of Russian in the university system had been a shambles: it was not managed rationally, it was based on over-optimism, over-enthusiasm, and on the ambitions of individual institutions and their leaders. In other words it had been a recipe for eventual disaster. The arguments for Russian in education are very strong indeed, but there must be *some* consideration of costs and some relationship between provision and demand—and the national need. If special treatment was to be allowed for Russian in terms of resources for small groups of students in multifarious institutions, what about other subjects?

In the event, the UGC and most others involved handled the unpleasant matter of rationalization well. There was no compulsory redundancy of Russian staff. Early retirements accounted for some of this. Transfers of staff from one university to another strengthened the receiving departments. Provision for the subject was much diminished, but a significant number of departments survived. In one case (Sheffield) the university refused to contemplate closing the department, and to this day (2008) it remains strongly in place with no fewer than five staff at professorial level. None the less, the Atkinson Report heralded a dramatic decline in the presence of Russian in the British university system, and in the years since its appearance, more than two dozen departments have disappeared. We may eventually be able to estimate whether this has worked to the benefit of the subject or to its decline.

Chapter 8

Change, Decline or Consolidation? The Last Three Decades

It is disturbing that the study of the main language of the second most powerful country in the world has declined to such a low level.
     SECOND REPORT FROM THE PARLIAMENTARY FOREIGN
     AFFAIRS COMMITTEE ON UK-SOVIET RELATIONS, 1986

THE end of the 1970s left university Russian and Slavonic Studies departments licking their wounds. It marked the beginning of a distinct reduction in provision for the subjects in terms of the number of universities offering Russian. In secondary schools, however, while there was a diminution in the numbers, it was a few years before serious decline developed. Looking at the three decades since 1980 overall, we can see that in the latter part of this period Russian collapsed almost entirely in Scottish, Welsh and Irish schools, while it clung precariously to life in England. It is not easy to define the actual reasons for decline, but we shall look at a number of matters which may have influenced it. Nevertheless, we must admit the possibility that a certain degree of irrationality is involved.

The political and social situation in the Soviet Union since 1980 and later in the Russian Federation was and remains a subject of the greatest interest, which may have been expected to stimulate study of the Russian language and of the nation where it is spoken. After the long years of 'stagnation' under Leonid Brezhnev and his two short-lived immediate successors, there came the accession to power of Mikhail Gorbachev and his institution after 1985 of *glasnost'*, a period of much freer debate than had ever before been permitted. I was myself fortunate to have been teaching young people in schools in Moscow and Leningrad briefly in 1988. For a younger person it would have been a 'formative experience'. *Zastoi,* stagnation, had at least meant stability of a sort, maybe greater stability than that enjoyed in the west at the time. I was amazed to watch *perestroika* (restructuring of society) as events unfolded, not only in education, but in every sector of Soviet life. The demise of Communism in Eastern European countries fuelled the flames; the coup in Moscow of August 1991 and its rapid collapse three days later must have had many friends of Russia moving from depression to jubilation when Dzerzhinskii's statue was seen on television being toppled by the police from its previous place of honour before the Lubianka. All this and subsequent events did in fact for a while stimulate uptake of student places in universities in Britain, including courses where politics, economics, or business were offered alongside Russian.

The Bare facts. Statistics of Russian in schools

In schools for the whole of this period Russian demonstrated the same instability of which teachers and researchers had been complaining over the years. Under the auspices of ATR and its eventual successor body, members carried out surveys of schools where Russian was taught in 1979, 1983, 1985, 1989, and 1992,[1] uneasily eyeing the situation as it developed. As those concerned in assembling the information learned from experience, the accuracy of this research improved over the years, and the last of this series (1992) is certainly the most accurate. That is not to deprecate the earlier reports. That of 1979 discovered 371 schools in the United Kingdom where Russian was taught. In 1982 it was 392, in 1985 387: 3 in Northern Ireland, 39 in Scotland, 4 in Wales, the remainder in England. The surveys of 1988/89 and 1992 showed that over this short but crucial period in Russian history, the number of schools in the UK teaching the subject rose slightly from 299 to 307. However, in those few years 89 schools nationwide discontinued Russian and 97 started it. Moreover, it was in the independent sector that the overall gain took place (twelve lost, 31 gained), while in the maintained sector 77 were lost and only 65 gained.

The 1985 survey is the first in which the ages at which school pupils started Russian were established, and an attempt to estimate the actual numbers of pupils learning the subject was made. As one of the authors of the 1985 and 1988 reports and the sole author of the 1992 survey and the report on it, I can assure the reader that blood was sweated and much computer time expended to achieve the result, and that I believe it to be as close to reality as is possible in a world where busy teachers cannot always be persuaded to supply necessary information. In 1985 there were 11,070 pupils learning Russian, 8,785 in maintained schools and 2,285 in independent schools. The 1988 survey showed a slight increase on this to a total of 11,580 (8,884 maintained, 2,696 independent). In 1992 13,231 pupils were learning Russian overall. This increase was probably mainly due to a number of comprehensive schools where brief 'taster' courses in Russian were offered, along with similar courses in other languages, all with the purpose of informing the choices pupils would make later. This venture, I emphasize, should not be dismissed as a dangerous 'smattering', irrelevant to what might be thought of as 'proper' learning of Russian. A small survey of undergraduates who enrolled for Russian in 1992 and 1993 on *ab initio* courses demonstrated conclusively that almost any introduction to Russian, however slight, at school overcame the notion that Russian was hopelessly difficult, and that such introduction stimulated

---

[1] See in the Bibliography: ATR (item for 1979), West (1983 and 1985), Muckle (1989 and 1992); for analyses of the data published in these booklets, see articles by the same authors.

demand for Russian at university.[2] The notion expressed by educators of an earlier age, that a 'smattering' was to be deplored, is therefore false.

These figures relate to a period now fifteen years in the past. What exactly is the position in the early twenty-first century? It is more difficult now to arrive at an exact picture. The data were assembled in 1992 and earlier by asking examinations boards to provide lists of schools which entered candidates, and it was checked by writing to or telephoning the schools and teachers concerned. Only one person (a minor official at an examinations board) ever refused to provide information on the subject; the fact that the information was wanted by the Committee on Area Studies chaired by the Prince of Wales was later sufficient to persuade the official concerned to reveal the less-than-vitally confidential information she was guarding so loyally. Things have changed since 1992, and data protection legislation provides the reason or the excuse to conceal facts which cannot infringe any real need for privacy and might inform the teaching profession about the state of Russian. None the less, valiant attempts have been made more recently to assemble a reliable list of schools offering Russian, and a list has been passed to me from a body known as the Russian Network.[3] Since the downfall of communism in Russia a new factor has arisen: the presence in Britain of Russian-speaking children of immigrants from thwe Federation. It may be that some of the schools in the most recent list are providing Russian as a native language (or 'heritage' language) or even simply offering the school premises as a centre for examinations in Russian. The extent to which this is happening may not, however, substantially challenge the accuracy of the list.

This latest list has what we have come to regard as the usual feature: a high degree of instability. It is fairly clear that it is not complete, but significantly the 134 schools listed in 2007 include 59 (44%) that were not in the 1992 list—so nearly half of the schools listed had begun Russian since 1992.[4] Again, the constant turmoil of reorganization which is endemic in British education may have resulted in some schools changing their names, so perhaps the situation is not quite so unstable as it seems. Nevertheless, the volatility is an aspect of the situation which has not changed since 1960.

---

[2] 'Starting Russian at University: expectations and reactions of students', *Rusistika*, no 11, 1995, pp. 43-49.

[3] www.schoolsnetwork.org.uk

[4] This figure should be taken alongside the data from the CILT Language Trends Survey, which is referred to later.

CHANGE IN SCHOOL EDUCATION and the consequences for the study of Russian.

Curricular and other issues

Both primary and secondary schools in the 1980s were facing a new and interesting challenge with consequences for every subject in the curriculum. This took differing forms in England and Wales and in Scotland. No part of the United Kingdom had ever had a statutory school curriculum, a fact which most other European countries found inexplicable. Scotland was not thought to need one, ostensibly because that country had only one examinations board at each grade (ages 16 and 17), which ensured a certain degree of uniformity. None the less, a series of measures in that country established policies and practices which look very like a national curriculum.

At age 18 in the rest of the UK it used to be argued that the universities controlled the curriculum by their entrance requirements. It seemed obvious in many quarters, however, that total freedom in England and Wales had led to unacceptable disparities in pupil attainment. This may have been more of a problem in the primary sector, where the structure of a child's learning day was left entirely to the teacher. Educators and politicians of all parties were agreed that a 'national curriculum' should be compiled and given the force of law. All children should be tested at certain ages in major curricular areas and the results of the schools published and placed in order of merit. The examinations taken by (far from all) pupils at age 16, at the time CSE and GCE O level, were also to be reformed into a General Certificate of Secondary Education (GCSE) with completely new syllabuses for every subject and a new philosophy, in which inviting pupils to show what they had learned and could do rather than exposing their ignorance was to be the aim. This in itself was a formidable task.

In the last two chapters we followed the movement among modern language teachers to modernize the aims, methods and the philosophy of their subject. Russian teachers were prominent in these moves. Schools, with many honourable exceptions, had tended to neglect the speaking of languages, had stressed translation, and had sometimes forgotten that pupils are often judged in real life by their ability to cope with everyday situations in a foreign country. We saw that in the nineteenth century the whole idea of modern languages in a university was denigrated as 'a courier's Tripos' and that leaders of the Russian-teaching profession at that time saw no need for a test of oral skills. These attitudes had long since been discarded, and the 1980s were to show how drastic this challenge to obsolete notions was to become: some might think too drastic.

When it was accepted that the education profession had to establish a national curriculum for schools in England, the Department of Education and Science (as it was then known: DES) was commissioned by government to establish a framework for the teaching of all subjects. The Working Group which it set up for modern languages, consisted of university academics, teachers, representatives of local education authorities, and language advisors, and it was chaired by

Professor Martin Harris, a university vice-chancellor, to cover *all* languages in secondary schools. This group examined the situation, and discussed the philosophy, aims, methods, content—everything relating to modern foreign languages in secondary schools. There were about a dozen members, one of whom (Robert Pullin) represented the interests of Russian, plus another sixteen persons co-opted to help the sub-groups; one of these (Judith Haywood) was a school teacher of Russian. The work undertaken by this group was intensive in the extreme: residential weekend meetings, evening sessions attended by members who had travelled long distances to be there. Personal relations are said to have remained cordial throughout, despite academic or professional disagreements.

It was made clear to the working group that whatever decisions they arrived at had to apply to *all* of the nineteen languages in the schedule,[5] and no language could be an exception. Extensive initial advice was presented for consultation early in 1990, and the final unanimous report,[6] which runs to over 130 pages, is dated October 1990. It indicates the majority state of opinion at the time on the study of foreign languages in schools. The Report mentions specific languages only in passing and as examples of general statements; however, each language is allocated a page summarizing its particular characteristics and some of its advantages and difficulties as a school subject. In 1990 it was assumed that one foreign language would be studied by all pupils from age 11 to 16 as a National Curriculum requirement. A section is devoted to 'The place of the second foreign language in the school curriculum' (pp. 86-88), and it may be assumed that Russian was likely to fall into this category, in view of the small number of schools where it was available as a first foreign language.

The Secretaries of State to whom it was addressed are reminded that languages serve 'the need of the individual and of the country'. Schools should be flexible over the point at which a second language is introduced. The Report does not declare that only able linguists should be allowed to start a second language, but adopts the more egalitarian formula that it should be 'offered to those, who in learning the first, have given evidence of enthusiasm and commitment.' As many pupils as possible should be offered the chance to learn a second language. The Report urges the strengthening of languages other than French and presses for diversification of provision. The Committee was clearly aware that this would only be possible in certain circumstances: 'If diversification is properly planned and resourced centrally as well as locally as part of an integrated school policy it is likely to have important consequences for the availability of second foreign languages in schools.' (p. 86)

---

[5] Arabic, Bengali, Chinese (Cantonese and Mandarin), Danish, Dutch, French, German, Modern Greek, Gujarati, Modern Hebrew, Hindi, Italian, Japanese, Panjabi, Portuguese, Russian, Spanish, Turkish, Urdu. It is clear that many of these languages are included as 'community' tongues for bilingual children who may be fluent speakers of them, but not yet literate. Some may indeed be both this and viable foreign languages for children with no prior experience of them.

[6] DES and Welsh Office, *Modern Foreign Languages for ages 11 to 16*, 1990.

Here we have yet again the apparently insuperable difficulty which has always faced Russian in schools, and this time the problem is seen not just concerning Russian, but on a much wider scale. An 'integrated school policy', 'proper' planning and resourcing, and the will to see that they happen have never commended themselves to education in England and Wales. While this Report was appearing, the government of the day was allowing, and indeed in many ways encouraging, schools to opt out of the control of local authorities, and consequently to make planning and integration across schools impossible. Yet, before the National Curriculum Working Party met, the DES and Welsh Office issued *MLISC: a Statement of Policy*, which trenchantly stated: '*[The dominance of French] is not satisfactory*. LEAs and schools should ensure that a reasonable proportion of their pupils of all abilities study a language other than French as their first foreign language. [...] We do not underestimate the extent of planning required [...] to bring about *the diversification which is necessary*.' Elsewhere: 'The *need for diversification is pressing*'. Also: 'Expertise in Italian and Russian is the least used. *This resource should be tapped.*' [All emphasis mine—JM.][7] The DES knew what was needed, but was incapable of formulating a course of action to serve that need.

How was Russian—and all languages—to be taught within this framework? The composition of the Working Group, consisting as it did of heavyweight academics, school teachers, heads of different types of schools, teacher-trainers, educational advisors, inspectors and administrators, and lay persons, would suggest that there would be disagreement about this. The predominant philosophy of the day in 1989-90 was that languages must be for *all*, and should be somehow made accessible to all pupils in secondary schools; the traditional view of the academics that learning a language was a serious business which required application and targets for really purposeful study lost out against the background of anti-élitist feeling. Any possible compromise on the lines of there being two types of language study in schools: elementary taster courses, and at a later stage achievement-oriented serious courses was not acceptable. A participant in the debate remarked that it was in essence a political exercise, in that the basic assumptions of educators at the time inevitably influenced the nature of the policy which was eventually established. The egalitarian idea did not survive fifteen years: by the middle of the first decade of the twenty-first century, the Government had decided that a modern foreign language should not be compulsory for all in the fourth and fifth years of secondary education in England.

The National Curriculum did not, of course, apply to Scotland. There the turmoil was perhaps a little less intense in the 1980s, though before the excitement over a national curriculum began in England, Scottish schools were faced with the Munn and Dunning Reports in 1977, which were described in the previous chapter. Nevertheless, policies were enacted in Scotland which closely

---

[7]MLISC, pp. 8-10.

resembled a national curriculum: between 1987 and 1991 there was the establishment of curriculum guidelines for all subject areas from age 5 to age 14. In the particular area of languages, three policies were promulgated in Scotland: 'Languages for all' (LfA), making four years of language study compulsory in secondary education, 'MLPS'—modern languages in the primary school, and diversification of languages (which was the most difficult policy to implement, since it was found hard to sustain in the face of MLPS and LfA.)[8] Clearly English and Scots were thinking along similar lines; the same applied to reform of the examination system.

It is not hard to see that subjects such as Russian were likely to suffer in both countries in this environment. When civil servants draw up regulations, even in close collaboration with educators, problems, injustices, and even absurdities arise. When languages are not mentioned in any statutory document, a school may offer Russian without infringing regulations. As soon as officials become involved, they start wanting to be specific—which languages? A school with numerous ethnic minority pupils may want to offer Hindi. Is this to be seen as a 'modern foreign language' and taught as such, or is it a 'community' or 'heritage' language, taught with the aim of making children literate in a tongue they already speak fluently at home? At least one local authority's education committee chairman decreed that they were one and the same thing and insisted that the same classes should be open to all pupils of whatever ethnic background: hence the absurdity. Should European Union tongues be given special status? Are some foreign languages more 'important' than others? Yes, said the officials, and Russian was placed at first in the less important bracket. This would scarcely have mattered, as the regulation was framed in such a way that schools could have done as they liked in most circumstances, but the message that Russian was of lesser importance was both erroneous and damaging to the prestige of the subject. Perhaps this serious effect on Russian as a school subject was analogous with the blows it suffered when schools were made comprehensive: it was a 'detail' which got overlooked or brushed aside while administrators dealt with what they saw as major issues.

Inspection of schools

The 1990s saw a significant change in the inspection régime as it affected schools. It will be recalled that during the First World War HM Inspectorate reported on and actively encouraged the experiments then being carried out in the teaching of Russian. After the Second World War it has been argued that they actively supported the expansion of Russian—while often denying they were doing so. Until nearly the end of the century the inspectorate had this important role in advising and encouraging experiment and innovation; it was not purely

---

[8] A very useful short summary of these and other policies is contained in Table 3.1, p. 31, of McPake et al., *Foreign Languages in the Upper Secondary School*.

a matter of assessing, of criticizing the performance of schools and rebuking recalcitrant teachers. By about 1990 a new spirit emerged. Children had to be tested, schools compared with each other, and set in competition. Traditionalist conservative 'think-tanks' decided that the inspectorate had been too 'trendy' and permissive, and the more loud-mouthed of their members—profoundly ignorant of the reality of the situation, as they were—succeeded in persuading a government headed by a prime minister who had never even completed his own secondary education that HM Inspectorate should be emasculated and replaced by an Office for Standards in Education. Henceforth raiding parties of inquisitors were to descend on schools to ascertain whether they were 'delivering' the National Curriculum; after four and a half days of deliberation they would depart, never to be seen again. With the best will in the world, there was no hope of any continuing influence from an inspectorate in this model. Yet another potentially beneficial external influence on schools was removed, leaving individuals to act without consideration of the wider context. Russian suffered in consequence.

The End of ATR and the formation of ALL

In the late 1980s the Russian-teaching profession was beginning to lose some of its voice. For many years before 1989 the Association of Teachers of Russian had been wooed by other schools' language-teaching associations to unite with them in a body which came to be called the Association for Language Learning (ALL). For several decades there had been a number of associations which language teachers in schools could join. The dominant language in British schools has always been French, and there was a routine assumption in educational quarters that 'modern languages' mostly meant 'French and possibly German'. What policy decisions there were were usually framed with this assumption in mind. The senior group was the Modern Language Association (MLA), which had held the banner of modern languages aloft since well before the end of the nineteenth century; for this it deserves credit. We have none the less noted that there were elements within it in the 1930s and 1940s which were sceptical of Russian and more than a little patronizing. It would have been surprising indeed if such a group could have campaigned for Russian and the other languages with as much enthusiasm as they did for French. The MLA at one point even antagonized teachers of German, a dynamic nucleus of which formed an Association of Teachers of German (ATG) in 1958, which, while it came to work fairly closely with MLA eventually, maintained a separate existence for some years. Russian, Spanish, Dutch, and Italian had their own associations. There was also another association devoted to modern methods of teaching languages: the Audio-Visual Language Association (AVLA) later renamed British Association for Language Teaching (BALT), devoted to fostering contemporary technology in schools. These associations tended to have quite a number of members in common, as school teachers most often taught more than one language and valued the publications both of MLA and BALT. Teacher-trainers, administrators and local authority advisors often joined everything, simply in order to keep in touch. The argument for a unitary association was therefore strong, if not overwhelming.

There was also the fact that Scotland on the one hand and England and Wales on the other had differing interests. It was not only the separate education systems, but certain cultural differences: a conference from 2 January necessitating participants travelling on New Year's Day was unthinkable for the Scots. ATR worked happily enough as a United Kingdom organization, except that it never quite managed to hold a conference in Scotland until BUAS invited school teachers to their meeting in Aberdeen in the 1980s. Well, Aberdeen *is* in Scotland, but even Scottish teachers as a whole felt that noble city was a very long way from the centre of affairs, and few attended.

For over twenty years a loose association of language-teaching associations had been in existence: the JCLA (Joint Council of Language Associations), under which umbrella the annual conferences of such bodies as ATR were organized. There were some very good people working in JCLA. Many were earnestly trying to establish a new association which would speak for the interests of *all* languages. Nevertheless, there were conflicting interests, and it must be said that the atmosphere in meetings of JCLA was occasionally tense, and one did not always have the feeling of being among friends.[9]

The model for ALL, it may be supposed, was the Association for Science Education, but, then, Chemistry, Physics and Biology are complementary subjects while French, German, Spanish, Russian and the rest may have conflicting interests. It was argued that there would be strength in unity, that money for research would be available to a joint body, but not to a crowd of disparate associations. It will be recalled that, while there were Russian teachers in the Modern Language Association in the 1930s to 1950s, Russian had a raw deal. There were misgivings, but the wind of change in the 1980s seemed to be blowing in the direction of ALL, and eventually the decision was taken by ATR to enter into the new body. The vote was decisive, but not unanimous. The consequences of this decision are now a matter of controversy.

Assessment: new methods

Closely related to the issue of the curriculum for ages 11 to 16 and, for that matter, beyond, is the question of its assessment in nationally organized public examinations. It may seem odd that the establishment of a new examination for pupils at age 16 and the reform of examinations for the post-compulsory stage of schooling preceded work on the national curriculum. The General Certificate of Secondary Education (GCSE) was first run in 1988, and in the same year A level GCE was taken according to significantly revised syllabuses. At age 16 the Government allocated the tasks of establishing new national criteria to working parties based on the various examination boards. The working party for modern

---

[9]This is a personal judgement, perhaps a biased one; I was briefly Chairman of JCLA—JM.

languages consisted of about eight people chaired by a non-linguist. Each board nominated one member of the working party; some were board secretaries with a particular interest in languages, others were teachers or applied linguists. The inevitable controversies arose between traditionalists and reformers, and compromises had to be reached. The new difficulty was the need to make the examination accessible to sixteen-year-olds of all abilities. As with the national curriculum, the criteria for all languages had to be the same.

In earlier chapters we have seen that many teachers had long been trying to change the old-fashioned O level examination, along with its A level successor. In the early 1960s an O level examination consisted of translation into Russian, a free composition, translation from Russian into English, an oral examination lasting a few minutes, dictation, and perhaps written or aural comprehension tests of some sort. It would have been intended for the more able, perhaps even the most able, pupils only. From 1965 CSE exams (for the middle range of ability) had become a laboratory in which teachers were able to experiment with new tests and exercises based often on syllabuses they had compiled themselves. There was also a strong and popular 'graded test' movement, the aim of which was to give pupils targets to aim for every few months, rather than a distant examination several years ahead. The first GCSE examinations, intended for pupils of all or nearly all abilities, built on this experience. Along with A levels usually at age 18 there was an innovation: the AS (Advanced Supplementary) level bridging the gap between GCSE and A level.

In bald summary, the features of the new GCSE included the following. Since it was impossible to imagine an examination suitable for all abilities, the modern languages working party decided there were to be two tiers: foundation and higher. All pupils were to take the foundation papers, and the more able would be entered for the higher level. The purpose of this was to ensure that the situation would not arise where able pupils could not order a meal or buy a railway ticket in the foreign country (tasks set for foundation level), while otherwise coping with much more sophisticated matters (in the higher tier). A minimum vocabulary (of about a thousand Russian words for higher level and four hundred for foundation) was specified, as were the grammatical structures to be assimilated. Listening, speaking, reading and writing activities ranged in difficulty from the simplest—aural recognition of words and simple phrases, the writing of captions or short messages, matching headlines to news items, and answering orally simple questions sometimes based on a picture—to the most difficult: noting details from spoken texts, writing an article for a school magazine in the foreign country, summarizing a printed article, or explaining orally what a Saturday job will entail. There were coursework options in both writing and speaking, with criteria for assessment carefully specified.

It is difficult to estimate the benefits and disadvantages of the introduction of the new syllabuses. At least much more communication was introduced into the exam than before; stress on the spoken language was on the whole beneficial, and prescribed activities were in many ways more related to real life and the situations the pupils might encounter when in the foreign country. On the other hand, there were complaints that pupils did not learn the necessary grammatical structures for further advanced study and that some pupils could obtain a high grade in the exam, which led them to believe, wrongly, that they would do well at Advanced level.

As for A level syllabuses, a participant in the five-year-long process undertaken by the Joint Matriculation Board to revise theirs speaks warmly of the experience, declaring it to be the best project he ever undertook.[10] The debate centred on the way progressive classroom teaching could be fostered by the examination, and teachers in secondary and higher education were engaged in solving the problem. Other boards clearly adopted similar approaches. The resultant syllabuses for both A and AS level have the following salient features among others: a stress on the use of the language for discussion and debate in writing and speech and for realistic interpreting tasks, a more searching oral examination, the necessity of teaching with maximum use of the foreign language, a variety of options for pupils who might wish eventually to use the language in business, to study economics, politics, or international affairs or, for that matter, literature and the arts, and a constant focus on the culture, life and society of the country—here we are again with Bernard Pares's 'nation study'. Sixth-form studies which had once concerned translating into Russian tricky *Times* fourth leaders or paragraphs of Jane Austen and Mrs Gaskell could not be further from the new notion. My informant regrets that the new ideas never worked out fully in practice, as teachers and pupils adopted stereotyped ways of working and pupils' reading was limited as 'strategic learning' came into force. In general, however, the changes at A and AS level worked for good, and the teaching in some (but not by any means all) universities was left behind—to the dismay of many new undergraduates who had hoped that the classroom practices they had come to expect would be carried on in higher education.

The simultaneous changes in Scottish examinations at age 16 and 17 reflect similar trends in educational thought. The former Ordinary grade was gradually replaced by a 'Standard' grade exam from 1988, the aim of which was—very much as for GCSE in England—to enable pupils to show what they knew and could do, whatever their attainment level. The revised Higher grade, introduced from 1990, aimed to make content more accessible and relevant, but it must be remembered that this exam was taken at age 17, one year after O grade. It was perceived by teachers to be particularly difficult, as its rationale was thought to conflict with that of S grade, being distinctly more academically challenging. The CSYS was discontinued, and a new Advanced Higher (or 'higher still') examination was introduced; nevertheless, Highers were still regarded as the gold standard for university entry, and some teachers and academics regard with scepticism the notion that Advanced Higher is of first-year university standard.

---

[10] I am indebted to Alan West for this observation.

The criticism has been levelled at both English and Scottish examinations at age 16 that they do not sufficiently encourage exploration of Russian life and reality along with the language. This misgiving is less valid after age 16, but the sort of topics younger pupils prepare for oral presentations: 'our house', 'our school', 'my favourite sport or hobby', indicate a degree of introversion. This need not be a problem if the textbooks and teaching materials used by teachers of Russian present the country in a lively, interesting, and realistic way. It is not a problem either if teachers make a point of raising simple cultural or 'lifestyle' issues with their younger classes. Many of them do, but some do not: they may feel strongly that it is a low priority compared with the hard graft of teaching the language.[11]

Changing higher education

Higher education in general was faced with change in several important respects. The government of Margaret Thatcher had to cope with a burgeoning sector, and was encouraging the notion that further and higher education should be entered by young people on a mass scale, as well as by older mature students who had missed the opportunity to go to university at the more usual age. The problem was paying for it. When only six percent of eighteen-year-olds went into higher education, grants and bursaries were not too difficult to provide, but when the percentage became thirty or forty, it was another matter entirely. Add to this the often passionately-held belief by politicians that universities should provide 'value for money' and be 'accountable', and problems arise. While few would deny that institutions must be held responsible for the quality of the educational service they offer, it is often very difficult to prove to those with little understanding of what education really is that value *is* being given for money, and that economy is not achieved merely by stuffing more students into a classroom, cutting the library budget, and making staff work longer hours. Language began to be used which many felt to be inappropriate to real learning: education was seen as a commodity to be 'delivered', students were thought of as 'customers' buying a 'product', and the world of commerce was looked to by some as a model of how universities (and schools too) should be run. Meanwhile the more enlightened business people were realizing that educational institutions had a great deal to teach business—possibly more than business had to teach education. This notion, however, carried little weight in government circles.

The Atkinson Report was probably the first ominous indication in Russian and Slavonic Studies of the strength of the crude notion of 'value for money' and its consequences for the subject. Russian would never have survived in the uni-

---

[11] This remark is based on years of observation of lessons given by student teachers, and may be influenced by the special situation implied. None the less, it is argued that teaching about the country is a strong motivating feature in school study of Russian. Such was a finding of the Scottish report outlined below.

versity system in the first half of the twentieth century if this principle had been ruthlessly applied. In those more liberal days it was possible to argue, perhaps humorously, that one student to one teacher was the ideal ratio, and so when there was a strongly perceived need for Russian in the 1950s and later, the infrastructure was there to begin to provide it. Atkinson was only the first element in the reduction in numbers of Russian departments; individual universities were looking closely at many departments, testing them for 'cost-effectiveness'. Government was already providing new weapons for hostile vice-chancellors to use, while—it is fair to say—those weapons might also be used in defence of the threatened departments. These were the external assessment of research output and of teaching quality. One vice-chancellor went so far as to speak of a sustained campaign of harassment of universities by the government. While forty years ago the point of studying at a university was to be taught by those who were making or discovering the knowledge, Sir Keith Joseph, once Secretary of State for Education, challenged the notion that all higher education staff should be involved in research, as opposed to what he called 'scholarship'—keeping abreast with the original work of others. Times had clearly changed.

Moreover, in the early 1990s the higher education sector was changing markedly. Until that time the so-called 'binary system' had been in operation: there were universities and there were polytechnics. The word 'polytechnic' had been around for a long time, but in this context it referred to the colleges set up in the 1960s to provide mainly technical education, some, or even much of it of university standard, but also courses of many different types at a lower level. The degree-level work was accredited by a national body, the Council for National Academic Awards (CNAA), or by universities which the polytechnic concerned had approached to do this work. By the 1990s the egalitarian spirit found the two-tier system objectionable, and it was decided that the polytechnics should be declared to be universities, provided they could demonstrate certain criteria. A number of polytechnics were teaching Russian, sometimes very well. A handful of new university Russian departments was therefore added to the list. Courses offered by the former polytechnics tended to differ from those in universities. In some, but not by any means all, the teaching staff were less committed to research than their university colleagues. However, as the students they were able to recruit were less academically well qualified on entry, their teaching, especially language teaching, tended to be marked by closer engagement with the students. Since very many of these students were studying *ab initio*, this was particularly necessary.

Russian studies in higher education: Government concern and attempts at oversight

A major sign of the profession fighting back against Atkinson was the success of lobbying by BASSEES along with other agencies to keep the whole topic in the eye of the education and research establishment. The first fruit of this was a *Review of Soviet and East European Studies*, which came to be known as the

Wooding Report. By the mid-1980s it became obvious that contraction of provision for Russian and other Eastern European languages at a time when M. S. Gorbachev was instituting change in the Soviet Union with an obvious knock-on effect in other state-socialist countries, was inconsistent, if not actually irrational. The contraction was not due purely to the Atkinson Report; universities not attacked by it were closing Slavonic Studies departments. Meanwhile, the British Government was investing both diplomatic effort and money into the region, and did not need much persuading that the issue should be looked at again. The Review was set up in 1989 and was carried out by Dr Norman Wooding, representing the world of business, Sir Bryan Cartledge from the diplomatic profession and Professor Malcolm Jones from the universities. The report ran to eighty pages plus appendices; it contained statistics of the numbers of students involved at both undergraduate and post-graduate level, similar information about schools, demographic breakdown of teaching staff, findings about the employment of graduates, questions of trade, and of the organization of university teaching in Russian.

The authors of the report later felt that events in Eastern Europe and the USSR had overtaken its recommendations within a few years. These included a plea for 'intervention to improve the present state of Soviet and East European studies,' mainly for funding for lectureships, fellowships, and studentships. Universities were urged to provide courses in Russian with the natural sciences, commerce and management, to establish links with business as well as with outside cultural bodies. It was proposed that a body should be set up to monitor the state of Russian and East European studies.

Response to Wooding was mixed. Partial funding was found by the DES for ten lectureships for an initial three years. The Economic and Social Research Council (ESRC) and the British Academy showed interest in projects in Eastern Europe. Some individual universities responded by establishing or re-establishing chairs. In addition, the Report improved morale among university teachers after the Atkinson débâcle: the Report contained descriptive paragraphs about the existing university Russian departments which were constructive. It also represented a certain continuity in lobbying, which eventually led to a later report by the Higher Education Funding Council for England (HEFCE). The point about monitoring represents a constant problem in Slavonic Studies, in that throughout the second half of the twentieth century government had repeatedly perceived a crisis in the field, which had been followed by action, followed again by inaction and neglect, leading to further crisis—and so the cycle had continued. However, a new element emerged, in that an Area Studies Monitoring Group was set up on the initiative of Professor Howard Newby of the ESRC. This covered a wide variety of area studies, and was chaired by HRH the Prince of Wales, who had expressed sympathy with its aims. Though the Group did not long survive Newby's move from the ESRC, it led through further lobbying to the HEFCE Review of Former Soviet and East European Studies of 1995, which did in fact result in several millions of pounds in funding for specialist posts in higher education. This funding was to represent a preference for social scientists and for East European rather than Russian specialists, but a small number of Russianists were in fact appointed.

From the mid-1980s regular assessment of the research carried out by staff in university departments was made. The theme of this book is the *teaching* of the Russian language, but as for universities, research and teaching are closely linked, and it would be impossible to ignore this aspect of the work of the Russian-teaching profession. It was, after all, the Scarbrough Report of 1947 which set *teachers* of Slavonic Studies the task of establishing an academic tradition in *research*. However, the Research Assessment Exercise (RAE) did not actually look at this aspect. Its aim, like that of many policies in the Margaret Thatcher era, and that of her successors, Conservative and Labour, seemed to be to set institution against institution, rather than to achieve more worthwhile ends.

The exercise was carried out in 1986, 1989, 1992, 1996, 2001, and 2007. The first, as might naturally be expected, was the subject of much resentment and derision across the system as a whole. The identity of the assessors was anonymous and has never been revealed. Departments were classified as 'outstanding', 'above average', 'average' and 'below average'. (Three Russian departments were named outstanding, one above average, and fourteen average.) While the conventional view of the procedure was that it was rubbish, many of those who professed to hold this view were quite unseemly in their delight if their own department achieved a high grade. The anonymity of the assessors was a matter for concern: the validity of an assessment must be considered in relation to the identity of the assessor. This objection was met in the succeeding exercises, when names were known: two Slavists only in 1989, six in 1992, seven (plus outside specialists) in 1996, nine in 2001. In 1989 and 1992 departments were graded from 1 (the lowest) to 5, and in 1996 and 2001 the grades were further refined: 1, 2, 3a, 3b, 4, 5, and 5*. There were three 5* grades, six 5, seven 4 and one 3a in 2001. This loss of the 'tail' may be explained because of a feature of recent exercises: departments were not obliged to enter all of their staff for assessment, if they regarded certain members as non-active in the field of research. Most importantly, funding of particular departments came to depend on the grades awarded by the assessment panel, tempered by the number of staff assessed in the compilation of that grade. Satisfactory or not, this seems, by the early twenty-first century, to have become accepted by default.

These successive assessment exercises caused vice-chancellors and heads of department much nail-biting. The pressure that this placed on individuals as well as departments is surely difficult to defend in view of the inconsistencies and imponderables of the whole operation. The grading system, as we have seen, was regularly refined. To achieve one grade less than expected, or hoped for, might not be very damaging to a department in a university where internal transfer of funds might take place, but the effect of receiving one grade lower than hoped for on SSEES (a free-standing institute of the University of London) in 1996 was serious. SSEES has now joined University College.

While all this was going on, in 1995-96 all university departments in England were additionally subjected to assessment of the quality of their teaching (TQA), mainly undergraduate teaching. It was assessed on a peer-review basis, with four external representatives operating under a convenor from another discipline. The resultant overview report comprises a valuable account of the state of university teaching in Slavonic Studies, which, it must be said, reflects credit on the staff assessed. For anyone who read for a degree before the 1970s, it also reflects the immense changes in university teaching and assessment methods since then. Each department was assessed not according to any pre-decided formula, but in relation to its own stated objectives. The *Subject Overview* reported widespread use of innovative teaching methods and materials, often produced in house. Language instruction was well integrated with other parts of the curriculum; practical language skills were mostly stressed, and residence in Russia required. 'The quality of teaching in many institutions was high, and most staff and students display[ed] an enthusiastic commitment to their subject'. Instead of traditional examinations, 'a range of assessment methods, including coursework, a dissertation and examinations' were employed by most institutions.[12]

Not everything was perfect. Yet—what good did this report of excellent achievement do? The trouble with awarding grades to departments for their 'performance' is that orders of merit are assembled by journalists and published. Potential students may attach too much importance to the grades received. However, even excellent grades did not prove advantageous. The writer of these lines was a minor participant in the assessment procedure, and I am dismayed that one department we assessed very favourably was closed a few years later. It was taking on less well-qualified students, teaching them Russian from scratch, and raising them to a more-than-acceptable standard. Contemporary educational orthodoxy as well as good common sense believe that is exactly what such an institution should be doing.

A Single voice for university teachers of Russian

It was not only school teachers who were swept along in gusts of ecumenical fervour. The British Universities Association of Slavists (BUAS) and the British National Association for Soviet and East European Studies (BNASEES), two organizations with different centres of interest, sought to unite. Again, there were misgivings: BUAS was an organization in which whole departments of Slavonic Studies participated; BNASEES members were often singletons with a Soviet Studies interest in larger social science departments. While some on one side feared being swamped by mainly young and unproven social scientists, on the other the language and literature people (dominated by professors—all presidents of BUAS had to be of professorial status) were perceived as antiquarians out of

---

[12] HEFCE, Subject Overview Report.

touch with the real world. It would be wrong to exaggerate this unease, as it was not significant enough to prevent amalgamation.

There were good reasons for unity: political reasons primarily. Two successive higher education ministers, George Walden and Robert Jackson, had urged the two organizations that if they spoke with a united voice they were much more likely to be listened to by government than if they remained separate. Happily, both organizations were almost exactly equal in membership, their bank accounts were comparable in health—there was no reason for resentment in either of these respects. Academically it would be possible to construct a case on either side, but any argument was unlikely to be conclusive.

The result was that in 1988 the two groups combined as the British Association for Soviet, Slavonic and East European Studies (BASSEES). The word 'Soviet' was dropped shortly after the winding up of the USSR. If not every member was entirely happy that the interests of both bodies would be served by amalgamation, BASEES has proved a vibrant and active organization. Government bodies *did* listen to it, and the Wooding and the HEFCE Committees were evidence of this.

BASEES study groups, whether inherited from the one or the other founding body, its annual conferences, and its participation in international congresses represent a lively programme of activity. A newsletter of 2008 reports a significant increase in membership. It should be remembered, however, that BASEES is primarily an organization devoted to research. Moreover, its focus area encompasses the entire Slavonic and East and Central European field and has tended to change to some extent in the past decade and a half. It maintains its 'distinctive perspective from the point of view of language-based area studies'.[13]

Public bodies, modern languages and Russian

Throughout the twentieth century we have seen that Russian studies in particular and language learning in general have been the subject of numerous enquiries. These have sometimes been set up directly by government, as were the Leathes, Scarbrough and Annan reports, or at other times semi-official or otherwise highly respected bodies have been persuaded to carry out enquiries of one sort and another. We have mentioned the HEFCE report of 1995 on former Soviet and East European studies; the 1990s and 2000s spawned other reports on languages by the Scottish Council for Research in Education (*Foreign Languages in the Upper Secondary School*, SCRE, 1999, sponsored by the Scottish Office Education and Industry Department), the Nuffield Foundation (*Languages: the Next Generation*, 2000), the Department for Education and Skills (*Languages for All: Languages for Life*), and Lord Dearing, commissioned by the Department for Education and Skills (*Languages Review*, known widely as the 'Dearing Report', 2007). Though much of what these reports have to say is relevant to the whole

---

[13]Terry Cox, 'Editorial', *BASEES Newsletter*, New Series, vol. 12, no. 2, pp. 11 and 16.

country, their geographical coverage varies. The SCRE document is centred on Scotland, the Nuffield report was conceived on a nationwide basis and was chaired jointly by a respected television presenter and the Master of Churchill College, Cambridge. *Languages for All* and The Dearing Report are official publications by an English and Welsh government department. The standing of these reports is beyond question, but their influence patchy. As ever, the real issue is whether government or anyone in a position to take action will do so. In relation to numerous reports of the past century, we have seen the truth of the bitter little exchange from a satirical television series of the 1980s. It went something like this:

> PRIME MINISTER: Why doesn't the [name your government department] do something about it?
> CIVIL SERVANT: But, Prime Minister, the department doesn't exist to *do* anything.
> PRIME MINISTER: Why *does* it exist, then?
> CIVIL SERVANT: It's there to explain *why nothing can be done*.

Teachers of languages have had ample cause to discover that these words spoken in jest are true indeed.

We shall look briefly at each report in turn and note what attention they devote to the study of Russian among the main languages they discuss. The SCRE report set out to investigate why senior pupils were deserting languages at SCE Higher grade in the late 1990s, at a time when entries at Standard grade French, German, Italian and Spanish were more numerous than ever before— though not in Russian. The researchers carried out interviews of teachers, school leaders, pupils and parents, and investigations in twelve case-study schools. They concluded that students did not see modern languages as an essential skill in the short term (to achieve entry to higher education and to find satisfying employment), and that there was a 'climate of negativity' about the ability of Scots to learn foreign languages, leading to a lack of confidence in their ability to communicate in them. Perhaps neither of these findings is particularly surprising, but the research unearthed other very interesting points. Pupils were often genuinely interested in the country whose language was being learned, and they were often not satisfied with the attention the teachers paid to cultural matters. Teachers were found not to 'market' modern languages and to overstate the difficulty of languages at Higher grade; they 'need[ed] to encourage [pupils] more actively.' (p. ix) Teachers often seemed defeatist, believing that schools could do little to improve the situation. Teaching methodology was not an issue; society and schools, on the other hand, need to challenge 'current negative stereotypes of ourselves as linguistically incompetent parochialists and [develop] imaginative approaches to raising the profile of foreign languages in education and in cultural contexts, particularly the media.' (p. xii)

This is, of course, all as relevant to Russian, which was very little taught in these twelve schools, as to any other language. Contained within the report are certain significant facts: Russian was taught in only one of these schools, but had once been taught in no fewer than nine of them. There were four teachers still in the schools qualified to teach Russian, but not doing so. Parents interviewed had raised the points that Russian was likely to be useful in business as markets in the East opened up; it was cited as being of particular use in the fishing industry. Examination statistics reveal the gruesome facts that there were only 11 Standard grade entrants for Russian in 1997 as opposed to 40,380 in French; there were 22 Higher candidates (many presumed to be native speakers resident in Scotland) as against 4,840 in French. National Certificate entries presented 'little encouragement for Russian.' (pp. 4, 5, 6, 7, and 10-11)

While the Nuffield Report is extremely well written and well argued, the preceding consultative document *Where are we Going with Languages?*[14] which contains a series of essays by experts in various fields is even more interesting. Sir Trevor McDonald and Sir John Boyd assert in their Chairmen's Introduction to the Report: 'English is not enough [...] There is enthusiasm for languages, but it is patchy. Educational provision is fragmented, achievement poorly measured, continuity not very evident [...] We want to see language skills built into the culture and practice of British business.' (pp. 4-5) Throughout the Report they call for diversification of language provision, a policy which has always been seen as working to the advantage of Russian. 'The education system is not geared to achieve this.' (p. 6) They say that the government has no coherent policy; there is no nationwide strategy for children to start languages early; secondary pupils lack motivation and nine out of ten stop learning languages at 16. In higher education attempts to run a twentieth-century programme for languages 'is hamstrung by outdated funding and management structures'. (pp. 6-7) Among their recommendations, they echo the SCRE report in calling for a campaign to promote positive attitudes towards languages; they seek a national languages strategy, the appointment of a 'languages supremo', an early start (at age seven) for language learning, for a wider range of languages to be taught, and for languages to be made a specified component of the 16-19 curriculum. (pp. 8-9)

The Report fires a broadside at the notion that foreign languages are not a necessary skill for British people because the rest of the world learns English. The UK cannot be 'reliant on the language skills of visitors'. Moreover, as English is used as a lingua franca between non-native English speakers increasingly, 'it is no longer UK English or even US English. And as UK English continues to become effectively a dialect of international English, like all dialects its currency will become localized.' (p. 15) This was a new argument which had only recently been aired: it makes the valid point that, as others learn and take over our language, we in effect cease to own it.[15] Already the 'airspeak' and 'seaspeak' in which international transport is conducted are cases in point; their relation to English is tenuous, to say the least. Anyone who has tried to negotiate

---

[14]See Moys, 1998.

[15]See Graddol, 'Will English be enough?' in Moys.

with the Asia-based helpline of an internet service provider will have experienced this phenomenon.

What do McDonald and Boyd have to say about Russian? They give credit to the diplomatic and defence schools of languages, and mention the Russian fluency of General Jackson, who headed the British army in Kosovo. (pp. 16 and 17) They deplore the decline in applications to study languages at university. 'The declining national capability in German and Russian is a matter of serious concern, given the strategic importance of these languages for the UK.' (p. 55) In this Nuffield Report Russian is again and again placed with Arabic, Chinese, Japanese and Portuguese—all important languages, needless to say—as tongues which pupils might take up *later* in their school career. Before 1990 Russian was bracketed with French, German, Spanish and Italian—the five languages accepted as established, however tenuously, in the lower and middle secondary school. Nuffield, however, strongly calls for money for Russian: 'Special funds should be agreed to support the teaching of languages such as Chinese, Japanese, Arabic, Portuguese and Russian, which are spoken by huge numbers of people in countries of significant economic and political interest to the UK.' (p. 48, also see p. 90) A particularly imaginative recommendation reads: 'The government should invest in the formation of small specialist teams of teachers to work in partnership with national agencies and bodies such as the BBC, the Open University and higher education language centres [... to] develop materials for use in training teachers to teach languages, both in the classroom and in the virtual classroom. This would be of particular benefit for less commonly taught languages, such as [...] Russian.' (p. 72)

A year or two later the Department for Education and Skills issued *Languages for All: Languages for Life*, Nottingham: DfES Publications, 2002. This may be seen in part as a retort to the statement in the Nuffield report that 'The Government has no coherent approach to languages.' (p. 6) This 'strategy for England', as its sub-title claims, lacks the forthright approach of the Nuffield authors, and is marked by the bland language of the civil servant; if 'complacent' is too unkind a judgement, it is self-justificatory. It is scarcely a very imaginative document, but it goes along with the current trends in language policy. Primary school language, 'languages for all' but emphatically not 'one size fits all', raising the profile of languages and increasing motivation, jolting industry out of its linguistic complacency, new forms of 'recognition' (a new word for assessment.) A new feature is that of urging all types of institution, schools primary, secondary and specialist, further and higher education, and schools abroad to collaborate. The teaching of content in other curriculum subjects in the foreign language is advocated. Diversification of languages is not stressed, and in fact there are no proposals at all to plan for a balanced provision. French, German and Spanish are given as possibilities for primary teaching, and a case study of a city where diversified provision has been planned and put into practice is given. (p. 21) If this document contains little encouragement for Russian (which is mentioned only three times), at least there is no discouragement: a third of the specialist language colleges (secondary schools) in existence in 2002 are said to teach Russian (p. 23), and the British Council was set to promote a Russian-language immersion course in Russia from 2003. (pp. 28 and 44)

As if the Government had not had enough advice on modern languages from these sources, in early 2007 the Secretary of State for Education and Skills had Lord Dearing's *Languages Review*. In the meanwhile, the government had disregarded Nuffield's appeal not to remove the requirement for pupils to study a language even to age 16 in the national curriculum. Indeed, the drop in take-up of languages at this stage from 80% (the percentage which actually entered GCSE) to 51% was said to have provoked the Dearing review.

Dearing held back from recommending the reinstatement of a compulsory foreign language for all pupils aged 14 to 16. He encouraged the development of primary-school language teaching. A variety of assessment options is called for. 'Flexible approaches' to language organization, allowing for second languages to be started more widely, are advocated. Initiatives whereby other subjects are taught in the foreign language should be encouraged. A wider range of languages should be taught; community languages (and Russian is seen as one of these) should be encouraged, through support for 'supplementary schools.' Funding, training for teachers to teach primary languages, provision of resources on line and of model teaching programmes; and a new 'major initiative', the establishment of an Open School of Languages, is proposed. The extension of extra funding for language ventures (the specialist language colleges had been receiving an extra £30,000 per annum) was urged. Support for necessary educational change by a number of bodies should be reviewed and 'a more coherent model for supporting change' should be developed. Higher education is urged to make foreign languages a criterion for selection of undergraduates.[16] And what of Russian in particular? Scarcely a word; but then no other language figures, as there is no proposal to plan provision of specific languages. There is an oblique reference to 'Mandarin, Urdu and other major spoken world languages' (p. 15) and to Russian as an ethnic community language. (p. 16—In the heyday of ATR Lord Dearing would never have got away with such minimal reference to Russian.)

It remains to be seen whether all this on the whole admirable matter will result in any more than the DfES[17] explaining 'why nothing can be done'.

---

[16]As this chapter is revised, it is announced in March 2008 that even Cambridge University is dropping its requirement of a foreign language for undergraduate entry. The reason given is that the government is pressing Cambridge to admit more students from state schools, but that the foreign language teaching in those schools is so poor that the requirement of a language discriminates unfairly against them. This ought surely to be a problem for the government, not for Cambridge University.

[17]The English Department for Education has (2007-8) again changed its name, this time to the Department for Children, Schools and Families. There are good practical reasons why it is regrettable that the word 'education' does not appear in the new title.

Dearing did take up many of the points in Nuffield, though Nuffield's sparkle and breadth of vision encompassing the whole of society rather than just the schools is missing. It has not been forgotten by many who were alive in the 1960s and 1970s that primary school French (and it *was* French pretty well exclusively) was all the rage then, but that it collapsed because it was not properly planned, supported, financed, or thought out; moreover, by general agreement, it damaged languages other than French. That was over thirty years ago, and much of the active teaching profession has passed on into retirement. Just as the foot-and-mouth disease crisis of 2001 took by surprise the civil servants in government agriculture who had not been around in 1967 when the previous outbreak took place, and who were slow to take the enquiry report off the shelf and consult it, how many of our educators and administrators remember the way it was in 1974, and will they have learned any of the lessons? The answer remains to be seen.

A View from ground level. The study of Russian since the end of the 1980s

We have examined the major changes in the educational scene in Britain in recent decades from the point of view of the policies they exemplify and of the organization of schools and universities on the macro level. Approaching closer to the classroom, a warmer and more personal picture may be seen. The best source for building up such a picture, since the *ATR Newsletter* was discontinued, is the pages of *Rusistika*, the new Russian journal of ALL, which has appeared in over thirty numbers since June 1990. *Rusistika* combined the functions of the *JRS* and the *ATR NL*, publishing many learned and professional articles on Russian language teaching, on the language itself, literature, life and culture, while at the same time reporting on the mundane but no less interesting day-to-day affairs of Russianists in ALL. One notable missing feature is the minutes of Russian Committee meetings, which appeared regularly in the *ATRNL* from the late 1960s. Nevertheless, a fairly clear if sometimes not totally complete picture of activities emerges from the pages of the journal.

Was the campaigning work of ATR enabled to continue under its new ALL 'patronage'? How about its support for teachers, the exchange of information, encouragement of curriculum development and the like? The sub-committee structure of ATR and the way committee members were allocated to specific duties of this sort does not seem to have been replicated in ALL. The Conference programmes in recent years have contained scant mention of Russian. Financial support for the *kruzhki* (circles), the local groups which had sometimes been only loosely attached to ATR as Russian-speaking clubs, cultural organizations open to members and non-members of ATR alike, was not forthcoming from ALL. They could not be comfortably absorbed into the organization of that body, as teachers of French and German did not seem to need or to be interested in such circles. It will be recalled that ATR set up the local *kruzhki* very early in its existence, and that they became a strength of the Association. Their loss would have been a disaster; happily some of the local circles remained in existence, and

Rusistika published regular summary reports of their activities. A committee member, Mrs Joan Smith, made it her duty to keep in touch with them. There was collaboration with the GB-USSR Association and its successors the Britain-Russia Centre, the Great Britain-Russia Society, and the Scotland-Russia Forum; the Society for Cultural Relations (SCR, later Society for Co-operation in Russian and Soviet Studies—SCRSS) continued its activities and to maintain its premises in Brixton with the invaluable and extensive library in the basement. A good number of teachers of Russian in the London area continued to meet. A significant feature of the work of *kruzhki* in provincial centres was the importance of 'vital outward-looking' local university departments, which provided a meeting place as well as members and moral support.[18] When a university Russian department was closed, sometimes the *kruzhok* also collapsed, illustrating yet again the interdependence of the higher and secondary sectors.

A significant issue of external support for Russian in schools was raised by an article in the first issue of *Rusistika* by D. J. Pearce.[19] Mr Pearce was a 'permanent supply teacher in charge of Russian' for Barnsley LEA; he described an imaginative scheme for providing Russian in the town, which had begun in 1986 with one teacher teaching 17 pupils in one school. By 1990 two teachers in four schools were teaching 67 pupils. The schools were all 11-16 establishments, which fed a tertiary college in the borough. Pearce advances several reasons for the success of the scheme to 1990: enthusiastic support from head teachers, advisers, education officers and politicians; the existence of a town twinning arrangement which gave Russian a high profile locally; and most of all the fact that initially half of the salary of one of the teachers was to be paid from LEA funds, not the finances of one particular school. This is the model for the introduction of Russian which teachers had pressed for over the years.

However, Mr Pearce also sounded the warning bell. Just as the scheme was developing nicely, the system was faced with moves in national education politics which threatened its further development. 'LMS' was introduced: local [financial] management of schools, an apparently democratic step whereby funds were granted directly to schools, and LEAs found their central budget was all but disappearing. While a borough authority might find it possible to allocate substantial funds amounting to half a teacher's salary in order to get a scheme such as this going, an individual head teacher and his governors would most likely find providing a teacher for a small group of Russian pupils an unaffordable luxury. Near the end of the article we read: 'The task is now to find a way [to follow the plan through] within the constraints of the new system of school financing.' Once again in the history of Russian teaching we find that teachers on the ground (even with keen support from their local mentors) have

---

[18] Chamberlain, p. 20.

[19] 'Russian in the era of khozraschyot', *Rusistika*, no. 1, June 1990, pp. 6-8.

to struggle with a system that appears actively to work against their subject and, it must be added, both the local and national interest.

I was able to track David Pearce down in September 2007 and discover the end of the story. He described Russian in Barnsley as 'a bubble that burst'. At its peak there were as many as 400 pupils learning Russian in the borough, with five teachers all attached to specific schools. GCSE entries reached 120, A levels nine per annum. By 1995 'serious' study of Russian had collapsed in Barnsley. The 'capping' of school budgets was fatal to the subject. Pearce, having had a roving brief, was assigned to the tertiary college, and gradually restricted in his ability to launch out into feeder schools and help with Russian. The National Curriculum effectively killed third foreign languages, league tables discouraged them even further; two of the school heads keenest on Russian retired. Worst of all, one school which had intended to run German and Russian as its two foreign languages encountered entrenched opposition from the French lobby, which could not conceive of a school without French and fought the proposal tooth and nail. Disappointing as the failure of this experiment was, it does present a model for the school teaching of Russian at some future time, when the policy issues may have been resolved. The failure was not due to incompetent teaching, nor to the fact that pupils found Russian any harder to succeed with in public examinations, nor to any unpopularity with pupils.

Events in Russia in the early 1990s brought about important changes in the environment in which Russian teaching was carried on. We have already noted the boost to Russian studies in universities in the early 1990s. After the attempted coup of 1991 and the collapse of the Soviet Union, however, economic and monetary chaos, poverty and hardship, shortages and non-payment of wages and salaries became the subject of lurid stories in the Western press, while 'new Russians', like some of their western counterparts, found ways of feathering their nests from the plunder of former state assets. Some of them even came to Britain and bought such things as football clubs. The Russian president was put under enormous pressure by western right-wing leaders to bring about instantly the sort of economic reform they had themselves taken years to achieve. The result was desperate hardship for many Russians, as the state could not pay salaries and pensions—they were sometimes months or years in arrears. Around this time a Russian deputy minister commented in relation to the establishment of educational exchanges: 'Provided the pace of change in our country does not reach the speed of light, there is much work to be done.'[20]

It very nearly did reach that speed. Civil and political turmoil was experienced as Yeltsin quelled his opponents. Opportunities for business ventures in Russia soon became possible for foreigners. For teachers of Russian things changed too. Exchanges and relations with Russian educational establishments were no longer centrally controlled and could in theory be set up at will. While

---

[20] Reported in *Rusistika*, no. 6, 1992, p. 52.

visa controls and getting into the country were still strict, it became possible to lodge in people's flats or in non-tourist hotels. Everyday life in Russia for the visitor—shopping, getting meals and the like—became very much easier. Most of all, freedom of expression, the open discussion of varying views and the loss of the need to know a 'code' when interpreting the opinions of Russians with whom one was in contact, seemed at that time to be developing in a healthy manner. The downside included matters such as the collapse of certain sides of the publishing industry and the uncertainty of the delivery of periodicals abroad—vital matters for scholars, and symptomatic of the chaos affecting many aspects of Russian life at the time.

Professor Kostomarov declared a little later, in 1996, that the Russian language was now happily 'bereft of the political implications which had earlier distorted its image'.[21] If this was ever really true, it did not remain so for long. The happy side of the new situation led briefly to enthusiastic enrolment in Russian classes, but a more measured reaction ensued. A. D. P. Briggs wrote in 1993: 'Gorbachev's Russia, glamorous and exciting [...] declined into a Russia perceived as dull and unhealthy. Now it also looks dangerous.'[22] And indeed, the bloodshed of October 1993, the Chechen wars, terrorism, murder, unscrupulous moneymaking by a few 'oligarchs', the emergence of a strong undercurrent of jingoistic nationalism and the cult of personality, growing religious intolerance (surprisingly, perhaps), and now murder outside the borders of Russia and in particular in our own country, have all soured the public perception of Russia. Some of these phenomena are more apparent than real, and the Western press, as ever they did, concentrate on the dark side. Nevertheless, they demonstrate that interpreters of Russian reality are as necessary since the end of Communism as they were before.

As one scans the pages of *Rusistika* and other journals for teachers and academics, it becomes quite remarkably clear that, whatever the state of Russian provision, a great deal of activity was being undertaken by teachers in both secondary and higher education to provide teaching materials. The British Library catalogue lists commercially published grammars and works on Russian language since 1990 by at least seven authors and teams of authors for university studies, five courses for school pupils, and six for the FE, business and leisure student. One or two of these are reissues of earlier work, but even that shows that a demand exists. While the National Curriculum and GCSE were being planned, along with parallel moves in Scotland, teachers were writing or adapting courses suitable for the new situation. David Rix and Robert Pullin, lecturers in education at York and Sheffield Universities, and themselves textbook authors,[23] maintained for some years up to 1994 a circle of support groups for writers of such materi-

---

[21] Quoted by Terence Wade, *Rusistika*, no. 14, 1996, p. 51.

[22] 'Wounded again—the marble swan of freedom', *Rusistika*, no. 8, 1993, p. 56.

[23] Pullin, *Putyovka* and *Privyet!*

als, based from the south-west of England to Scotland, backing them up with in-service conferences at which work could be discussed, improved, assessed and disseminated. These teacher-authors worked largely on a non-profit-making basis, and in fact at some financial cost to themselves: 'little funding and endless dedication', as one reviewer wrote. One group of secondary teachers rewrote and freely adapted the Nuffield/Schools Council course *Vperyod!* of the 1960s. As their work was not in the narrow sense 'commercially viable', the materials had often to be produced by the good old Soviet and Russian tradition of *samizdat*. Some materials for the post-16 age-group were written and published outside of the charmed circle of well-known educational publishers. In the face of all this, it seems odd that one writer in *Rusistika* referred to a 'distinct lack of Russian textbooks', while at the same time declaring that there were 42 of them. Teachers are never satisfied.[24]

At the same time more than one group of university teachers were working on the production of *ab initio* Russian materials in response to the clear necessity of attracting students to university departments to start Russian from scratch, and to have appropriate study materials for them to work with. Gone are the days when dons thought that *ab initio* language work was drudgery for university lecturers and that they should not be expected to sully their hands with it! SSEES and the University of Portsmouth were prominent in writing such material for their own and others' undergraduates.[25] Meanwhile, a successful series of books for further education students has gradually appeared, and the BBC reissued the materials accompanying their most popular television course. An important grammar has appeared, along with others for reference and progressive study:[26] dictionaries and works on aspects of the Russian language have also been published. One section of *Rusistika* for 2001 reviews or lists no fewer than eight new textbooks, study materials or teaching aids. The following year it was stated, 'Teachers will be spoiled for choice [for] new teaching materials.' These are important achievements, and it can safely be said that the overall quality of published work on the Russian language has improved out of all recognition over the past century.[27]

The activities of the international body MAPRYaL continued to have a supporting influence on the Russian-teaching profession and their students throughout these decades. Regular conferences took place, and British delegates often made distinguished contributions to the proceedings. This point is worth making, since there had always been a tendency on these occasions for East European delegates to go through the motions, and to produce stereotyped *soobshcheniia*

---

[24]F. Wright, pp. 12 and 13.

[25]See items by Aizlewood, and by Rodimkina, Riley and Landsman in the Bibliography.

[26]Wade, *A Comprehensive Russian Grammar*, and ancillary materials; Derek Offord, *Modern Russian, An Advanced Grammar*.

[27]Courses and grammars are listed in the final section of the Bibliography.

('communications') which no-one was interested in, and during which the audience chatted. In the early 1970s Bertram Pockney had received a standing ovation for his presentation of the cartoon films, 'The Martian in Moscow'; in the 1990s Terence Wade and Michael Kirkwood in particular showed that British scholars were a power to be reckoned with in relation to language teaching. A second aspect of MAPRYal activities was the biennial *olimpiada* for school pupils. This Russian word, common in the USSR when referring to national competitions for schoolchildren in anything from mathematics to Russian literature, aroused some opposition from the Olympic Committee in one European country. 'Olympiad' they regarded as their copyright! The Russian language was not changed to please them.

Six is perhaps a very small number of pupils, even considering the relatively small number of school students learning Russian in Britain. But the ATR and ALL regularly held competitions in Britain to select this number to send to Moscow for the finals. Having been a judge on one occasion, I can confirm that the standard was very high at the British finals. Britain sent some excellent candidates to Moscow. There the lucky—or the deserving—six had an experience which more than one of them described in print.[28] What fun it must have been! The social events, the dances, the *kontserty khudozhestvennoi samodeiatel'nosti* (do-it-yourself ceilidh-like performances) which the British must have found so embarrassing while gritting their teeth in order fully to enter into the spirit of the occasion. ('The audience burst into spontaneous applause when they heard we were to perform Queen's *Bohemian Rhapsody* and were still polite enough to applaud when they had actually heard it'), the harmless leg-pulling by the boys of their (female) Russian 'minder' who had the greatest difficulty in persuading them to get out of bed in the morning. The partly sardonic, partly enthusiastic, modest accounts of these competitors of their performance before the examining 'commissions' are heart-warming, and any teacher can be glad even if only six British school pupils on each occasion had the opportunity to participate.

Reading of all this enthusiastic activity by teachers, authors and pupils, it is hard to face the decline in schools Russian provision by the mid-1990s. GCSE entries dipped to 1,733 in 1998, significantly fewer than the entries in Urdu, Italian, Chinese and Panjabi, and, of course an infinitesimal figure when compared with the 338,000 for French and the 136,000 for German.[29] There were 839 full and part-time undergraduates reading Russian in 1996-97; comparisons here are difficult to make, as combinations with other subjects (including other Slavonic languages) vary so much, and the way full-time equivalents are calculated is complex, but as a rough measure, there were nearly 7,000 reading French

---

[28] For example, a report by a seventeen-year-old contestant Adam Fergus, 'VII Mezhdunarodnaia olimpiada ... What it was really like', *Rusistika*, no. 13, 1996, pp. 34-36; another by a participant two years later, Andrew Daniels, 'Ninth international Russian-speaking olympiad, *Rusistika*, no.18, 1998, pp. 33-34.

[29] Boaks, in Moys, p. 36.

and over 2,600 German.[30] For every one undergraduate there had been 48 offering French at GCSE. For every undergraduate studying Russian there had been two at GCSE. Ninety-seven percent, therefore, dropped French between GCSE and university. The figures suggest that only 48% dropped Russian, but one must allow for the fact that many of the undergraduates are studying *ab initio*—yet some of these will have done GCSE Russian at school without having the opportunity to do A level. The figures—as well as a heap of experiential, anecdotal, and other factual evidence—show that when Russian tends strongly to take hold of the imagination of the learner, he or she sticks with it.

Quite apart from the Nuffield, DfES, and Dearing Reports, the first decade of the twenty-first century brought some interesting and some ominous developments for Russian teaching. One in particular was the decision to make the GCSE examination in Russian a 'single-tier' subject, that is: only the 'higher' candidate could enter. This notion, in the first instance, conflicts with the principle of 'Russian for all', as the school child who was not capable of reaching 'higher' standard was debarred virtually from the start. In consequence it was not possible in many comprehensive schools to assemble Russian classes in what was considered to be 'viable' numbers. The resultant situation is obvious: Russian becomes 'unviable' in most schools, where it is essential to show that one teacher is daily and constantly facing thirty pupils. Moreover, as a result of this decision, Russian is now classified with Polish and the like as a 'heritage' language, and English-speaking candidates are competing with Russian native speakers. It was never really intended, or it certainly should not have been intended, that this was the way GCSE was conceived. Some hope may be held out in relation to a second aspect of twenty-first-century policy, the development of specialist language colleges, which has done something to encourage the study of Russian in Britain.

---

[30]Towell, in Moys, p. 46.

Chapter 9

What is the Position of Russian in Britain Now and Where is it Going?

I have enormous confidence—and faith—in the people of that vast country. And whatever political system Russia ultimately chooses will be one that all of us respect and one that, whether we like it or not, none of us can afford to ignore.'
PRINCE MICHAEL OF KENT, *writing in 2007*

THE YEAR 2007 was officially designated Год русского языка (Russian Language Year: RLY) in the Federation. This presents an opportunity for reflections on our findings in this historical survey of Russian in Britain. Why did the Russian government feel it needed to celebrate the Russian language in this way, and why was it thought the time was ripe in 2007?

It should not be forgotten that nearer two hundred than one hundred different native languages are spoken within the borders of the Russian Federation. It used to be stated that Russian had been 'freely chosen' as the intra-national language of the USSR. The alacrity with which every other republic except one, Belarus, dropped Russian as an alternative state language once the Union collapsed shows how 'free' that choice was perceived to be. The tsarist régime saw the Russian language as 'the cement of the Empire.'[1] Though Lenin was often said by Soviet writers to have been a lover of the Russian language,[2] he encouraged the use of the mother tongues of non-Russian Soviet nationalities as a way of gaining support among those nationalities. All languages were to be equal; 'any talk of superiority of Russian culture [was] an attempt to foster domination' and was to be eschewed in all circumstances. However, Russian perhaps inevitably became the predominant state language, whatever republican or local media and educational institutions taught, spoke, and did. It was, as the only practical possibility, the language of the Soviet Army. Lenin well knew that Russian was seen by non-Russians as a symbol of tsarist oppression; his linguistic policy won support for the Revolution among people from these nationalities who had originally been

---

[1] Isabelle Kreindler, 'The Changing status of Russian in the Soviet Union', *International Journal of the Sociology of Language*, 33, 1982, p. 7.
[2] It is hard to find real evidence for this. Lenin did once write in passing: 'The language of Turgenev, Dobroliubov and Chernyshevskii is a great and mighty one.' ('Is a compulsory official language needed?', in *Lenin on Language*, Moscow: Raduga, 1983, p. 135.) This scant quotation was so often used by Soviet linguists that one suspects no other could be found.

hostile.[3] Yet the dominance of Russian inside the borders of the USSR and in the satellite states of Eastern Europe after the Second World War caused resentment. When Russian political control was removed, the language went with it. 'Russian has been sidelined', wrote Conor Sweeney, a correspondent on the Reuters website (1 July 2007). The 'cement' of the Empire or the Union had become, in the prophetic metaphor of one linguist, the acid which dissolved it.[4] At the same time the Russian-speaking population is falling by seven hundred thousand a year.[5]

Sweeney's headline is 'Russia promotes language as symbol of resurgence', and he argues that such promotion matches the increasing economic and political confidence of Russia: 'The Kremlin believes it can start rebuilding the credibility of Russian as a means of communication outside its own borders, with business and not communist ideology driving the revival.' This, of course, is a journalist's view; perhaps he does not fully understand the emotional importance to a Russian of the Russian language. Russians imagine that all nations feel the same about their own languages. A remarkable book by Madame N. Jarintzov entitled *The Russians and their Language* appeared in 1916. She writes, 'These thoughts [contained in the book] concern the spirit of our land, which is interwoven with its language to the highest imaginable extent'.[6] The aims of Russian native language teaching in Soviet schools in the 1980s included that of giving pupils a feeling for its beauty and the desire to strive for mastery of its richness.[7]

Some might mock some of the nationalistic and whimsical sentiments expressed on the RLY website: 'Russian was the first language spoken in space'; 'My language is your friend', 'How our language will resound', 'We shall preserve you, Russian speech'. These are the titles of competitions or events. But what is really wrong with them? The intention appears to be inclusive and internationalist, rather than to humiliate and belittle, as is sometimes liable to happen in linguistic campaigns in other countries where people should know better.

The RLY website lists eleven festivals and creative projects, eleven conferences and congresses, nine publishing and media activities, and 103 events organized by the Ministry of Foreign Affairs, all these in a very wide variety of countries as well as Russia, but very few in Britain. The supreme irony is that this website is published in two languages: Russian and another, and readers will have no difficulty guessing *which* other language. Could a Russian Language Year not happen without that 'killer' language at its side, ready to pounce? Happily the Russians have got some of their own back on the English language by providing delightfully bizarre translations. One anticipates with excitement the

---

[3] Kreindler, pp. 8-9.

[4] Yaroslav Bilinsky, 'Expanding the use of Russian or Russification?' *Russian Review*, 40, 1981.

[5] http://reuters.com/article/inDepthNews/idUSL2821441620070701 dated 1 July 2007 5.45 p.m.

[6] Jarintzoff, p. 2.

[7] Muckle, *A Guide to the Soviet Curriculum,* esp. pp. 62ff.

promise of 'shootings on the Red Square', until closer examination of the Russian original (съёмки на Красной площади) indicates that what will be 'shot' in that auspicious place are not recalcitrant traitors to the cause, but film and television interviews. The events promised include: book exhibitions and festivals, poetry events, literary conferences, musical concerts, folklore festivals, courses and competitions for teachers and students of Russian, a press congress, and a forum of translators of Russian literature. Establishment of a Russian cultural foundation on the lines of the Alliance française and the Goethe-Institut is promised. (The British Council is not mentioned.) Imaginative steps in this direction can only benefit the study of Russian abroad, including Britain.

However, the sudden announcement on 12 December 2007 that the activities of the British Council in Russia are held by the Russian government to be illegal and must most of them be ended is a highly unwished-for development which could cancel out the expected benefit of a Russian foundation. Very shortly before this, the Russian 'immersion' course for school pupils first announced in 2003 had been advertised as a going concern for 2008. The Russian government can scarcely have objected to this particular initiative. It was, however, rumoured in the press that the authorities' real objection to the British Council is its success in promoting British culture; isolationism and xenophobia in certain quarters in Russia have led to the unpleasantness.

The present situation in the United Kingdom and Ireland

It is not a simple matter to sum up the centuries of experience of teaching and studying the language and of research into that language, the people who speak it, their history, culture, scientific achievements, and intellectual and spiritual constitution. Achievements there certainly have been and continue to be, but the optimism of the 1960s is no longer present in the way it was then. The generation which experienced that optimism has by now retired, and new teachers, learners and scholars have arisen to take their place, in smaller numbers, but they *are* present.

Educational establishments in Britain where Russian is taught have declined substantially in number in the last twenty years. In Wales they have largely disappeared. There is only one university in the whole of Ireland—Dublin—where Russian is taught to degree level. The figures for schools in Northern Ireland rose from 2 in 1960 to a peak of 9 in 1969 and fell again to 4 in 1992. This conceals the fact that the tiny handful of schools were forever changing: only the Methodist College, Belfast, appeared in every list from 1965 to 1992. Numbers of pupils opting for Russian had been small, but in 2008 the position of Russian there is encouraging, with full classes of pupils who continue with the study of Russian even when the opportunity is offered to drop it. Success in university entrance applications is high. In further education in Northern Ireland, it is possible to learn Russian in non-degree classes at Queen's University and elementary Russian at the recently re-named Belfast Metropolitan College, which has three part-time teachers.

Trinity College, Dublin (TCD) has proved the most enduring centre of Russian studies in Ireland. Russian has also been taught at the National Institute for Higher Education (later University) at Limerick, at Cork (long ago) and at the Letterkenny Regional Technical College (until the late 1990s). Russian was taught at Queen's University, Belfast, between 1968 and 1997, and at the New University of Ulster (Coleraine) from 1967 to 1982. Russian never became firmly established in these institutions; one member of staff described the experience as being 'rather like standing on a sandcastle we had built and watching the tide wash it away.'

At different times since the mid-1970s, however, there has been much activity in Ireland. An Irish Slavists' Association was set up in 1975 open to members on both sides of the border. The wish to learn Russian has been shown pretty constantly by adult students working simply out of interest. TCD offered an evening diploma in Russian, a two-year course for two nights a week. Interest in this died down, but when it revived in the mid-1990s evening classes offered tuition at four different levels from beginners to advanced. Classes in Russian are offered in other towns and cities in evening institutes and community colleges.

The resurgence of interest in Russian in Ireland may be due to the relatively large number of recent Russian immigrants in the country. A Saturday and Sunday school is run by the Orthodox Church in Dublin. A number of Irish parents have adopted Russian orphans. Meanwhile the National Council for Curriculum and Assessment approved a syllabus for Russian in the school Leaving Certificate which was first taken in 2003; entrants have gone from 55 in the first year to 111 in 2005, 158 in 2006, and 181 in 2007, 78.5% of whom were awarded the highest grade.[8] It is assumed that the vast majority of entrants are the children of Russian immigrants, as this high level of achievement might suggest.

At the same time the Irish Department of Education and Science has since 2000 been funding a Post-Primary Languages initiative as part of the National Development Plan. Russian figures in this, and materials are being developed for use in schools. Under this dispensation, pupils aged 15 to 16 are encouraged to try new subjects in their 'transition year', which they are not allowed to offer for the Leaving Certificate. A score of Irish schools have expressed the wish to participate in this innovation, which, it is hoped, may lead to certificated courses when curricula are developed.

In Wales Russian survives in the odd school. It is in Scotland that devastation has been seen in schools. Around 1960 it had even been considered possible that Russian might become a main first foreign language in secondary schools in Scotland; one cannot say how seriously this idea was ever regarded. However,

---

[8] http://www.examinations.ie

now three universities, Glasgow, Edinburgh, and St Andrews, continue to teach the language to degree level. Glasgow recently won a bid for substantial funding in partnership with several other Scottish and two English universities, and in consequence has been able to establish a solid basis for Slavonic and East European languages. On the other hand there has been a notable contraction of provision in Edinburgh. In December 2007 St Andrews was stronger, featuring nine academic staff on its website, two of whom were lectors and two more of whom had honorary positions.

Fourteen universities in England continue to offer Russian on undergraduate courses, and these include some strong departments (by the standards of Russian).[9] The most recent figures presented by the Universities and Colleges Admissions Service (UCAS) for Russian and East European Studies from 2000 to 2007 show an increase of 40% in applications and of 15% in acceptances.[10] Some of this is due to the appearance of a new constituency: the children of the ever-growing number of immigrants from Russia and from other former Soviet republics with a background in Russian language study, or perhaps with native command of Russian. Admissions tutors in 2007 reported 'no doom and gloom', and commented that applications for research degrees are booming in area studies. Membership of BASEES was reported to have increased significantly in March 2008.

There would appear to be at least as many secondary schools in England offering Russian as in the late 1950s and early 1960s. The Centre for Information on Language Teaching (CILT) carries out an annual Language Trends Survey.[11] The most recent of these at the time of writing, 2007, has discovered that, in England in a sample of 678 maintained and 182 independent schools, 6 percent of the former and 19 percent of the latter provide Russian at some level. (Equivalent figures for Mandarin are 9% and 8% respectively, for Japanese 7% and 18%, for Urdu 6% and 4%, and for Arabic 3% and 8%.) Six percent of English maintained schools amounts to 202 actual schools, which is considerably more than the 164 which were teaching Russian in 1992. This suggests that, on the face of it, the extrapolation must have produced an inaccurate figure. However, the explanation may well be that these schools are teaching Russian to a few pupils only. CILT's report further indicates that half of these schools teach Russian outside the organized curriculum, which may mean that some at least (though not necessarily, of course, all) of the pupils are native Russian speakers who are developing their literacy; many who speak fluent Russian can barely write their names in block capitals. This agrees with the findings of Nick Brown

---

[9] Figures from the website of UCAS, which coordinates admission of undergraduates.

[10] www.ucas.ac.uk. These figures (for Russian and East European Studies exclusively) must be taken as no more than a very rough guide to the situation. UCAS do not show combinations of Russian with other subjects, which the vast majority of students undertake.

[11] Results appear at http://www.cilt.org.uk/research/languagetrends/2007/secondary.htm. Links may be followed to a wide variety of other sources of relevant information.

of the Specialist Schools and Academies Trust, who has discovered one hundred British schools where Russian is taught in the normal curriculum.[12] The figures certainly show that the subject is not dead in English schools.

Comparable figures in other western countries may be of interest. Websites of professional organizations betray exactly the same difficulties of compilation as are experienced in Britain: authorities and schools do not necessarily reply to enquiries, and the information is therefore incomplete. However, for what it is worth, the facts are: in the USA in 2005, in 28 states of the Union, 126 schools responded that they were offering Russian and that there were 7,863 students enrolled in Russian classes. This would appear to be a drop from the 306 schools with 10,371 learners reported in 1996, but it is likely that the 2005 figures were based on a significantly smaller response to the questionnaire. The Association française des russisants presents the current figures for seventeen *académies* (regional education authorities) out of twenty-five: 3 primary schools, 197 secondary, and five higher education establishments were offering Russian, though as Paris was one of the *académies* not to have replied so far, it may be assumed that the real figure is much higher. Germany boasts a much healthier total: the Deutsch-russisches Forum knows of 1,948 schools which offered Russian in 2004. This high figure is surely a residual consequence of Russian having been compulsory in the East under Socialism; it was often stated that German educational establishments deserted Russian for English after the dissolution of the DDR, but this retreat was clearly not complete.[13]

Examination entries for Russian in Scotland have reached a nadir. According to published but unconfirmed statistics, one pupil only took Standard grade SCE in 2007. Higher grade entries were 16, plus 4 for Advanced Higher; it may be assumed that many of these are 'heritage' candidates for whom S grade is inappropriate. The Scots have not published figures for students in further education colleges since 2001, but here there is a glimmer of optimism: in that year there were 92 such students, while there were only ten entering S grade in schools. (The majority of those FE students were aged over 40 and almost all the rest between 25 and 40.)[14] In England and Wales examination entries are not unhealthy (see below). It is important to bear in mind that foreign languages in general in secondary education are in decline: in August 2007, when GCSE results were published, serious concern was expressed at the drop in numbers for French (to below 300,000) and German (to below 100,000). Only 46% of pupils in England took a language, or more than one, at GCSE in 2007; the figure for 2001 had been 78%, for 2004 68%, for 2006 59%, and for 2006 51%.

---

[12]Website: www.schoolsnetwork.org.uk

[13]These figures come from the Committee on College and Pre-College Russian (CCPCR): www.american.edu/research/CCPCR; www.deutsch-russisches-forum.de; www.int-evry.fr/afrr.

[14]Figures from Scottish CILT: http://www.scilt.stir.ac.uk/Languages_in_Scotland/

To examine the figures for examination entries for the GCSE in Russian is instructive. They are not insignificant: an average of 1,713 per year between 2000 and 2005, approximately 84% of whom were school pupils aged 15-16. (The peak was double this at 3,370 for GCE O level in 1970). AS level Russian entries increased from 226 in 2001 to 467 in 2005 and 543 in 2006 (the most recent available figure at the time of writing); A level figures were 531 in 2001 and 729 (unconfirmed) in 2007. There were 1,775 entries for GCSE Russian in 2006, including 1,396 school pupils aged 15-16, 78% of the total. In 2007 the total was 1,897, but the figure of school pupils is not yet published.[15] The website of the Specialist Schools and Academies Trust indicates that numbers of candidates for the International Baccalaureate have reached about three hundred annually, and about the same number have entered for the Certificate in Business Language Competence (CIBC). In 2006 258 entered for the ABC in Practical Languages.[16]

ALL was able in 2006-07 to organize a Russian essay competition, and the section for school pupils attracted a very respectable 135 entries, including a variety of excellent ones.[17] Children who were Russian native speakers entered this essay competition in a separate category for such candidates.

Perhaps the most innovative development for school pupils is an initiative fostered by the British Council: its Educational partnership programme (EPP). This has three aspects: the first two are study visits for head teachers and school staff, with the aim of building relationships and 'future collaborative curriculum work.' The third is the Russian Immersion Courses: 'Students from schools in England attend immersion courses in Russia that combine intensive Russian language studies with an active programme of cultural activities.' This has not been in existence for long, but the first indications are that it is extremely successful. Political events at the close of 2007, however, cast a shadow over the activities of the British Council in Russia, and it remains to be seen whether this project will suffer in consequence. There are, however, rumours in early 2008 of possible financial support for Russian teaching from a new player on the scene: the Yeltsin Foundation.

The increase in applications for research degrees and in the membership of BASEES is interesting: it is due to the creation of new posts in research (in Eastern European studies as well as Russian), and these young people are working for the most part in area studies rather than on literary topics. If they go into

---

[15] The most informative statistics on examination entries in Russian for recent years are published on the websites of CILT and Scottish CILT. Government sources do not separate Russian from 'other languages.' Until 2005 the AQA was responsible for collating data, and I am grateful to Chris Higgins for supplying detailed information.

[16] www.schoolsnetwork.org.uk, as at 9 August 2007.

[17] Natalia Tronenko, 'ALL first Russian essay competition', *Language World*, Summer 2007, p. 7. A full report, names of winners and their winning essays were published in Tronenko, 'First ALL Russian essay competition', *Rusistika*, 32, 2007, pp. 15-17. The exercise was repeated in 2008.

university teaching, it will not be in language departments, but in social sciences, history, economics, politics and the like. However, they will at one remove contribute to Russian language studies. The HEFCE Report of 1995 further encouraged research in area studies by some provision of funding. Success in the establishment of an academic tradition may further be demonstrated by the rich contents of twenty-first century publishers' catalogues of new books on Russian studies. This comes at a time when financial constraints on publishing are increasing rather than the opposite.

Nevertheless, on the face of it, it would seem that there is no cause for despair. We may have even more cause for optimism: do these figures tell the whole story? The Muscovy merchants learned from scratch with no academic guidance at all. Heard, Darlington, Pares, Forbes and Morfill and their ilk—and all those serving officers who qualified as linguists—had to show initiative in order to acquire Russian in the nineteenth and early twentieth century. Prisoners of war in 1914-18 and the autodidacts between the wars, enthusiasts who learned on their own, using the many published teaching aids, and who attended evening classes for what assistance they could get in Russian conversation, have all figured in this narrative. Are there such people around today?

The answer must surely be 'yes', even if numbers are not enormous. What evidence is there for this view? The figures for examination entries clearly also include mature entrants from further education colleges and independent students: as always, private coaching in Russian is both available and sought. One publisher's website lists seventy FE colleges to teachers and students of which he has sold Russian books recently.[18] Short intensive residential weekend and vacation courses continue to be advertised and run by universities, adult education colleges and friendship societies. Authors and publishers of self-study manuals report healthy sales and royalties for their books and other teaching materials. Not everyone who buys a copy of a title promising 'learn Russian on your own' succeeds in doing so, but the purchase at least indicates interest. It may well be that fifty years of Russian in schools and colleges has created a climate of opinion by which people feel, despite all the journalistic clichés about Russian being a 'fiendishly difficult' language, that it is worth giving it a go.

'Friendship' and cultural societies with Russia still exist and still flourish. The Great Britain-Russia Society (GBRS) and its Scottish fellow, the Scotland-Russia Forum (SRF), the Pushkin Club, and SCRSS are all dynamic organizations with a reasonable proportion of Russian-speaking members; as well as mounting talks and symposia, and promoting conversation in Russian, the GB-RS publishes an impressive *East-West Review*, the Scots issue a lively *Scotland-Russia Forum Review*, the SCRSS still maintains its richly stocked mainly Russian-language library and runs language courses, meetings, concerts, and conversation evenings as it always did. Most of these bodies maintain very frequent electronic mailings

---

[18] www.ruslan.co.uk as at 18 August 2007.

to members of events of Russian interest, and they have in 2007 and 2008 run conferences or residential courses on the Russian language. These organizations, along with town-twinning groups and some entirely *ad hoc* clubs, entertain visitors from Russia, look after cultural emissaries such as theatre or dance groups, orchestras, ballet companies, make expatriates feel at home, and guide and look after tourists.

There has been a small Russian community in Britain for over a century, dating back particularly from the days of political, ethnic, and religious repression from the mid-nineteenth century onwards. Numbers were never large, and as recently as the 2001 census, Russian residents here amounted to no more than 15,644 (only half the estimate for 1938 reported in Chapter 4), the vast majority of them below the age of 44. However, numbers have increased substantially, and the best estimates we now have—though very approximate—indicate that by December 2006 there were as many as 300,000 residents in the UK who consider themselves Russian, some say half a million or even more. A hundred thousand of these arrived in the two years 2005 and 2006. Seventy percent live in London, 10 percent in Manchester, 8 percent in Scotland (mainly Glasgow and Edinburgh), and Birmingham, Brighton, Bristol and Cambridge all have sizeable communities.[19]

'Heritage' learners of Russian are in consequence more visible than in earlier times. This manifests itself in part because of the existence of 'supplementary' (as they are termed) Saturday or Sunday schools for the children of Russian immigrants or of parents working here for an extended period. Such schools there have doubtless been in the past, but they have been fewer in number,[20] but there is a particular need for them now since the children may well be returning to Russia to continue their education in due course. The children may, of course, be of any age, and many of them attend regular schools too where they may or may not obtain help with literacy in Russian. Examiners at Advanced level GCE and their teachers in schools often report absolutely lamentable written Russian from some of these students, while their spoken Russian is, not surprisingly, excellent. It is a problem that British teachers of Russian have not usually encountered previously, and one which they consequently find refreshing to tackle. Some of the Russian supplementary schools are now admitting British native pupils whose parents would like them to learn Russian. It will be

---

[19] International Organization for Migration, *Mapping Exercise for Russian*, London, July 2007. See http://www.iomlondon.org/doc/mapping/Russia%20Mapping%20Report.pdf, pp. 6 and 7.

[20] Until very recently there did not appear to be a coordinating body for the work of these Russian supplementary schools. Websites give the flavour of their work: for example, the school at Cambridge www.camruss.com/school.htm, www.azbuka.org.uk; there are four others in the London area, and one in Edinburgh, which had forty children at the end of 2007. A meeting which took place on 17 November 2007, entitled the 'First Forum of the Russian-speaking Community in the United Kingdom: ways of consolidation', sought to establish a framework for cooperation among all types of expatriate groups. See Andrew Jameson, 'The Russians are coming', *SCRSS Information Digest*, Spring 2008, pp. 9-10.

interesting to see if this interesting development results in any significant progress.

This evidence of activity in Russian teaching and learning reveals a landscape which is far from barren. It is not purely a matter of the numbers of people involved: one must also consider the intensity of the activity and its quality. After the First World War, when the fever for Russian had died down to a large extent and numbers of pupils and classes declined, it was often reported by colleges that the students in the Russian class were small in number, but very good in quality, and extremely keen. This sentiment has been a refrain throughout the history of the Russian language in Britain. In early 2007 a teacher in Derby, whose school had relegated Russian to extra-curricular lunchtime classes, reported that none of his tiny group ever missed these voluntary sessions, which must have added a considerable extra load to their GCSE work and his teaching programme, and that they were all keen and reasonably hardworking. There does seem to be something about the subject which, while it appeals to a smaller section of the population, somehow inspires great fascination and dedication.

In connection with this factor, the late David Rix remarked memorably on occasion that the real justification for Russian teaching was that there were people wanting to learn it and people who wanted to teach it. It is clear in 2008 that the surviving universities are hearing from numerous prospective entrants, as the figures quoted above show. A good few schools, as we saw in Chapter 8, have introduced the subject as others have dropped it, and post-graduate students are still offering for teacher-training in Russian. Russian, in other words, is far from dead, but the travails it has endured are a warning to other 'new' subjects in the school and university curriculum of the British Isles.

Public policy, public opinion, private initiative, and personal prejudice and the Russian language in Britain

If we are to learn anything from this historical account of the study and teaching of the Russian language in Britain, we must attempt to reach some conclusions about the factors which fostered and which have obstructed the growth of Russian studies in this country. It is often difficult to separate appearance and reality, particularly when we analyse the influences which have worked for or against Russian as a subject in the curriculum of educational establishments. All of these factors have been highlighted throughout this book, but maybe it will be helpful to summarize them and then consider the more important ones more carefully.

A brief interpolation is appropriate at this point on the subject of the British and language-learning in general. It is often said that the British are 'no good at languages'; there is a persistent belief that we are congenitally incapable, or reluctant for reasons of traditional attitudes, of studying and succeeding in mastering foreign languages. There is little point in arguing about this matter, since it is so bound up with prejudice; the indisputable fact is that the crucial feature is *motivation* and attitude rather than innate linguistic ability. Recent research commissioned by the British Council investigated attitudes towards language learning and international affairs in ten countries. Children in the United Kingdom were the *least* favourably disposed to take an interest in international affairs; the most was represented by Nigeria, followed by India, Brazil, Saudi Arabia, Spain, Germany, China, the Czech Republic, and the USA. Scottish, Welsh and Northern Irish children were slightly more internationally aware than English. However, 70% of British children thought a language might be important for their future working life (here English were more convinced than Scottish children). This is surely not *too* bad a percentage: better than one might have thought. Russian did not figure among the languages they thought it might be important to learn: here Chinese scored 6% in the UK, in Scotland 9%. You may make of this what you like, but the Chief Executive of the British Council commented, 'It is vital that we encourage our young people to have an interest in and engagement with the world around them.'[21] When the government removes the requirement for schoolchildren to study a language to age 16, further reinforcement of insularity is achieved.[22]

In summary, then, what have we discovered are the factors which have retarded or inhibited the development of the study of Russian in Britain, and which still do? Some are so obvious we need devote no more space to them: Russian is seen as less vital to cultural understanding than French or German, and as being less 'useful'. Teachers of other languages are sometimes hostile to Russian; head teachers can scupper Russian in a school easily, undoing years of constructive labour supported by a predecessor. Universities may target Russian departments for economies if they appear temporarily weak.

We shall deal later with the perceived difficulty of Russian, but this perception creates the notion that it is for an intellectual élite. Worse, it is seen as an 'élit*ist*' subject. What this word means in the context is hard to see, but its use creates a nonsensical notion: that it is wrong to teach it because it works to the *advantage* of an élite, and therefore has no great place in a comprehensive system of education. Moreover, Russian is a subject with appeal only to some pupils, therefore schools recruit small classes which are non-viable economically, and the subject is in consequence perceived as not very important, a by-way of the curriculum, a 'way-out' field of knowledge, a 'frill'.

A series of educational reforms all worked against Russian. Local financial management of schools effectively prevented them combining to provide Russian

---

[21] See http://www.britishcouncil.org/home-press-121107-internationalism-research.pdf

[22] In March 2008 during the state visit by the President of France, *The Times* reported that every single member of the Labour and Conservative front benches needed to listen to his formal speech in French through the earphones which provided an English translation. What does this say about motivation, international awareness, and the failure of the British system to teach the cream of our intelligentsia a subject—French—which every one of them must have studied at school?

classes in order to overcome the 'non-viability' problem. Primary school modern languages, meaning French in effect, inhibit all other secondary languages. The weakening of the HM Inspectorate and its replacement by OFSTED removed a strong supporter of subjects like Russian. The tendency of recent governments to place more influence in the hands of local governing bodies has not been beneficial in all respects: these bodies can be parochial in their attitudes, having no sense of the national interest—indeed, they have no stated obligation even to consider the national interest.

School visits and exchanges, and study terms for undergraduates are easier to arrange than once they were. However, health and safety legislation inhibits visits organized by teachers; fear of litigation if anything goes wrong discourages teachers from this type of activity.[23] Russia is notorious for a cavalier attitude to safety, so things are rather more likely to go wrong than in other countries.

Now to certain crucial issues for Russian:

Is Russian a difficult language?

The profound conviction that Russian is a very difficult language for English native speakers to learn has always proved difficult to counteract. We have seen that when Russian was proposed in the early twentieth century as a subject for university study, there were persons who immediately expressed the view—based on no personal knowledge—that it would be 'impossible' for English students to learn it. This deeply held misconception remains rooted in the mind of those ignorant of the facts. There is no point in simply railing against those who express forthright opinions while knowing nothing of the matter. Let us here examine the proposition that Russian is much more difficult than other tongues which are widely studied in schools, colleges and universities.

Teachers of Russian have themselves to blame for some of this, and they have occasionally been their own worst enemy. They have denied the difficulty of Russian when arguing for its inclusion in the curriculum, but have stressed its complexity when seeking timetable time, funding and staffing. Either Russian *is* significantly more difficult than other languages taught or it is not. Which is it?

It depends to some extent on the attitude and, crucially, motivation of the learner. The unwilling or uninterested student will find it an unrewarding study. All other things being equal, we can, however, make certain assertions which will find acceptance by most who know the field. What are the real difficulties?

The cyrillic script is often mentioned as an obstacle; it is not. Adults find it far more difficult to master than children. Twelve-year-old school pupils of moderate intelligence relish learning the Russian alphabet and do so in a few days, while many older people, perhaps more set in their ways, sometimes fail at the starting post. Once the alphabet has been learned, spelling is fairly easy;

---

[23] and the threat is now faced that all parents receiving foreign exchange pupils in their homes may have to be formally (and expensively) cleared for criminal record purposes.

it is not totally 'phonetic' in representing pronunciation, but is logical. Pronunciation presents fewer problems than, say, French, and the aural recognition of the spoken language is not particularly hard. Syllabic stress presents some challenges—mostly if one is working exclusively from the written language.

There is no definite or indefinite article in Russian, so *der, die, das, die* or *le, la, les, un, une, des* are issues which do not impinge upon the learner. Gender presents little difficulty, being almost always determined by the ending of the noun in the nominative case. There are six cases of nouns, and rules about endings are easy enough; however, exceptions to these rules are legion, and are encountered in several very common nouns. The genitive plural is a pain in the neck, but—if well taught—is not an insuperable difficulty. Adjective endings are logical, but to a beginner they may appear complex.

Verbs are often regarded as a major problem. Why this should be is something of a mystery. The learner of French is presented with tenses and moods galore: present, imperfect, perfect, pluperfect, conditional, conditional in the past, past historic, future, and subjunctives to match. The linguist Walter Grauberg writes: 'If one were to take any regular French verb conjugated with *avoir* in the *-er* conjugation and count the number of separate forms, a staggering total of 77 written and 51 spoken forms for the active voice would result, counting identically spelt or pronounced forms only once!'[24] Some, to my mind, grossly overestimate the difficulty created by the fact that Russian verbs belong to one of two 'aspects', perfective and imperfective.[25] It is sometimes forgotten that the term 'aspect' is used by linguists to refer to very many languages (including English and those commonly taught in Britain), and that learners of other European languages have some similar difficulty in deciding between imperfect and perfect tenses, and then manipulating the forms. In Russian the imperfective verb *delat'*, to do, has an infinitive, six forms in the present tense, four in the past and imperatives; the future is formed with an auxiliary (the same for every imperfective verb), making 19 forms so far, far fewer than Grauberg's 77. If we add to this the forms taken by the *perfective* verb 'to do', *sdelat'*, we have none in the present (because perfective verbs have no present tense), six in the future and four in the past. Counting the infinitive and two imperatives, that is 13: total 32. Add the single word *by*, which forms the conditional and subjunctive, and we have 33: 44 fewer than a regular French verb. So why are Russian verbs thought

---

[24]Walter Grauberg, *The Elements of Language Teaching*, Clevedon, etc: Multilingual Matters Ltd, 1997, p. 43.

[25]In this I take issue with that outstanding Russian linguist Michael Kirkwood in his fascinating inaugural lecture as Professor at Glasgow: he writes that the correct choice of one aspect or another 'involves quite dramatic psychological adjustments' ('Learning and teaching Russian', p. 15.) I just do not see it—not in most everyday contexts, at least. I am prepared to agree with his comment on the 'seemingly quite ridiculous system of numerals.' But *Russians* get these wrong, and they avoid the difficulties wherever possible, as can foreign learners.

to be so complicated? The French language could take a few lessons in economy from Russian!

The Russian verbs of motion (a handful of them, at least, to walk, to ride, to fly, to crawl etc.) are often quoted as a minefield for the learner, and so they are. But there are ways around them most of the time, and they should not be allowed to create too much of an obstacle to the learner. The fact that they often do is probably the fault of the more old-fashioned published grammars.

Syntax, particularly word order, is an interesting feature of the language. Because of the way nouns change their endings to indicate case, the order of words in a sentence may be much more flexible than in English. English native speakers, who expect the order of words in Russian to resemble the English order, may be nonplussed by simple sentences. *Ivan liubit Mashu*, Ivan loves Masha, can as easily be expressed as *Mashu liubit Ivan*: the case-endings clearly indicate the meaning, whereas in English it is the word-order that does. This is a simple example, but in much more complex sentences it is clear that English-speakers have to be sensitive to the form of the nouns and pronouns and largely disregard the word order, or they may totally misunderstand the utterances.

Perhaps the most difficult aspect of learning Russian is mastering and remembering vocabulary. There are many Russian words, and common words at that, which resemble English words, but there are very many more that do not. Some basic concepts are conveyed in words which sound very strange to English ears. One eminent professor of Russian confessed (on the radio, no less!) that 'the first time [he] tried to learn Russian' he was brought to a standstill, a *stop*, by the word for 'stop': *ostanavlivat'sia* (six syllables).[26] A feature of intensive Russian courses, such as those carried out in the armed services in the 1950s, was the forced feeding of Russian lexis. Clearly this was seen as an obstacle to be overcome by tackling it head-on.

The force of tradition.

Russian as a new item in the school curriculum encounters the opposition of those for whom traditional subjects have a strong grip on their imagination—or lack of it. The public acceptance of Latin and French is in no small part due to these subjects being seen as traditional. There are genuinely good reasons why they should be securely established in the educational system, though not necessarily taught to every pupil in every school. However, the notion expressed by a letter-writer to the *Times* in 1958 (already quoted) that for French and Latin to give way, if only slightly, to Russian or another language was to turn back a thousand years of history asserts a blinkered understanding of the cultural sources of our own civilization. Sloppy thinking should not be allowed to stand in the way of curricular innovation. Russian has not had long enough and has not had

---

[26]The late Professor Dennis Ward, broadcasting in the 1960s.

sufficiently wide acceptance to be seen as an established feature of the curriculum. In the public mind it still seems an oddity.

Curricular innovation of any sort in Britain is not a straightforward issue. The first draft of these lines was written in July 2007; at that time 'new subjects'—if that is what they are—for the school curriculum were being promulgated: global warming, debt management, healthy eating, Mandarin. The same government announcement trumpets 'flexibility and choice'. This is a splendid slogan; in the past something like it got Russian into schools and then out again just as quickly. The same may well happen to some of these other innovations.

The supply of teachers for Russian.

This is another matter where reality and perception diverge spectacularly. There have always been plenty of teachers of Russian to supply the needs of schools which wanted to teach it: research has shown and continues to show this to be true, in report after report. No research project ever carried out failed to discover numerous teachers qualified in Russian who were not teaching it. Yet at the same time school head teachers have regularly complained that they could not fill vacancies, while newly-trained teachers of Russian complained that they could not find posts. One must ask, did the heads try hard enough to find suitable teachers, and did the new teachers' nerve give way when seeking jobs? More crucially, did heads offer potential teachers of Russian opportunities which were not just challenging, but attractive?

It is not only a matter of jobs for newly-trained teachers. The willingness and ability of experienced teachers to move within the profession must also be considered. School teachers of Russian are all teachers of something else as well, usually French. French may start as the insurance policy, guaranteeing a job for a newly-trained language teacher. It may then become the subject which ensures promotion within the school and from school to school; promotion into middle and senior management depend more on subjects seen as 'mainstream'. Another curious feature of a very complex situation, for which I can offer no explanation, is that when a classicist is promoted to deputy head or head teacher, Latin is strengthened in that school; when a Russianist gains such promotion, the same does not usually happen to Russian.

In short: yes, there were and probably still are plenty of teachers of Russian, but for the reasons stated, they tend often to be in the wrong places.

Students and their motivation.

There is absolutely no point in arguing for Russian in the education system if no-one wants to learn it. While many other subjects in the school curriculum are taught to relatively unresisting captive audiences, Russian usually has to recruit positively and retain learners by infecting them with enthusiasm. Pupils will perhaps join a French class when compelled to do so without too much protest, but Russian? They have to be persuaded.

Part of Russian's problem is that pupils *can* be persuaded, but not always in large enough numbers to form what is today considered a viable class. We have nevertheless already commented on the dedication of many of the pupils who do take the language up, and on the fact that a much higher proportion of them continue with it beyond the age of sixteen than do learners of other languages. One former school teacher of Russian has commented that the interest shown by pupils in, for example, meeting Russians who are visiting their town or attending Russian events of one sort and another so far exceeds the keenness of other language learners for similar experiences is 'what gets up the noses of some other language teachers.' The spirit of adventure enjoyed by some learners is typified by the Leeds class who with their (woman) teacher disguised themselves with Russian furry hats and, feigning ignorance of English, gained admittance to the away enclosure at Elland Road when United were playing Moscow Spartak; they quickly learned Russian football chants and even appeared on local television as 'visiting Russians'.[27]

The fact that most undergraduates now take up Russian *ab initio* similarly means that a positive choice has to be made by them; it is easier to continue with a subject studied already at school, or, if not, to change to something easier than Russian. Students of Russian usually select themselves and persevere of their own volition; if they do not do so in huge numbers, that is scarcely surprising.

Were (and are) the teachers good enough?

In researching this project, a collection was made of reminiscences by teachers of Russian and of obituaries and tributes on retirement paid to some of the stalwarts of the profession.[28] Many charismatic personalities emerged. Reports by school inspectors indicate that lessons in Russian were every bit as good as those in other languages. But for Russian, *was this good enough?* Has the commitment of *all* the teachers always been sufficient to ensure continuation of Russian teaching? A subject with a tendency to instability in the curriculum needs something approaching one hundred percent inspired teachers, or teachers who are dedicated to defending and fostering the subject. A voluntary subject and one seen as an unusual option must *attract* learners—and keep them attracted—if it is to survive. Teachers are needed who combine the merits—but not the faults!—of Lev Tolstoy, Anton Makarenko, Peter the Great, even Ivan the Terrible. Study of individual schools reveals again and again that when an ineffectual teacher takes over the subject, Russian dies. Even the presence of an excellent teacher may not be sufficient to guarantee survival—the schools of Britain are littered with teachers who have not managed to keep the subject alive, despite noble efforts and undoubted talent. No-one suggests mathematics or English should be discontinued if a poor teacher takes the subjects over. We may

---

[27] Private information for which I am indebted to Ms Sue Coatman.

[28] This file is to be deposited in the Leeds Russian Archive.

even conclude that the versatility of Russian teachers, the fact that they have expertise in other languages as well, offers an opportunity to educational authorities to close the subject down without incurring the charge of depriving a teacher of his livelihood.

Has backup for Russian teaching in terms of material and professional support been sufficient?

By this heading we mean training, mutual assistance, teaching materials, and assessment instruments. It is possible to answer with an almost unqualified 'yes'. Initial teacher training in Russian has been available from the late 1960s, in-service training has been provided by a variety of higher education establishments, and by teachers' organizations, especially ATR. The same organization ran local groups and advice services which at their best were networks which were helpful both on the professional and the personal level. Once Russian took off in schools, teachers started writing textbooks, readers, audio-visual courses, and ancillary materials; it was always possible to complain about limitations, but in fact, in relation to the size of the operation, there was a considerable amount available. British publishers, happily, considered that their prestige was enhanced by having Russian textbooks in their lists; this was just as well, since they can scarcely have made much money by issuing them. Soviet publishing houses produced a great deal for learners of Russian; some of it was only moderately suitable, but the best became popular with teachers and enriched the choices available to them. Soviet material was made available by the now defunct firm of Collet's often at very low prices until the early 1990s.

If there was an aspect of external support for Russian which was lacking, it was in the easy availability of exchange opportunities. Soviet officialdom was never very good at seeing that free and open interchange between themselves and the outside world should be encouraged, being deeply suspicious of outsiders, and fearful that their young would be corrupted by contact with capitalism. While British learners of French, German or Spanish could travel repeatedly to the country, might live in families there, and not be subject to unwelcome surveillance, a once-in-a-lifetime short tourist visit was all they were likely to get in Russia. Before the 1960s even that was out of the question. We have seen that town twinning and stays in Pioneer camps did take place occasionally; university teachers sweated blood over the arrangements for undergraduate residence and study in Russia, and a special inter-university committee was set up to lobby for, facilitate, and organize this aspect of higher education study which is seen as vital in Britain, but was not considered so in the Soviet Union. At the time of writing, procedures for acquiring Russian visas are becoming not less, but more difficult, and the expense is considerable. Paranoia and isolationism rule where openness to the outside world is concerned. Meanwhile, other former Soviet republics have abolished visa requirements.

What part have public policy and international relations played in the development of Russian in education?

Earlier chapters have shown that interest in Russia began in the sixteenth century as a result of English trading enterprise. Centuries later, in 1914, it was the desire of Britain to appropriate the Russian market from the Germans which led to the first spectacular increase in the study of Russian; as political conditions inhibited trading and other relations, an equally spectacular decline set in. Russian as a language for use in diplomatic and military intelligence became visible in the eighteenth century (though it doubtless existed, hidden from view, long before that). The enthusiasm for Russian among army and naval officers from the 1870s reflected British fears about Russian ambitions in the Indian subcontinent; in the mid-twentieth century signals intelligence came into its own. Parallel with military learners of Russian, some diplomatic personnel have not neglected the language, though there is evidence that at some periods in history only a minority of British Embassy staff have been fluent.

Further as to trade in the present: does the British public today perceive Russia as a trading partner? It did in 1914, unquestionably, when British business suddenly realized it should learn Russian to set up new trading links. Does the British public and British business today realize that a foreign language such as Russian is necessary to make trading relations operate to our advantage? Report after report declares that 'English is not enough.' Trade with Russia accounts for a relatively small percentage of British exports, but not an insignificant one. A 2006 report on the shortage of foreign language skills and its effect on the European economy persistently places Russian in the top ten languages for trade: where a firm lacks Russian linguists, business is lost, where it has them it influences them to enter Russian markets. The 'backlash against Russian' in the former Eastern bloc and the Baltic states is now said to have largely dispersed, and Russian is used extensively in Eastern Europe. Chinese, Russian, Spanish and Portuguese are becoming more important on the internet. Only five percent of British firms adapt their websites for foreign markets, however.

Schools, colleges, and universities contribute significantly to 'Russian for special purposes'. We have completely rejected the nineteenth-century view that universities have 'nothing to do with diplomatic or any other [vocational] purposes' and that they exist purely to offer a very small élite among young people from the upper classes an opportunity to prove themselves in intellectual gymnastics. Today higher education institutions do have the very important additional purpose of feeding into the public consciousness an understanding of the knowledge that they assemble, to inform the national consciousness of world affairs, culture, history and so on. In other words, the education service helps to disseminate knowledge including that about Russia which interests, informs and influences public attitudes and hence policy. Having said all this, it must also be admitted that the funding bodies tend to find the requirement to perform this public duty something of an embarrassment in an environment where they now adopt an uncompromising 'market forces' attitude to subject provision.

Throughout this book we have constantly asked ourselves whether external political events and the current perception of Russia influence the wish of potential students to learn Russian. Does the behaviour of Russia as a world power incline us to learn Russian or discourage us from so doing? Our conclusion must be that it does in some cases, but inexplicably not in others. French language teaching does not suffer when France seems to be opposing British interests; German declined only slightly in popularity even when Britain was at war with Germany—so these comparisons do not help all that much. Alliance in 1914 popularized Russian, political turmoil in the 1920s discouraged it. The sputniks raised considerable interest, as did Gorbachev; yet the period of the disagreeable post-war rantings of Stalinist lackeys were when Russian really began to take off. So—yes, politics do have an effect, but not an easily explicable one. In more recent years, civil unrest under Yeltsin, wars in Chechnya, the rule of Putin, and diplomatic unpleasantness have all affected relations. Have they seriously influenced the learning of the Russian language in Britain? To some extent they probably have—but in what way? Russian foreign and internal policy may repel while at the same time arousing interest in what is going on. Unlike France and Germany, to which we are thoroughly used, and the point of whose languages we never question, Russia is a 'special case', one that is noticed when it is in the news and forgotten at other times. She has not yet established herself in the British psyche as representing normality; if she ever does, attitudes to the language may change.

Support for or obstruction of Russian from within education.

We have seen that Russian entered the curriculum of universities a hundred and more years ago as a result of the campaigning of certain prominent figures, whose enthusiasm swayed academic opinion. These people could not have achieved much entirely on their own. Often they had rich allies from the business world. Almost invariably there was strong support from a few academics, specialists in other subjects or senior figures in the university in question: H. A. L. Fisher at Sheffield, Ronald Burrows at London, Sir Donald Macalister at Glasgow, Principal Hugh Stewart and Professors Pinto and Hewitt at Nottingham (both specialists in other subjects who were interested enough to actually take over the teaching of Russian during the Second World War), Sir Michael Sadler at Leeds, and others elsewhere. This was paralleled in the schools when Russian emerged there; here the attitude of the headmaster or mistress was crucial, even more so than that of the governing body. There are known cases of heads refusing to accede to governors' advice to stop Russian. There are cases when a stubborn deputy head in charge of curriculum stopped Russian even though it was doing well. It is also helpful to a Russian teacher if rank-and-file colleagues, as well as senior managers, support the subject. The teacher's skill, energy and professional dedication are vital in gaining this support, as is his or her willingness to take on extra-curricular responsibilities for sport, music, theatre and the like—to be a popular colleague, in other words.

Support for Russian was also seen from HM inspectors and local authority language advisors. The national Inspectorate was mainly very supportive of Russian from the 1960s onwards, as were many advisors. However, as we have seen, central government and local authorities, the masters of these people, were apt to be ambivalent, sometimes offering active help and advice, at other times stating that they had no powers to intervene in curricular matters. In the 1990s HM Inspectorate was virtually replaced by OFSTED, and instead of there being some guarantee of continuity in oversight, the previous mainly benign régime was replaced by a system of hectic brief inquisitions. The most OFSTED inspectors can do to be of service to Russian teaching is encourage the school to continue with it by writing into the report the strongest arguments for continuing with the subject that the inspector can square with his conscience. It is not an entirely happy position to be in.

Some teachers attribute decline of Russian in their school to hostility from colleagues who represent other vested interests. In a crowded curriculum, it is inevitable that such conflicts will sometimes arise. Teachers of other languages or of other subjects sometimes feel threatened, especially if Russian is doing well and winning keen recruits. The Russian teacher may be isolated as an 'oddball' and a very junior member of a language department; only if he is head of modern languages (unlikely, as such posts usually go to teachers of mainstream languages for whom Russian is not their first priority) is he in a strong position. If a similar situation obtains in a university, it is likely to be even worse, as academics are typically jealous of the resources other departments are awarded and can become intensely hostile if any inequity is perceived or imagined.

In fairness to both sides, it should be remembered that if a 'vested interest' means 'a strong personal concern in a state of affairs', as the dictionary defines it, then it is justifiably held by teachers of Russian as firmly as by anyone else. In short, the concept is not helpful in analysing the situation.

Could Russian enjoy another renaissance? What can we learn from our historical study?

The sense of the foregoing section is that in certain conditions Russian has been, is and may continue to be a viable subject in educational institutions at secondary and tertiary level. The first of those conditions is that the student and the teacher have to have a realistic conception of the difficulties presented by the task of learning the language: namely, that it is not an enormously difficult language for the English native speaker to tackle, but that, like all foreign languages, the learner requires application and motivation in order to be reasonably successful. The second factor is that a steady supply of teachers should be available; we have argued here that these teachers always did exist, but that it does not always appear to be possible to connect them with the learners, for various reasons. Those teachers were trained and no less competent than teachers of other subjects, but our third point is that a particularly high standard of both dedication and skill on the part of the teachers is needed for continuity in provision to be achieved; ideally more than one teacher of Russian should be present in any one school. The fourth condition has been met: it is for textbooks, materials, methods, opportunities for in-service training all to be available. What we have may not be perfect, but it is good enough, or can be adapted and updated, and teachers of Russian have shown themselves more than capable in the past of clubbing together to write materials and to offer mutual support through discussion and advice. Moreover, they have often done this largely without profit or generous payment, seeing the work as service to the cause.

The fifth issue is not crucial, though it might appear so: the climate of public opinion can encourage the right conditions for successful Russian teaching, but there is little the individual teacher can do about this. The third, fourth and fifth condition lead us to the sixth factor: the need for teachers of a subject like Russian to band together strongly and campaign for their cause. This teachers of Russian did through ATR, and the amalgamation of that body with ALL in 1989 is regretted very widely indeed—almost universally by ATR's surviving former members. An association of Russian teachers has a focus which is missing from a wider grouping. One retired professor commented privately that ATR fostered a unique sense of solidarity and comradeship, which he and many others found inspiring. There were moves in April 2008 towards a new grouping of Russian teachers in schools and further education in England; whether or not this organization comes to have much influence, its possible formation indicates a certain dissatisfaction with the *status quo* and the feeling that something of the past can perhaps be rescued. Both the British Council and the Department for Children, Schools and Families were represented at the April meeting, and some participants felt the mood of it to be fairly optimistic.

The seventh condition is that there must be support for Russian within the system and within the particular educational institution; Russian teachers must make friends for the subject among their colleagues and leaders. As the Russian teacher is likely to be something of a 'loner', he must try hard to be part of the wider team and work towards building support if it is not readily forthcoming. Educational conditions militate against this condition, in that financial and organizational autonomy is increasingly being placed in the hands of individual schools, the inspectorate has largely lost its advisory role, local authorities are having their oversight circumscribed, and the lack of financial viability of many Russian classes cannot easily by countered by inter-school collaboration.

There is a crucial final condition which we shall come to shortly. But first, do we need to make the case for Russian yet again? Surely not. The bibliography at the end of this book contains numerous items showing that teachers and advocates of Russian language and civilization have repeatedly made that case. Has it changed now? Very similar arguments have come from Heard in 1827 through Morfill (1890), H. G. Wells (in his letter to *The Times* in 1914), and numerous others (Bolsover, Burgin, Chamberlain, Edwards, Hill, C. V. James, Jones, Lampert, Morley, Muckle, Peace, Pockney, Pollock, Pullin, Scott, Sedgefield, Storr-Best, Strong, Underwood, Waterhouse, the SSEES students' pamphlet) since then. While conditions have changed over the decades, those arguments are all as valid and strong as ever. We must trade with Russia, we must treat diplomatically with her, and we must be sure while doing both of these things that we are not being taken for a ride. We must make friends with the Russian people. There are still scores of millions of native speakers of Russian, we need to understand Russian history, science, technology, economy, religion, literature, and thought; Russian scientists, psychologists, engineers and technologists demand the attention of professionals in their field; Russian music, art and literature offer intellectual and aesthetic enrichment to the earnest student and to anybody else, for that matter. While once we needed to understand the affairs of the socialist state, we now have a different political entity to engage with, which stridently demands our attention; we must also know how much of it resembles that of the past and how much is a new departure. Translation is no substitute for direct contact. A mature student of Russian who had ventured into a provincial town south of Moscow, writes: 'You don't have to stray very far from Economic Fortress Western Europe to enter a strange world which, perhaps more than ever, cries out for interpreters and champions.'[29] Though conditions may seem to have changed drastically, not one of the arguments put a hundred, or fifty, or thirty years ago for the study of Russian has lost its force, and many have, if anything, gained in intensity. Yet the profile of the Russian language in Britain is reduced from what it was in earlier years.

And why is this? Why did Russian language studies blossom but fail to flourish as richly as was once hoped? The answer lies in a major weakness of the educational systems of the British Isles. It was because the introduction of Russian to schools and universities was not planned and never *managed*, and probably never will or could be. As early as 1945 one veteran Russianist aptly remarked:

> Some 27 years ago such studies were encouraged on a considerable scale, Russian classes being held in universities, technical colleges and schools, both public and secondary. But these efforts led nowhere: there was no direction, no organization. This time [i.e. after 1945] there must be a carefully thought-out plan.[30]

No such luck! Enthusiasts started up Russian departments in higher education; all credit to them. Then a government commission reasons cogently and explicitly that we must avoid over-proliferation of departments, we must ensure that due attention is devoted to non-literary studies as this is something the country is in particular need of; however, in no time universities go their own way, the thirteen departments which Scarbrough thought was too many already became nearly fifty, with a strong bias towards literature. In schools Russian was started

---

[29] Chris Bissell, 'In at the deep end', *Rusistika*, no 9, 1994, pp. 51-54, see pp. 53-54.
[30] W. J. Sedgefield, letter to *The Times*, 9 March 1945, p. 5.

and stopped again at a dizzying rate; it often depended on the fortuitous availability of a teacher, the support of a head—both of which might stop at any time. Local authorities, if they intervened at all, often enough represented nothing more than parochial interference. The whole scene was entirely at the mercy of individuals, many of them unpredictable or uncommitted, and few of them bearing the national interest in mind. And we are back in this position today: the national 'Strategy for England', while tentatively suggesting French, German and Spanish as candidates for primary-school language teaching (readers will remember that this is the latest 'solution' to our inability to encourage and foster language learning),[31] is markedly reluctant to recommend planning in regard to the choice of languages. It is suggested that the choice might be left to primary and secondary teachers getting together locally 'in clusters' to discuss the issue. In other words, the parochialism and lack of national perspective which are endemic in British education will reign supreme. A scheme by Liverpool City Council for supporting nine centres of excellence, consisting of three schools each for French, Spanish and German, is held up as an example of 'excellent practice.'[32] Russian was tried in a primary school in Sussex in the early 1960s (it is currently offered at three primary schools in France), and it doubtless can work;[33] however, to press for primary Russian is surely unrealistic for all sorts of reasons.

A sympathetic reader of a draft of a chapter in this book objected that I had described this situation as a 'shambles.' His reason for the objection was, 'Well, that's how we do things in Britain.' That is the whole trouble. There is no provision in the system for managing curricular change such as the introduction of Russian. No agency outside itself could stop a university opening a superfluous Russian department or prevent it appointing experts in a field already well catered for elsewhere. Even Atkinson, in a belated and botched attempt to manage the situation at last, could only *recommend* action to vice-chancellors, advice which some of them and the UGC ignored. Should not some national agency have taken responsibility for planning sensible provision of a subject, instead of denying that it could do any more than express an opinion? In the resultant confusion, with all the personal and professional harm it causes, is not 'shambles' the correct word to describe it? In July 2007 Dr Martin Stephen writing in the *Daily Telegraph* described the proliferation of dubious types of secondary school as 'a dog's dinner'. He referred to a situation which is largely the result of government intervention which was only *partly* planned, and cer-

---

[31] An earlier attempt to introduce primary French in the 1960s-70s failed, since it was neither properly planned nor managed. Secondary teachers of French were faced with classes of children, from those who had done no French at all to others who had had three years. Some had been taught by qualified teachers, some not. The effect on pupil and teacher morale was devastating. There is no sign that this sorry episode has been remembered, never mind that any of the lessons have been learned.

[32] DfES, *Languages for All*, pp. 10, 18, 20 and 21.

[33] L. J. Jemetta, 'Using the Nuffield Course with nine-year-olds', *ATR Occasional Papers*, I.iii, 1967, pp. 3-6.

tainly not managed. The British Government declared in July 2007 that it wanted to encourage Mandarin in schools. Indeed, the CILT 'Language Trends' survey shows that more schools are offering Mandarin than Russian. We wish enthusiasts for Oriental studies well—but if we could achieve only limited success with Russian in fifty years, what hope is there for Chinese as a foreign language in schools? Where are the teachers, the materials, the experience, the support from the public, or from within the schools, and from the whole fragmented system? Do politicians ever think out the consequences of what they are proposing?

Measured by the number of institutions offering courses in the Russian language and in the civilization to which that language is the door, Russian in Britain in 2008 is in decline. But that is entirely the wrong way to look at the situation. Let there be no mistake: this book records a magnificent achievement to which thousands of British linguists have contributed. Scholars have added an incalculable store of knowledge to the national understanding of Russia, teachers have opened the minds of students to a unique world of which they would otherwise have known nothing, and learners—quite apart from the enjoyment they experience by contact with all things Russian—have also spread around a sense of the accessibility, the warmth, the infinite variety of Russia and all that she encapsulates.

Winston Churchill is often stated to have described Russia as a 'riddle wrapped in a mystery inside an enigma.' He said nothing of the sort. He was confessing in October 1939 to his inability to forecast the future action of the Soviet government *in the specific circumstances of the day*. We may none the less accept his engaging phrase as an expression of our own difficulty in interpreting the culture and civilization of Russia. British achievements in the study of Russian and Russia over the past few centuries have undoubtedly made that 'riddle' less insoluble than it was, and have made it possible to begin to unwrap the enigma and to attempt to reveal the mystery. If the study of Russian were to cease in Britain tomorrow, it would be lamentable, but it would not take all of that away.

But Russian is not going to die out in Britain tomorrow. If the story told in this book shows anything, it is that the language and all it represents can arrest the attention of many British people, once they have reason to take notice of it, and it can exercise a fascination over them, which they find an extension of their own personality and culture and an enrichment of their lives.

Bibliography

THE Bibliography is arranged as follows: articles, monographs, and symposia are placed first. Next come reports and documents from governmental sources along with reports by official and voluntary bodies. Archival, oral, and other unpublished work follows; instructional materials conclude the Bibliography.

Abbreviations used in titles of journals, publishers, etc. (See also the Index).

ATR	Association of Teachers of Russian	*MLT*	Modern Language Teaching
HMSO	Her/His Majesty's Stationery Office	*NL*	Newsletter
		OP	Occasional Papers
J	Journal	*Pr*	Press
JRS	Journal of Russian Studies	*RSA*	Royal Society of Arts
L	London	*SALT*	Scottish Association for Language Teaching
Lg	Leningrad		
M	Moscow	*SEER*	Slavonic and East European Review
MLs	Modern Languages		
MLiS	Modern Languages in Scotland	*SPb*	St Petersburg
		UP	University Press

Articles and books

Anonymous and unattributed items

'A Language worth knowing' [leading article]. *The Times*, 6 October 1958, p. 11

The Case for the Teaching of Russian in Schools. A Memorandum prepared by the Students' Union Society of the School of Slavonic and East European Studies, University of London. L: no date, [1949?]

'Hush! Russian spoken here. Fife's school of secrets'. *The Bulletin*, 19 Nov. 1957, p. 9

'Joint Services School for Linguists', *Crail Airfield*. Information leaflet from Crail [Fife] Museum Trust, 2004

'The Learning of Russian. Needs for the future', (from a correspondent). *Times Educational Supplement*, 4 Jan. 1916, p. 6

'Reopening of Edinburgh University Class. Sir Alfred Ewing and the study of Russian'. *The Scotsman*, 13 October 1916, p. 6

'Russian in the Schools. Too few teachers and books', by a Special Correspondent. *Manchester Guardian*, 9 August 1958

'Sozdanie assotsiatsiia rusistov'. *ATR OP*, I(4), pp. 1 and 28.

'Strange languages in an old-world Fife village', by a 'News' Reporter. *Edinburgh Evening News*, no date in source: [assumed April/May 1956]

Language Centre, University of Essex, *Report of the Contemporary Russian Language Analysis Project*. Colchester: [publisher as author], 1972

Authored works

M. Aid and C. Wiebes, 'The Importance of signals intelligence in the Cold War'. *Intelligence and National Security*, 16(1), 2001, pp. 1-26

R. J. Aldrich, *Espionage, Security and Intelligence in Britain 1945-70*. Manchester and New York: Manchester UP, 1998

——— 'GCHQ and Sigint in early Cold War; 1945-1970'. *Intelligence and National Security*, 16(1), 2001, pp. 67-96

M. P. Alekseev, 'Angliiskii iazyk v Rossii i russkii iazyk v Anglii'. *Uchenye zapiski Leningradskogo Gosudarstvennogo Universiteta*, seriia filologicheskikh nauk, vypusk 9, Lg 1941, pp. 77-127.

M. S. Anderson, *Britain's Discovery of Russia 1553-1815*. L: Macmillan, 1958

C. Andrew and D. Dilks (editors), *The Missing Dimension. Governments and Intelligence Communities in the Twentieth Century*. Basingstoke: Macmillan, 1984

G. Bannister, 'Prepodavanie russkogo iazyka v Irlandskoi Respubliki'. *Russkii iazyk za rubezhom*, 1976 no. 3., pp. 127-128

H. C. Barnard, *A History of English Education Since 1760*. L: London UP, 1961

C. G. Bearne, C. V. James (eds), *Modern Languages for the 1980s. Report of a Colloquium held at the University of Sussex, 16-18 Sept. 1976*. L: CILT, 1976

T. J. Binyon, 'From Cheshire with love' [on National Service Russian]. *The Guardian*, 4 October 2003, p. 31

Jeremy Black, 'Anglo-Russian relations 1414-1750: a note on sources', in Janet M. Hartley, *The Study of Russian History from British Archival Sources*, L and New York: Mansell, 1986, pp. 67-87

J. K. Blackadder, 'Visit of Manchester schoolchildren to Leningrad: July 1964'. *ATR J* 12, 1965, pp. 43-46

D. D. Blagoi, *Istoriia russkoi literatury XVIII veka*, izd. 3e. M: Gos. uchebno-ped. izd. Min. pros. SSSR, 1955; re: Trediakovskii pp. 120-121, re: Karamzin pp. 524-525

Peter Boaks, 'Languages in schools', in Moys, pp. 34-43

F. Bodmer (ed. L. Hogben), *The Loom of Language*. L: George Allen & Unwin, 1943, esp. pp. 415-416.

G. H. Bolsover, 'Russian and East European studies in the universities'. *Universities Quarterly* 7(3), May 1953, pp. 224-232

Christopher Brandie, 'Russian teaching in Scottish schools'. *Rusistika* 21, 2000, pp. 3-6

Sir George Buck [credited on title page as 'G. B., Knight'], *The Third Vniversity of England*. L, 1615

Leslie Burgin, 'More of us must learn foreign languages'. *Daily Mail Yearbook for 1944*, p. 39

Angus Calder, *The People's War. Britain 1939-1945*. L: Pimlico Pr, 1969

Cambridge, University of, 'Report of the Special Board for Medieval and Modern Languages of the Medieval and Modern Languages Tripos'. *Cambridge University Reporter*, no. 26, 27 Feb. 1917

David Chamberlain, 'ATR atrophied or a trophy in the cabinet?' *Rusistika* 30, 2005, pp. 20-21

——— 'The Past, present and future of Russian'. *ATR J* 16, 1967, pp. 3-5

J. W. M. Chapman, 'Russia, Germany and Anglo-Japanese intelligence collaboration, 1898-1906', in Erickson, pp. 41-55

Winston S. Churchill, *The Second World War*, VI vols. L: Cassell, 1948-54

J. Clark, 'Munn and Dunning and modern languages'. *MLiS* 15, 1978, pp. 53-57
D. J. Cole, *Geoffrey Prime. The Imperfect Spy.* L: Hale, 1998
Bernard Comrie, Gerald Stone, Maria Polinsky, *The Russian Language in the Twentieth Century* [second edition, revised and expanded, of *The Russian Language Since the Revolution*]. Oxford: Clarendon Pr, 1996
Mark Cornwall and Murray Frame, *Scotland and the Slavs: Cultures in Contact 1500-2000*. Newtonville MA: Oriental Research Partners and SPb: Dmitriy Bulanin Publishing, 2001
S. F. Cotgrove, *Technical Education and Social Change.* L: Allen and Unwin, 1958
Anthony Courtney, *Sailor in a Russian Frame.* L: Johnson, 1968
A. G. Cross, *Anglo-Russica. Aspects of Cultural Relations Between Great Britain and Russia in the Eighteenth and Early Nineteenth Centuries.* Oxford, Providence: Berg, 1993
A. G. Cross, 'A Banner with a strange device: *Sauve qui peut*'. *JRS* 40, 1980, pp. 3-12
——— 'Arcticus and *The Bee* (1790-4). An episode in Anglo-Russian cultural relations'. *Oxford Slavonic Papers, New Series*, II, 1969, pp. 62-76
——— *'By the Banks of the Thames'. Russians in Eighteenth-century Britain.* Newtonville MA: Oriental Research Partners, 1980
——— 'By the Neva, by the Aire' [inaugural lecture], reprint [from *University of Leeds Review*]. Leeds, 1982
P. T. Culhane, 'Research in O level examinations'. *ATR J* 14, 1966, pp. 22-24
J. B. C. Davidson, 'The implications of the Dunning Report for modern languages'. *MLiS* 15, 1978, pp 20-30
J. M. C. Davidson, 'ATR Survey of supply, demand and utilization of Teachers of Russian in secondary schools', *JRS* 21, 1971, pp. 56-68
James Davie, Neil Landsman, Lindsay Silvester (eds.), *Russian Language Teaching Methodology and Course Design*. Nottingham: Astra, 1999
Robin Davis, *The Grammar School.* Harmondsworth: Penguin, 1967
Richard Daugherty, *National Curriculum Assessment. A Review of Policy 1987-1994.* L: Falmer Pr, 1995
Terry Doyle, 'Filming in the Soviet Union—never take *nyet* for an answer' *Britain-USSR*, 57, 1980, pp. 7-8
W. B. Edgerton, 'The history of Slavistic scholarship in the United States', *Beiträge zur Geschichte der Slawistik in nichtslawischen Ländern*. Vienna: Verlag der Österreichischen Akademie der Wissenschaften, 1985; Schriften der Balkankommission, Linguistische Abteilung XXX, pp. 491-528
Reese Edwards, *The Secondary Technical School.* L: Univ. L Pr, 1960
T. W. Edwards, 'The Case for Russian'. *MLs*, 38(1), March 1957, pp. 23-27
Geoffrey Elliott and Harold Shukman, *Secret Classrooms. An Untold Story of the Cold War.* L: St Ermin's Pr, 2002
Kenneth Ellis, *The Post Office in the Eighteenth Century.* L: Oxford UP, 1958
L. and M. Erickson (eds.), *Russia. War Peace and Diplomacy. Essays in Honour of John Erickson.* L: Weidenfeld and Nicolson, 2004
Dimitry Fedosov, *The Caledonian Connection: Scotland-Russia Ties Middle Ages to Early Twentieth Century: A Concise Biographical List*, Aberdeen: Centre for Scottish Studies, University of Aberdeen, 1996
Sir Charles Firth, *Modern Languages at Oxford 1724-1929.* L: Oxford UP, 1929

Giles Fletcher, *Of the Russe Commonwealth*, facsimile edition of the 1591 original, ed. R. Pipes and J. V. A. Fine Jr. Cambridge MA: Harvard UP, 1966
────── ed. E. A. Bond, *Russia at the Close of the Sixteenth Century*. L: Haklyut Society, 1856
Nadezhda Fops and Oksana Morgunova, 'Kak napisat' Nobelevskuiu lektsiiu po-russki' [re: Edinburgh Russian School]. *Scotland-Russia Forum Review*, 17, 2007, pp. 6-7
Murray Frame, 'Dundee and the "Grand Purveyor"', in Cornwall and Frame, pp. 191-206
Edward A. Freeman, 'Literature and Language'. *Contemporary Review*, 52, 1887, pp. 549-567
Joseph T. Fuhrmann, 'Alexis and the West', in Fuhrmann's *Tsar Alexis. His Reign and his Russia*. Gulf Breeze FA: Academic International Pr, 1981, pp. 47-51
H. Hamilton Fyfe, 'The Russian Riddle'. *MLs* 1(4), April 1920, pp. 100-102
J. L. Gaddis, 'Intelligence, espionage and Cold War origins'. *Diplomatic History*, 13(2), 1989, pp. 191-212
D. Galton 'The Anglo-Russian Literary Society'. *SEER*, 48(101), 1970, pp. 272-282
Richard Garnett, *Constance Garnett. A Heroic Life*. L: Sinclair-Stevenson, 1991
Peter Giles, 'Russian Studies at Cambridge'. *The Times (Russian Supplement)*, 26 April 1915, p. 15
John Howes Gleason, *The Genesis of Russophobia in Great Britain*. Cambridge MA: Harvard UP, 1950
Anthony Glees, *The Secrets of the Service. British Intelligence and Communist Subversion 1939-51*. L: Cape, 1987
P. H. J. H. Gosden & A. J. Taylor (eds.), *Studies in the History of a University 1874-1974*. Leeds: E. J. Arnold, 1975
V. G. Goudin, 'Record of the teaching of Russian'. *MLT* 13(6), Oct 1917, pp. 165-169
David Graddol, 'Will English be enough?' in Moys, pp. 24-33
V. H. H. Green, *The Universities*. Harmondsworth: Penguin, 1969
Stephen Hagen, 'What does global trade mean for UK languages?' in Moys, pp. 14-23
Richard Hakluyt, *Voyages and Documents*, selected by Janet Hampden. L, New York, Toronto: Oxford UP, 1958
C. M. Handley, 'Diversification of language provision: the place of Russian at Camden School for Girls', in Muckle, *Russian in Schools*, pp. 18-19
Sir Philip Hartog, *A Conspectus of Examinations in Great Britain and Northern Ireland*. L: Macmillan, 1937
B. E. Hawkins, *Russian Language Training in the Services. A Personal Memoir*. No place of publication [Beaconsfield], no date [c. 1990]
Sir William Hayter, 'Modern languages and modern politics'. *MLs* 41(1), 1960, pp. 4-8
H. M. Hayward, 'The Curriculum in Russian Studies', *Universities Quarterly* 7(3), May 1953, pp. 240-246
A. A. Haywood, 'Russian at Firth Park Grammar School, Sheffield'. *ATR Broadsheet* 8, pp. 52-54
John [Ivan] Heard [Gerd], 'Pervaia v Rossii lankasterskaia shkola'. *Istoricheskii vestnik* 9, 1887, pp. 650-656
Elizabeth Hill, *Why need we study the Slavs?* Cambridge UP, 1951
────── *[Memoirs]* see Jean Stafford Smith
Jerome Horsey, 'The Travels of Sir Jerome Horsey, Knt.' in Fletcher, *Russia at the End of the Sixteenth Century*

Geoffrey Hosking, *Russia, People and Empire 1552-1917*. L: Harper Collins, 1997

Michael Hughes, *Inside the Enigma. British Officials in Russia, 1900-1939*. L and Rio Grande: Hambledon Pr, 1997

T[homas] H[unter: authorship assumed from internal evidence], 'Russo-Scottish Society. The Future Relations of the Countries'. *The Scotsman*, 22 March 1916, p 6.

Michael Hyndman, *Schools and Schooling in England and Wales. A Documentary History*. L: Harper and Row, 1978

Peter Jackson, 'Signals intelligence gathering at Uetersen', Chapter 21 of Jackson's *Royal Air Force Uetersen. The Story of an Unusual Station*. Oxford: published by the author, 2005, pp. 319ff.

C. V. James, 'Annan and after'. *ATR J* 12, 1965, pp. 15-21

——— 'The Case for Russian'. *ATR Broadsheet* 7, 1962, pp. 46-53.

——— 'Lies and statistics'. *ATR Conference NL*, 1972

——— 'Otkuda vy?', *JRS* 18. 1969, p. 3 [Russian title, text in English]

——— 'Shag vpered i dva nazad'. *Britain-USSR*, 48, 1975, pp. 1-2 [Russian title, text in English]

——— 'The State of the Union'. *ATR OP*, 3(1), 1969, pp. 1-2, 15-23, 33-36

Joyce James, 'Survival on the Russian front'. *MLiS* 23, 1983, pp. 104-107

Susan James, 'Russian in Castle Vale School, Birmingham'. *JRS* 33, 1977, 10-12

Madame N. Jarintzov, *The Russians and Their Language*. Oxford: Blackwell, 1916

E. W. Jenkins, *From Armstrong to Nuffield. Studies in Twentieth-century Science Education in England and Wales*. L: John Murray, 1979

Malcolm V. Jones. 'The Fascination of Russian culture', in Muckle (ed.), *Russian in Schools*, pp. 92-94

——— 'Slavonic Studies in the United Kingdom since the Second World War: a personal view', in Giovanna Brogi Bercoff *et al*, eds., *Contributions à l'histoire de la slavistique dans les pays non slaves*, ii (Vienna: Austrian Academy of Sciences, 2005), pp. 267-301

David Kahn, *The Codebreakers. The Story of Secret Writing*. New York: Scribner, 2. ed., 1996, esp. pp. 171-172 and 614-615

Olga Kaznina, *Russkie v Anglii*. M: Nasledie, 1997

William Kenefick, 'Aberdeen was more Red than Glasgow. The Impact of the First World War and the Russian Revolution beyond Red Clydeside', in Cornwall and Frame, pp. 158-189

Michael Kirkwood, 'Learning and teaching Russian: from practice to theory'. *Rusistika* 10, 1994, pp. 14-25

Martin Kitchen, *British Policy Towards the Soviet Union During the Second World War*. Basingstoke: Macmillan, 1986

Mark Knight, 'A Short history of the Department [of Slavonic Studies]'. *Slavonica*, Dept. of Slavonic Studies, University of Nottingham 6(1), 1977, pp. 1-9, 15-19

S. Konovalov, 'Anglo-Russian relations, 1617-18'. *Oxford Slavonic Papers*, I, 1950, pp. 64-103

V. Kostomarov, 'Tsentr russkogo iazyka: zadachi i plany'. *ATR OP* 1(1), pp. 7-10

Isabelle Kreindler, 'The Changing status of Russian in the Soviet Union'. *International J of the Sociology of Language*, 33, 1982, pp. 7-39

M. Kuz'min, 'Angliiskoe obshchestvo kul'turnykh sviazei s SSSR'. *Voprosy istorii* 2, 1966, pp. 203-206

E. Lampert, 'Russian studies'. *The Tablet (Educational Supplement)* 27, 23 February 1980, pp. 185-186

Walter Laqueur (ed.), *The State of Russian Studies*. Cambridge MA: MIT Pr, 1965

Janko Lavrin, 'Difficult beginnings'. *Slavonica*, Dept. of Slavonic Studies, University of Nottingham 6(1), 1977,. pp. 12-14

Michael Lee, 'The Joint Services School for Linguists'. *The Linguist* 38(4), 1999

John Lewis, *The Left Book Club. A Historical Record*. L: Gollancz, 1970.

J. B. G. Linton, 'The Munn Report'. *MLiS* 15, 1978, pp. 41-46

Mikhail Lomonosov, 'Iazyk' [Language], in Meilakh, pp. 42-44

W. S. Macgowan, 'Report of the [MLA] sub-committee for Russian Studies'. *MLT* 14, 1918, pp. 93-94

Joanna McPake, Richard Johnstone, Lesley Low and Lindsay Lyall, *Foreign Languages in the Upper Secondary School. A Study of the Causes of Decline*. Glasgow: Scottish Council for Research in Education, 1999

J. A. R. Marriott, *Anglo-Russian Relations 1689-1943*. L: Methuen, 1944

Alan Marshall, 'Intelligence and the Post Office', in Marshall's *Espionage in the Reign of Charles II*. Cambridge: UP, 1994, pp. 11-25

Margaret Mathieson, *The Preachers of Culture. A Study of English and its Teachers*. L: George Allen and Unwin, 1975

C. D. Meader, 'Russian Studies in America'. *Russian Review* [Liverpool] II(ii), undated [1913?]

V. A. Mealor, 'The Intensive course for teachers at Liverpool College of Commerce'. *ATR J* 11, 1964, pp. 36-37

B. Meilakh, *Russkie pisateli o literaturnom trude, I*. Lg: Sovetskii pisatel', 1954

Prince Michael of Kent, 'Some Russian reminiscences'. *East-West Review* 15, 2007, pp. 4-13

Harry Milne, 'Russian in Leith Academy'. *JRS* 33, 1977, 7-9

——— 'Russian as a first foreign language', in Muckle, *Russian in Schools*, pp. 8-13

Rosamund F. Mitchell, 'The Dunning Report and modern language teaching'. *MLiS* 15, 1978, pp. 58-65

R. J. Montgomery, *Examinations. An Account of their Evolution as Administrative Devices in England*. L: Longmans Green, 1965

Bob Moon, Patricia Murphy, John Raynor (eds.), *Policies for the Curriculum*. L (etc): Hodder and Stoughton/The Open University, 1989

William R. Morfill, *An Essay on the Importance of the Study of the Slavonic Languages*. L, 1890

G. D. Morley, J. Y. Muckle, 'The Place of modern languages and of Russian in the curriculum'. *ATR NL*, October 1978, pp. 14-16

W. John Morgan, 'Independent workers' education', in Morgan, *Communists on Education and Culture*. Basingstoke: Palgrave Macmillan, 2003, pp. 3-15

Alan Moys (ed.), *Where are we going with languages? Consultative Report of the Nuffield Languages Enquiry*. L: Nuffield Foundation, 1998

James Muckle 'The Archives of ATR 1959-1989'. *Rusistika* 6, 1992, pp. 2-4

——— and Daphne M. West, 'British Schools in Which Russian is Taught: A Report on the Survey'. *JRS* 49 (1985), pp. 3-17

——— 'British Schools in Which Russian is Taught: A Report on the 1988 Survey'. *JRS* 56 (1989), pp. 4-18

——— *A Guide to the Soviet Curriculum*. L: Croom Helm, 1988

―――― (ed.), 'Is Russian only for the most able?'. *JRS* 33, 1977, 5-12
―――― 'Russian in the university curriculum: a case-study of the impact of the First World War on language study in higher education in Britain'. *History of Education* 37 (3), 2008, pp. 359-381
―――― *Schools, Polytechnics and Universities where Russian is Taught*. Nottingham: Bramcote Pr, 1992
―――― 'Survey of Schools, Polytechnics and Universities Where Russian is Taught', *Educational Research* 36(1), 1994, pp. 39-50.
―――― 'Teachers of Russian and Their Careers'. *Educational Research* 27(3), 1985, pp. 210-219.
―――― 'What have teachers of Russian achieved in fifty years?' *Rusistika* 30, 2005, pp. 15-19
J. Y. Muckle, *British Schools in Which Russian Is Taught*. Nottingham: ATR, 1989
―――― *Russian in Schools. A Handbook of Information for Head Teachers, Inspectors, Educational Advisers, and Curriculum Planners*. Nottingham: ATR, BNASEES, BUAS, GB-USSR Association, 1982
James Munn, 'The implications of the Munn Report for modern languages'. *MLiS* 15 1978, pp. 53-57
Keith Neilson, *Britain and the Last Tsar. British Policy and Russia 1894-1917*. Oxford: Clarendon Pr, 1995, esp. pp. 51-109
David O'Connor, 'Russian Language Training in 1893'. *The Rose and the Laurel* [journal of the Intelligence Corps: Crown Copyright], 2002.
Jacob Ornstein, *Slavic and East European Studies: Their Development and Status in the Western Hemisphere*. Washington DC, Dept. of State, External Research Staff, Office of Intelligence Research 1957, External Research Paper 129
G. S. Osborne, *Scottish and English Schools. A Comparative Survey of the Past Fifty Years*, L: Longmans Green, 1966
Joslyn Owen, 'Modern languages in new education: the link between present and future'. *Language Learning J*, September 1990 [no. 1?], pp. 2-4
Margaret Page, 'The ATR and Russian in the English secondary School 1959-1989'. *Rusistika* 26, 2002, pp. 18-22
W. S. Page, *The Russia Company from 1553 to 1660*. L: Brown, undated [1911?]
Anton Palme, 'The Progress of Russian Studies in Germany'. *Russian Review* [Liverpool] 3(1), undated [presumed 1914], pp. 131-136
Bernard Pares, 'Forty Years On'. *SEER*, 18(52), 1939, pp. 55-72
―――― *My Russian Memoirs*. New York: AMS Pr, 1969 [reprint of 1931 ed.]
―――― *A Wandering Scholar*. Syracuse NY: Syracuse UP, 1948
Albert Parry, *America Learns Russian. A History of the Teaching of the Russian Language in the United States*. Syracuse NY: Syracuse UP, 1967
Monica Partridge, [interview with Mark Knight]. *Slavonica* [Dept. of Slavonic Studies, University of Nottingham] 6(1), December 1977, pp. 17-18
R. A. P[eace], 'ATR Survey, 1963-64'. *ATR J* 11, 1964, pp. 52-57
―――― 'Now is the time to act'. *ATR Broadsheet* 3, 1960, pp. 34-36.
D. J. Pearce, 'Russian in the era of khozraschyot'. *Rusistika* 1, 1990, pp. 6-8
David Peat, 'Minority Languages in Schools. Russian on the brink'. *MLiS* 23, 1983, pp. 101-103
A. E. Pennington, 'A Sixteenth-century English Slavist'. *Modern Language Review* 62, 1967, pp. 680-686.

G. W. Pincock, 'Some thoughts on reading the Munn Report'. *MLiS* 15, 1978, pp. 31-36

B. P. Pockney, 'The Case for Russian (or Russian is a key language in any future we may have...)'. Guildford: University of Surrey, pamphlet [inaugural lecture], no date [1984]. Summarized in *ATR NL*, May 1985, no. 1, pp. 17-19

Richard Pollock, 'Russian and Education: hindsight, oversight and foresight'. *JRS* 26, 1973, pp. 21-36

Bernard Porter, *Plots and Paranoia. A history of political espionage in Britain 1790-1988*. L: Unwin Hyman, 1989

Bob Powell et al., 'Responding to the National Curriculum: some perceptions of teachers in training'. *Language Learning J* 4, Sept. 1991, pp. 16-18

Ian Press, *A History of the Russian Language and its Speakers*. Munich: Lincom Europa, 2007

Bob Pullin, '*Putyovka* and *Privyet!* Teacher-led materials development groups and professional development: a case-study of the York-Sheffield Project'. *Rusistika* 10, 1994, pp. 38-46

R. T. Pullin, 'The National debate on education and Russian'. *JRS* 33, 1977, pp. 3-5

David Raffe (ed.), *Fourteen to Eighteen. The Changing pattern of schooling in Scotland*. Aberdeen: Aberdeen UP, 1982

D. R[ichards], 'Russian in the universities, 1964'. *ATR J* 11, 1964, pp. 30-34

D. J. Richards, 'Russian in the universities today'. *Forum for Modern Language Studies* 1, 1965, pp. 87-94

———— 'Russian and the aims of Modern Language Studies', *ATR Broadsheet* 4, 1960, pp. 23-25

David Rix, Robert Pullin, 'Russian renaissance?' in David Phillips (ed.), *Which Language? Diversificationand the National Curriculum*. Sevenoaks: Hodder and Stoughton, 1989, pp. 32-43

John Roach, *Public Examinations in England 1850-1900*. Cambridge: Cambridge UP, 1971

J. O. Roach, *Language Studies and International Relations*. L (etc.): Harrap, 1944

I. W. Roberts, *History of the School of Slavonic and East European Studies 1915-1990*. L: SSEES, 1991

E. Rooney, 'Will modern languages survive the Munn Report?'. *MLiS* 15, 1978, pp. 37-80

W. F. Ryan, 'Rathbone's *Surveyor* (1616/1625): the first Russian translation from English?'. *Oxford Slavonic Papers* 11, 1964, pp. 1-7.

Michael Sanderson, *The Missing Stratum. Technical School Education in England 1900-1990s*. L, Atlantic Highlands, 1994

———— *The Universitiesand British Industry 1850-1970*. L: Routledge & Kegan Paul, 1972

Karl Schlögel, 'The Futility of one professor's life. Otto Hoetzsch and German Russian Studies, in Manfred Sapper et al., *Sketches of Europe*. Berlin: Osteuropa, 2005: compilation booklet distributed at the Berlin Congress of ICCEES, 2005

James Scotland, *The History of Scottish Education: II. From 1872 to the Present Day*. L: University of London Pr, 1969

J. P. Scott, 'The study of Russian'. *MLT* 12(1), 1916, pp. 10-15

W. J. Sedgefield, 'The Study of Russian'. *University Review* 5 (1907), pp. 405-428

Hugh Seton-Watson, 'Russian History and Society'. *Universities Quarterly* 7(3), May 1953, pp. 232-239

R. W. Seton-Watson, 'The Origins of the School of Slavonic Studies'. *SEER* 17(50), 1939, pp. 360-371

J. S. G. Simmons, 'H. W. Ludolf and the printing of his *Grammatica Russica* in Oxford in 1696'. *Oxford Slavonic Papers* 1, 1950, pp. 111-113.

—— and B. O. Unbegaun, 'Slavonic manuscript vocabularies in the Bodleian Library'. *Oxford Slavonic Papers* 2, 1951, pp. 119-127

G. M. Sinclair, 'Modern languages in Scotland: a historical review'. *MLiS* 13, 1977, pp. 106-117

T. I. Skalkina (editor-in chief), *Rossiia i Britaniia XVI-XIX veka*. M: Drevlekhranilishche, 2007

B. Slepchenko, 'Garantii pravil'noi otsenki uspeshnosti ekzamenuiushchikhsia'. *MLT* 13(6), Oct 1917, pp. 163-164

Jean Stafford Smith (ed.), *In the Mind's Eye. The Memoirs of Dame Elizabeth Hill*. Lewes: The Book Guild, 1999

R. E. F. Smith, *A Novelty: Russian at Birmingham University 1917-67*. Birmingham: U of Birmingham, 1987

A. Sokolov, *Navstrechu drug drugu. Rossiia i Angliia v XVI-XVIII vv.* Iaroslavl': Verkhne-Volzhkskoe knizhnoe izdatel'stvo, 1992

Count Nicolas Sollohub, 'Is Russian Too Difficult? Teaching naval cadets'. *Times Educational Supplement*, 24 Jan. 1948, p. 51

N. S. Sollohub, *A Survey of Russian Teaching in British Secondary Schools*. Nuffield Foundation, Nuffield Foreign Languages Teaching Materials Project Reports and Occasional Papers 23, York [assumed], 1967

Iu. S. Sorokin (ed.), *Literaturnyi iazyk XVIII veka*. Lg: Nauka, 1982

R. C. d'Esterre Spottiswoode, *Reminiscences*. Edinburgh, L: Edinburgh Pr, 1935

W. T. Stead, *Truth About Russia*. L: 1888

Ludmila Stern, *Western Intellectuals and the Soviet Union, 1920-40. From Red Square to the Left Bank*. Abingdon: Routledge, 2007

Gerald Stone, 'The History of Slavonic Studies in Great Britain (until the Second World War), in J. Hamm and G. Wytrzens, *Beiträge zur Geschichte der Slawistik in nichtslawischen Ländern*, Vienna: Verlag der Österreichischen Akademie der Wissenschaften, 1985; Schriften der Balkankommission, Linguistische Abteilung XXX, pp. 361-397

Lloyd Storr-Best, 'Russian as a school subject'. *MLs,* 27(2), April 1946, pp. 55-57

H. A. Strong, 'Some thoughts on the teaching of Russian in England'. *MLT* 12(6), 1917, pp. 139-141

A. P. Sumarokov, 'Epistola I: (o russkom iazyke)' in Sumarokov's *Izbrannye proizvedeniia,* Lg: Sovetskii pisatel', 1957, pp. 112-115

Penny Summerfield, Eric J. Evans, *Technical Education and the State Since 1850: Historical and Contemporary Perspectives,* Manchester and New York: Manchester UP, 1990

Richard Szawlowski, Hanna Terlecka, 'Western Research on Russia until 1939. I. Developments up to 1914'. *Canadian Slavonic Papers* 9(2), 1967, pp. 145-169

Veronica Tennant, 'Teaching Russian in a London comprehensive school'. *Anglo-Soviet J* 51(1), September 1980

Garth M. Terry, 'The Department of Slavonic Studies', in Cynthia Marsh and Wendy Rosslyn (eds.), *Russian and Yugoslav Culture in the Age of Modernism*, Nottingham: Astra Pr, 1991, pp. 147-155. Graduates 1932-1991, pp. 157-165

B. H. Tolley, 'The Department of Slavonic Studies', in Tolley, *The History of the University of Nottingham*. Nottingham: Nottingham UP, 2001, II, pp. 80-87

Richard Towell, 'Languages in higher education', in Moys, pp. 44-53

Yury Tolstoi, *The First Forty Years of Intercourse between England and Russia 1553-1593*. Documents collected, copied and edited by G. Tolstoi/*Pervye sorok let snoshenii mezhdu Rossiei i Angliei 1553-1593*. SPb 1875 [bilingual publication]

M. V. Trofimov, 'Russian language. Political and economic importance'. *The Times Russian Supplement*, 17 Dec. 1915, p. 11

M. V. Trophimoff [sic], 'Practical training in Russian'. *MLT* 8(7), pp. 200-209

Ivan Turgenev, 'Russkii iazyk' [the Russian language], in Turgenev's *Sobranie sochinenii*, M: Gos. Izd. Khud. Lit, vol. 8, 1956, p. 507

A. Logan Turner, *History of the University of Edinburgh 1883-1933*. L: Oliver and Boyd, 1933, p. 192

B. O. Unbegaun, 'Introduction' and 'Bibliographical note', in *Henrici Wilhelmi Ludolfi Grammatica Russica*. Oxford: Clarendon Pr, 1959, pp. vii-xx

E. G. Underwood, 'Place of Russian in school curricula'. *MLT* 13(3 & 4), 1917, pp. 65-68

Vengerov, *Istochniki slovaria russkikh pisatelei*, I. Note/biblio. on James Heard

Jacques Veyrenc, 'Histoire de la slavistique française', *Beiträge zur Geschichte der Slawistik in nichtslawischen Ländern*, Vienna: Verlag der Österreichischen Akademie der Wissenschaften, 1985; Schriften der Balkankommission, Linguistische Abteilung XXX, pp. 245-303

G. O. Vinokur, *The Russian Language: A Brief History*, translated by Mary A. Forsyth, ed. James Forsyth. Cambridge: Cambridge UP, 1971

——— 'The Russian and his language'. *Life and Letters Today*, Oct. 1942, pp. 6-11.

Meriel Vlaerminke, 'The subordination of technical education to secondary schooling', in Summerfield, pp. 55-76

Terence Wade, 'Eyes right for Russian'. *The Linguist* 45(1), 2006, pp. 20-21

——— 'Strathclyde Survey'. *JRS* 19, 1970, pp. 77-80

D. Mackenzie Wallace, *Russia*. L/Paris/New York: Cassell, 1905

G. Waterhouse, 'The Place of Russian'. *MLT* 13(7 & 8), Nov-Dec 1917, pp. 219-221

Foster Watson, *The Beginnings of the Teaching of Modern Subjects in England*. L: Pitman, 1909

[Wavell], 'Archibald Percival Wavell, First Earl Wavell, 1883-1950'. *Dictionary of National Biography* 57, Oxford: Oxford UP, 2004, pp. 764-768

Rebecca Wells, *The Jacobites and Russia 1715-1750*. East Linton: Tuckwell Pr, 2002

D. M. West, *British Schools in Which Russian Is Taught*. Nottingham: ATR, 1983.

——— *British Schools in Which Russian Is Taught*. Nottingham: ATR, 1985.

Marcus Wheeler, 'Irlandskaia assotsiatsiia slavistov'. *Russkii iazyk za rubezhom* 2, 1976 p. 119

——— *Russia—East or West*. Belfast: Queen's University, 1969

——— 'The Russians are Coming'. *Queen's University Belfast Gazette* 14, 1969, pp. 4-9

T. S. Willan, *The Early History of the Muscovy Company*. Manchester: UP, 1956

——— *The Muscovy Merchants of 1555*. Manchester: UP, 1953

William Sharpe Wilson, 'British influence on Russia'. *The Times (Russian Supplement)*, 26 April 1915, p. 15
A. C. Wood, *A History of University College Nottingham 1881-1948.* Oxford: Blackwell, 1953
Leslie Woodhead, *My Life as a Spy.* Basingstoke: Macmillan, 2005
C. L. Wrenn, 'The Earliest English students of Russian'. *Brno Studies in English*, 8, 1969, pp. 197-203
F. Wright, 'The teaching of Russian in England today'. *Rusistika* 23, 2001, pp. 11-16

Government, Parliamentary and Civil Service papers, Reports and Documents. Reports by Voluntary Bodies

Reports of committees and commissions appointed by Governments are listed by the name of the chairman or principal or sole compiler: Annan, Darlington, Hayter, Leathes, Norwood, Scarbrough, etc.

Agreement between the Government of the UK of GB and NI and the Government of the USSR on Relations in the Scientific, Technological, Educational and Cultural Fields 1960-61. L: HMSO, December 1, 1959, Command Paper Cmnd. 917 [Examples of later Cultural Agreements are to be found as papers Cmnd 808, 853]
Agreement between the Government of the UK of GB and NI and the Government of the USSR on Relations in the Scientific, Technological, Educational and Cultural Fields for 1983-85. L: HMSO, 1983, Cmnd. 8981.
Anglo-Soviet Communiqué on the discussions of the Prime Minister of the United Kingdom, Mr Harold Macmillan, and the Foreign Secretary, Mr. Selwyn Lloyd, with the Chairman of the Council of Ministers of the USSR, Mr. N. S. Khrushchev [with Agreement on Cultural Exchanges]. Soviet Union No. 1 (1959). L: HMSO, March 1959, Cmnd. 689
[Annan Report] *The Teaching of Russian.* L: HMSO, 1962
Association for Language Learning, *Why learn Russian?* Document untraced
Association of Teachers of Russian and British Universities Association of Slavists, *Russian in School, Why Not?* [no place or date of publication], c. 1972
ATR, 'British Schools where Russian is taught', unpublished typescript, 1979
——— 'Survey of supply, demand and utilization of Teachers of Russian in secondary schools'. *JRS* 21, 1971, pp. 56-68
[Atkinson Report] *Report on Russian and Russian Studies in British Universities,* University Grants Committee [no place of publication], 1979
Board of Education, Circular 797: *Memoranda on Teaching and Organisation in Secondary schools. Modern Languages.* L: HMSO, 1912
——— *Reports of the Board of Education* for 1915-1916, 1916-1917, etc. to 1950. Command papers 8594, 9045 etc.
[E. Bullough, Sub-committee Secretary: name not credited on title page] *The Teaching of Russian. Memorandum issued by the Modern Language Association Sub-committee for Russian Studies,* February 1917 [no place of publication]
Calendar of Home Office Papers 1770-1772. L, 1878
CILT and InterAct International, *ELAN: Effects on the European Economy of Shortages of Foreign Language Skills in Enterprise,* Internet, December 2006, http://www.ec.europa.eu/education/policies/lang/doc/elan_en.pdf

Civil Service Commission, *Reports of the Civil Service Commissioners*, 1880-1901
[Darlington, Thomas] *Report on Education in Russia.* L: Board of Education, 1909. Special reports on educational subjects no. 23; Cd 4812. L: HMSO, 1909
[Dearing Review] Department for Education and Skills, *Languages Review.* Crown Copyright 2007
Department of Education and Science, *Circular 9/89. Modern Languages in the National Curriculum,* [official document reprinted in] *British J of Language Teaching* 27(2), Autumn 1989, pp. 110-113
———— *Mathematics, Science and Modern Languages in Maintained Schools in England. An Appraisal of Problems in some Key Subjects by HM Inspectorate* [no author, publisher, place of publication, but presumed HMSO], Jan. 1977
———— *Report by HM Inspectors on Modern languages in the Sixth Form, carried out Jan 1983-April 1984,* mimeographed document, Crown Copyright 1985
———— *Report by HM Inspectors on a Survey of the Teaching of Russian in the North Midland Division,* carried out during the school year 1969-1970. L: Department of Education and Science, 1970. S 21/87/01 DS 30/70
———— and Welsh Office, *Modern Foreign Languages in the School Curriculum, a Statement of Policy.* L: HMSO, 1988
———— and Welsh Office, *Modern Foreign Languages for ages 11 to 16. Proposals of the Secretary of State for Education and Science and the Secretary of State for Wales,* [no places of publication: York and Cardiff?]: DES and Welsh Office, 1990
Department for Education and Employment, *Modern Foreign Languiages. The National Curriculum for England, Key stages 3-4.* L: HMSO, 1999
Department for Education and Skills, *Languages for All: Languages for Life. A Strategy for England.* Nottingham: DfES Publications, 2002
[Dunning Report] *Assessment for All.* Scottish Education Department, 1977
Education in England and Wales, being the Report of the Board of Education for the Year 1917-18. L: HMSO, esp. pp. 23 and 25
E. Green (ed.), *Calendar of State Papers Dom. 1633-1634.* L 1862
[Hayter Report] University Grants Committee, *Report of Sub-committee on Oriental, East European and African Studies.* L: HMSO, 1961
Higher Education Funding Council for England/Department of Education for Northern Ireland, *Quality Assessment of Russian and Eastern European Languages and Studies 1995-96,* Subject Overview Report QO 7/96. Bristol: HEFCE, 1996
———— *Review of Former Soviet and East European Studies.* Bristol: HEFCE, 1995
House of Commons. Education, Science and Arts Committee, Session 1980-81, *Secondary School Curriculum and Examinations: 14 to 16 year old age group.* Minutes of Evidence, Wed. 8 April 1981, Memorandum Submitted by the Association of Teachers of Russian, pp. 135-138. House of Commons Paper 110-v. L: HMSO, 1982
———— Second Report from the Education, Science and Arts Committee, Session 1981-82, *The Secondary School Curriculum and Examinations: with special reference to the 14 to 16 year old age group. I: Report.* House of Commons Paper 116-1. L: HMSO, 1982 [?]
———— Foreign Affairs Committee. First report. *Eastern Europe and the Soviet Union.* Report, together with the Proceedings of the Committee, Minutes of Evidence and Appendices. L: HMSO, 1989 esp. pp xl-xli and 264-5

BIBLIOGRAPHY

Incorporated Association of Assistant Masters, *The Teaching of Modern Languages.* L: University of L Pr, first ed. 1949, second ed. 1952, third ed., 1956, pp. 286-289, fourth ed., 1967 pp. 286-301
—— in Secondary Schools, *Memorandum on the Teaching of Modern Languages.* L: University of L Pr, 1929
Incorporated Association of Head Masters, *Modern Languages in the Grammar School. report of a working party of DIVISION XII (Lancashire and Cheshire)* of I.A.H.M. (published with the assistance of the Nuffield Foundation), 1963, pp. 15-16
—— *Modern Languages in the Grammar School. Report of a working party of Division XII* of I.A.H.M., revised edition, February 1966, pp. 19-21
J[oint] C[ouncil] of L[anguage] A[ssociations] 'Open Letter to the Secretary of State', *British J of Language Teaching* 27(3), 1989, pp. 169-170
[Leathes Report] *Report of the Committee appointed by the Prime Minister to enquire into the position of modern languages in the educational system of Great Britain.* L: HMSO, 1918. Command paper 9036
Ministry of Education, *Modern Languages. Ministry of Education Pamphlet no. 29*, L: HMSO, 1956
—— *Russian Studies*, Circular no. 81, 15 Jan. 1946. L: HMSO, 1946
Modern Language Association, 'Memorandum on the teaching of Russian' (adopted by the General Committee). *MLT* 13(3 & 4), 1917, pp. 75-85
—— 'Report on Conference of teachers of Russian', *MLT* 13(6), 1917, pp. 158-164
Modern Languages. Ministry of Education pamphlet no. 29. L: HMSO, 1956, pp. 8, 15-16, 96
Modern Languages in Comprehensive Schools. A Discussion Paper by Some Members of H.M. Inspectorate of Schools Based on a Survey of 83 Schools in 1975-76. L: HMSO, 1977
[Munn report] *The Structure of the Curriculum in the Third and Fourth Years of the Scottish Secondary School*, SED, Edinburgh: HMSO, 1977
The Munn and Dunning Reports. The Government's Development Programme, Mimeographed Document: SED, no date [presumably 1981]
[Norwood Report] *Curriculum and Examinations in the Secondary School.* L: HMSO, 1943, esp. pp. 113-118
[Nuffield Languages Enquiry] Sir Trevor McDonald, Sir John Boyd, *Languages: the Next Generation. The Final Report and Recommendations of the Nuffield Languages Enquiry.* L: Nuffield Foundation [CD version corrected], 2000
[Scarbrough Commission] *Report of the Inter-departmental Commission of Enquiry on Oriental, Slavonic, East European and African Studies*, L: HMSO, 1947
Scottish Central Committee on Modern Languages, 'Survey of Scottish language teacher opinion: the Munn and Dunning Reports'. *MLiS* 16, 1978, pp 22-33
Scottish Education Department, *Effective Learning and Teaching in Scottish Secondary Schools. Modern Languages*, Report by HMI, [Edinburgh] HMSO, 1990
—— *Modern Languages in Further Education. Report of a Working Party.* Edinburgh: HMSO, 1970
—— *Modern Language Courses for Non-certificated Pupils. A Document for Discussion.* Edinburgh: HMSO, 1975
—— *Modern Languages in Secondary Schools.* Edinburgh: HMSO, 1950, p. 30
—— *Modern Languages in Si and Sii of the Comprehensive School. Report of the National Steering Committee for Modern Languages.* Edinburgh: HMSO, 1970

────── *The Place and Aims of Modern Language Teaching in Secondary Schools.* Edinburgh: HMSO, 1972

────── National Steering Committee for Modern Languages, *Alternatives to French as a First Foreign Llanguage in Secondary Schools.* Edinburgh: HMSO, 1971

[Thomson Report] *Secondary Education. A Report of the Advisory Council on Education in Scotland.* Edinburgh: HMSO, 1947, Cmd 7005

[Wooding Report] *Review of Soviet and East European Studies.* L: Universities Funding Council, 1989

Archival, oral, unpublished, manuscript and miscellaneous sources:

Nicola Allen, *The History of RSA Examinations,* unpublished typescript provided by the RSA, 2004

Archive of the Anglo-Russian Literary Society, SSEES, University College, L

Association of Teachers of Russian: Discussions with DES following Annan Report, 1964, National Archives, ED 181/103

Association of Teachers of Russian: archives held at the Leeds Russian Archive, Special Collections, Brotherton Library, University of Leeds

R. Avery, 'Russian language teaching at Defence School of Languages Beaconsfield', 16 September 2007, unpublished typescript provided by the author

Board of Education internal papers relating to four Reports on education in Britain, including that of the Committee chaired by Leathes. National Archives: E12/234, RECON 2948, ED 24/1173 4079, ED 24/1174 4085

Board of Education Office Memorandum no. 55. 'Office Committee on the "Four reports" (Natural Science, Modern Languages, English, Classics). Report of the Committee'. Mimeographed typescript, 44 foolscap pages, dated June 1922; document unnumbered

Board of Education: file on Study of Russian and other Slavonic languages in secondary schools and evening institutes. Correspondence with SSEES, Open document, 1916-1935. National Archives ED 12/228

Borough of Leicester Education Committee Minutes, 1915-20, held at Record Office for Leicestershire, Leicester and Rutland, 19 D 59/VII/400-

Robin Breen, Lyudmila Gilmour, Marcus Wheeler, 'Northern Ireland Russian Circle', typescript information sheets and announcements, dated 1999 and 2002

British Council, with assistance of Academica Rossica, SSEES, Russkii mir Foundation, Yeltsin Foundation: Account of a workshop on 'Russian language and culture in the UK—next steps'. Typescript dated variously, latest 22.6.08

Committee on Russian Studies, 1946, National Archives, FO 371/56827 and 56828.

Derby Chamber of Commerce, Minutes: held at Derby City Record Office

Derby Technical College and Evening Branches, prospectuses for sessions 1914-1915 to 1919-1920. Held at Derbyshire County Record Office, Matlock

Friends Service Council, *British-Soviet Teacher Exchange 1976,* unpublished flysheet with application form, 4 pp.

Dave Haysom, 'Linguists, Languages and Schools.' Unpublished electronic document on Russian in the RAF, c. 2002

Walter Grauberg, 'Language teaching in the UK—21 years on', typescript 27pp., University of Southampton Language Centre, 1990

Bibliography

Michael Kirkwood, 'The University and the Wider World 1970-2001. Russia and Eastern Europe.' Unpublished typescript on the development of Slavonic Studies at the University of Glasgow, January 1998

Janko Lavrin: transcript of tape-recorded interview with Lavrin by G. S. Smith, in Leeds Russian Archive

Leicester Chamber of Commerce Minutes, held at Record Office for Leicestershire, Leicester and Rutland, at Wigston Magna, Leicester.

Materials relating to the teaching of Russian in Britain: map, list of universities and colleges where Russian was taught, list of names and addresses of teachers in these institutions and in private practice. *Russian Review* [Liverpool] 3(1), undated [presumed 1914], opening endpapers [published in several issues of the journal with appropriate amendments and additions]

Nottingham Chamber of Commerce Minutes of Council Meetings, 1915-1918. Two bound volumes of printed minutes. [Hallward Library, University of Nottingham: uncatalogued]

Robert T. Pullin, 'Russian Teaching in the United Kingdom. Its Development and Present Problems', unpublished typescript document, 1975

Royal Society of Arts, L: Annual reports, examination syllabuses, examination papers for Russian, etc.

Johann Nestor Schnurmann, grant of nationality 1889, National Archives HO 144/307/B5569

'Schools teaching Russian'. www.schoolsnetwork.org.uk

Basil S. Slepchenko: curriculum vitae of 1931 (unpublished typescript, 1 p.)
———— testimonial by A Bruce Boswell, 28 Nov. 31 (typescript, 1 p.)

Vasilii Semenovich Slepchenko, known as Basil Slepchenko, Grant of British nationality by naturalization, 28 June 1930. National Archives, certificate 18419, HO 144/11688, disclosed by request under Freedom of Information Act

Society for Cooperation in Russian and Soviet Studies, archives of minutes, annual reports, journals. At SCRSS headquarters, Brixton, London

Gerald Stone, *Slavonic Studies at Oxford: a Brief History*, [mimeographed documentation for a public exhibition] Oxford, 2005.

University College, Nottingham. Uncatalogued records in Hallward Library, University of Nottingham:
Minute books: Council and committee minutes, 23.3.1915-16.1.1923: manuscript book containing carbon copies of typewritten minutes.
Prospectuses for the thirty-fifth to forty-first sessions. Printed booklets.
Annual Reports to the University College Council, 1915-. Printed books.
Book of newspaper cuttings relating to the College.

Statistical Records

Ministry of Education, *Education in 1951 (etc.) being the report of the Ministry of Education and the Statistics of Education for England and Wales*, L: HMSO

Scottish Educational Statistics, 1967-72, Edinburgh: HMSO.

Scottish examination entries for 1986-, website www.sqa.org.uk.

Russian exam entry data 1998-2005, provided by CILT and available on www.cilt.org.uk/research/statistics

Reports of the Board of Education, 1919-1950 for England and Wales: examination statistics, L: HMSO

Royal Society of Arts, examination entries (unpublished) supplied by the Society in manuscript form

Statistics of Education, [1960s-], L: HMSO

Other statistics quoted in this book, if not attribued directly, were provided from unpublished sources by the authorities concerned.

Dictionaries and Grammars in approximate chronological order

The purpose of this list is to indicate the degree of activity in the writing and compilation of teaching materials for use in Britain over the last two hundred years. It is not comprehensive and is not intended to be complete, nor is it a list of recommended publications. Works included meet at least one of the following criteria: they are (1) translating dictionaries, (2) descriptive grammars, (3) progressive grammars, 'methods' and courses, and they are (4) of British (part-) authorship, or were (5) published in Britain, or (6) aimed at British learners, or (7) works which had impact on teaching in Britain. Readers and supplementary materials as well as studies of one special aspect of the Russian language have been omitted, unless criterion (7) is met.

Chronological arrangement is felt to be appropriate for reasons of interest. Note particularly that some works went into multiple editions and the consequent revision varied in nature; for some works it is impossible to discover exact dates of first publication. The date of the first edition is given on the left, and of other editions when known after the bibliographical details. Care should be taken in interpreting these data: for example, while very little new material was published between 1918 and 1934, perusal of earlier entries will reveal a large number of reprints.

It is hoped that this list will indicate the magnitude of British interest in the Russian language at different times in history; the nationality of the authors (when it can be accurately recognised!) may be of significance; titles sometimes make clear the emphasis of the authors' aims of instruction ('communicative', 'conversational', 'business' or 'commercial', 'army and navy officers', 'science Russian', and so on.)

1696 *Henrici Wilhelmi Ludolfi Grammatica Russica Oxonii A.D. MDCXCVI.* [Facsimile reprint by Oxford: Clarendon Pr, 1959]

1800 Adam Kroll, *A Commercial Dictionary of the English and Russian Languages.* L: Chappel

1808 Grammatin, Nikolai, *A new Dictionary English and Russian, composed upon the great Dictionary English and French of M. Robinet.* M: Dubrovian and Merzliakov

1822 W. H. M. D., *A Manual of an English and Russian Grammar.* SPb: N. Gretsch

1827 James Arthur Heard, *Practical Grammar of the Russian Language.* SPb, 1827

1846 *A New Pocket Dictionary of the English and Russian and the Russian and English Languages.* Leipzig: Tauchnitz

1853 Carl P. Reiff, *English-Russian Grammar or Principles of the Russian Language for the use of Englishmen.* Carlsruhe [1857, 1862]

1867 Aleksandrov, F, *A New Practical and Easy Method of Learning the Russian Language.* L, Leipzig: publisher not stated [1879—publisher L: Thimm, 1889]

- 1878 Henry Riola, *How to Learn Russian. A manual for Students* with a Preface by W. R. S. Ralston. L: Kegan Paul, etc. [1883, 1884, 1890, 1895, 1913, 1915]
- 1882 A. Ivanoff, *Russian Grammar...translated for the use of English students.* L: Kegan Paul [1915]
- 1884 Ivan Nestor-Schnurmann, *The Russian Manual.* L: W. H. Allen and Co.
- 1886 F[rank] Freeth, *A Condensed Russian Grammar for the Use of Staff-officers and Others.* L: Trübner and Co.
- 1889 William R. Morfill, *A Grammar of the Russian Language.* Oxford: Clarendon Pr
- 1890 Pietro Motti, *Russian Conversation-Grammar for General Use, with an Appendix for tradesmen...* Heidelberg: Groos [1899, 1901, 1906, 1922]
- 1890 Alexander Kinloch, *Russian Conversation-Grammar*, with exercises, colloquial phrases, and extensive English-Russian vocabulary. L: W. Thacker and Co. [1902]
- 1890 Theodore Maxwell, *Terminologia Medica polyglotta.* A concise international dictionary of medical terms [Russian included]. L, Paris, Philadelphia: Churchill
- 1897 S. W. Linden, Th. Th. Kavraisky, *Pocket Dictionary of the English and Russian Languages*, L: Hossfeld [1911]
- 1898 Arthur Mears, *English and Russian Military Vocabulary.* L: Nutt
- 1899 Alexis Mansfeld, *A Russian Course of Commercial Arithmetic and Business Operations.* M: Klimenko [exact date untraceable]
- 1903 *Hossfeld's New Practical Method for Learning the Russian Language.* L: Hirschfeld
- 1906 Victor Ferguson, *A Dictionary of Russian Military and Naval Terms.* L: HMSO
- 1909 Leo Meycliar, *English-Russian and Russian-English Engineering Dictionary.* L: Spon
- 1910 *Hill's Modern Pronouncing Dictionary of the English and Russian Languages.* L: Hill
- 1911 D. Bondar, *Bondar's Simplified Russian Method Conversational and Commercial.* L: Effingham Wilson. [1915, 1917, 1918, 1932, rev. Segal: 1942]
- 1913 M. Golovinsky, *A New English-Russian and Russian-English Dictionary.* L: Siegle, Hill
- 1913 S. I. Lyubov, *Hill's Russian-English (English-Russian) Vest-pocket Dictionary and Self-instructor.* L: Hill
- 1914 Neville Forbes, *Russian Grammar.* Oxford: Clarendon Pr [1917, 1919]
- 1915 *Active Service Pocket Dictionary, giving useful words and phrases in English, French, German and Russian, with pronunciation.* L: Gale and Polden
- 1915 Charles Hugo, *Russian Grammar Simplified.* L: Hugo [1920, 1921, 1935]
- 1915 M. B. Karrachy-Smitt, *Lessons in Russian... A Graduated Russian Course.* L: Sampson, Low
- 1915 Boris Manasevich, *A Russian Manual for Self-Tuition.* L [?]: Trübner [?]
- 1915 Louis Segal, *The Self-educator in Russian.* L: Hodder and Stoughton [1918, 1931, 1932, 1937, 1942. See also 1961: Segal and Whibley]
- 1915 Susan M. Taylor and Capt. [J. S.] Keyworth, *Easy Russian for our Men Abroad, and How to Pronounce it.* L: Kegan Paul
- 1916 A. L. S., *Laurie's Elementary Russian Grammar.* L: Laurie
- 1916 S. I. Lyubov, *The Pictorial Russian Course.* L: Hill
- 1916 Leonard A. Magnus, *A Concise Grammar of the Russian Language.* L: Murray
- 1916 P. M. Smirnov, *A Progressive Russian Course.* L: Blackie

1916 Eric Gordon Underwood, *A School Russian Grammar*. L: Blackie
1917 Bernard Hopfen, *Nelson's Simplified Russian Grammar*. L, Edinburgh: Nelson
1917 W. I. Kon, *A Short Russian Grammar*. L: Melrose [1919]
1918 R. T. Currall, *Practical Russian Grammar*. L: Harrap [1920]
1923 John Marshall, *Russian Grammar Self-taught*. L: Marlborough [?]
1930 V. K. Müller, S. K. Boyanus, *Anglo-russkii slovar'*. M: Sovetskaia entsiklopediia [1931, 1933, 1937, 1943, 1946, 1953, 1960, 1962... 1977]
1934 Anna H. Semeonoff, *A New Russian Grammar*. London: J. M. Dent [1937, 1941, 1942, 1945, 1946, 1960]
1935 *Linguaphone Introduction to Russian Grammar*. Linguaphone Institute [1947]
1937 G. A. Birkett, *A Modern Russian Course*. L: Methuen [1940, 1946, 1950, 1960]
1937 Charles Duff, *The Basis and Essentials of Russian*. London: Nelson [1938]
1938 I. Kolny-Balotsky [also spelt: Kolni-Balozky], *A Progressive Russian Grammar*. L: Sir Isaac Pitman [1944, 1946, 1953]
1939 S C. Boyanus, *Spoken Russian: A Practical Course*. L: Sidgwick and Jackson [1945, 1952]
1939 M. V. Trofimov, *Handbook of Russian. Vol. II: Accidence and Syntax*. Manchester: Sherratt and Hughes
1942 Louis Segal, *New Complete Russian-English Dictionary*. L: Lund Humphries [1943, 1948, 1951, 1953, 1958, 1959]
1943 Nevill Forbes, revised Elizabeth Hill, *Elementary Russian Grammar*. Oxford: Clarendon Pr
1943 Maximilian Fourman, *Teach Yourself Russian*. L: Hodder and Stoughton [1952, 1954]
1943 Mark Sieff, *Colloquial Russian*. L: Kegan Paul
1944 I. Freiman, *Elementary Russian Grammar*. L: Lindsay Drummond
1944 Nikolai Sollogub, *Russian in a Nutshell*. L: Hutchinson
1946 E. A. Moore and Gleb Struve, *Practical Russian*. L: Arnold
1947 L. S. Miller, *Russian by Yourself. A Quick course in Reading for Adult Beginners and Others*. L: Bell
1949 Maximilian Fourman, *Science Russian Course*. L: University Tutorial Pr [1961]
1949 A. I. Smirnitskii, *Russko-angliiskii slovar'*. M: Gos. Izd. inostrannykh slovarei [1952, 1958, ... 1985]
1949 M. V. Trofimov, *Russian Conversational Course. Grammar*. L: Linguaphone [1960]
1949 Maurice O'C. Walshe, *A Concise Russian Course*. L: Hirschfeld
1957 B. Unbegaun, *Russian Grammar*. Oxford: Clarendon Pr [1962]
1958 *Collins Gem Russian Dictionary (English-Russian, Russian-English)*. L, Glasgow: Collins [1963, 1971, new edition 1996, 2003]
1959 F. M. Borras, R. F. Christian, *Russian Syntax. Aspects of Modern Syntax and Vocabulary*. Oxford: Clarendon Pr [1971]
1959 Ronald Hingley, *Russian for Beginners*. L (*Radio Times* pamphlet): BBC
1960 Charles Duff and Dmitri Makaroff, *First Year Russian*. L: Cassell
1960 A. A. Haywood, *A First Russian Book*. L: Harrap [1961, 1970]. *A Second Russian Book* followed in 1961 [1964, 1966, 1969] and *O Level Russian* in 1966
1960 Dennis Ward, *Russian for Scientists*. L: University of L Pr
1961 Louis Segal, K. H. Whibley, *Elementary Russian Grammar. [New] edition of Segal's Russian Grammar and Self-educator*. L: Lund, Humphries

BIBLIOGRAPHY

1961 J. L. I. Fennell, *The Penguin Russian Course*. Harmondsworth: Penguin
1962 Charles Duff, Dmitri Makaroff, *Russian for Adults*. L: English Universities Pr
1962 R. Hingley, T. J. Binyon, *Russian. A beginners' Course*. L: Allen and Unwin
1963 *First Year Russian*. BBC and University of Essex joint project. [later published as L. M. O'Toole, P. T. Culhane, *Passport to Moscow*. L: Oxford UP, 1972. The second year course was published 1968 by O'Toole, later reissued with the title *Passport to Odessa*, OUP, 1976]
1963 G. Davydoff, P. Pauliat (adapted F. G. Gregory), *Ivan and Katya*. L: Harrap
1963 Yu. A. Markov (adapted J. M. C. Davidson, L. A. Volossevich, C. V. James, *Russian Audio-visual Course*. Oxford: Pergamon
1963 A. Menac, Z. Volos, *Audio-visual Method of Russian*. L: Harrap
1963 F. F. Seeley, *The Gateway Russian Course*. L: Methuen
1965 Michael Beresford, *Complete Russian Course for Scientists*. Oxford: Clarendon Pr
1965 Alexander Blum, *Concise Russian-English Scientific Dictionary for Students and Research Workers*. Oxford, New York: Pergamon
1965 Alfred Dressler, *An Introduction to Russian for Social Studies*. L: English Universities Pr
1965 J. C. Harding, *Russian One*. L: Harrap
1966 V. Arakin, I. Samoilova, *My First [etc.] Russian Book*, M: Prosveshchenie
1967 Joshua Cooper, *Russian Companion Part One*. Oxford, etc: Pergamon
1967 Frank Higenbottam, *Teach Yourself Russian Through Reading*. L: English Universities Pr
1967 Eugene Jackson, Elizabeth B. Gordon, *Russian Made Simple*. L: W. H. Allen
1967 Nuffield Foreign Languages Teaching Materials Project: Russian, *Vperyod! Nuffield Introductory Russian Course*. L: Macmillan, Lund Humphries (series of books, booklets, audio-visual aids, etc.) [See also *Iskra*, c. 1983]
1967 A. G. Waring, *Russian Science Grammar*. Oxford: Pergamon
1970 M. H. T. and V. L. Alford, *Russian-English Scientific and Technical Dictionary*. Oxford etc: Pergamon [1974]
1971 M. Vyatyutnev et al., *Russkii iazyk 1. Audio-vizual'nyi kurs dlia zarubezhnykh shkol*. M: Russkii iazyk
1972 Ealing Technical College Division of Russian Studies, *Ealing Course in Russian. An Audio-visual Course for Beginners*. Madrid: Editorial Mangold
1972 V. G. Kostomarov (ed.), *Russkii iazyk dlia vsekh. Russian for Everybody*. M: Russkii iazyk
1972 Marcus Wheeler, Boris Unbegaun (editors), *Oxford Russian-English Dictionary*. Oxford: Oxford UP [1984; see also *Oxford English-Russian Dictionary* below]
1973 Michael Frewin, Alla Braithwaite, *Ochen' priyatno. A BBC radio course for beginners in Russian*. L: BBC.
1973 William Harrison, Yelena Clarkson, Stephen le Fleming, *Colloquial Russian*. L: Routledge & Kegan Paul [1978]
1973 William Harrison, Stephen le Fleming, *Russian-English and English-Russian Dictionary*. L: Routledge & Kegan Paul
1974 Michael Frewin, Alla Braithwaite, *Svidanie v Moskve. A Second-year Russian Course*. L: BBC
1974 University of Birmingham, *Language Laboratory Course in Russian for Social Scientists*. Birmingham: University Department of Russian

1975 Jessie Coulson, *Pocket Oxford Russian-English Dictionary*. Oxford: Clarendon Pr
1977 R. Bivon, *Advanced Russian Grammar*. Norwich: University of East Anglia
1977 Patricia A. Heron, *Reading Russian. A Course for complete beginners who wish to acquire the ability to translate scientific texts*. Birmingham: University of Aston
1980 Terry Culhane, Roy Bivon, *Russian Language and People*. L: BBC [1995, 2006]
1981 *Pocket Oxford Russian Dictionary*. Oxford: Clarendon Pr [1994, 2000]
1982 Elizabeth A. M. Wilson, *Modern Russian Dictionary for English Speakers*. Oxford: Pergamon; M: Russkii iazyk
1983 *Iskra* (series of books comprising a classroom course in Russian for younger secondary pupils based on Nuffield Course *Vperyod!* (see 1967 above). [Appeared in self-published form; later pub. Thornes; see below 1992; pub. Murray, 1996, as *Novaya Iskra*]
1984 Paul Falla, *Oxford English-Russian Dictionary*. Oxford: Oxford UP. [Reissued jointly with *Russian-English Dictionary* by Wheeler *et al.* 1993; 1997, 2000, 2007]
1984 D. J. Rix, Yu. Yu. Desheriyeva, L. B. Trushina, *Dialogue One*, M: Russkii iazyk; L, Wellingborough: Collets
1988 Nicholas J. Brown, *Russian in Three Months*. L: Hugo [c. 1997]
1990 Nicholas J. Brown, *Get By in Russian*. L: BBC [1993]
1990 Michael Ransome, Daphne West, *Poshli dal'she. A Complete Language Course for A level Russian*. L: Collets
1991 Daphne M. West, *Teach Yourself Russian*. L: Hodder and Stoughton [1995, 2001, 2003]
1992 Nuffield/Schools Council Russian Teachers' Association, *Iskra: a Communicative Russian Course*. Cheltenham: Thornes [1992]. [See also c. 1983. and 1996]
1992 Terence Wade, *A Comprehensive Russian Grammar*. Oxford: Blackwell [2000]
1993 Halya Coynash, *Breakthrough Russian*. Basingstoke: Macmillan
1993 Svetlana le Fleming and Susan E. Kay, *Colloquial Russian*. L: Routledge [1997, 2003]
1993 Derek Offord, *Modern Russian. An Advanced Grammar Course*. L: Bristol Classical Pr
1994 Olga Bridges, Pauline Rayner, Irina Tverdokhlebova, *Business Russian: A Complete Course for Beginners*. L: Hodder and Stoughton
1994 Melanie Hardman, Andrew Jameson, *Russian for You*. Lancashire College
1994 Keith Rawson-Jones, Alla L. Nazarenko *Essential Russian*. Oxford: Berlitz
1995 John Langran, Natalya Veshneva, *Ruslan Russian 1: a Communicative Russian Beginners' Course*. Birmingham: Ruslan [1997, 2001, 2005]
1995 Della Thompson (ed.), *Oxford Russian Minidictionary*. Oxford: Oxford UP [1996 reissued as *Oxford Paperback Russian Dictionary*; 2002]
1996 Nicholas J. Brown, *The New Penguin Russian Course*. L: Penguin
1996 Nicholas J. Brown, *Russian Learners' Dictionary. 10,000 Words in Frequency Order*. L: Routledge
1996 Rachel Farmer, *Beginner's Russian: an Easy Introduction*. L: Hodder [2003]
1996 John Langran, *Ruslan 2*. Birmingham: Ruslan [2000, 2007]
1996 Derek Offord, *Using Russian: a Guide to Contemporary Usage*. Cambridge: Cambridge UP
1996 Ken Smith (ed.), *Novaya Iskra*. L: Murray [2002]

BIBLIOGRAPHY

1996 Daphne West, Michael Ransome, *Tranzit. A Bridge to Advanced Russian Language Studies*. Nottingham, Ilkeston: Bramcote [2003, 2008]

1997 Della Thompson (ed.), *Oxford Starter Russian Dictionary*. Oxford: Oxford UP

1998 Roger Cockrell, *The Exeter English-Russian Dictionary of Cultural Terms*. Exeter: University of Exeter Pr

1998 Alla Rodimkina, Zoya Riley, Neil Landsman, *Russia Today*. SPb: Zlatoust [1999, 2000]

1998 Della Thompson (ed.), *Oxford Colour Russian Dictionary*. Oxford: Oxford UP

1999 John Murray, Sarah Smyth, *Basic Russian. A Grammar and Workbook*. L: Routledge

1999 Larissa Ryazanova-Clarke, Terence Wade, *The Russian Language Today*. L: Routledge

2000 William Harrison, Stephen le Fleming, *Intermediate Russian Grammar*. Cardiff: University of Wales Pr

2000 Svetlana le Fleming, *Russian for Business Studies*. L: Bristol Classical Pr

2000 John Murray, Sarah Smyth, *Intermediate Russian*. L: Routledge

2000 Ian Press, *Learn Russian*. L: Duckworth

2000 Daphne M. West, *Teach Yourself Beginner's Russian Grammar*. L: Hodder & Stoughton

2000 Elisabeth Smith, *Instant Russian*. L: Hodder [2003, 2006]

2001 Nick Ukiah, *Take off in Russian*. Oxford: Oxford UP

2002 Michael Ransome, Daphne West, Rachel Smith, *Kompas. An Advanced Russian Course for Schools and Colleges*. Ilkeston: Bramcote [2006]

2002 Sarah Smyth, Elena V. Crosbie, *Rus: a Comprehensive Course in Russian*. Cambridge: Cambridge UP

2002 Natalia Veshneva, *Through Russia, with Love. A Complete Course for Beginners in Russian*. L: Melrose

2003 Tom Dickins, Irina Moore, *S azov (Russian From Scratch)*. Internet publication now available at www.gefix.net/sazov

2005 John Langran, *Ruslan 3* [2008]

2006 Robin Aizlewood, *Routledge Intensive Russian Course*. L: Routledge

2006 Della Thompson (ed.), *Oxford Beginners' Russian Dictionary*. Oxford: Oxford UP

2008 Michael Ransome et al., *Navigator. AS level Russian*. Ilkeston: Bramcote Pr

Index

A[dvanced] level 131, 143, 150, 168, 169, 175, 183, 203, 204, 205, 218, 222, 229; see GCE
ab initio Russian at universities 141-3, 151, 174-5, 192, 196, 207, 220, 222, 238
abbreviations xii
Aberdeen University 143, 203
Aberystwyth, University of Wales 143
Académie française 18
Academy, Russian, and its publications 18, 24, 172
Adamson, Miss 67
adult education classes 92, 95, 96, 137, 138, 146, 151, 153, 172, 173, 226, 230
Advanced Higher grade 205
Akhmatova, A ix
Aldrich, R 132-3 and n.
Aldworth, W 34
Aleksandrov 28
Alekseev, M P 7, 9, 13, 19
Aleksei, Tsar 7-9, 24n
ALL: Association for Language Learning 202-3, 216, 221, 229, 243
Alliance française 225
Allied Control Commission 120, 125,
Alternative Ordinary grade 164,
Anderson, M. S. 3, 4, 9, 13, 14
Andreyev, C 122
Anglo-Russian Friendship Committee 54
'Anglomania' 18-19
Annan Report 136, 140-1, 149, 156-60, 161-2, 168, 175-7, 184, 211,
Anti-Fascist Committee for Soviet Youth 145
Archangel 1, 128
ARCOS raid 82
ARLS: Anglo-Russian Literary Society 37n, 49, 53,
armed services and Russian: 51, 107, 32ff., 33, 35-6, 49, 51, 58n., 98ff., 107, 118-20, 126-136, 148 (USA), 178-181, 214, 240 See also RAF
Armstrong College 73, 80
AS: Advanced Supplementary (later 'Subsidiary') level 204-5, 229
Askwith, Lord 82
assisted places 184
Associated Examination Board 164
Association for Science Education 203

ATG: Association of Teachers of German 202
Atkinson Report 183, 190-4, 206-8, 245
ATR: Association of Teachers of Russian 69, 151-2, 158-66, 168-72, 176-7, 182, 189-90, 193, 196, 202-3, 215-7, 221, 239, 243
attitudes towards language learning 233
Attlee, C 144
audio-visual study materials: see educational technology
Austria, Russian in 189
AVLA: Audio-visual Language Association 202
BALT: British Association for Language Teaching 202
Bangor, University of Wales 143
Barnsley 217-8
Barrie, J M 53
BAS(S)EES: British Association for (Soviet), Slavonic and East European Studies 211, 227
BBC External Services 97
BBC 214, 220
bditel'nost' 167
Beaconsfield, Defence School of Languages 179-81
Beerbohm, M 53, 79
Belfast Metropolitan College 226
Belfast, Queen's University 80, 144, 226
Bell, A 22
Bennett, A 53
Beresford, M 171
Berlitz schools 51
BFSS: British and Foreign School Society 23, 24
Bibliographies, notes on xi-xii, 247ff.
Bird, G 134n.
Birkett, G A 76, 93, 95-6, 104-5, 154
Birmingham, schools, colleges, Russian community 62, 65, 69, 169, 189, 231
Birmingham University 73-8, 80, 95, 97, 108, 117, 141, 143, 158, 168, 170-1
Blair, J 36
Blair, R 58, 87
Blake, G 120
Blunt, A 134
BNASEES: British National Association for Soviet and East European Studies 210

Bodmer, F 114, 115n.
Bodmin 128-9, 135
Bolsover, G 131, 142, 244
Bondar, D 28, 50, 103, 104
Boot, J 75
Borras, F 123, 151
Boswell, B 76, 95
Bowen, G 36,
Boyanus, S K 104, 154
Boyd, J 213-4
Bradford 60, 62, 66-9
Bratstvo (Fraternity) Club 55
Bratus, B V 171
Brennan, H 76, 93, 95
Brezhnev, L 195
Briggs, A P D 219
Bristol, city and schools 66, 231
Bristol University 74, 143
Britain-Russia Centre 217
British Academy 208
British Council 149-50, 215, 225, 229, 233, 243
Brown, N 227
Bryce Commission 48
BUAS: British Universities' Association of Slavists 150, 189, 191-3, 203, 210
Buchanan, G 38
Buck, G 8
Burgess, M vi
Burgin, L 110
Burrows, Gen. 125
Burrows, R 57, 76, 241
Burton, R 35. 36, 45
Butler, R A 108; Education Act 103
Callaghan, J 110
Cambridge Russian community 231
Cambridge University 40-3, 45-7, 57-8, 65, 73-4, 76, 80, 88, 95-6, 98, 107, 117-123, 125, 127, 130-1, 140, 143, 150, 156, 212
Cartledge, B 208
Catherine II, Empress
Cazalet, E A 49
Cecil, R 82
Chambers of Commerce 61, 71-2, 74-5
Chancellor, R 1-4
Charles I, King 8
Chayter, H J 98, 139
Chekhov, A 104, 147
Cheltenham College 35, 45, 50, 65
Chicherin, G 100
Chicksands (RAF) 179
Chilston, Lord 102
Churchill, W 37, 83, 109, 124, 128, 246
Circular 797 (Board of Education) 64

Circular 81 (Ministry of Education) 115, 117-8, 137-7, 139-40
City of London College 50
Civil War, Russian 58, 63, 80, 82
Clarendon Commission 48
Clews, J 144
CNAA: Council for National Academic Awards 174, 207
co-education 184, 185
Cocks, C 9
Cole, D 134
Collet's 162, 239,
commercial/technical schools/colleges and modern languages 48; and Russian 59, 60-4, 66, 69, 71-2, 75, 79, 90, 92-4, 96, 103, 117, 137, 146, 153
commercial benefactors of Russian 46
Committee for Research and Development in Modern Languages (CRDML) 159
Committee on Area Studies 197, 208
comprehensive education 116, 162-3, 176-7, 183-4, 188-9, 196, 201, 222, 233
Conrad, J: *Under Western Eyes* 30
Contemporary Russian Language Analysis Project (CRLAP) 155-6
Coulsdon 128
Courtney, A 118, 120
Crail 135, 179
Crankshaw, E 103
Crimean War 43-4
Cross, A. 14n.
cryptology 15-16
CSC: Civil Service Commission, exams and reports 32, 33, 36, 86, 107, 118, 124, 131, 179
CSE: Certificate of Secondary Education 164, 183, 188, 198, 204,
CSYS: Certificate of Sixth-Year Studies (Scotland) 169, 205
Culhane, P T 164, 173
cultural agreements with USSR 149, 165, 168
curriculum, national in schools, statutory instruments 198-204, 210, 213-5, 218, 219, 226, 237
Curzon, Lord 30
Czechoslovakia 181, 191,
Dabert 66
Daily Express 138
Daily Worker 135
Darlington, T 30n, 39-40, 230
Dartmouth RN College 116
Davidson, P 2
Davidson, J M C 177
Deane, J 16

Dearing, Lord, and Report 211-2, 215-6, 222
Denikin 83
Dent, W 99
Department for Children, Schools and Families 215n.
DES: Department of Education and Science (England and Wales) 158 and n., 159, 160 and n., 189, 198, 200, 208
Department of Education and Science (Ireland) 226
Derby, schools and colleges 60, 61, 67, 232
DfES: Department for Education and Skills (England and Wales) 215
Dickens: *Tale of Two Cities* 40
dictionaries, provision, compilation and use of 19-20, 21, 23, 27-8, 81, 89, 103-4, 164, 220 and Bibliography
difficulty and imagined difficulty of Russian 25, 89, 94, 110-12, 114-16, 142, 145, 147, 151, 153, 157, 176, 184, 186, 196, 230, **234-36**, 242
Digges, D 8
diplomatic and consular Russian 37-41, 118
direct grant 184
diversification of language provision 113, 159, 175, 186, 199-201, 213-4
Donetsk 166
Dostoevsky, F M 31, 71
Dublin, city 51, 120, 190, 226
Dublin, Trinity College 144, 225-6,
Duddington, N, 37: see also Ertel'
Duff, C 104
Dukhovskoi, Gen. 34
Dundee 54, 59, 63
Dunning report 186, 188, 200
Duranty, W 83
Durham University 73, 143, 173
Dutch/German language 3
East Anglia University 143
Eden, A 124, 136n.
Edge, R R 50
Edgerton, W 148
Edinburgh, city and schools 34, 51, 54, 62, 65, 86, 92-3, 104-5, 166, 188, 231
Edinburgh University 45, 62, 74, 76, 80, 106, 143, 227
educational technology 121, 154
Educational Partnership Programme 229
Edward VI, King 1, 2, 3
Eisenhower, D D 119
Elizabeth I, Queen 3-6
Elizabeth, Empress 15, 24n
Elliott and Shukman 122, 127-8, 133

English language used in Russia 18-19
Ertel' family 36-38, 109
ESRC: Economic and Social Research Council 208
Eton College 65, 68, 101
European Community 162
Evans, R J M 150
evening schools/classes: see adult
examinations and qualifications: see CSC, RSA, GCE, GCSE, SCE; other: 51, 70, 131
exchanges with Russia 137-8, 144-5, 149-50, 153, 159, 161-2, 165, 168, 183, 219, 234
Exeter University 143
FCO (Foreign and Commonwealth Office) language school 180
FE: further education, see adult
Fedor, Tsar 3
Fedosov, D 9, 14
Fen, E 109 and n., 129
Fennell, J vi, 123, 143
First examinations, see School Certificate
Firth Park School 66, 68, 93, 94
Fisher, H A L 76, 241
Fishmongers, Worshipful Company 45, 74
Fletcher, G 6
Forbes, N 42, 53, 68, 76, 81, 93-5
FO: Foreign Office; Committee on Russian Studies 136-7, 140
France, Russian in 73, 97, 189, 228, 245
Freeborn, R 123
Freeth, F 27, 28, 33
French language, used in Russia 15-18
Friedman, M 75
Fyfe, Hamilton 83
Gagarin, Iu 147
Galsworthy J 53
Garnett, C 31, 53
GB-USSR Association 189, 217
GCE: General Certificate of Education, see O[rdinary], AS [Advanced Supplementary] and A[dvanced] levels
GCHQ: Government Communications Headquarters 129, 134n.
GCSE: General Certificate of Secondary Education 163, 186, 198, 203, 204-5, 215, 218-9, 221-2, 228-9, 232,
George II, King 16
George, Prince 10
German language in Russia 3, 18
Germany: British attitudes to Russia 46
Germany, Russian in 73, 97, 189, 228
Gladstone, W E 41, 142
Glasgow (University) 63, 73-4, 76, 80, 93, 95, 108, 117, 123, 140, 143, 227

Glasgow (city) 51, 54, 59, 63, 93, 231
glasnost' 195
Gleason, J H 29
Glees, A 139
Goethe-Institut 225
Goldsmith, O: *Vicar of Wakefield* 24, 'The Hermit' 26
Gollancz, V 83-4
Gomel' 22
Goncharov, I 11
Gorbachev, M S 195, 209, 219, 241
Goudy, A P 45-6, 53, 76, 81, 94-5, 119
Gouin schools 51, 105
graded test movement 204
grammar schools, introduction of modern languages 48
grammar and grammar books 10-12, 18, 19, 21-28, 35, 43, 44, 48, 68, 71, 89, 101, 103-5, 109, 129, 130, 154-6, 219-20, 236
Gray, T, 'Elegy' 26
Great Britain-Russia Society (GBRS) 230
Great Northern War 13
Greatwood, E A 159, 160n.
Grech, N 24-5
Grey, E 30
Grierson, J M 33, 35
Guthrie, M 14
Hackel, Mrs 131
Hardinge, C 38
Harris, M 199
Harrison, W 173
Harvey-Jones, J 120 and n.
Hawick 62
Hawkins, B 127, 179
Haysom, D 127
Hayter Report 116, 136, 140-1, 143, 174, 175, 192
Hayward, H M 142
Haywood, A A 109, 117, 154
Haywood, J 199
Heard, J ix, 21, 22-27, 29, 43-4, 230, 244
HEFCE: Higher Education Funding Council for England, and report 208, 211, 230
'heritage' language, Russian as 197, 201, 222, 228, 229, 231,
Higher grade 149, 188, 205, 212, 228
Higher School Certificate 71-2, 94, 141
Hill, C 139
Hill, E vi, 96-7, 107, 109, 119-21, 125-8, 139-40
Hingley, R 42n., 142, 144, 172
Hitler, A 98, 107, 108, 111, 128
HMI: His/Her Majesty's Inspector(ate): see inspection of schools

Hodgetts, E R B 29, 34
Horsey, J 1, 5-6
Hugo, C 104
Hull University 143
Hume, G 56
Hungarian uprising 147, 181
IAAM: Incorporated Association of Assistant Masters 145, 148
Ilchester, Earl, Oxford bequest, 40, 41, 43
immersion courses 215, 225, 229
in-service work with teachers 90, 153, 168, 171, 220, 239, 243,
Ingram, J 119, 121
initial teacher-training 170-1
inspection of schools and HM inspectorate 158, 159, 169, 176-7, 185, 188, 189, 200, 201-2, 234, 238, 242-3
Institute of Linguists 85, 116
intelligence, military and diplomatic viii, 13, 15, 16, 34, 46, 99, 100, 120, 122, 127-9, 132-3, 175, 182
intensive courses 157-60, 168, 174, 177, 191-2, 229-30, 236,
interpreters, English and Russian 3, 4, 6, 7, 10, 16, 33-6, 44-5, 54, 83, 98-100, 107, 118-21, 123, 125-7, 130-3, 135, 174, 179-80, 205
Ireland, Republic, Russian in 51, 62, 74, 144, 190, 225-6
Ireland, Northern, Russian in 80, 144, 153, 163, 174, 195-6, 225-6
Irish Association of Slavists 144, 226
Isis case 133-4
Ivan III, Tsar 3
Ivan IV, Tsar 1-3, 5
Ivan Czarowitz, play, 14
Jackson, Gen. 214
James, E J F 117
James B A 120
James R 8
James, H 53
James, King 6
James, C V 89, 149, 151-2 and n., 158-61, 173, 177, 244
Jarintzov, N 81, 224
JCLA: Joint Council of Language Associations 203
Johnson, Hewlett 83, 84
Joint Matriculation Board 163, 205,
Jones, M V 208
Joseph, K 207
JSLS: Joint Services Language School, 122; see Tangmere, Chicksands
JSSL: Joint Services School for Linguists 121, 127-36, 142, 143, 148, 149, 153, 168, 179

271

Kantemir, A 17
Karamzin, N 14, 25, 26
Keele University 143
Kennan, G F 126
Khrushchev, N S 135, 147, 149
Kidbrooke RAF courses 127-8, 132
King's College, Cambridge 156
King's College, London (see also SSEES) 69, 70, 73-6, 95, 100, 118
Kinloch, A 27-8 and n., 33, 34n., 38, 49
Kirkwood, J M 221
Klinger, F M 56
Kolchak, Admiral 36, 83
Kolny-Balotsky (spelt variously), J 68-9, 76, 95, 104-5
Konovalov, S 76, 95, 98, 139
Kostomarov, V G 169, 219,
Kroll, A 19
kruzhki (singular: *kruzhok*) circles, local groups 168-9, 216-7
kursant: student on course 130n.
Kursk, submarine 180
Laming Scholarship, Queen's College, Oxford 58, 73
Lancaster, J, and 'Lancasterian' system 22, 24, 27
Lancaster University 143
Languages for All (DfES report) 214-05
Lansdell, H 29
Laqueur, W 148-9
Laski, H 83
Lavrin, J 77, 95, 97
LBC: Left Book Club 84-5
le Fleming, S 173
LEA: local education authority
Leathes Report 77, 85-8, 90-2; Board of Education response 103, 140, 157, 211
Leeds (city, schools) 62, 155, 171, 238
Leeds Grammar School 1805 judgment 48
Leeds Russian Archive 216
Leeds University 68, 73, 74, 76, 78, 80, 95, 108, 117, 123, 142-3, 151, 241
Leicester 60-1
Leigh Grammar School 50, 93, 94
Lenin V I 63, 79, 82, 83, 223
Leningrad 137, 144, 165, 166, 168, 195
Letterkenny Technical College 226
Leverhulme, Lord 74
LfA: Languages for all (Scotland) 201
Limerick, University 226
Linguaphone Institute 104
Liverpool School/College of Commerce 47, 51, 158
Liverpool Russian-speaking club 169
Liverpool University 40, 45-7, 50, 51, 61, 65, 73-8, 80, 95, 108, 117, 119, 143

Liverpool, education in 87-8, 245
Livingstone, R 87
Lloyd George, D 55
Lloyd, T 128, 132,
LMS: local [financial] management [of schools] 217-8
Lockhart, J H Bruce 114, 115
Lockhart, R Bruce 37, 38, 114
Lomonosov, M ix, 13, 17-18, 22, 151
London Chamber of Commerce 51
London County Council 138
Ludolf, W H 10-13
Lvoff, Prince 55
MacGregor-Hastie, R 159
Macalister, D 74, 241
Macdonald, Ramsay 100
Macmillan, H 149
Maddison, J 14-15
Magnus, P 87, 91
Malcolm, J 108
Manchester Guardian and Russian teaching 49, 124, 125, 147, 149-50,
Manchester, Russian community 231
Manchester schools 65-7, 166
Manchester School of Commerce 50, 73
Manchester University 47, 74, 76, 77, 80, 95, 108, 117, 123, 143, 171
MAPRYaL: *Mezhdunarodnaia assotsiatsiia prepodavatelei russkogo iazyka i literatury* 169, 182, 220,
Marx, K 63
Mary I, Queen 3
Mather, W 55, 74, 75
Matthews, W K 110n.
Maude, A 78
McDonald, T 213-4
Meades, P H 121
Methodist College, Belfast 225
Michael, Prince of Kent 180, 223
military: see armed services
Milne, H 166, 169 and n.
Ministry of Information 97
Minns, E 45
Minto, Lord 30
Mirsky, D S 18, 76, 78
Mitchell, R 186
mixed-ability teaching 184-5
MLA: Modern Language Association 62, 63, 65, 70, 82, 100-1, 103, 113, 116, 152, 202; Russian (Slavonic) sub-committee 55, 59, 64, 69, 81, 100, 115
MLISC: Modern languages in the school curriculum, document 200
MLPS: Modern languages in the primary school, see primary
Modern Languages. Pamphlet 29 146-7

272

Molotov, V M 124
Morfill, W 28, 43, 44, 45, 47, 50, 76, 230, 241, 244
Morgan, K V 101
Morning Post 106n.
Moscow Youth Congress 1957 145
Motti, P 27. 28
Müller, Max 40
Müller, V K 104
Munn, J and Report 186-7, 200
Musgrave, H 80
nation study (Pares) 47, 78, 164, 205, 230
National Council for Curriculum and Assessment (Republic of Ireland) 226
National Institute of Higher education, Limerick 144
National University of Ireland 144
Nauchno-metodicheskii tsentr 169
NCLE: National Congress on Languages in Education 189
Neglect of Science Committee 59, 87
New University of Ulster 144, 226
Newby, H 208
Newton, J 16
North Luffenham (RAF) 179
Northamptonshire, Russian teaching 66-7
Norwood Report 110-13
Nottingham University and University College 60-1, 72-3, 75. 77-8, 80. 95-6, 108, 117, 119, 123, 143, 171, 241
Nottingham College of Education and Trent University 170
Nuffield Foundation reports and funding 146, 156, 163, 211, 212-6, 222
Nuffield Language Teaching Materials Project (*Vperyod!*), 155, 220
O grade (SCE) 205
O level 117, 149, 153, 163-4, 183, 186, 188, 198, 204, 229; see GCE
O'Toole, L M 191
Obernkirchen 129
Official Secrets Act 133-4
OFSTED: Office for Standards in Education 202, 234, 242
olimpiada: speaking competition 221
Onslow, Earl of 101, 102, 117
Open School of Languages 215
Open University 214
Orloff, N 47, 73-4
Osbourne, C 110
Oundle School 50, 52n, 65, 102
Oxford University Press 10, 43
Oxford University 40-43, 45, 46, 47, 51, 58, 68, 71, 73, 76, 77, 80, 93, 95, 96, 106, 110, 117, 118, 123, 133, 139, 140, 143, 150, 152, 172

Panin, N 16
Pares, B 46-7, 50-1, 52, 70, 75-8, 81, 93-6, 101-2, 138, 141, 163, 205, 230, 241
Patriot, The 106n.
Peace, R A 181, 244
Pearce, D 217
Peel, R 142
perestroika 195
Peter I, Tsar 9, 10, 11
Peter II, Tsar 16
Peterson, A D C 150-2
Philip II, King 3
Pixner, V 172
Pockney, B P 173, 221, 244
Portsmouth University 220
Post-primary Languages Initiative (Ireland) 226
Press, I 17
primary schools, languages in 185, 201, 214-6, 228, 233-4, 245
Prime, G 134n.
prisoners of war 62, 230
Prokopovich, F 14
Pullin, R 155, 199, 219, 244
Pushkin, A S 16n., 18, 71, 105, 147, 151, 171
qualifications of teachers 69-70
RAE: Research assessment exercise 209
RAF and Russian 107, 118-123, 125-36, 142, 179-1; see Chicksands, North Luffenham
RAF Gatow 134 n.
RAF Linguists' Association 133
RAF Uetersen 132
RAF Wythall 132
Raffi, A 69, 100, 120
Rankin, J 46, 74
Ransome, A 78
Rapallo Treaty 99
Rason, E G 35-36
Reading University 143
Red Clydeside 63
Reiff, C P 25, 27, 38
research (all fields) 76, 97, 121, 129, 133, 135, 139-41, 147, 155, 159, 163-4, 169, 174-5, 192-3, 196, 203, 207, 209, 211-2, 227, 229-30, 233, 237
Revolutions, Russian 46, 51, 63-4, 77, 79-81, 223
Ridley, M 8
Riola, H 27, 32, 33, 38
Rix, D 155, 219, 232
Roach, J O 113
Roberts, J 74-5
Royal Institute of International Affairs 97

RSA: Royal Society of Arts 51, 62-3, 71-2, 93, 118
Russia and Britain in Asia and Europe 29ff
Russia/Muscovy Company 3, 5, 8, 19, 54
Russia Society, (and —— of Scotland) 54-6, 68-70, 90, 98, 108
Russia Today Society 108
Russian community in Britain 85, 231
Russian cultural foundation 225
Russian language, different terms for 3
Russian language, varieties of 3, 4
Russian Language Year (RLY) 223-5
Russian Ministry of Defence 181
Russian Network 197
Russian Review (Liverpool) 49-50
Russian revolutions: 1905 46,
Russo-British Chamber of Commerce 56
Russo-Japanese War 30, 35, 46
Russo-Scottish Society: see Russia Society
Russophobia viii, 29
Rutkowska, T 172
S Wilts Grammar School for Girls 190
Sadler, M 30, 39, 241
Sandhurst 32
Sands, E 123
Sargent, O 136
Saulus, V P vi
Scarbrough Report 116, 117, 136ff., 138-43, 161, 173-5, 192-3, 209, 211, 230, 245
SCCML: Scottish Central Committee on Modern Languages 187
SCE: Scottish Certificate of Education. See O grade, S grade, H grade, CSYS
Schnurmann, I Nestor- 27, 35 and n, 36, 45, 50, 58, 65, 119
School Certificate 71-2, 94, 117
school leaving age, raising of 183
schools, introduction of Russian to 47
Scotland and Scots, Russian language in and among: *passim*, 2, 7, 9-10, 14, 19, 54-5. 59-60, 62-3, 68, 86, 88, 92-4, 104-6, 110-13,143, 145, 149, 151, 153, 163-4, 168-9, 172, 174, 177, 182-3, 186-9, 195-6, 198, 200-01, 203, 205-6, 211-13, 217, 220, 226-8, 230-1, 233
Scotland-Russia Forum 217, 230
Scottish examinations boards 169
SCR: Society for Cultural Relations with the USSR; later SCRSS: Society for Cooperation in Russian and Soviet Studies 84, 85, 106 and n, 108, 118, 217, 230-1
SCRE: Scottish Committee for Research in Education 211-3,

SCRSS: see SCR
Second Front Now movement 109
SED: Scottish (formerly Scotch) Education Department 86, 88, 112, 145, 158, 169, 186, 188
Sedgefield, W J 47, 76, 125
Segal, L 69, 77, 104
Selborne Commission 41
Selby-Bigge, L 88, 91
Semeonoff (Semeonova), A H 104, 105, 117, 129, 131, 154
Seton-Watson, H 142
Seton-Watson, R W 76
Shakespeare, *Henry V*: 15, *All's Well*: 32, *Winter's Tale*: 92
Shaw G B 83
Shchelkalov 6
Sheffield schools and city 62, 66, 68, 71, 93, 117, 166
Sheffield University 73-4, 76, 78, 80, 93, 95-6, 108, 119, 138, 171, 194, 220, 241
Shukman, H 145
Sieff, M 51, 69, 109
Sigint: see intelligence
Skinner, B F 122
Slavonic, Church language 3, 4, 17
Slavonic and East European Joint Consultative Committee 189
Slavonic [and East European] Review 96, 97
Sleight, A H 114
Slepchenko, B 60-1, 69, 72, 77, 95
Smith, J 217
Smith R E F 95, 97, 138
Sokolov, A B 4, 5n., 6n.
Sollohub, N 116, 146
Southampton University 74, 143
Specialist Schools and Academies Trust 227-8
Spens Report 103
spoken language, teaching, examining 42, 46, 48, 71, 72, 88, 90-1, 125, 127, 129-31, 154, 155, 158, 163-4, 198, 204-6
Spottiswoode, R C d'E 33-34, 35, 36
spying: see intelligence
Squire, P S xi, 123
SSEES: School of Slavonic and East European Studies, formerly School of Slavonic Studies 73-4, 77-8, 95-7, 101-2, 106, 108, 116-20, 123, 131, 140, 142-3, 209, 220, 244
St Andrews University 45, 74, 131, 143, 227
Staff College 32, 33
Stalin, J V 37
Standard grade 205, 212-3, 228

Stanhope, Lord 102
Stead, W T 29, 29n
Stepniak-Kravchinskii, S 31
Stern, L 83, 84, 106n.
Stolypin 142
Stone, Gerald 43
Strachey, J 83
stranovedenie 170,
Strathclyde, University of, intensive courses 158, 177
Strauss, E 151, 171, 172,
Suburb, Foreign 7
supply of teachers 237, 66-7, 69-70, 114, 177-8, 185, 191, 213, 214, 237, 242
Sussex University 143
Svenske, C 24
Swansea, University of Wales 143
Sweeney, C 224
Sylvester, D 4-5
Tameside judgment 183
Tangmere (JSLS) 179
Tappe, A W 25
Taylor, R, Oxford bequest 40
technical schools/colleges: see commercial
Thatcher, M 129, 206, 209,
'thaw' 165
Thomson Report 110-13, 188
Thornton, W 33-34
Tillyard, J 61, 76, 105
Tolstoi, Yu, 3
Tolstoy, D 142
Tolstoy, L N 31, 39, 104, 147, 151, 238
TQA: teaching quality assessment 210
transliteration xii
Trediakovskii, V K ix, 17
Tripp, Miss 137
Trithen F 40, 43
Trofimov, M V 50-1, 56-7, 67, 69, 70-1, 76-7, 95, 98, 104, 139
Trotsky, L 63
Tsekerov 67
Turgenev, I S vii, ix, 31, 147
UCAS: Universities and Colleges Admissions Service 227

UGC: University Grants Committee 175, 190, 192, 194, 245
universities: introduction of Russian 40ff.
universities: Modern Languages in 40ff.
universities, reform of 41ff.
USA, study of Russian 73, 97, 148-9, 228
Vater, J S 25
Vickers, D 74
Vinogradov, Academician 171
Vlasto, A 131
vocabularies and glossaries, 7ff
vocational purposes of language study 42, 46
Vyshinsky, A 122-3, 126
Wade, T L B 221
Wales, Prince of 197, 208
Wales, Russian in *passim*, 62, 153, 163, 174, 185-6, 195-6, 225-6, 233
Wallace, D Mackenzie 29, 39
Walpole, H 38
Wavell, A P 36-37
Webb, S and B 83
Weir, W 74-5
Wells, H G 52-3, 65, 83, 87, 244
WHMD 21-2, 25-27
Wilkinson, E 110
Williams, H 29, 29n, 78
Willoughby, H 1
Winchester College 102, 117, 151
Wolseley, Lord 33, 34
Woodhead, L 132-3 and nn.
Wooding, N. and Report 208, 211
Woolf, L 109
Wright, P 122
Yeltsin, B, and Foundation 218, 229, 241,
York University 143, 155, 169, 170, 220
Yudenich, Gen. 83
zastoi (period of 'stagnation') 195
Zhukovskii, V 24, 26 and n.
Zinoviev letter 82